CHAPTERS OF ACCIDENTS
A Writer's Memoir

CHAPTERS OF ACCIDENTS

A Writer's Memoir

Alexander Baron

Edited by Colin Holmes and Nick Baron
With an Introduction by Colin Holmes

VALLENTINE MITCHELL
LONDON • CHICAGO

First published in 2022 by Vallentine Mitchell

Catalyst House,
720 Centennial Court,
Centennial Park, Elstree WD6 3SY, UK

814 N. Franklin Street
Chicago, Illinois,
60610 USA

www.vmbooks.com

British Library Cataloguing in Publication Data:
An entry can be found on request

ISBN 978 1 80371 029 7 (Paper)
ISBN 978 1 80371 030 3 (Ebook)

Library of Congress Cataloging in Publication Data:
An entry can be found on request

Figure 1. Alexander Baron at the time of writing his memoirs, mid-1990s.

Contents

List of Illustrations

Note on Referencing

The Introduction is accompanied by footnotes, used mainly to reference the source of quotations which are not drawn from the memoir.

The memoir *Chapters of Accidents* that follows has two forms of referencing apparatus. First, it has footnotes to provide explanations and contextual information regarding terms, events and people mentioned. Following the text of the memoir, the reader will also find an appendix (pp.342–63), presenting extensive endnotes referenced to the memoir text by page number and the opening words of the relevant paragraph. These reproduce, with editorial commentary, extracts from notes that Baron composed for planned revisions to the memoir after he completed its second draft in November 1997, but which he was unable to incorporate into the text before his death in December 1999. For a discussion of Baron's notes for revision, see the preamble to the appendix.

Acknowledgments

The editors and publisher acknowledge the generous support for production of this volume provided by the Sybil Shine Memorial Trust. Both editors also express their gratitude to Martin Paisner for his efforts in assisting with the publication of this memoir.

The editors also wish to thank the Baron and Kelmanson families for their co-operation with the research for this volume, for provision of some of the photographs and documents used as illustrations, and for valuable suggestions and corrections.

We owe a further debt of gratitude to the many librarians, archivists and academics who have helped in the course of our research.

Nick Baron expresses his thanks to the following for their support, expertise and friendship over many years of collaboration: Andrew Whitehead, Ken Worpole, Ross Bradshaw, Susie Thomas, Sean Longden, Nadia Valman, Anthony Cartwright, Rachel Kolsky, Natania Jansz, and the late and much-missed Robert Hastings.

Both editors wish to thank Stewart Cass, Toby Harris, Sue Garfield, and Jenni Tinson of Vallentine Mitchell publishers for taking on this project and providing such professional and friendly support for its completion.

Introduction: A Writer's Journey

Colin Holmes

Staline, Notre Soleil!

[A French slogan during the period of the Popular Front.
Chapters of Accidents, p.168]

I was with Gollan when he received a deputation of left-wing writers. He was the soul of concern for their problems and of interest in their work, for which he was full of praise. He listened to them with an air of respect, made a few suggestions modestly and offered them warm thanks before they went off. We listened to them going down the bare wooden staircase. When they had passed the lower landing, he said, 'Bastards!' expressing my thoughts as well as his; for he had trained me.

[*Chapters of Accidents*, p.209, recalling
an incident in the 1930s]

...Communists can only recognise certain categories of thought, those in which they have been trained, and can only express themselves in the private language of the Party, a dreary mechanical jargon that in itself limits their thinking. I did not want to speak this language any more or to have to listen to it.

[*Chapters of Accidents*, p.333–34, writing
of his thoughts in 1946]

1.

Authors' reputations can wax and wane.[1] Who now recalls Jack Common, a writer much admired and discussed by George Orwell? The standing of John Petty, whose *Five Fags a Day* received considerable publicity on its publication in 1956, has also failed to stand the rigorous test of time. How many people today turn to the writings of Stan Barstow, who, in novels such as *A Kind of Loving*, captured a northern culture in the late 1950s and 60s? For all the Osbornes and the Sillitoes there are those whose reputations soon fall by the wayside.

Alexander Baron, born Joseph Alexander Baron Bernstein, is sometimes referred to as another forgotten, hardly remembered author. But nothing could be further from the truth. His first novel, *From the City, From the Plough*, published in 1948, remains a million–selling classic account of soldiering during the Second World War. Indeed, a case could be made quite easily for it being the best novel by an English writer of a soldier's life during that conflict. Like another classic, Alex Bowlby's 1969 autobiography *The Recollections of Rifleman Bowlby*, it is history written from the bottom up, recalling not the gallant deeds of officers and shifts in military strategy—so fascinating to military historians—but the daily travails of the poor bloody squaddies who trudged off to war between 1939 and 1945. Three other Baron novels, *There's No Home* (1950), *With Hope, Farewell* (1952) and *The Human Kind* (1953), complete his work linked to the recent War.

However, Baron was not an author with a single theme, a star who first flashed across the literary landscape in the late 1940s and early 1950s and then crashed to earth. He published fourteen novels, and produced many well-known film and television screenplays, in a writing career that stretched to the mid-1980s. In addition to his war literature, Baron's accounts of life in London, particularly in the East End, remain important statements of literary intent and importance. His novels *Rosie Hogarth* (1951), *The Lowlife* (1963), *Strip Jack Naked* (1966) and *King Dido* (1969), all feature in this tradition. These writings too, retain their strong advocates and, as with the war novels, it is easy to understand why.

2.

Who was Alexander Baron? His father, Barnett Bernstein, was born in Poland on 3 January 1894 in Brok, a *shtetl* about forty-five miles

---

1   All unreferenced quotations in the Introduction are from *Chapters of Accidents*.

north-east of Warsaw, near the city of Łomża. This area then formed part of the Tsar's Empire. The family lived "in dire poverty" and during Barnett Bernstein's earlier years his father remained largely absent, conscripted into the Tsar's army. When the Russo-Japanese war broke out in 1904, Barnett's father had simply had enough. He decided to flee, cast the soil of Russia from his feet. He formed part of that great outward migration from Russia, between the 1880s and the outbreak of the First World War. He finished up in England. Had he intended to make a fresh start here? Or, like many "greeners" who left the Tsar's Empire during these years, did he have his ultimate sights set on America, the *goldene medineh* but eventually decided to settle for less?

After living first by himself in London, he sent for his family, including Barnett. They lived in Hare Street, Bethnal Green and, when Barnett became old enough to work, he went into the fur trade, a well-known niche for Jewish bosses and workers, where he became a skilled cutter.

Alexander's mother, née Fanny Levinson, had been born on 14 May 1895 in Corbet's Court, Spitalfields, to parents who had come to Britain from Lithuania, also then part of the Russian Empire. The Levinsons lived in the East End of London in Tenter Street. Her son always writes of her as a genteel person: "She was innately ladylike." She must have found it difficult therefore to cope with her job in a canvas and cordage factory near the docks. Sheffield had its buffer girls, who buffed metals in the cutlery trade and these women, immortalised in art by William Rothenstein, developed a fearsome reputation. The kind of factory which employed the young Fanny Levinson also had its strong women, "traditionally East End Amazons." But she obviously possessed an inner resilience to cope.

She was twenty-one and Barnett twenty-three when their son was born in 1917, just over a year after their marriage. The First World War had already come to the Home Front and a pregnant Fanny Bernstein went to Maidenhead to stay with relatives of friends whom they knew in London. There, it was hoped, she would be free from the dreaded air raids, a new feature of modern warfare, later to be depicted by Picasso in *Guernica*. She gave birth to her son in Maidenhead on 4 December 1917.

It might be assumed, given the flight of both the Bernsteins and Levinsons from the Tsar's Empire, that this great westward migration would come to dominate their thoughts and everyday conversations. In Barnett Bernstein's case particularly, since when he began to court Fanny Levinson, he remained technically "on the run", avoiding military service in the Russian Army. The Revolution of 1917 put an end to his fears on this score. But in fact, the Great War rather than the Bolshevik Revolution marked the

Figure 2 "She was twenty-one and Barnett twenty-three when their son was born in 1917, just over a year after their marriage." Fanny and Barnett Bernstein with the newborn Alexander, early 1918.

historic milestone they frequently recalled. They came to regard it as a watershed and this sense of "before and after" transmitted itself to their son.

> When I listened to my parents and their friends during my childhood, their talk created in my mind a [prewar] vision of a lost paradise of music-halls, Hampstead Heath, golden sovereigns, charabanc outings and dancing the Valeta.

With hearing so much talk about the recent conflict, the young Baron thought for some time that the War continued and lived in constant fear of an air raid. Or, after listening to his parents discussing the devastating Silvertown explosion in West Ham on 19 January 1917, which killed seventy-three people in a munitions complex, that another massive bang in the night might suddenly erupt to disturb and disorientate him.

The obsession with war remained for some time and as a young lad he became fascinated by aerial warfare. He began to haunt the aerodromes at Croydon and Edgware. He spent hours reading aviation literature in the Science Museum. He built model aircraft. He prided himself on being able to identify all types of planes.

Behind this fascination lay another. The derring-do of young pilots seized and populated his imagination. He projected himself into this role. "My most potent daydreams were about the airmen of The Great War." To this end he wrote later:

> I bought American magazines, *Wings, Aces, Battle Aces*, paying sixpence for each and getting threepence back in part exchange... In the Reader's Library edition I bought *The Dawn Patrol* by John Monk Saunders. I read it to rags and I saw the film five times, the first version with Richard Barthelmess as the self-sacrificing Captain Courtney. I saw life in terms of a legend of heroes of eighteen led by old men of twenty-five. I could think of nothing to recommend life after the age of eighteen and I aspired to a hero's death in flames at that age.

I felt something similar after reading *Enemy Coast Ahead* by Guy Gibson, published in 1944, often contemplating the long list of Gibson's airforce comrades who had "copped it" (to use their language) on bombing missions over Germany.

In Baron's case, this obsession continued. His memoir recalls that a little later, when at secondary school, he wrote a short story, *The Long Dive* and a novel, *A Lightning before Death*, both of which dwelt on death in the air. Not that his interest lay entirely in aerial tragedy. At secondary school, Richard Aldington became for a time his literary idol, particularly on account of his 1929 novel, *Death of a Hero*. As Baron saw it:

> It is the story of a writer, George Winterbourne, who is presented as a doomed child of his time from his birth in the late nineteenth century to his death on the Western Front.

Death in action yet again. "We were carried away by the novel's charge of anger. We were all George Winterbournes."

His obsession with aircraft and flying remained with him and on the second day of the Second World War, he attempted to join the RAF but problems with his eyesight told against him. Instead, he became a soldier, initially in the 172 Pioneer Corps and later, as he had long wished, as an infantry man, the army's gun fodder.

He survived the War without life-threatening injury. But not all his contemporaries did, and, when recalling it, he often returned to the theme of death. Edwin Fairchild, a friend from his teens, became a pilot and Baron tells us, "…was killed when his bomber was shot down over Germany." He also learned that Dennis Hoyland, "…a big fellow, with a kind, strong Saxon face and a tumble of fairish hair…" counted as another friend lost. Before the War, Baron had visited him in Balliol. After being demobbed and in a fragile state of mind, Baron rang the Hoylands' address. A manservant answered the call and told him laconically and painfully: "'I'm very sorry, sir, Master Dennis was killed in the war.'" It could hardly have helped Baron's fragile mental state to learn as much.

3.

When musing on the air force, the heroic feats of airmen, or a soldier's death on the Western Front, Baron was living in Hackney, a district just north of London's East End. *Chapters of Accidents* paints a vivid tableau of his everyday life there.

His parents were not especially religious. Barnett Bernstein remained a free thinker and Fanny had been educated at a Christian school. Baron observed his mother's light hair and "fresh Nordic looks" and later concluded that in the distant past his Jewish forebears had intermarried with other groups living in Lithuania. And in his memoir he felt obliged to add: "The Orthodox Jewish notion of a long-preserved racial purity that must be maintained is nonsensical and dangerous."

The family still celebrated Jewish festivals and as a child in Foulden Road, Hackney—the first home he remembered—he enjoyed the spring cleaning and the search for the last crumbs of bread around the time of Passover. But his parents never strictly enforced fasting at *Yom Kippur*. And when the family took holidays at seaside resorts, such as Margate, they sometimes stayed in Gentile boarding houses. Moreover, *Chanukah* struck the young Baron as nothing compared with the overwhelming delights of Christmas:

In the weeks before Christmas we mixed the pudding until the time came for my father to drop silver threepenny bits into it. We went to the pantomime and the circus, we put up coloured paper chains in the kitchen; and at school, before we broke up for the holidays, we hung decorations and sang carols…

Here we can observe acculturation at work but within the new the old could still stir itself. Baron began to study for his *barmitzvah*. Significantly, however, he never went through with it, one day informing his parents that if they insisted on the ceremony, he would commit a grotesque act of sacrilege by placing a ham sandwich on the Scroll. Reluctantly, his parents resigned themselves to his decision and so, he wrote later, "I went unbarmitzvahed. I do not know if I am still a Jew in the eyes of the religious."

This incident created a degree of family tension but *Chapters of Accidents* also dwells on the pleasures of family life.

As he grew up, Baron became especially close to his mother. She awoke in him an interest in Dickens and from her he developed a fascination with the weekly publication, *The Magnet*. She had been an avid reader since the magazine first appeared in 1908 and through its pages her son devoured Frank Richards's stories of Greyfriars School. Moreover, with her Christian education, his mother would often sing hymns, as well as popular songs of the day, such as, "Swanee" and "Keep the Home Fires Burning." Her voice continued to echo in his memory.

It would indeed be difficult to overestimate the early bond shared by mother and son. Recalling these years, he wrote:

> I was still very much part of her. Children are as cognisant of smells as animals and her smell was an aura of comfort in which I could take refuge. Sometimes, giving me what she called a catlick, she spat daintily on a handkerchief and wiped my face. This handkerchief and her saliva had a smell which returns to my nostrils as I write. To me she was a deity bestowing cleanliness, the authoritative firmness of her hand itself a reassurance, yet so dainty and ladylike.

We enter here an almost Proustian world of recall.

When recapturing other features of his childhood, he often paints vibrant pictures of street scenes and domestic life in which colours and scents are never far away. The flower garden at 6 Foulden Road, Hackney, fascinated him. He drew sensual pleasure not only from the perfumes but also from

Figure 3 "…his life offered much to make him content." Baron aged about ten, with his younger sister Ida.

the bright patterned leaves of the lupins, geraniums, pansies, carnations, and roses. This fascination owed much to one of his teachers at Shacklewell Infants' School who regularly brought flowers into the classroom. These plants "mesmerised me, such an endless array of glistening petals, bright colours and distinct, delicate perfumes." And when at home, mingling with the natural perfumes of the garden, came the constant waft of manufactured aromas from a sweet factory twenty yards away which resulted in the air becoming heavily scented by lemon drops, wine gums and raspberry lumps.

With a hardworking father who earned enough for the family eventually to employ a maid, his closeness to his mother, a younger sister, born five years later, and a warm extended family, his life offered much to make him content.

> Then there were our birthdays, when we had kitchen parties with Bob Apple, I-spy, fairy cakes and lemonade; school terms and holidays; the annual week at the seaside and the fever of getting ready for it; Spring Cleaning in the house while steam rollers rumbled up and down the street amid a stimulating smell of hot tar, laying new yellow gravel in the road; bath night, the weekly arrival of *The Magnet* and the tram ride to the East End every Saturday [to see grandparents]; and innumerable small rituals like shelling sweet-smelling peas and tasting the pods, or my mother's baking days, with samples to taste and more unforgettable aromas.

But none of us can stay forever in this womb that is forever Eden. We become institutionalised from an early age. As Wordsworth wrote long ago:

> Shades of the prison-house begin to close
> Upon the growing Boy...[2]

4.

School beckoned, first at Shacklewell Infants' and later at the Grocers' in Hackney Downs, a grammar school with a mixture of fee-paying and scholarship pupils.

---

2 Wordsworth's lines on the prison walls closing on the young child are taken from his "Ode: Intimations of Immortality from Recollections of Early Childhood" (1807).

He recalled first having sight of the Grocers' Company's School on a day when his mother had arrived at Shacklewell School gates to take him for a picnic on Hackney Downs. From there he glimpsed the Grocers' red "Victorian-Gothic building" set in its own grounds. "That's where you're going one day," his mother remarked.

In September 1929 he did indeed begin his secondary education there as a scholarship boy. Baron viewed his new school as Greyfriars, which he and his mother had read about every week when they greedily turned the pages of *The Magnet*. To his young eyes, the Headmaster, William Jenkyn Thomas, assumed the persona of Dr Locke in Frank Richards's creation.

Grocers' had been established in 1876, twenty years after the company had founded the public school at Oundle. This offshoot in the East End catered "for the sons of tradesmen, minor professional men and better paid city clerks." The LCC had formally taken it over in 1907 and this transfer led to it being named Hackney Downs School. Even afterwards, though, its pupils would often refer to it as the Grocers'. The school suffered a major fire in 1963, and in 1995, reflecting its recent poor performance, the Conservative government closed it.

Before then, its alumni had included the playwright, Harold Pinter, the nutritionist John Yudkin, the artist Leon Kossoff, the publisher, Frank Cass, as well as a long list of others, some famous, others infamous. The historian Geoffrey Alderman, author of the school's history, counts as one of the former.

The school offered the young Baron a wonderful new world, with black gowned teachers floating through the school dispensing their knowledge. But the Grocers' catered not just for the mind: it offered an impressive array of sporting and leisure facilities. Fanny Bernstein must have been overjoyed to see her son take his place among such surroundings and Barnett Bernstein could continue to dream that one day his son would fulfil all the family's ambitions.

At first it appeared Baron's life might unfold in this way. He did well initially at the Grocers' but his life soon took a different turn. In 1957 Richard Hoggart wrote in *The Uses of Literacy* that a working-class scholarship boy's attachment to school can act as a destructive as well as a liberating influence. And it certainly did with Baron:

> School displaced home as a centre of my life. It was the place where I at last fitted in. In time our family home became only an annexe to it, a place where I was little more than a lodger.

Figure 4 "The school offered the young Baron a wonderful new world…" The obsessive reader and incipient writer, just turned 15.

That sense of a growing, unbridgeable difference gradually increased when, after matriculating and entering the sixth form, he began to explore life in London, far beyond the East End and also embarked early on a political career which would soon consume much of his energy.

When younger, he had haunted London's aerodromes and the Science Museum. He now ventured to Sadler's Wells to appreciate the ballet; he visited the Tate to ponder over its national treasures; he took himself off to the Academy Cinema to watch continental films; he joined the New London Film Society; he began to attend the theatre. These wider interests affected in turn his time at the Grocers'. He became less concerned with the set curriculum of his studies (English, French, Latin and History) and, along with some other sixth formers, became interested in exploring culture more generally.

In parallel with this wider cultural awakening, Baron became more politically conscious.

5.

His first year at Hackney Downs is one of the most significant in the history of the twentieth century. That year, 1929, witnessed the Wall Street Crash. Whereas Baron's parents and their friends referred to the Great War as a watershed, a marker between a settled world before and an uncertain future which followed, many Americans took the financial collapse as their benchmark; a situation wonderfully captured by J.K. Galbraith in his 1955 study, *The Great Crash*. The question: "Would it be 1929 all over again?" henceforth haunted collective memories in the United States whenever economic turbulence threatened. And in the 1930s, as the consequences of the '29 crash rippled through society, the exuberant, extravagant days of, *The Great Gatsby* (1925) became replaced in popular imagination by heart-wrenching songs such as, "Buddy can you spare a dime?" (1932) and in literature by John Steinbeck's classic tale of the economic depression in *The Grapes of Wrath* (1939).

Britain could not divorce itself from these events in America. The old stock market adage, "When Wall Street sneezes, the rest of the world catches a cold," certainly proved true. In the summer of 1931, Ramsey MacDonald's minority Labour government collapsed when it became split over its response to the economic crisis which had now been transferred beyond America. A National Government dominated by Conservatives, replaced it and in September 1931, decided to go off the gold standard, to which in 1926 Churchill, then Chancellor of the Exchequer, had decided, whether through a misguided sense of national pride or hubris, Britain should once again be linked. Pay cuts descended. Unemployment increased.

Baron's father could not escape these economic problems. His trade fell off but, thanks to his employer, he survived as a caretaker to an empty factory. He was one of the fortunate ones. Meanwhile, his son visited London's public libraries to read whatever he could on the country's condition. Years later he wrote: "Perhaps these events did in the end lead me to think about the world outside my head."

This shock of 1931 soon became eclipsed by other events which hastened Baron's political consciousness. In a 1984 interview with Margot Kettle, he remarked that around the age of fifteen or sixteen, he discovered the USSR and Socialism and, as a result, read avidly about them. In particular, he turned to journalists, such as Walter Duranty and Maurice Hindus for information on the Soviet State.[3] Whereas his parents had focused on the Great War and its consequences as a dominant influence on their times, Baron came to think – at least for a time – of the Soviet Union and Socialism as the foci around which his own life turned.

He began attending the Hackney branch of the Independent Labour Party and, significantly, went to meetings of the Friends of the Soviet Union, then being held in East London. He later admitted believing in the exculpatory accounts he heard there and read elsewhere of life under Stalin. If eminent figures, the likes of the scientist J.B.S. Haldane and the novelist Romain Rolland sang its praises, who was he to dispute them? If a great literary figure, such as Maxim Gorky could defend the appalling rigours endured by inmates of the Gulag when constructing the White Sea Canal, asserting that it amounted to, "…the greatest enterprise of moral redemption in history," then so it must be.

His growing interest in Communism occurred in tandem with his increased awareness of events in Central Europe. When the Nazis came to

---

3   Baron refers to Walter Duranty and Maurice Hindus influencing is early thinking on the Soviet Union in a 1984 interview with Margot Kettle, which can be read in the People's History Museum, Manchester at CP/IND/KETT/03/05. This source also offers Baron's reflections on his days in the CPGB (see p.27). Duranty (1884–1957), worked in Moscow between 1922 and 1934. He would subsequently visit the USSR until 1940 on assignment for the *New York Times*. He came to be regarded as an apologist for the Soviets. See S.J. Taylor, *Stalin's Apologist. Walter Duranty:* The New York Times's *Man in Moscow* (New York, 1990). Maurice Hindus (1891–1969), a Russian American writer, faced criticism from the Soviets for not presenting what they regarded as an objective view of events in their country.

power, his initial response had been intensely personal. He had heard so much about the beauty of Germany from friends who had enjoyed cycling holidays there and felt acutely deprived of this future pleasure by a regime hostile towards Jews.

His awareness of these dangerous developments now being unleashed in central Europe soon began to firm up. He was waiting for a tutorial at the Grocers' one day in 1934 when he picked up a copy of the *Daily Express* and read a report by Sefton Delmer on the Austrian government smashing the Socialist City Council in Vienna, bombarding workers' flats and executing its political opponents. This news appalled him. These events in Vienna marked a Damascene moment on his political journey. It was an experience he shared with Kim Philby, for whom what happened there also became a crucial turning point.

That morning, after reading Delmer's report, Baron noticed a poster advertising a meeting on "The Struggle in Austria," to be addressed by Dorothy Woodman. His decision to attend it influenced his subsequent life in at least two respects.

It was there he first saw Ted Willis:

> ...a young man wearing shorts and a red sports shirt, with a bicycle which he leaned against the wall... He had dramatic good looks, with black glossy hair and a gypsy complexion... I did not take notice of the visitor's name that night, but I was to hear it again; it was Willis.

Ted Willis, who later became well-known through writing television's *Dixon of Dock Green* series, soon began to feature prominently in Baron's life. Willis had entered the meeting that evening to enlist support for the women then on strike at a clothing factory in Tottenham. After this motion had been passed, he left but not before Baron, overcoming his natural shyness and public reticence, spoke up in support of the strikers and, in doing so, fractured the "lethargic silence" which lingered in the room after Willis had spoken.

Baron's unexpected intervention led to the second important consequence which followed from this meeting. One attendee invited him to her flat in Stamford Hill for a coffee and to meet her husband. The couple were active Communists, and in the next few weeks Baron visited them on several more occasions. The husband, John Douglas, served as a leading officer in the Communist Youth International, a sub-section of the Communist International (Comintern). Both husband and wife had worked in Moscow and Baron soon realised that their flat acted as a point of arrival for visitors, probably couriers, who arrived from the Soviet Union. At this point he had not embraced Communism. He had maintained his ILP connections and become a member of the Labour League of Youth. However, through Douglas and his wife, he met someone who would become his political Mephistopheles.

I had always regarded John Gollan as the epitome of the dull, desiccated Communist Party apparatchik – which in some respects is accurate, even though in 1956 he succeeded the long-serving Harry Pollitt as General Secretary of the CPGB, in effect its leader. But from Baron's memoir it becomes clear Gollan could exercise a powerful influence over those he met. From their first contact at the Douglas's flat, he began the task of taking the impressionable Baron under his wing, recognising that, though still young, he could be moulded to serve the Party's cause. By the time of their meeting, Gollan already knew Ted Willis and doubtless envisaged a future when their young talents could be harnessed in tandem. Gollan never made any demand that Baron should join the Party, presumably believing on tactical grounds he could exercise a greater influence by remaining off the membership list. But Baron became quickly – though not immediately – smitten by Gollan and the gaunt-faced, yellow-fingered, chain-smoking, gently spoken Scot retained a fierce grip on his protégé's life until 1948.

The point at which Baron's involvement with Gollan began, ushered in a dramatic time both in British and European history. In parallel with events in Italy (think Mussolini) and Germany (think Hitler), some British political figures began to regard Fascism as the way forward. In 1932 Oswald Mosley had founded the British Union of Fascists (BUF), the country's most important Fascist movement of the twentieth century. Echoing the increasing antisemitism in Hitler's Germany, Mosley's movement soon became drenched in such sentiment.

Baron witnessed one of the key flash points of these years, the Battle of Cable Street in October 1936 when "The Leader," as Mosley became known, attempted to march his black-shirted troops in a demonstration of strength through East London. Such experiences cemented Baron's CPGB links. Fascism threatened Jews, just as Hitler did in Germany, and the CPGB stood out strongly against Fascist policies.

How precisely did Baron participate in this political battle that began to rage in the early 1930s and persisted for the rest of that decade? His memoir, recounting these days, serves as a valuable addition to the history of British Communism.

Baron's original intention after leaving school had been to enter university to read History. But swept up in the politics of his day and with Gollan constantly hovering over his shoulder, from 1934 he renounced this option, even though he passed his Higher Matriculation Examinations at the Grocers'. In 1935, rather than enter university, he began to work at County Hall in a clerical capacity for the London County Council. The laxity or generosity of his employers – depending on how one views it – allowed him time to pursue a vigorous political life. His parents remained completely nonplussed by the life he had chosen to lead. How quickly their earlier hopes and aspirations for him had vanished.

Baron's activities in the 1930s involved using his pen rather than a sword. He worked on *Advance*, a publication of the Labour League of Youth, in which he and Willis became central figures. Baron eventually worked as its editor. His political involvement increased still further in 1938 when the CPGB manoeuvred him into the post of assistant editor of *Tribune*, the fortnightly publication of the Labour left. By the late 1930s, this publication, like *Advance*, functioned under Communist influence. However, on May Day 1939 Baron relinquished his post at *Tribune* to work for *Challenge*, the CPGB's publication aimed at members of the Young Communist League. He was paid £2.10 shillings a week by the Party, even though still not a member. Through his central involvement here as editor, along with Mick Bennett and Ted Willis, all operating under the watchful eye of Gollan, he circulated among the leadership of the Party. Of his own admission, he knew the organisation entirely from above, rather than from a rank and file perspective.

Baron's concern at and opposition to Fascism in Britain marked only one of his activities in the 1930s. As Fascism spread its octopus-like tentacles in Europe, international influences became important in his life, especially between 1935 and 1939, years which, he believed, ushered in a "sort of golden age of Western Communism." Following the 1935 Seventh World Congress of the Communist International, Moscow now advocated the Popular Front. This involved Communists collaborating with other sections of the Labour movement, with the aim of capturing and dominating these other groups. Baron fully participated in this strategy both in Britain and France, visiting Paris and Toulouse on Popular Front business. He saw himself here marching with the shock troops of revolutionary change.

> Bliss was it in that dawn to be alive
> But to be young was very heaven.[4]

---

4   "Bliss was it …" is Wordsworth in "The Prelude" (1850).

Figure 5 "Bliss was it in that dawn to be alive..." Baron aged about sixteen years, when he became active in left-wing politics.

He drove himself hard to this end, engaging in what he later called a "frantic daily round of activity", sometimes working twenty-one hours a day.

Another international issue of the 1930s also entered Baron's life, the Spanish Civil War, which "burned before our eyes like some mesmeric conflagration." In effect, between 1936 and 1938 Fascism and Communism fought a fierce proxy war in Spain. Baron never went to Spain to fight in this conflict. Some of his friends, however, had their lives brutally cut short on Spanish soil. As Baron reflected on these personal tragedies and asked: "'Why not me?'" he drew some comfort from the fact that he was too young to go. Later, he also seized hold of the observation made in January 1939 by Andrei Andreyev, then head of the cadres in Moscow, that it remained important to "consider the problem of retaining leadership cadres in case of war, mobilisation and possible transition to illegal status."[5] Gollan, Baron's

---

5   Baron's notes for revision of the memoir quote Andreyev's comments on Spanish Civil War recruitment, which he discovered in a published volume of Comintern documents: Harvey Klehr, John Earl Haynes, Fridrikh Igorevich Firsov, *The Secret World of American Communism* (New Haven, London, 1995), Document 27, p.91.

advisor, mentor and protector, would certainly have taken this view. Through their constant politicking, Baron and Willis were helping to ensure that one day a rich political harvest would be gathered in. They were too valuable to lose. Rank and file members might be encouraged to enlist, so might intellectuals. Gollan despised intellectuals. Did the likes of Christopher Caudwell and Ralph Fox who died in Spain, ever realise as much? Did many of the academics, artists, composers, musicians, and writers who for years laboured enthusiastically in the Communist vineyard in Britain ever reach that awareness? In his later life, Baron recognised how fortunate he had been never to go to Spain. His conscience could also live with the fact that he had never recruited a single person for its everyday hazards.

Baron's unremitting political activity quickly brought him into contact with leading British Communist figures of his day. He brushed shoulders with Emile Burns, Ranji Palme Dutt, that totemic figure in the CPGB, and Esmond Romilly. He also met and was influenced by D.F. Springhall, "Springy," who moved seamlessly between Moscow and London: he received a seven years' prison sentence in 1943 as a Soviet spy. Labour figures who crossed Baron's path included Clement Attlee, Stafford Cripps, Hugh Dalton, the publisher, Victor Gollancz, Herbert Morrison, George Strauss, who put up most of the money for *Tribune* and that, "cosmopolitan cocktail" Konni Zilliacus. International figures he met during the years included the novelist, André Malraux, whom he encountered in Paris when engaged on Popular Front business, in which Malraux also participated, and Krishna Menon, later to assume a key political roll in an independent India.

Aspirations, hopes and dreams help to sustain us, but we need to remain constantly aware of disappointments. Moscow's plans for a Popular Front in Britain failed to take root. Baron had campaigned in vain. The Labour Party came out strongly against any move in that direction. At its 1939 conference, ultimatums were issued, and Stafford Cripps and his associates, strong advocates of the Popular Front, faced expulsion from the Party. Baron's hopes for Spain also crumbled. When on tactical grounds Stalin withdrew his support for the Republicans midway through the conflict, their battle was virtually over.

Even so, unfinished business remained in Europe. Hitler's power in Germany continued to increase and, fearful of its consequences, the CPGB assumed an active role in opposing Fascism in Britain, especially in the East End where Baron had grown up. But events in Europe threatened more. Hitler's ambitions, which had implications for Britain, were not easily contained and in 1939 Germany invaded Poland. Following this assault,

Baron vividly recalled hearing Neville Chamberlain's sombre radio announcement on 3 September 1939: "...and consequently this country is at war with Germany."

Baron now resolved to join the fight against Fascism by entering the armed forces. We know he had long harboured a deep fascination with the air and aeroplanes and had earlier dreamed of an airman's death in flames. Hence it was on the second day of the War that he took himself off to Kingsway to volunteer for the RAF, only to be rejected. When the recruiting sergeant witnessed Baron's bespectacled face he remarked dryly, "Run along, son. Don't waste your time."

Rejected for the RAF and working for a party which, having initially supported the War, on Moscow's orders soon opposed it, Baron now continued with his political life but under less easy circumstances. In this tense wartime situation, Britain's Communists came under MI5 surveillance. The authorities remained constantly vigilant against anyone and any group viewed as hostile to the state.

Not surprisingly, therefore, Baron soon received a visit from a Special Branch officer who enquired delicately why he had not already been called up. Baron informed him of his attempt to do so. However, it is no coincidence that along with Mick Bennett and Ted Willis, he soon received a buff envelope, requiring him to enlist for military service. Through this initiative, Special Branch, acting on behalf of the Government, was helping to decapitate the YCL. Even so, Baron received this official communication with "a great drench of pleasure." The feelings which had stirred within him when a little earlier he had attempted to join the RAF had surfaced again when watching the bedraggled survivors of the Dunkirk disaster arriving back in London. He wished he could have been among them. Now the opportunity to serve had presented itself. He wrote later of:

> ...the feeling of sheer escape that buoyed me up, escape perhaps from the ghost of depression that had been haunting me, or even, unknown to me, from the life I had been leading.

For years he had served as a soldier in the Communist cause. Now he could become a soldier in the British army. A new chapter beckoned in his life which would change it forever.

When in 1940 Baron entered 172 Pioneer Corps, he would finally taste the military action he had often dreamed of as a schoolboy. He also believed initially a service career would offer an extension of his personal political development.

> ...a Party man must equip himself to become a future leader
> of the masses, and that included the mass of soldiers. I wanted
> to get used to battle and to test my courage under fire. One
> day, I thought, we would need the support of fighting soldiers,
> the best of them, and they would only listen to and follow
> those whom they respected s brave men and capable leaders.

Tom Wintringham, Communist, revolutionary and writer, viewed the War
in a similar light. To him, the Home Guard could become an effective
Citizens' Defence Army, helping not only to repel any fascist invaders but
also serve as a vital future tool in the continuing fight for social change and
justice.

During his early army days, Baron sold copies of *Challenge* to fellow
soldiers and in 1942, under a pen name, wrote a series of articles for it. A
year later when he participated in the campaign in Sicily, he carried in his
knapsack a handbook on the 1936 Soviet Constitution. In his words, "I was
still then ... one of the faithful." A story called "Toy Shop," which he wrote
on the Sicilian campaign, appeared, without his knowledge, in the *Daily
Worker*.[6]

Yet certain actions by him are more important for what they reveal about
his developing attitude to the CPGB and towards the ideology he had
doggedly pursued and promoted for years. Following the entry of the USSR
into the War as a result of Hitler's attack on the Soviet Union in June 1941,
Baron wrote to the authorities underlining that he could now be relied upon
to "refrain from any political talk and activity."

> This letter, which I never mentioned to anyone in the Party,
> was a turning point in my life for I honoured it to the letter, at
> least, according to my lights, until the end of the war, and
> consequently came to feel less and less like a Communist
> among soldiers, more and more like a soldier among all the
> rest.

The full implications of what he had written gradually showed in his
behaviour.

---

6   The story is reproduced in Susie Thomas, Andrew Whitehead and Ken Worpole (eds),
     So We Live: The Novels of Alexander Baron (Nottingham, 2019), pp.82–85.

Figure 6 "The army gradually replaced the Party as the object of loyalty." Baron with army friends (see also Figures 29, 30 and 36).

Under Gollan's influence, he had for years read no books except works approved by the Party as politically "correct." But now he began once again to discover literature as a "magic casement".[7] He revisited Dickens. He turned to Baudelaire's *Les Fleurs du Mal*, poems which reflected that deep love of French culture he had first absorbed at Hackney Downs School. Also, after the Soviet Union had entered the war in 1941, he read Tolstoy's *War and Peace*.

During his early life, Baron had found a sense of belonging through institutions. As a non-believer, he could never have discovered it within the religious structures of Judaism. But when young, he had found it at the Grocers' School. Communism, through which race and ethnicity would be rendered irrelevant, had then for years been his adopted home, as it had for many others seeking certainty and security. The historian Eric Hobsbawm discovered something similar in that ideology. But now the Party's grip on Baron was loosening. In his words, "The army gradually replaced the Party as the object of loyalty."

---

7   My comment on Baron rediscovering literature as a "magic casement," draws from Keats's "Ode to a Nightingale" (1819).

Incidents around D-Day in 1944 also underline the important shift then taking place in his outlook. In that year, when busy training for the Normandy landings, he visited London on leave and met up with Mick Bennett, his close colleague and friend from their days at *Challenge*. Bennett remarked that there wouldn't be a Second Front any time soon. He had learned as much from Harry Pollitt who in turn had been offered that detail by Manny Shinwell, the War Minister.

> A year ago [Baron wrote] I would have plunged into argument and given an account of what we were doing on the south coast. Indeed, I would have thought it my duty earlier to let the Party know. Now I decided to take my cue from Manny Shinwell. I held my tongue.

It is a significant observation…

Before the landings, Baron enjoyed a period of leave and, again significantly, spent it with his family in Newbury, to which they had been evacuated from London, rather than with his CP comrades. Finally, just prior to D-Day, his command dispatched him on army business to London. His responsibility involved handing over papers to the Second Echelon, "a shadow organization that had been set up to take over most of the paperwork of units going into the field." Once again, he wrote,

> I did not want to meet any Party people even by accident and stayed in the Second Echelon building until it was time to catch the train back. I did not give the matter a second thought. I had simply stopped trusting the Party.

In the summer of 1944 D-Day, the opening of the Second Front, was finally launched, and Baron played his part in this long-threatened and dangerous assault. Fragments of what he experienced on the Normandy beaches and during the hard-fought grinding advance inland appear in *Chapters of Accidents*, as well as his novel, *From the City, From the Plough*.

Soon afterwards, the army transferred him to the infantry which had suffered heavy losses as Allied forces pushed further into occupied Europe. Baron had wanted initially to be an infantry man but now, he transferred reluctantly, preferring the company of his mates in the Pioneers. Even so, with this move he entertained hopes of being deployed in the forward areas. However, along with the other Pioneer NCOs transferred with him, he found himself put aboard a tank landing craft which, to his surprise, chugged its way from Ostend to Tilbury. Like so much army life, it all seemed totally surreal.

Back in England he received fourteen days' leave and an incident at this time further fuelled his growing alienation from Communism. One day he met someone, now an infantry sergeant, whom he knew from their days in the YCL. They decided to visit William Rust, editor of *the Daily Worker* and a key figure in the Party until his early death in 1949, to voice their concerns about soldiers' welfare. *Chapters of Accidents* provides a graphic account of that meeting.

> We asked Rust if he would pass on to Willie Gallacher the MP [for West Fife] a request to put in a word behind the scenes to get more warm clothing sent to the soldiers at the front, who were freezing. Rust sat in a low-slung chair warming his bottom with an electric heater. He told us not to worry about things like that. The Red Army was winning the war. We left in silence.

Baron's hostility towards Rust leaps off the page here. Their brief later correspondence in 1948 over the question of the status of Berlin also carried distinct sulphurous overtones. The wartime meeting between the two had loaded another log onto the fire glowing inside Baron which several years afterwards clearly still burned away inside him.

The transfer to England effectively marked the end of Baron's wartime service. But not immediately. He was sent to a training battalion in Northern Ireland, prior to his dispatch to "the other side" as the Quartermaster-Sergeant put it. However, an incident which occurred as he walked along the main road to the camp, near Newry, deemed otherwise: a heavy truck skidded and hit him. In his memoir, he recalled "a black interruption to life" in the wake of this accident and remarked that "my latest concussion might have been one too many." On D-Day his landing craft had been hit ...

His account of this time in *Chapters of Accidents* strongly suggests that by now his nerves had been shot to pieces. In army slang of the time he, "had got a twitch on." Signs of this problem had been apparent earlier when he had visited a department store in Antwerp and had panicked, imagining a rocket powering through its glass roof. By now, "innumerable fine wires inside me were being tightened on violin pegs." Soon afterwards he became aware of being, "...lonely, miserable, angry, disappointed and tired." Not surprisingly, the authorities rejected his application to transfer to British troops still fighting in Burma.

In his distressed condition he sought medical help and was advised to take a long convalescence. What followed around this time remained unclear to him fifty years later. It seemed beyond rational recall. He was clearly suffering from what would now be called post-traumatic stress.

In view of his condition, his demobilisation, scheduled for April 1946, went through three weeks earlier. When the committee enquired if he needed anything to begin civilian life, he asked merely for a typewriter.

At this point he clearly remained unwell.

> I went to the demobilization centre and travelled up to London… I arrived at Waterloo Station. Not long afterwards, I met a man who had been in the tanks, a hard-bitten fellow who said to me, "It was lucky they'd taken my pistol off me, or I'd have shot myself sooner then walk under that arch at Waterloo." I knew how he felt. I was reluctant and frightened when I walked out of the station.

For complex reasons he had been keen to enter the war and found a sense of comradeship and belonging during that conflict. However, though he hadn't been shot down in flames, as his young self frequently envisaged, he had paid a heavy price for his involvement.

Moreover, ever lurking in the background and contributing to his unsettled, anxious self, remained the tangled issue of his future relationship to the CPGB. It needed to be resolved—and soon. By now, he wrote, "most of the thousand threads that bound me to the Party had been broken." He knew that he had no wish to re-enter the Party machine and even less to settle for being a rank-and-file foot soldier for Communism. But the resolution of this difficulty still lay ahead of him.

7.

In this demoralised, uncertain state of mind, someone from his past provided a much-needed short-term lifeline. Baron chanced to meet Ted Willis in Kingsway. Baron had gone there to the Imperial Typewriter Company premises for the machine he had requested on demobilisation. Willis now earned his living by writing film and radio scripts. He had also assumed the role of artistic director at Unity Theatre, which had started life in 1936 and was run by a strong nucleus of Communists. He invited Baron to assume the editorship of the group's monthly magazine, *New Theatre*. Within six weeks he had become the Theatre's Chairman.

Baron spent the next couple of years with the Unity people. And it was here that he first met his future wife, Delores. Throughout this time, he maintained his CPGB links, but they no longer fastened deep within him. Once when he called in at King Street the staff there thought he had returned to duty. Not so, and he turned down invitations to take on Party posts, including on *The Daily Worker*. But that big issue of his relationship with the Party could hardly be avoided forever. And it wasn't.

Willis had mentioned to John Gollan that their old comrade appeared to be in a strange state of mind. Gollan duly arranged a meeting, clearly hoping to reassert his influence. A get-together between Baron and the man who had "mesmerised" him soon followed. Gollan invited Baron to become his assistant, a post which would involve supervision of the Communist Youth Movement. However, with his recent experiences as a soldier to fortify him, Baron refused. He explained that he now wanted to be a writer.

> [Gollan] said in a sickened tone, 'Oh Christ!' Then, in his old persuasive way, 'That's not a job for you. What does a writer do, even a good writer, even one of ours? He describes the world. You are one of the people who have to change it. And one day to run it.'
>
> I said nothing.
>
> He leaned across the table and went on, 'Look at me. An Edinburgh slummie. I am one of the five hundred men who matter most in the world.' Later he said, 'I don't care about that Willis. He's all right on a platform with the lights on him. But you are one of us.'

Following their confrontation, Gollan asked Baron to see a doctor, obviously hoping that he might then reconsider his position. But the psychiatrist advised that Baron be left alone for a year or two. Gollan agreed, probably reluctantly.

Just over a year after this major disagreement Gollan and Baron were both invited to supper, chez Willis. Baron remained unmoved, his position unchanged: "I was no longer in awe of him or tongue-tied. I was for once as fierce and eloquent as he was." Gollan left, according to Willis, "white-faced with emotion."

Baron and Gollan met only once more, *en passant*, at King's Cross Station. By this time, the latter had become General Secretary of the CPGB. Now recognising he had lost the battle with Baron, he "chatted gaily," shook hands, wished his former colleague all the best, caught his train to

Edinburgh and disappeared out of Baron's life – but not his thoughts – for good.

8.

This rupture marks the end of Baron's direct involvement with the Party to which he had devoted much of his youthful energies during what he would later call the "most intensely-lived" days of his life, when he fervently believed in the message of historical materialism, that a new and better world would be brought into being, a "joyful and fraternal" future.

But later? When Margot Kettle interviewed Baron in 1984, he expressed his horror that he and others had been drilled into what he now described as, "…a narrow, mean and fallacious theology". Even so, he admitted:

> …behind it there were many things which are part of my mode of thinking still, and a way of looking at all human activity which I think enlarged me, and which I certainly regard as valuably formative in my life.

Just over ten years later, when he embarked on writing *Chapters of Accidents*, he could be found rummaging in his past and being reminded of evidence which now alienated him from his exuberant political youth. Events of the Spanish Civil War assumed an importance here. How could the Party have ever justified siphoning off funds intended for children suffering in the Republican cause? How could Harry Pollitt ever have contemplated raiding the International Brigade Dependants' Fund? Baron was troubled particularly by realising that if at the time he had known of these matters, he would have given them his approval. His understanding of Communist ethics would have permitted him to do so. Bravely, he also recognised in old age that had he been active in the Spanish cockpit he might, like Monty Rosenfield, one of his CPGB comrades, have acted as an informer for the secret police who constantly prowled the ranks of the International Brigades looking for the slightest evidence of political unreliability.

Spain did not feature alone among his later concerns. Would his Communist ethics also have led him to support the CPGB's calculated deception of Jewish businessmen who were conned into believing they were providing funds to secure the emigration of persecuted Jews from Germany, whereas their donations, just like some of the Spanish money, disappeared seamlessly, without trace, into the general coffers of the Party? Any addition to Moscow's gold proved welcome.

Baron's wartime blanking of the Holocaust also worried him when, years later, he worked away on *Chapters of Accidents*. He wrote: "Even the most humane of Communists took into themselves the brutal indifference of the Party towards human suffering."

9.

Soon after losing the services of Baron, Gollan had to contend with another departure. Ted Willis, who had apparently ceased to be a Party professional around 1942, left the Party entirely to concentrate on a writing career. In Baron's dark post war-days, Willis had thrown him a lifeline and he soon carried out another favour for his friend.

During his evidently difficult years just after the War, Baron had been beavering away, quietly, secretly, on a novel. One evening, deep in his cups, he blurted out his secret to Ted and Audrey Willis. They enlisted another friend, Roger Woddis, to read the manuscript. Both he and Willis urged Baron to send *The Fifth Battalion*, as he had called it, to a publisher. Jonathan Cape, the third house to which he dispatched it, replied that after considering the advice of their reader, Daniel George Bunting (who wrote under the name, Daniel George), they would accept the manuscript for publication. It was Cape's wife who came up with its eventual title: *From the City, From the Plough*. Not only the title changed. Baron had written under the pen name John Masterman, in order to divorce its authorship from his Communist past. Unfortunately, John Masterman already existed as an author and Cape asked Baron to pick another name of not more than five letters. Bernstein became Baron. "The book came out in the year that I severed my last tie with the Party and I seized the chance to shed my Communist identity and start life again with the new name." He left his job at *New Theatre* following the book's success and would devote the rest of his life to writing. His memoir ends at this point.

10.

Baron left the CPGB much earlier than many other intellectuals. John Saville and E.P. Thompson took their leave after the Soviet invasion of Hungary in 1956. So did Christopher Hill and Victor Kiernan. Chimen Abramsky left with a heavy heart in 1958. Eric Hobsbawm never relinquished his membership.

From 1948, his new life as a writer, functioning outside the Communist orbit, led to a succession of novels. During these years he also wrote

Figure 7 "[He] would devote the rest of his life to writing." Baron, London, 1956.

anonymous reviews for *The Listener*. He served on the editorial board of the *Jewish Quarterly* and contributed to it. He composed film scripts, including *Robbery under Arms* (1958) and *The Siege of Sidney Street* (1958–9) – which I recall seeing at the time – a cinematic account of the well-known East End incident in 1911 involving anarchist émigrés from the Tsar's Empire. He also produced the script for Carl Foreman's *The Victors*

(1962), a screen adaptation of his novel, *The Human Kind*. The rise of Independent Television from the 1950s and 60s offered further opportunities and he found work writing for ATV and Rediffusion. Television viewers who then watched – and still watch – Jeremy Brett as Sherlock Holmes and Edward Hardwicke as the faithful Dr John Henry Watson were sometimes savouring a script Baron had written, as were viewers of some early *Poldark* sagas or of *A Family at War*. Later he obtained many commissions from the BBC, which involved mainly adaptations of literary classics such as *Ivanhoe, Oliver Twist, Jane Eyre, Vanity Fair* and *Sense and Sensibility*.

11.

While much of Baron's film and television work continues to attract critical acclaim, it is his novels which have stood the test of time. His literary output has long attracted admirers and been the subject of much discussion. There is no need here to travel in detail over that territory. But *Chapters of Accidents* provides a crucial background for understanding some of the central recurring themes to be found there: working class life in London, political engagement and disillusionment, and the experience of war.

12.

Baron's first novel, *From the City, From the Plough* (1948), clearly drew upon those wartime experiences in Sicily and Normandy, particularly the latter, that he recollects in the central section of his autobiography. In fact, he would sometimes refer to the book as his "Normandy novel." *There's No Home*, which followed in 1950, reflected his time in Sicily. In *Chapters of Accidents* he describes the relations between the women of southern Italy and their liberators and his second novel treats the same theme in its narrative of the affair between Sergeant Craddock and Graziella. *Rosie Hogarth*, his third novel, published in 1951, Festival of Britain year, contains scenes of postwar East End tribalism. These impressions had crowded in on him when growing up in Hackney, and when he returned home after the War. In this novel, Jack Agass's difficult transition to civilian life after the War clearly mirrors Baron's own problems, about which his memoir is disarmingly frank. In *With Hope, Farewell* (1952) there are also reflections drawn from Baron's early experiences, evident in his accounts of East End life and Mosleyite activity. Interestingly too, the recent War also returns. The novel introduces us to Mark Strong who had earned distinction in the

War as a fighter pilot. There is a reminder here of Baron's early love of the air, his boyhood fantasy about dying in aerial combat, and his thwarted attempt to enlist in the RAF on the second day of the War.

Baron's novels continued to appear thick and fast in the 1950s. His next book was *The Human Kind* (1953), a collection of stories that also drew closely on his impressions and memories of the War. In *Chapters of Accidents* he recalled a day in Normandy in 1944 when he lay in a grassy dip next to a heap of dead German soldiers.

> Their faces were chalky white, their mouths grinned open and fair hair stuck out in untidy fringes from under the rims of their helmets, but I reflected that they must have been a fine-looking lot. I was still a Communist and I do not suppose that my thoughts ran any further than this, but later, in retrospect, I saw them as also, very likely, young people of an excellent sort, misled like us by blind faith and like us poisoned by wicked lies.

Almost ten years after this experience, he wrote a story in *The Human Kind* expressing similar sentiments to those which had occurred to him on the battlefield. The tale, "The Way a War Ends," derived from an account Baron had heard of a recent fatal knife fight in occupied Berlin between a British soldier and a Red Army conscript. Yet only a little earlier these young men had been allies in the battle against Nazism. War brutalises, ideologies deceive, as his reflections on lying next to those German dead in northern France had brought home to him.

Two historical novels followed that explored another recurrent concern of Baron's work – the relations between men and women. *The Golden Princess* (1954) tells the story of Conquistador Hernán Cortés and his Aztec consort La Malinche, and *Queen of the East* (1956) centres on the conflict between Zenobia of Palmyra and Roman Emperor Aurelian.

Baron's next novel returned to political themes. *Seeing Life* came out in 1958 and turns heavily on his earlier experiences. It is critical of the CPGB and one of its characters, Hagerty, is almost certainly based on John Gollan, whose influence had weighed heavy over Baron throughout his political career in Britain and proved so difficult to lift. Listen to these lines:

> He recruited me. He trained me. I did a good deal of work for him when I was abroad. We were friends for sixteen years. When I told him one night I was leaving them, and the last

argument had failed, he opened the door and told me to get out. I should say he forgot me then … But you know I have never forgotten him.[8]

Gollan, Baron's Mephistopheles, 'lives' in this conversation.

Three novels appeared in the 1960s. *The Lowlife* (1963) is widely regarded as one of his finest. It affords penetrating insights into London lives which has led Iain Sinclair to write of it as "his delirious Hackney novel" and "one of the best fictions, the truest accounts of the borough."[9] That area is seen through the eyes of Harryboy Boas, a later incarnation of the *spielers* who had once populated the East End. But it does more. It reflects Baron moving in step with his times through though his betrayal of the Caribbean migrants then arriving in greater numbers in London – and elsewhere – through the 1950s, Pakistani café owners, Italians, the occasional Pole and Maltese gangsters in Soho.

Strip Jack Naked (1966), a sequel to *The Lowlife,* proved unsuccessful. But *King Dido* (1969) showed Baron back on top form. Set in Edwardian London, it is a powerful tale of underclass crime in the East End, where Baron's grandparents had settled. He portrays Dido, a character perhaps based partly on his uncle Hymie, running protection rackets around Hare Street, near Brick Lane, which in his memoir he would describe as: "…a cobbled street lined by high three-storey buildings blackened by soot from the railway that run behind the backyards." As a child, Baron would often visit his paternal grandparents here. This area clearly remained vivid in his memory.

Baron's London novels reflect a writer in full command of his terrain. They ring true and sound authentic. The characters, the narrative, the language all emphasise as much. It is not always the case with authors. In certain spy novels for example, a genre which remains extremely popular and attracts sales, it is sometimes possible to detect that a guidebook has been used to provide the colour and context of the story. Even an extremely well-known writer in this field was mortified to discover, when visiting a city described in one of his novels, that information lifted from a travel guide proved totally inaccurate. These jarring notes can occur, even though one leading real-life spy remarked that attention to small detail is the mark

---

8   The passage on Baron's fictional break from Gollan appears in his novel *Seeing Life* (London 1958), p.132.

9   Iain Sinclair's warm appreciation of *The Lowlife* can be read in the 2010 Black Spring Press paperback edition of that novel (pp.x,xiv).

of the true professional. Such attention to detail is strikingly evident in John Harvey's superb collection of detective stories based in Nottingham – the Resnick novels. And it is in Baron's literary work.

In the following decade Baron wrote three novels. *The In-Between Time* (1971) shifted his focus away from the East End to the "gilded ghetto" of North London. But in other ways it drew heavily on the experiences he recalled in *Chapters of Accidents*. Vic Mason is active in the Labour League of Youth, an organisation which occupied a fair amount of Baron's time in the 1930s. Mason is turned down for the Spanish Civil War: Baron never was. But a rejection for military service finds an echo in Baron's own life in his abrupt dismissal when volunteering for the RAF in 1939. The novel also reveals yet more antagonism towards the CPGB which is clearly drawn in part from Baron's developing re-assessment of his past life.

In 1976 Baron published *Gentle Folk*, a novel about middle-class life and social mores on the eve of the First World War, intended as a companion to *King Dido,* each treating different aspects of the 'condition of England' at that fateful moment. The final novel Baron published in his lifetime revisits the Spanish Civil War. *Franco is Dying,* which appeared in 1977, is set two years earlier with the Caudillo seriously ill. Frank Brendan, a Briton who had fought in Spain in the 1930s returns to the country and meets up again with a Spanish Communist at a time when Communism remained banned by Franco. In Andrew Whitehead's opinion, it is "…an excellent and dark political thriller."[10]

When writing it, did Baron relive his feelings, rehearsed in *Chapters of Accidents*, about never joining in this conflict? As he typed away on his novel, did he think of his friend, the tousle-haired Sidney Avner, "Big Sid," a member of the YCL who had perished early in the Spanish conflict? Did his mind return to Bill Featherstone, of the Paddington branch of the LLY, who had joined the British battalion in 1938? When Baron began his autobiography, Featherstone was known to have simply disappeared in the Spanish conflict but beyond that detail he had become one of history's invisible people. It transpired later he had been liquidated as a bad individual, an unreliable volunteer, by an American Communist who served in Spain as a secret police officer, presumably acting under the ultimate control of the NKVD. Whatever passed through Baron's mind, we know that the events in Spain continued to disturb. A prequel to *Franco is Dying,* Baron's novel

---

10   For Andrew Whitehead's comments on *Franco is Dying*, see: www.andrewwhitehead. net/alexander-baron (accessed 16 June 2020).

The War Baby appeared posthumously in 2019; it further reveals the continuing grip of the Spanish cockpit on his thinking and writing.[11]

13.

When he had completed *Franco is Dying*, Baron had no intention of allowing the fly to die in the ink-well on his desk. On his death, he left several unpublished manuscripts.[12] One of these was a gargantuan, unfinished, deeply hostile history of the "mystique and legend" of Communism, titled *The Party. A Study in Presumption*. Another was his memoir, whose research and writing occupied him during the last years of his life. He finished a second draft of *Chapters of Accidents* in late 1997. It appears here complete for the first time.

14.

Baron's memoir offers a vivid tableau of life in the East End of London in the early twentieth century, revealing the tussle between the resilience of conventional Jewish values, linked to the continual immigration into London between 1880 and 1914, and the persistent tug of assimilation which followed. His memoir also traces the tensions between school and home during his life at the Grocers' School. Education then, as later, could create its own frictions.

Chapters of Accidents provides a rich mine of information too on the early British Communist Party, which takes us beyond its well-known figures who feature remorselessly in the literature. True, John Gollan, one of these "políticos," appears frequently but Baron introduces us to other, less well-known figures who greased the wheels of the Party's machinery through all its national and international vicissitudes in the early twentieth century. Activists like Alex Massie and Maggie Jordan clearly left a strong impression on him. Other members such as Ray Matlock disgusted him.

Then there is the War which saw Baron serving as a foot soldier between 1940 and 1945. "Jews don't fight", "Jews are cowards", "Jews create wars for their own financial benefit, paid for by the blood of others!" These antisemitic sentiments possess a long, tenacious history. Yet Baron yearned for military service and, as his memoir reveals, embraced it wholeheartedly.

---

11 Alexander Baron, *The War Baby* (Nottingham, 2019).

12 These can be found among the sixty boxes of Alexander Baron's archive and library now held in Special Collections in Reading University Library, Reference MS 5126.

The army offered him a new home to replace that of the Party and, as his readers, we encounter a conscript's everyday experiences, traumas and memories as captured through the ever-observant eyes of Corporal J.A. Bernstein.

15.

An East End childhood, Shacklewell Junior School and the Grocers', Communist Party days, wartime service in the Army, the break with a Communist past. Yes: they provide key stages in Baron's life until 1948. But our lives are not so easily sectioned off, hermetically sealed. His postwar novels often drew heavily on his earlier East London experiences. His days in the CPGB also provide inspiration for his later imaginative work. His first book, a best-selling novel, which allowed him to open a bank account and clearly marked a significant tipping point in his life, could never have been written without that steadily accumulating store of detail he derived from his army days in Britain and Europe. "Only connect!" E.M. Forster wrote in *Howards End* and there is a clear interconnectedness in Baron's work.[13] The past, his past, drips steadily into the present. Which is how his work should be viewed.

16.

Alexander Joseph Bernstein, known in his Communist days as Alex Bernstein, in his army days as Corporal J.A. Bernstein, and later still as Alexander Baron, the novelist, died in London just over twenty years ago on 6 December 1999.

Colin Holmes
University of Sheffield, 1 March 2022.

---

13   E.M. Forster's "Only connect!" features in *Howards End* (Harmondsworth, 1971 ed.), p.174.

Chapters of Accidents

A Writer's Memoir

PART ONE:
Goodbye, Eden

Chapter 1

I was born on 4 December 1917 at 30, Penyston Road, Maidenhead, in Berkshire, eleven months before the end of the Great War. My mother went there to get away from the air raids. She stayed with relatives of Mr. and Mrs. Simmonds, a couple whom she and my father knew in London. Mr. Simmonds was a policeman. She arrived in Maidenhead a week before I was born and went back to London with me three weeks later.

My father, Barnett Bernstein, was born in Poland. He came to England when he was thirteen. My mother, Fanny Levinson, was born in Corbet's Court, Spitalfields. She was twenty-two and my father was twenty-three when I was born, a little more than a year after their marriage.[1]

My father worked as a fur cutter. We lived for a year with his parents above their cobbler's shop in Hare Street, Bethnal Green. Whenever there was an air raid at night my mother carried me a few hundred yards to the railway arches in Brick Lane. People came in crowds to shelter under the arches until the All Clear sounded. Sometimes her younger sister Hetty was with her; and since I was a very fat baby they had to take turns to carry me the short distance. I was only in my first year, but they told me that I used to point at the searchlights that combed the sky and shout, "Up! Up!"

A name loses its potency after it has been used for a while. 'The Great War': the words meant what they said to the generations who lived in that war. It continued to be known by that name until the war of 1939 began. It was the Great Divide in many lives. People spoke of "before the War" and "after the War" as two different eras, even when the shock of it had faded. To them the Second World War, with all its terrible air raids, was an anti-climax. "Before the War," even to the poorest people, became a Golden Age. When I listened to my parents and their friends during my childhood, their talk created in my mind a vision of a lost paradise of

---

1   In fact, their marriage certificate is dated 4 March 1917.

Figure 8 "For several years after the end of the war, I am sure until I was four years old, I thought that it was still going on." Baron aged about four years.

music-halls, Hampstead Heath, golden sovereigns, charabanc outings and dancing the Valeta.[2]

For several years after the end of the war, I am sure until I was four years old, I thought that it was still going on. The grown-ups talked about it with such immediacy that I had no sense of its being over. They recalled the Silvertown Explosion when a huge munition works had blown up in London, and the night the Zeppelin, one of the German airships that were bombing London, came down in flames.[3] When I was small, long after the war, I was frightened sometimes that there might be more air raids or another mighty bang in the night. For a few years after the Armistice great numbers of wounded men were still to be seen in the streets wearing hospital blue, an outfit of bright blue jacket and trousers with a white shirt and a red tie. When they were no longer to be seen I thought that men in the blue uniforms of the new Royal Air Force were the wounded.

After the war my mother's family, the Levinsons, lived in Tenter Street, in Spitalfields. It was known as the Old Tenterground.[4] I saw my uncles Alf and Joe there, still in uniform, and one day an American soldier, in a different uniform which I still remember, stood in the doorway and swung me up to the ceiling. He was a young nephew of my grandmother. His name comes back to me, Abe.

Hare Street, where my paternal grandparents lived, was a cobbled street lined by high three-storey buildings blackened by soot from the railway that ran behind the back yards. It was near the huge Shoreditch goods yards. Railway wagons came down the street all day long, the horses' hooves clashing on the cobbles, the carters often walking alongside holding the horses' reins. These men all wore army uniforms, old soiled tunics hanging half open, with the tarnished brass buttons still on them, service caps crumpled in the manner of the trenches stuck on the backs of their heads, and military greatcoats in the winter. My grandfather Bernstein's shop was a gathering-place for them. I sat perched on the counter with these huge men towering all round me. I listened to them talking about the trenches and I looked up at their weather-beaten faces believing that they were still soldiers.

---

2   The Valeta is a ballroom dance, rather like a waltz. It is danced in triple time.

3   The Silvertown explosion at a Brunner-Mond munitions factory reflected inadequate safety controls. The sensitivity of the incident was such that the official report into events was delayed until 1950.

4   Tenterground. An area of Spitalfields initially where newly made cloth was dried.

Piles of old war-time periodicals still lay about in every home. Wherever we visited, it seemed to me, there were copies of the *Penny War Weekly* for me to pick up. They were full of drawings that fascinated me. Shells burst in neat black and white asterisks. British soldiers were either very young and clean-cut or, if older, wore thick, ragged Old Bill moustaches. Germans were villainous. Wounded had neat white bandages round their heads or arms in slings. Our officers led their men with pistols upraised amid shot and shell. Jack Cornwell, V.C., stood to his gun at Jutland, alone among the bodies of his shipmates scattered upon the deck. Piper Laidlaw, V.C., strode through the smoke at Loos playing the pipes in front of his battalion. The men of 'L' Battery at Mons served their eighteen-pounders to the last. I must have been tiny when I first turned over the pages of these papers. I stared and stared at the scenes which remained in my mind for years, exciting and sometimes upsetting me.

*****

Until just before her wedding day my mother worked in a canvas and cordage factory near the docks. This was rough work. The women who did it were traditionally East End amazons. My mother looked like a young lady who made posies for a florist; her job in the war was making shrouds for dead sailors. Nothing, however, could have ruffled her serenity. She was innately ladylike, as was her closest sister Hetty.

She and my father, both superb dancers, met at one of the genteel East End dances of the time. He contrived to court her although he was, in a manner of speaking, on the run. That is to say, he lived away from his parents' home so that if an official communication came there they could claim that they had no idea of his whereabouts.

My father had been declared unfit for military service by a medical board. His weak heart was not feigned. When he was thirty-six he had a terrible heart attack that laid him on his back for months. He had another at the age of seventy-nine, when a hospital doctor warned me that he would not live for another three hours. He died at eighty-three of something else. He was a wiry, muscular man. He had, from his childhood, worked harder than all but a few do nowadays. His hands were calloused, with hard yellow lumps at the joints; but I dare say a long route-march in full pack would have killed him.

What he feared was the convention signed between the British and the pre-revolutionary Russian Government under which Russian males in Great Britain could be sent back to Russia to fight there. Once he was summoned,

Figure 9 "Until just before her wedding day my mother worked in a canvas and cordage factory near the docks. This was rough work." Barnett Bernstein and Fanny Levinson on their wedding day, 1916.

he might find that his British certificate of exemption was useless; he knew the Russian attitude to cannon-fodder, and to Jews.[5] He lodged in Hackney with a family of German Jews, the Marburgs. There was plenty of work for him in the backstreet work-shops of the neighbourhood.

---

5   For the issue of conscription which affected Baron's father, see Colin Holmes, *Anti-Semitism in British Society, 1876–1939* (London, 1979; reissued 2015), chapter 8; and Harold Shukman, *War or Revolution. Russian Jews and Conscription in Britain, 1917* (Edgware, 2006).

Chapter 2

By the time I was old enough to perceive my father as a person I saw him as a brisk, always faultlessly-dressed Englishman who took pride in having achieved membership of the lower middle class and who in speech was only distinguishable from the native-born in being more articulate and a trifle

Figure 10 "By the time I was old enough to perceive my father as a person I saw him as a brisk, always faultlessly-dressed Englishman." Barnett Bernstein in his youth.

Figure 11 "My father was hardly four years old when his grandfather took him on the tramp to relieve the family of two mouths to feed." Baron's paternal great-grandparents, Chie and Golda Bursztyn, in Poland probably around 1880.

too precise in his pronunciation. He spoke only occasionally of his early life and each time he gave me another glimpse of it he increased my wonderment that such experiences as he described could have befallen him. I sensed in his tone that he felt a little like that himself. "Could this have been me?" he seemed to be musing.

He was born in a Jewish *shtetl*, or village, near the River Bug, about forty-five miles from Warsaw.[1] He named the nearest town as Brok. He was one of five children. It was clear from his narratives that the family had lived in dire poverty. During four years of his childhood his father was away on military service in the Czar's army. I assume from my father's account of their circumstances during this time that no dependants' allowances were paid to the families of the conscripts. There was no leave, either. When a regiment came on manoeuvres to its home district, the wives of the soldiers trudged into the forests with sacks on their backs to find their menfolk, During one such encounter a younger brother of my father was conceived.

My father was hardly four years old when his grandfather took him on the tramp to relieve the family of two mouths to feed. They went from farm to farm repairing clothes for the Polish peasants. The peasants gave them food in payment for the work and let them sleep in barns. My father said that he did not remember the peasants ever being unkind. He learned to sew and stitch with his grandfather, and on the road the old man taught him the only Hebrew he ever learned. There was no religion in his own household. As I shall relate, my family on both sides have been irreligious people. Nevertheless, after a couple of years of this tuition he knew all the Hebrew prayers and rituals well enough to despise, in later London times, the illiterates (as he called them) who gabbled Hebrew without understanding it when he was called upon to join them in a *minyan* (a religious quorum of ten males) or at some synagogue ceremony. He never picked up more than a few words of Russian or Polish. His father came home from the army speaking Russian and during my childhood taught me some. My father's native tongue was Yiddish. Years later the painter Josef Herman told me that my father's Yiddish was of a classical purity.[2]

---

1   *Shtetl.* A small village or town in Eastern Europe with a predominantly Jewish population.
2   Josef Herman (1911–2000). Royal Academician, born in Warsaw, who arrived in England during the Second World War. His art is noteworthy for carrying political messages. He lived for some years in Wales. The National Museum, Wales holds a sizeable collection of his paintings and sculptures.

I asked my father once if he had ever been to Warsaw. "Only once," he answered. "I went with some of the other boys to look at Peretz's house." Peretz was a famous Yiddish writer.[3]

I asked, "Did you see Peretz?"

"Of course not. We looked at the house and we came home."

After my father's return to his mother he helped to eke out the family's food by foraging in the forest. He brought home mushrooms and berries and he became adept at catching fish. Sometimes he went down the river on the rafts of the timbermen. (My neat father, I could not get over it, a ragged little Huck Finn.)

I never asked my father questions. I have never known how to draw people out to talk. Perhaps I am the sort of writer who stimulates his imagination by not knowing about people and then surmising and dreaming. I never spoke to my mother about her life, either, and know only fragments of it. My sister was close to her and knows a great deal about her; but then, I rarely ask my sister questions. My parents are dead now and it is too late to find out what I do not know. I cannot say, then, how it was that when my father was eight he travelled on his own to Odessa — five hundred miles on the map measured with a ruler, perhaps eight hundred by any mode of travel. All he said was, "I was in Odessa, I was on my own, I must have been hungry, I fainted in the street."

He might have died and been thrown into a paupers' pit, as many were each day, but a passer-by picked him up and took him home. The man was a Jew, a herbalist. My father lived with the family, learned to make up country simples, slept in the shop on sacks of herbs and ate well by his standards from the food left by the family in the cooking utensils before he cleaned them.

While his father was still away in the army two of my father's younger brothers died of scarlatina. This enabled his mother to come to Odessa with the two surviving boys, twins, to find him. She rented a "corner". I have read about this in Russian literature. Four families each rented a corner of a room. Theirs was in a cellar with water-logged walls. The herbalist did not want to part with my father. He said that he had never come across a brighter boy and that he would teach him the trade if he remained.

They went back to my father's native village. My grandfather came back from the army. Soon after, the Russo-Japanese war began. My grandfather and his four brothers were all reservists. They fled together to England. My

---

3   I.L. Peretz (1852–1915). Regarded as one of the three great classical writers in Yiddish.

grandfather stayed, the brothers went on to America. He never saw any of them again. He was a good bootmaker and he set to work to prepare a home for my grandmother and the children.[4]

In 1907, after three years, he sent for them. He had taken a little shop in Hare Street, where he was to remain until he went into an old people's home. My grandmother was a deserter's wife. She had no hope of getting a permit to leave the country. With money sent by her husband she "went to the smugglers." A convoy of women and children, escorted by these dealers in every kind of contraband, plodded for two weeks to the frontier, walking only at night and sometimes waiting in hiding for days. My grandmother and my father carried all the family belongings on their backs. The twins, seven years old, often fell to the ground in the course of a night's march and had to be carried by the smugglers. They went on to Hamburg in a train, and were there loaded into the hold of a tramp steamer in which they were all sick for thirty hours on the journey to London Docks.

My grandfather met them there. He took them to Hare Street where the three children were scrubbed, fed and put to bed. Next day he put boots on their bare feet and took them to Petticoat Lane to buy them suits.

My father went for a year to the Jews' Free School. By the end of that time he had a good command of English and was at the top of his class in every subject. The headmaster implored my grandfather to let the boy stay. This was still the time when a promising child might be kept on as a pupil teacher, entering the profession with no other training, like Dickens's Bradley Headstone, and the headmaster said that he would keep my father by him and make a teacher of him; but my father had to go out to work. I think he later saw this as the great lost chance of his life.

He was apprenticed to the fur trade. This apprenticeship brought with it the further stage in his education that my father craved for; the acquisition of culture and gentility. His master was a German. The Germans were the aristocrats of immigrant Jewry, educated people, Europeans. He lived in the master's home, perfected his English and learned the entire repertory of correct dress, bearing and manners. Not that he and his family were

---

4   The Jewish migration to Britain is covered in L.P. Gartner, *The Jewish Immigrant in England 1870–1914* (London, 2001. First ed., 1960): J.D. Klier, "Emigration Mania in Late Imperial Russia. Legend and Reality, in A. Newman and S.W. Massil (eds), *Patterns of Migration 1850–1914* (London, 1996), pp.21–36. On London, a major centre of settlement, see A.J. Kershen, *Strangers, Aliens and Asians: Jews and Bangladeshis in Spitalfields 1660–2000* (Farnham, 2005); For a photographic record see W.J. Fishman, *The Streets of East London* (London, 1979) with photographs by Nicholas Breach.

deficient in culture; but theirs was not of the English sort. They read the great European authors in their home; in Yiddish. Their father took newspapers of a sort which would be called "heavy" nowadays, full of literary essays, stories and politics; in Yiddish, of course. He took the boys to the theatre. When my wife and I told my father at some time in the nineteen-sixties that we had seen Paul Scofield playing Lear, he said, "What? Have they translated that play into English?"

My father also became a master craftsman. During my childhood he was put under contract by a large firm of furriers. The contract seemed a wonderful document to me when I was small, a patent of honour on big, crackling pages of parchment paper with an enormous heading engraved in scroll work. He was a five-pound-a-week man, a title conferring import-ance in those days, and at one time I heard ten pounds spoken of. Even when the firm fell on bad times later on, during the Depression, and closed down for a while, they continued to pay him a wage so that he should not look for work elsewhere. Still on the payroll, on his own in the workshop, my father designed an attractive collar for them. The travellers went out on the road with samples that he made up, orders poured in and the factory was in full production again. A rich woman for whom he had made a sable coat wanted to set him up in a business of his own in the West End. She told my mother that he was one of the finest craftsmen in the country, an artist. I sat in a corner listening. He refused the offer. He was timid, as I have always been, and would never dare to try on his own.

Everything that he turned to he did well. He grieved sometimes in later life that he had not fulfilled the abilities that were in him. I do not know that this is so, for I shall have something to say about his limitations. Certainly he saw me as the one who might realise his own dreams. That was in part the story of my life; not only of my early life.

Chapter 3

Corbet's Court was a seventeenth-century alley in Spitalfields, among the buildings and yards of the great Truman-Hanbury brewery. It was lined with little dwellings, two rooms up and two down. It is gone now. My mother was born there in 1896 and spent her childhood there.

A smell of hops always hung about the brewery precincts. My mother remained a child of Corbet's Court all her life as I dare say Amy Dorrit remained a child of the Marshalsea for the rest of hers after Dickens' happy ending. Fifty years later at my mother's home in Hackney, she waited every week for the brewery dray to come by. It was one of those smart equipages which the companies keep on the road for publicity, freshly painted, stacked with new casks with polished brass bands, pulled by great shire horses with coloured ribbons plaited in their manes and strings of prize medallions hung round their necks. At the sound of hooves she hurried out of the house and walked up to the street corner alongside the wagon. Once in the 1950s when she was in Spitalfields, she explored around the brewery. She came home eager with pleasure. She had chatted with an old watchman who had been a lad at the brewery when she was a little girl. When she was dying in hospital at the age of seventy-nine, her mind apparently gone, I sat by her asking questions that might evoke a response; until she turned her head to me and recited, in a clear, child's voice, "Fanny Levinson, Four Corbet's Court, Spitalfields, London, East One." Then she relapsed into silence.

Her mother and father came from Lithuania. She was one of ten children. They all had blue eyes and several of them, like her, had light hair and fresh Nordic looks. These features are common among Baltic Jews. Their forbears have obviously mixed with the population around them. In the same way, Sephardic Jews whose ancestors came from the Mediterranean look like Iberians or Italians; and it is a commonplace that large numbers of Spaniards have Jewish blood. The Jews in Israel belonging to families gathered in from Arab countries are Arabs of a sort, often in temperament as well as appearance. The Orthodox Jewish notion of a long-preserved racial purity that must be maintained is nonsensical and dangerous.

Figure 12 "Her mother and father came from Lithuania." Baron's maternal grandparents, Jane and Isaac Levinson.

My grandfather sent my mother to a school in Deal Street, behind Brick Lane, at the back of the brewery. This was a Christian school, although the great Jews' Free School, which some of her brothers and sisters attended, was only a few hundred yards away on the other side of Commercial Street.

The children at Deal Street, mostly from brewery families, lived in some of the roughest slums in London. They were well taught. When my mother left school at the age of fourteen she read well and she continued to read a great deal. She knew the outstanding events in English history and where most of the countries and great cities and seas of the world were. She could do any kind of arithmetic rapidly and correctly. She was taught needlework, botany and singing. Her spelling was good and she had a neat, round hand of writing. I could never easily distinguish it from the handwriting of any of her three sisters; they were taught at different times by different teachers but on the same system.

I know that a lot of people who are struggling with the miseries of modern education console themselves by believing that education in the past (say, in my mother's time at the beginning of the century) was a dreadful, useless, Mr. Gradgrind affair. It was not. Right down to my own schooldays it produced a literate and numerate working-class and from 1870 onwards it was one of the great civilising influences in this country. The little girls of my mother's generation learned to wear clean petticoats and to be polite. The grown-up women I knew in my childhood were all products of that time, articulate, capable and ceremoniously courteous.

At Deal Street my mother had Christian scripture lessons and took part in School Prayers every morning. Twice during her schooldays she was sent away for a week by the Children's Country Holiday Fund. These were the only holidays she had. She was sent both times to stay with two elderly ladies at Seaford, in Sussex. They were pious Christians and taught her accordingly. For the rest of her life she looked back on these holidays with something like rapture, recalling the lovely house and garden. As she did her housework she liked to sing and as often as not she sang the Christian hymns of her childhood. She agreed readily when my father decided that I should go to the local Christian school in Hackney, I, too, went to scripture lessons and took part in School prayers. Ever since, I have enjoyed such things as hymns, Nativity plays and the ordered calm of church services.

My mother had a good knowledge of London. When she was young, children enjoyed the freedom of the streets, with nothing to fear except the wheels of passing carts and carriages. She and her brothers and sisters roamed all over London in a band. Her older brother Izzy, a scholarship boy, led these outings. He took the children to all the museums, parks and historic places.

They were allowed into the offices of the great shipping lines, to look at huge models of liners in glass cases and wall maps of the sea routes. Greenwich was familiar territory to them; they knew all the passages and bridges and basins of the Docks; and, most often of all, they wandered round inside the Tower of London on the free mornings and played in Tower Hill Park.

George Orwell has made the writer Frank Richards well known.[1]Richards was the creator of Greyfriars School. For more than thirty years he published a long weekly story about it in *The Magnet*. My mother was a reader of *The Magnet* from its first issue in 1908. (So, I found later, was the mother of my closest friend.) She started me on *The Magnet* when I was quite small and followed with me the fortunes of its schoolboy heroes The Famous Five.

These stories are now the subject of a cult; no doubt, too, of many PhD theses. They did not inculcate snobbery or encourage working-class servility towards what would be called the Public School Class. Their fantasies were in essence classless, for they were almost entirely concerned with rebellion, conspiratorial fun and friendship. The Famous Five travelled all over the world in their adventures and Richards saw to it that we learned a lot about the world from his stories. All the multitude of children who read *The Magnet* and papers like it read twenty-five thousand words of solid print each week. Not many children at the state schools nowadays could do that. So much for Mr. Gradgrind.

My mother and most of her brothers and sisters went to work in factories at fourteen but the Jewish ferment of betterment was present in the family. Izzy was at the Davenant Foundation School in Whitechapel. My mother was his pet. He and she read together and talked about life. He took her out to theatres and to suppers. While he was training (as a pupil teacher at his former elementary school) to be a schoolmaster he bought her a pretty costume of dark green velvet with a long hobble skirt. It was a lady's costume. She had a photograph of herself wearing it, sitting on the photographer's high stool with a potted plant on a stand next to her. She was always delighted to bring out this photograph and talk about her girlhood outings with her worldly brother.

---

1   Frank Richards (Charles St John Hamilton) (1876–1961). Frank Richards wrote for *The Magnet* and its sister paper *The Gem*. He also dashed off novels. His heyday was the early twentieth century when Billy Bunter and Greyfriars School particularly captured the imagination of young readers. See George Orwell, "Boys' Weeklies," Sonia Orwell and Ian Angus (eds), *The Collected Essays, Journalism and Letters of George Orwell*, Vol. 1, *An Age Like This* (Harmondsworth, 1979), p.502–40. This source includes a reply by Richards to Orwell.

Chapter 4

The earliest home that I can remember was at 11, Sandringham Road, in Dalston. We went there when I was two years old. We had been living in one room before that. We still had only one room, but now there was a scullery as well.

Hackney is talked of nowadays as part of the slummy East End (despite some infiltration by many young middle-class people) but in those days it was for the poor a socially superior district, a step up. Dalston was an abode of City clerks, skilled workmen, tradespeople and very minor professional people: part of Pooterland.[1]

Sandringham Road runs up a slope into the main Kingsland High Street. A chapel, since demolished, stood at the top with the minister's forbidding grey house next to it. The street seemed as wide to me as a boulevard, the slope like a hillside. I saw the few steps up to our street door as a lofty ziggurat. Inside, the stairs up to the top of the house soared as mysteriously as a staircase in a Piranesi drawing.

Our room was on the top floor, in front. The scullery was a narrow passage without a window, through which we entered the room. There was just space in it for a stone sink, shelves for crockery and a tiny table with our chairs.

There was a garret above, of which my father had the use. This enabled him to take in private jobs and work all hours at night. He also put in as much overtime as he could at the factory. He was saving up to buy a house. When he bought the house he continued to work all hours to pay off the mortgage. Working day and night was normal to him. Even in his one year at school he had worked at night for a man he referred to with no pejorative intention as a "sweater".

He sounded almost affectionate when he spoke of his times with the sweater. This man and all his own family lived on the premises and slaved

---

1   Pooterland is a reference to George and Weedon Goldsmith's comic novel, *The Diary of a Nobody* (1892), where the leading character is Mr Pooter, a lowly but aspiring clerk.

in a backroom workshop as hard as they forced their workers to slave. When his own children came home from school they were put to the machines till the early hours of the morning just as my father was. Workpeople and employers lived hugger-mugger together, cursing each other but as close in some ways as members of one family, eating together, involved in a mesh of affections, confidences, jealousies, intrigues, jokes, lending and borrowing and of course courtship. They were all as one in face of the arch-adversary, the factory inspector, who wanted to take the bread from their mouths. Against his coming they closed the windows with curtains and shutters after dark, kept watch, and if he came, all protested fluently that they were only friends visiting.

Our one room looked enormous to me. I do not know if I remembered the room we came from, in Abersham Road. Perhaps my mother told me about it, herself proud of the move; a little room, always dark, with hardly space to move among the furniture. I too was proud of our grand and spacious habitation. It seemed wonderful to look down at the street from this great height. To this day I cannot be sorry for the modern poor who live in conditions that we would have called palatial. It was an adventure each time I toiled up the steep, lofty-seeming staircase. The garret above, into which my father vanished as soon as he had finished his supper every evening, was a place of mystery to which I never dreamed of ascending.

The centre-piece of our room was a big double bed with iron rails painted pale green and surmounted by ornate brass knobs. Next to it was a cot with high railings in which I slept till we moved when I was nearly six. Between the windows was a dressing-table with three hinged mirrors. In front of each window was a bentwood chair. In the wall next to my cot was a small fire grate and a cupboard.

Except when we went shopping my mother spent all her days in this room. I never saw her resting. She was cleaning, cooking, baking and mending; and for hours playing with me. She sang all day long. Besides the Christian hymns she had learned at school, she sang airs that she remembered from the school song book, as well as ragtime tunes and songs of the Great War. Some popular tunes are still poignant to me because when I hear them I hear her; for instance, *Swanee*, which comes to me again in her clear young voice, from the scullery, against the rattle of plates.

For a long time the war songs added to my uncertainty as to whether the Great War was still going on or not. She sang "Keep the Home Fires Burning", "While the hearts are yearning", and "We won't be back till it's over, over there".

She frightened me with a tune which still sounds sinister to me, the first verse ending:

> *We will burn you all alive.*
> *We are the German soldiers.*

There was another verse in which the English counter-attacked and, full of relief, I shouted the words as she sang:

> *Shoot bang fire, shoot bang fire,*
> *We are the English soldiers.*

There was another which I took to be about the Great War until she explained to me that there had been another war in South Africa that ended when she was five:

> *Lord Roberts and Kitchener*
> *And Buller and White,*
> *They are our leaders*
> *In this terrible fight.*

Sometimes we sang together, I yelling joyfully, "Yes! We have No Bananas" or:

> *John Brown's baby's got a pimple on his nose,*
>   (repeated twice)
> *And they rubbed it in with camphorated oil.*

I was still very much part of her. Children are as cognisant of smells as animals and her smell was an aura of comfort in which I could take refuge. Sometimes, giving me what she called a catlick, she spat daintily on a handkerchief and wiped my face hard. This handkerchief and her saliva had her smell, which returns to my nostrils as I write. To me she was a deity bestowing cleanliness, the authoritative firmness of her hand itself a reassurance, yet still dainty and ladylike.

Sometimes she let me venture out of the house on my own. I did not go far up and down the street. Horses and carts and people went by, looming above me. Once an elaborate black carriage came slowly along the street, with a canopy supported by baldaquin pillars, beneath which a polished coffin rested on a dais, covered by floral wreaths. All the pedestrians paused as it passed them. The men raised their caps. I knew that there was a body in the coffin. When I was five and wore a school cap I raised it whenever a funeral passed by. Everyone paid their respects to the dead.

Once a band of big, rough boys, six-year-olds probably, took me across the street to explore an empty house. I was terrified as I trotted after them in and out of bare, echoing rooms, up and down wooden staircases. Afterwards we all returned to my own house, and gathered on the top of the front steps. One by one the big boys shouted words that terrified me even more. "Poop!" "Cuck!" "Fart!" My turn came. I wondered if my mother upstairs could hear. Guilty and miserable, I whispered, "Wee-wee."

Most of my memories, however, are of indoors, looking out from our room. My mother set a chair with its back to a window and I stood on it looking down at the immense street far below. It was empty most of the time. Occasionally a horse and cart came along, the small ones briskly, the larger ones at a slow plod-and-clatter. Mr. Brodsky the dairyman came by, riding his float like a charioteer, a Cossack with a swarthy face covered with boils under a wild head of hair. His son, later on, was in my class at school. The teacher called him a dirty little boy and I thought he was, too. She said she would not dream of drinking his father's milk. Nor would my parents, who patronised Mansfield the Gentile dairyman. Every morning the milkman's horse walked from one house to the next, stopping unbidden at each. The milkman went up the steps, carried back to his float the pewter cans with hinged brass tops that had been left on the doorsteps and filled them with a ladle from the brass-decorated churn in the middle of the float. Street vendors and other itinerants still came and sang their cries, the old-rags-and-lumber man, the any-old-iron man, the knife-grinder, cockles-and-mussels, cane-your-chairs, Indian-toffee, the ice-cream man ("Joe Assenheim's, they're lovely!") and sometimes a newsboy, running with one arm holding a bundle of newspapers and under the other a poster like a flapping apron, shouting "Speshul! Speshul!" Sometimes it was a forlorn street singer, an old man with a cracked voice or a woman with a baby in her shawl; or it was an organ-grinder playing and moving on intermittently. My mother was forever throwing pennies down into the street.

Opposite the top of the street was a cinema, the Kingsland Empire. I was not one of the infants conveyed every afternoon by their mothers to "the pictures." My mother would have nothing of that; but one no doubt lonely afternoon when I was two she gave way and took me. We saw part of a film; then I began to yell with fright and she took me home. Huge men in elaborate uniforms strutted at an unreal speed on a dazzling white sheet carrying a man trussed hand and foot. They came to a sort of stone urn, stuffed him in and flames leaped up from the urn. That, at least, was what I remembered. I cried at the memory of it and had bad dreams about it for a few years afterward.

On the corner in the main road was a draper's shop called Hull's. It consisted of two shops interconnected. The ways between the counters were narrow, little boxes containing the takings hummed to and fro on wires overhead, shelves lined the walls to the ceiling packed with fabrics in bolts of every colour, assistants flung bolts across the counter in torrents of colour in front of my mother. The smell of the fabrics comes back to me. The pungent scents of acid drops, peppermints and, strongest of all, pineapple drops, hung over the pavement in front of Sisley's next door. Home-made sweets were made in a back room and were to be seen in the window in rows of jars filled with jagged lumps in many colours. Many of my most acute and sometimes painful memories are prompted by the fleeting involuntary return of a smell or colour, acting like the taste of the madeleine. The undulled faculties of a child are as sensitive to enjoy colours as they are to record smells.

A long alley from our street led to Ridley Road market, where booths faced the stalls along the top of an embankment from which I looked down at the rail yards, a seemingly vast expanse of rails on which strings of goods wagons stood. In the open frontages of a butcher's shop at the corner hung split carcasses of cattle and pigs together with clusters of rabbits. Pigs' heads squinted from slabs and the butchers wearing straw hats and striped aprons stood in the doorway shouting, "Buy! Buy! Buy!" On the provision merchant's counter stood great cheeses and cylinders of yellow butter. The assistants cut pieces from the butter and patted them into shape with wooden blades that imprinted pretty pictures and patterns on them. Every fruit stall mounted a display composed with an artistry now lost. On dark afternoons in winter the naphtha flares hanging at every stall were lit and their great wild flames leaped up to my delight, making the mud glitter underfoot.

Once a taxi came down the street. The driver was some little boy's uncle. He crammed a dozen children in and took us for a ride round the block; an adventure. My father's factory was at Ludgate Hill in the City, work finished at midday on Saturdays and he always came home from "business" with a Dundee cake in a tin or a box of six chocolate cream buns. The Lord Mayor's Show went past his factory and I believed that he rode in it, in a coach. There were some blue and yellow cards on the dressing-table into which he stuck stamps every week. These were to do with rates and taxes. I assumed that the taxes were the same that I had ridden in.

My father bought me a big Meccano set. The pieces were unpainted at that time. He saw it in the window of a toyshop displayed in the form of the Eiffel Tower. The shop people dismantled it and sold it to him in whatever box came to hand, without any instruction book. As I have said, he had his limitations and he was too ignorant of such matters or too timid to go back to the shop and ask for an instruction book. We kept the set for several years, until most of the pieces were lost, but neither of us was ever able to construct anything exciting out of it. He took me to another shop, this one on Kingsland Waste, and bought an expensive toy motor-car for me. I liked to pedal it and sound the bulb horn, but I was disappointed as soon as I saw it. It was not made to look like a real car. It looked too much like one of the soap-box go-carts in which ragged boys were always swooping and whooping down the hill at the end of our street. In the parks I saw with envy other toy cars that looked like real ones.

When I was five my mother took me to a hospital, where I was fitted with a pair of gold-rimmed glasses. I never found out why it was the Royal Waterloo Hospital that we went to, a long and tiring journey from home, at the south end of Waterloo Bridge. We saw a kind doctor named Mr. Bickerton. Both of us loved him. We loved every good doctor, that is to say, every doctor who spoke kindly. Whenever we went back we had a penny currant bun each at the A.B.C. tea shop across the road, with a glass of milk for me and a cup of tea for my mother. In the hospital, we waited to be seen for hours on benches, moving up until our turn came. Old books were sold at a stall in the waiting-room at a penny each. My mother bought several of these for me, ancient school books, *Tales of King Arthur*, *A First Geography Reader*, *Aesop's Fables*. I could read. Did anyone teach me? Perhaps my mother taught me the letters. I do not recall that she did so. It seems to me that by looking at words I saw what they were. I had heard only talk of school; a remote prospect, still puzzling, for I had no playmates to tell me what school was like.

Hospitals were kept up by charity. One of the events that gave shape to our year in Dalston was the Metropolitan Hospital Carnival. Everyone knew the Met. It was not big and it was not far away. Anyone in distress could walk in there and be received kindly. We joined the dense crowds on the pavements as the procession of floats came by, all costumes, music, shouts, flung streamers; collection-boxes rattled at us. At the Royal Waterloo my mother had to go, each time we went, to see the Lady Almoner to make what was called a voluntary contribution. The Lady almoner sat behind a desk. My mother sat upright on a bentwood chair in front of the desk. I stood next to my mother. My mother offered a shilling. The Lady Almoner said, "Is that all you can afford?"

I saw my mother's lips clamp together. She clutched her purse with both hands. She said, "Yes, ma'am."

I listened to my parents talking about schools. Near to us was Sigdon Road School at which there were a lot of Jewish children. These children had Jewish scripture and Jewish prayers. A little further away, next to a notorious slum precinct, was another school, the Shacklewell.

My mother said, mildly, "It is a rough school."

My father said, "Let him rough it."

On the morning I started at the Shacklewell Infants' School I stood with my mother in the school hall, taking in the close, stuffy smell laden with chalk dust. A tall lady with her hair done up at the back in a bun led me by the hand to a classroom. There, another lady sat me at a little table at the front and gave me a frame of coloured beads on wires. The brightness of the colours wholly occupied me so that I took no notice of her or of the other children. In the break I went across the playground to a group of children, was admitted to a game as a matter of course and as a matter of course joined in.

One day I had to take a farthing to school. It was for charity. In return the teacher gave me a tulip to take home. I walked to the gate where my mother was waiting for me, holding it out in front of me, my gaze fixed on it. My mother often bought a penny bunch of daffodils at the market but they were pale things beside this splendid, sleek red flower. The same teacher brought flowers to school, pansies, which were a revelation of beauty to me, and bluebells when they were in season. She kept them on the windowsills in jam jars filled with water. Flowers mesmerised me, such an endless array of glistening petals, bright colours and distinct, delicate perfumes.

Soon after I had started at school I woke up one morning and was surprised to see that my father, who ought to have been off to work already, was still in the room, together with a strange, elderly woman. Then I saw my mother lying in the big bed, holding a bundle out of which a baby's face peeped. The women told me that I had a little sister. I was five years old and no longer an only child. I was bitterly jealous of the intruder.

Chapter 5

A crowd of poor patients always filled the little shop in Commercial Street which was Doctor Hume's waiting-room. Young wives with babies, sickly children, bent old women in shawls, huge porters from Spitalfields Market down the road packed the little room; and sometimes ragged, silent men and women from the slum streets of Whitechapel, or from the doss-houses, from whom their neighbours tried to keep at least a few inches of distance.

The shop window was painted green except for a strip of grimy pane at the top. The room was gloomy or dark most of the time. On dark or foggy days a street lamp outside cast a pale gas light into the room and the gas jet in the room popped and flickered. I must have seen electric lighting in big shops and public buildings but nowhere else could I imagine any other means of illumination than gas. At home I waited at the window when dusk came to see the lamplighter come down the street with his long pole.

Doctor Hume was a small Scot, with a red face shrunk like a prune and a few hairs on his head. He sat in an old armchair which was bursting underneath, his bottom almost on the floor. When he spoke to us he leaned forward, his eyes gleaming. He always wore the same crumpled suit of hairy brown tweed. The surgery was not far from the Tenterground and he was the protecting deity of my maternal grandmother Levinson's family. I shared their awe of him. I flamed with indignation when a woman in Petticoat Lane, talking to my mother, called him "that old drunk."

My grandmother's name was Jane. My grandfather was Isaac. They married when they were eighteen. A photograph with Cyrillic wording printed on the back shows them as a beautiful couple. He was tall, slender and dark-haired, with a stern, striking face. She was small, with mild blue eyes, her smooth shining, golden hair drawn back from her forehead. My earliest memory of them must be when they were about fifty.[1] My grandfather was as tall and upright as ever, his stern face tight on the cheekbones with a thick military moustache. My grandmother was a little old woman bowed by the bearing of ten children, her face wrinkled and sprouting little

---

1   See Figure 12, p.50.

tufts of grey hair. Years later she said to her daughter Hetty, "My girl, if I had known as much as you know, you would not be here now."

She panted and wheezed incessantly. She was not a healthy woman. Some of her children inherited her weak chest. My Uncle Harry had a cough and later on I heard the word "consumption." Grown-ups used it as casually as if they had said, "headache." Jack had asthma and was often to be seen with a towel over his head inhaling Potter's Asthma Cure. Doris, her youngest daughter, was only four years older than me and was the pretty playmate of my childhood. In later life she developed a chronic asthmatic complaint and died of it when she was sixty.

Doctor Hume was my grandmother's great support. She ran to him whenever there was a family problem and my grandfather was away. She really did run; I remember her feet scurrying under her fat old body, and the sound of her panting. It might be a dispute with the rent collector, or she might be clutching some official paper which she did not understand. If one of her family was out of sorts she cried, "Run to the doctor's shop, quickly!"

My mother often took me to see Doctor Hume. She would trust no-one else when I was small, although it was a tram journey to his shop. In my earliest years I was extraordinarily fat. A studio photograph (no-one we knew had a camera then) shows me standing on a chair, my body like a large egg, encased in a one-piece blue woollen garment. A year or so later I became exceptionally skinny. My parents were scared. They may have feared that I had inherited my grandmother's weak chest. Every morning for several years I was given two big spoonfuls of tasty malt. Less enjoyable were the laxatives with which my sister and I were dosed regularly, on principle, I suspect. These were an enthusiasm of my father who, poor man, conducted a public struggle with his bowels for as long as I can remember, quaffing a dram of liquid paraffin every night. He greatly alarmed me, too, from my early years, by describing luridly to me and warning me against a variety of illnesses. In the street he pointed to a large poster for Wright's Coal Tar Soap and said, "Never use that, or you will get cancer."

My chest was rubbed every night with camphorated oil and for most of the year, whatever the weather, my mother dressed me in one thick garment upon another. It surprises me to recall that until I was five I wore *tsitsis* under all the other layers. This is a ritual fringed garment like a bib enjoined by Mosaic Law. Nowadays it is worn only by the most pious Jews but in those days the immigrants and the first generation of their children still kept up the primitive superstitions they had brought with them. They went through motions against the Evil Eye and, I guess, took for granted that the *tsitsis* was an amulet to protect a little boy from harm. My mother may have thought of it so, or she may have put the garment on me out of piety towards her pious mother, whom she adored. After my grandmother's death my father, the freethinker, forbade all such practices.

I owe it to Doctor Hume that I still have my tonsils. Most children had their tonsils taken out as a matter of routine. Doctor Hume forbade it. Throughout my childhood I suffered from tonsillitis and sore throats. I was off school ill for long spells. A succession of doctors urged my parents to have my tonsils out, doctors who were tall, prosperous, well-dressed, commanding men; but each time my mother stood glum and resolute, her mouth clamped in a familiar obstinacy, until she answered, "Doctor Hume said, 'No!'"

Chapter 6

Soon after midday every Saturday I was posted at my window, standing on the chair, looking out for my father's return from "business". I was always proud to see him come, different from any other man in the street, upright, head up, with a rapid, strutting stride, wearing a light overcoat severely cut but fitting his slim body perfectly, his light grey trilby hat with a curled brim, with kid gloves, spats, stiff winged collar and diamond tiepin; and with the awaited box of cream buns held by its coloured silky ribbon in his right hand.

We had our lunch. It was called dinner, of course. Soup was served after the meat course, logically it seems to me, to wash it down. By this time I was already dressed in my Saturday best and my baby sister Ida, good-natured with a beautiful Levinson face and shining blonde hair, was properly robed; and afterwards, the great occasion of the week, the taken-for-granted, invariable, climactic ritual excursion, a journey by tram to the East End to visit both the grandparents' homes.

We always got off the tram in Shoreditch High Street to visit my father's parents first. To get to Hare Street we walked through Sclater Street, which was lined with bird shops. Parrots eyed us from their cages, hundreds of linnets and canaries sang to us and the street smelled of bird droppings.

Huguenot weavers once lived in Hare Street. Many of the houses had large windows in the top storeys where their workshops had been. The strong tang of railway soot was always in the air. Ever-present in the street, too, were the smells of the cart-horses and of fresh horse dung. All of these made a mixture exciting to me.

My grandfather Bernstein's shop was a grimy, gloomy cavern. Most of the space was taken up by great hides stacked against the walls. There was a battered counter lined with black oilcloth, its front covered with enamel advertising plates for the two boot polishes, Cherry Blossom and Nugget. The window was full of trays containing nails of all sizes, cards of blakeys, shoemakers' knives, piles of iron lasts and pairs of boot soles cut roughly to a number of sizes from thick leather. Shelves behind the counter were stacked with similar requisites. In these days most men, women and children wore boots and families in the neighbourhood could not afford to

Figure 13 "I was already dressed in my Saturday best and my baby sister Ida, good-natured with a beautiful Levinson face and shining blonde hair, was properly robed." Baron, aged about eight, with Ida.

have them repaired. The men came in with paper patterns cut out to show the sizes of sole and heel they wanted and they bought the leather, iron lasts, nails and knives with which to do it themselves. There were usually a few railway carters hanging about in the shop hobnobbing with my grandfather, tall, lean men like my other grandfather, soldierly, even those who no longer wore old uniforms, with weathered faces, strong bare necks and Old Bill moustaches. To the reek of tanning and old iron that filled the shop was added the smoke from their clay pipes and Woodbine cigarettes. A few years later during the General Strike of 1926 I have memories of the men in the shop, all of them on strike, talking in rough bewildered voices. We went home after our East End journeys during the strike on trams that were manned by cheerful men in the black suits, stiff collars and striped ties of city clerks, wearing the armbands of volunteers. Passengers, mostly of the working class, went on indignantly about "those strikers." A policeman rode on the rear platform but his protection was not needed. I saw clusters of strikers watching us from the pavements along Shoreditch High Street and the Kingsland Road but they all looked dispirited and never even raised a shout.

My father's parents lived in one room behind the shop and in a front bedroom on the first floor. There were tenants upstairs whom I only knew of by the sound of boots on the staircase and the bang of the outer door. Whenever a customer came into the shop a bell tinkled over the door and my grandfather went to serve. There was no running water inside the house. It was brought in from a tap in the yard. The lavatory was in the yard. This was a well-built brick cupboard with two diamond-shaped holes cut in the door. The w.c. seat ran from wall to wall. It was always kept scrubbed white by my grandmother. The smell in this place was like a strong smell of walnuts, not unpleasant, as I remember it. I liked going there and reading the squares of newspaper hung by a string from the wall. In the shop, sitting on the counter, I read the newspapers kept there for wrapping, usually the Labour paper, the *Daily Herald*. All print was irresistible.

My other grandparents' home had an outside lavatory which seized my imagination. In it I became Robinson Crusoe. It had been installed in the open air, at the end of a narrow passage, possibly next to the drain, and a sort of shanty had been improvised around it of planks and bits of waterproof.

Forbidden to me at Hare Street was the cellar. The door leading down to it under the stairs was bolted. My grandfather told me that the rats were down there. In the yard I squatted to peer down through a grating and smelled accumulated dirt, perhaps the dirt of two hundred years and I convinced myself that I could hear the scurry of countless rats. Prince, the yard dog, was chained to his kennel. He was a collie, my friend and sometimes guardian. When the grown-ups were busy they sat me on the flagstones with him and I played with him. I do not know when it was, later on, that I conceived a fear and dislike of dogs which persists.

Sometimes my father took me to the shop on Sunday mornings. The weekly street market was one of several which still draw great crowds to that part of Bethnal Green. My father and I helped at my grandfather's stall.

My part was to stand at a corner of the stall, which was higher than me, supposedly to watch out for thieves. I never caught one but I felt immensely responsible. I gleaned from snatches of grown-up conversation that my grandfather was under the protection of "them", a family of hard cases somewhere down the street. He did not pay for this; they had taken a liking to him.

My sister and I called him Zaida B. We called our grandmothers *Buba*, from the Russian *baba*, and our grandfathers *Zaida*. These were the only Yiddish words we used, apart from names of foodstuffs, like *cholent*, *tsimmes*, *latkes* or *lockshen*.[1] Zaida B. was a square, strong man with black hair and keen, quizzical eyes in a round face. A Siberian, I thought in later years. He knew little of London outside Hare Street. He told me once that he had gone to Piccadilly to look for the circus. Sometimes he went to sit on his own for a few hours in Victoria Park. His only other resort was the music hall, which he loved. Two of the famous music halls were still open during my early childhood. I was taken to the London, in Shoreditch. It was supposed to be the roughest. We sat in a gallery that to me was immensely high and seemed to overhang the stage upon which, in gaslight far below, singers and comics succeeded one another. The audience was well-behaved.

I liked to sit next to my grandfather, on the sofa of cracked black oilcloth, and listen to his stories. His dusty black working suit had taken a strong smell of tanner's chemicals from the leather which he held against his chest to cut. When my sister was older he told us both a continuing series of stories about The Fat Lady. At times he talked about his life. He was the only Jew I ever met who spoke with relish of his time in the Czar's army. He chuckled over his adventures. He told me about a sergeant who had bullied the conscripts. One night my grandfather stole the bolt of the sergeant's rifle and threw it into the Dnieper. For the crime of losing it the sergeant was reduced to the ranks. "And then did we give him a beating!"

He spoke with admiration of his big brother, Srulka, whom he had not seen since 1904.[2] One day while Srulka was still in London he was walking in Brick Lane with my grandfather. One of the brewery draymen going by on his high perch flicked at them with his long whip, a sport not uncommon at the time. Srulka caught the end of the whip with a turn of his hand, tugged, and brought the carter tumbling down to the cobbles.

---

1   *Cholent*. Traditional Jewish stew, traditionally consumed on Shabbat; *Tsimmes*. A sweet stew usually combining fruit and root vegetables; *Latkes*. Potato pancakes; *Lockshen*. Flat egg noodles.

2   Srulka is a diminutive of the boy's name Israel.

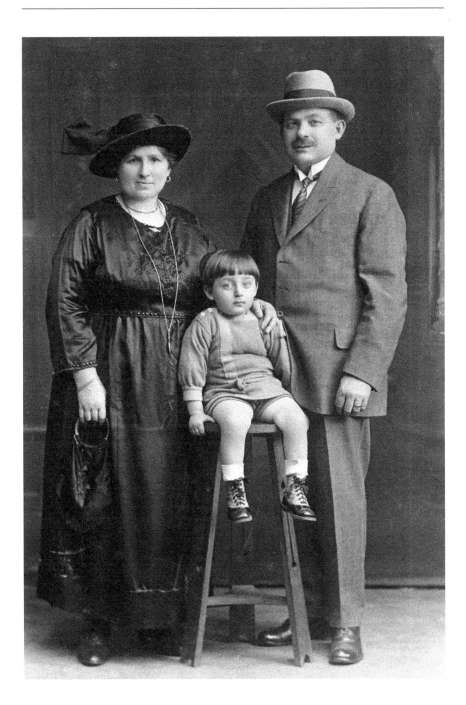

Figure 14 "Zaida B. was a square, strong man with black hair and keen, quizzical eyes in a round face." Baron aged about two with his paternal grandparents, Leah and Simon Bernstein.

My grandmother was pale and gaunt, with a seamed, parchment face. Her eyes were always sad. When I came she would lean down to me, take my face between her flat hands and kiss my forehead. She was so clean that she always smelt of Sunlight soap, the cheap soap which we bought in big yellow bars. Her anxious love repelled me. I have written a short story about her, an act of repentance. She said little, sitting upright and impassive in a corner of the back room, between a wall cupboard and the table covered with oilcloth which stood under the window. I never sensed any current of affection pass between her and her husband as I did between my other grandparents. They had been introduced to each other by a match-maker in Poland and I suppose had married as a duty. Nevertheless, taking each other utterly for granted, they were one entity, part of each other.

She kept hens in the yard. As soon as we came she was anxious to feed us. Everything had to be fresh. She took eggs from under the hens to boil for us. She bought live fish in readiness for our coming and kept them swimming round in an old enamel bowl until it was time to kill and cook them. In little shops kept by *landsleute* she bought sorrel to make a cold soup and kinds of currants unknown to us from which she brewed for us cordials of the forest.[3]

Sometimes we arrived to find a mysterious uncle present. His name was Hymie. For long periods he was not to be seen. The grown-ups did not mention him. Then one day there he was, sitting at the end of the old black sofa, next to the window, upright, silent, hands on his knees. A photograph of him on the mantelpiece showed him in the same pose and with his hair cropped close high up the back and sides as it was now, his hard face battered like a street-fighter's with a nose that looked as if it had been broken. But in the photograph he was spick and span, in a soldier's tropical kit, with his sun helmet on a stand beside him. Now he wore no collar and tie, he was unshaven and his jacket and trousers were crumpled and dirty. I sat across the room, usually on a stool by the kitchen range, staring at him. He grinned back at me bashfully. I was fascinated by him and mystified. As I see the little boy perched on his stool I read in his face a tug of strange feelings. I imagine some current of recognition passing to and fro between him and his uncle. That cannot have been so. I imagine it because I now remember Hymie as *mon semblable*.

After this first appearance, Hymie came to visit us from time to time. He always sat in the same stiff pose and the same silence but he now wore a

---

3   *Landsleute.* Fellow countrymen.

decent old suit of my father's with a collar and tie, and he had shaved. I could see my mother putting herself out for him; it seems to me that I discerned her pity for him. He could never respond with more than a shy grin and a few clumsy words.

Curiosity about him only came when I was older and I began to take notice of his disappearances. Once I heard from my grandfather that on Hymie's second day in the army during the Great War he hit a sergeant-major who had sworn at him. For this he spent a year in a military prison. Afterwards he was posted to the Middle East and fought in Palestine.

Later I heard the explanation of his disappearances, and why he had enlisted in the army as a volunteer when he was still under-age, only seventeen years old. He was a gambler. This is supposed to be the Jewish vice but he was the only one in our far-flung clan. He would live at home for a while, doing casual work for cabinet-makers. As soon as he had saved some money he would disappear, gamble away his money, pawn the clothes he wore to raise a stake and stay away, living among other ragged outcasts of the night, until hunger or illness drove him home.

After one of his sprees he came home in the usual state. My grandfather gave him a couple of pounds to buy a new set of clothes. He went off, gambled the money away and came home a few days later dressed in a khaki uniform, a Fusilier.

He remained a family outcast, seldom seen. He died in the nineteen-fifties, untended and in agony, of a burst ulcer. I saw the room in which he had died, in a slum as foul as any described by Dickens.

Hare Street has been renamed Cheshire Street. When I went there a few years ago most of the buildings were boarded up, as if awaiting demolition. The front of my grandfather's old shop was covered by corrugated iron sheets. The door frame was charred by a fire, as were the surrounds of the gaping windows on the upper floors. From the other side of the street I could see into the first-floor front room in which I sometimes slept with my grandparents, I in the bed with my grandfather, my grandmother on the floor next to us. The faded wallpaper was the same that I had known as a child, with diagonal rows of light blue rosettes enclosing chains of pink roses.

Chapter 7

The old Tenterground was demolished in 1928 to make room for a Council estate. It was here that, two hundred years before, the Huguenot weavers had stretched their cloth on tenterhooks. There is another Tenter Street, still to be found, near to Tower Hill. The Tenter Street of my mother's parents was known as the Dutch Tenterground because Dutch Jews had settled hereabouts. My Levinson grandparents, who came from Lithuania and consequently held themselves to be aristocrats, called them, contemptuously, "Dotchkies." Dotchkies sold salt herrings and pickled cucumbers from barrels in Wentworth Street. They gathered at the Netherlands Club in Bell Lane, which backed on to the Tenterground.

From White's Row, next to Spitalfields Market, we walked under a round arch with a house over it and came into a long, broad, cobbled precinct which I have since thought to be like Dickens' "Bleeding Heart Yard" in *Little Dorrit*. On our right was a row of decaying little dwellings with worn stone steps. My Levinson grandparents lived at Number 28, Brune House. Halfway to it lived old Mrs. Cooper, whose front room was turned into a general store. If she was at the door when I came, she called me in and gave me a halfpenny sherbet fountain. Across the street were three big, black, derelict buildings, their windows broken. At the far end the Tenterground was enclosed by another covered way with a house above it, a narrow passage that led into a yard, from which yet another covered passage led into noisy Bell Lane. On one side of the yard was a stable. I never saw a horse in this stable but the strong smell of rotten straw soaked in horses' piss remained until the block was pulled down. Across the yard was a dairy, a gloomy barn in which four brown-and-white cows were chained in stalls as strongly and agreeably odorous as the stable opposite. People came here with their jugs to buy warm milk. In Leyden Street beyond Bell Lane the poultry dealers were busy among stacks of crates in which living hens were kept. The smell here, sharp and stifling, was of hens' droppings. The air was loud with the squawking of poultry having their throats cut and the shrill voices of chaffering women. In the background was the uproar of Petticoat Lane.

Except when the weather was bad the Tenterground was always thronged and noisy. Life was lived outside the fetid, crowded houses. The women sat on home-made benches outside their front doors, carrying on screaming conversations with one another. Illegal street bookies were busy at the corners of the three side-streets opposite the houses, each with his crowd around him. Their sentries were posted at the far ends of the streets, on the lookout for the approach of a policeman. At whistles from the sentries, the crowds scattered and the bookies fled. Swarms of children at play set up a clamour. Hawkers with barrows cried their wares. Itinerant musicians played. The archway from White's Row was always crowded with chattering Lascars, Indian seamen with gaunt faces, who wore baggy blue cotton jackets and trousers, turbans or round red caps, gathered around a doorway under the arch for purposes I never understood. One day a travelling roundabout came, on a low cart pulled by a donkey. It stank with vomit but children crowded on to it, myself among them, surrounded by an envious ring of small onlookers.

I adored this bustling scene. When my grandmother Levinson saw me coming she rose joyfully from her bench on the pavement and I ran into her arms. She kissed me but she never fussed or gushed. She simply emanated love.

Five of her ten children lived at home. The five married children all came often, some bringing families. Kinsfolk, and the kinsfolk of kinsfolk, came and went, and the single children brought in troops of friends. The house was filled with life. My grandmother presided, beaming, sitting with an immense brown teapot always ready.

I was the first grandchild in a large family, and a Jewish family at that. I know that I was well aware of being the object of an abundance both of love and pride. It was no wonder, then, that I always chafed with impatience to leave Hare Street and to hurry, by way of Brick Lane and Hanbury Street, to Spitalfields, the Tenterground and the joys of the Levinsons' house.

I often stayed at Tenter Street. It was a tremendous treat. The front room downstairs led, with no door, into another. Most of the front room was taken up by a big bed in which my two youngest uncles slept. Jack and Alec were thirteen and fourteen or so when I first remember them. Into the small L-shaped bit of the room that remained, the daily life of the family and its visitors was packed. There were the usual kitchen range and cupboard in the wall, a small table under the window, two wooden chairs and two of the (in that world) universal home-made benches. The back room was long and narrow. It looked like a tunnel to me. I made my way along it past a sink and high old chests of drawers piled on top with rolled-up feather quilts to the two beds in which the unmarried girls slept, a big double bed at the end and a small bed along a side wall. Like the front room, this room was panelled with wood half-way up the walls. Sometimes I slept with Doris, sometimes in the large bed between Hetty and Annie. I felt warm, snug and safe between their big bodies. They gave off a strong, clean smell which I enjoyed, like that of raw tobacco. On the nights I slept in the front room with the two boys I lived in hopes of seeing the bugs of which I had heard them talk rather boastfully. I only ever saw one bug in that house. I was lying next to the wall, hopefully watching the jointing of the wood panels from which they were supposed to emerge. Then I saw a single little red creature, to me no different from a ladybird, clinging to the edge of my pillow. He struggled up on to the pillow, crept over its slope like a little mountaineer over a snowfield, went down into the valley between the two pillows, up on to the other pillow and across it until he disappeared over the far edge.

At bedtime my grandfather placed a bucket in the opening between the two rooms. It was behind a curtain. We all used it if we needed to pass water during the night. When we got up in the morning he had taken it away.

My parents took me home on a tram from Bishopsgate. Our way took us through Artillery Passage, a narrow footway with gunposts at each end. I lingered, until they pulled me away, at the gaslit window of a corner shop which sold not only sweets and Woodbine cigarettes but the *Police Gazette* which hung on display in the window, displaying melodramatic engravings of some gory crime. Sometimes in the darkness a troop of ragged boys ran past us, shouting, their bare feet slapping on the pavement. I envied them their bare feet and their freedom.

At the far end of the alley, next to a Salvation Army hostel, was a pub which every Saturday night became the centre of a down-and-outs' orgy. Shapeless women wearing men's caps and sacking skirts lurched out of the crowded bars with red-eyed, unshaven men, bawling songs or shouting in thick, frightening voices. I saw a man and a woman lying in the gutter clutching each other tightly. We had to step round them. I thought they were fighting. In one of the doorways in the alley a woman hoisted her skirts up and pissed like a horse. These were the people we feared. My father pulled me close and hurried me on.

Chapter 8

When my maternal grandfather-to-be, eighteen-year-old Isaac Levinson, was about to leave the Lithuanian town of Kovno for England, he bought a boat ticket and put the rest of his savings into a little cloth bag which his young bride wore on a necklet of string under her blouse.

As soon as he had found a room and a job in London he sent for her. Their first home was a room in Sandys Row, twenty yards from the corner of the infernal Frying-Pan Alley about which Jack London writes in *The People of The Abyss*.[1] They slept on the floor at first, with some orange boxes from Spitalfields Market for furniture.

My grandfather was a mechanic by trade. He was always a solitary man, set apart from others by his pride and his eccentricities. When he was young he frequented all the radical organisations in the East End but he was too scornful of them to join any of them. He was active in his trade union and by nature he was always one of the last to go back after a strike; but he looked on his fellow-workers as riff-raff and never mixed with them.

There was an ardent and vigorous Jewish trade union movement in the East End but as a skilled man he was eligible to join an English trade union. These unions were restrictive in their outlook and were particularly hostile to Jewish immigrants whom they saw as alien cheap labour. My grandfather would not have been put off by this. He was among them in pursuit of principles, not of congenial company; and among them he must have come across at least a few serious, principled, self-educated men like himself who respected him.

A tall, strong man who, when he was not at work, always wore a decent suit with a collar and tie and polished boots, he was often mistaken for a detective of the City of London Police, a force which in those days required its recruits to be at least six feet tall. He always walked with his head up, casting a fierce, authoritative look about him. In the streets where he was not known, bookies and their crowds fled when he was seen by the lookouts. On Sunday

---

1   Jack London (1876–1916). American writer. *The People of the Abyss* (London, 1903), draws on his experiences in East London, where he stayed in Frying Pan Alley.

mornings he often went to Tower Hill to join the band of six-footers who formed a ring to protect trade union meetings from the attacks of drunks and hired roughs. He said to me when he was older, "I have shaken hands many a time with Mr. Tom Mann and Mr. Ben Tillett."[2] These two men were the greatest among the generation of leaders who brought about a phenomenal growth of the British trade union movement between 1888 and 1914.

A big strike took place while my grandfather was looking after the machinery at a boot factory. He came out with the rest, but when the strike dragged on he went to New York to earn some money; he already had six children to support. He worked there in a construction gang; until one day, as he told me, he was climbing the staircase of his rooming house when he heard a baby crying in one of the rooms. He said, "I sat down on the staircase and I cried for my missus and my kids."

On his return to London he discovered that his employer had been calling on my grandmother to make sure that all was well with her and the children, leaving a sovereign (a one-pound gold coin) on the table each time. All the same, when the strike collapsed and the rest of the men returned to work, my grandfather refused to go back beaten. For the rest of his life he would not work for a boss.

The gramophone had come into fashion. My grandfather made one and went on making them, working in his back bedroom. He earned a living selling and repairing them; he also repaired boots and did odd jobs as a mechanic.

The gramophone introduced him to opera, which became his passion. Over the years he accumulated a fine collection of records. When I was small he already had a cupboard full of these, stacked on the shelves in labelled boxes. On a table in the parlour stood the gramophone that he had made for himself, a mahogany cabinet, a great, fluted trumpet and a mechanism that ran in faultless, oiled silence. Nobody but my grandfather was allowed to touch it. Before a performance we all had to sit in silence; a whisper brought a sharp glance from him, while he found a record, wiped it gently with a felt pad and placed it as gently on the turntable, selected the proper needle from a large array, fitted it into whichever of several sound-boxes he had chosen to use and wound the handle; then a voice filled the silence, Chaliapin, perhaps, or Melba or Caruso.

---

2   Tom Mann (1856–1941), Trade Unionist. Founding member of the British Communist Party. He stayed in the Party until his death. Ben Tillett (1860–1943). British Socialist and trade unionist. Often associated with the London dock strike of 1889 and the later industrial action by dockers in 1911 and 1912.

In the nineteen-twenties, when "the wireless" – radio – came in, he got hold of some blueprints and was soon busy in the back room making and repairing sets, which, like the gramophones, were bought by neighbours and their acquaintances.

He was one of those people who can take offence at some slight so tiny as to be discernible by no-one but themselves. Then he would simmer with black, stifled rages or retreat into sullen solitude to the dismay of those who loved him and especially of his wife, into whose simple and loving soul he must at times have struck terror.

He was a freethinker, but a Jewish freethinker who kept up religious observances as taken-for-granted tribal customs. He had his sons circumcised eight days after birth, he married under the Jewish canopy and took it for granted that his children would do the same and that death and burial were governed by Jewish rites.

Like many of his generation of immigrant men he had been educated at a Talmud and Torah school. Among the Jews, Lithuania was by tradition a centre of high culture. He was able to recite with authority the prayers in which he did not believe, as he demonstrated to us at Passover.

It may have been for my grandmother's sake that he presided over a great family Seder Night every year at Passover, or perhaps simply to hold a family reunion as secular Christians do at Christmas. Up to two dozen of us crammed round the parlour table, with improvised high chairs for the two babies, my sister Ida and my cousin Sidney Levinson. My grandfather gave out tattered *haggadahs*, service books printed years before in Eastern Poland and sold by pedlars. They were illustrated by crude woodcuts that looked mediaeval. My grandfather directed the rituals and intoned the prayers like a High priest. At the proper moment he called me to my feet to recite the Four Questions, which I did with great pride in Hebrew. I can remember a few lines of them still.[3]

Sidney was Izzy's son. He was taken prisoner by the Japanese in the Second World War. I was a soldier in Sicily at the time. I heard from my father that Sidney had been located in a prison camp and I wrote to his parents saying how glad I was that he was alive. By the time that my letter reached them, they had heard that he was dead. According to a survivor

---

3   The Four Questions. The question at the Seder (Passover) meal, "Why is this night different from all other nights?" has four responses which are usually offered by the youngest child capable of attending.

who came home at the end of the war, he had been too ill to work and the guards had finished him off with rifle butts.

*****

These gatherings stopped after my grandmother died in her sixtieth year, when I was twelve. It was only for her sake that my mother and father had kept up the religion and they too stopped doing so.

Until then we enjoyed every year the excitement of spring-cleaning the house and hunting out the last crumbs of bread before Passover, of opening the door to the Jewish grocer who brought in a barrow-load of Passover food; and of getting out the special Passover crockery and utensils. Each night during the Feast of Lights we lit beautiful coloured candles. Every Friday night we scrubbed ourselves and dressed in our best to sit down to a supper of cold fried fish and *challah*, the sweet plaited loaf glazed with eggs and sprinkled with poppy seeds. My mother lit two candles in brass candlesticks, bowed to them and lifted a little apron up to cover her face while she prayed. I knew that she had no Hebrew. The only prayer that she could have uttered was an entreaty, wordless or in English, for the preservation of her loved ones.

We were hypocrites on the day of the great fast, Yom Kippur.[4] We wore our best clothes and stayed indoors and food was hidden away in case anybody came; but my sister and I were well-fed at meal times and my father took an occasional surreptitious snack. My mother may have fasted, for her mother's sake.

My parents never ate pork or bacon but they explained that this was only out of habit. On holiday, we stayed as often as not at Gentile boarding-houses. At breakfast there, my parents asked for a boiled egg or a piece of smoked haddock. I was allowed to have bacon. Even the aroma of it was an exquisite treat. When I was in my 'teens my mother bought it for me at home.

Even our tongue-in-cheek observances helped to give a structure to the year. The disciplines, rituals and celebrations of a religion enable people to impose order upon the chaos of life. What is meaningless is given the appearance of meaning and ceases to frighten. Children eagerly enjoy the events of an ordered, religious year. Many people who do not believe choose to pretend, above all for the sake of the children. Why not? But I have never been able to.

---

4   Yom Kippur. The Day of Atonement. The holiest day of the year in Judaism. A time for prayer and fasting.

In any case our year was structured and full of excitements without the Jewish festivals. The Jewish Chanukah was nothing compared with Christmas, which came soon after.[5] In the weeks before Christmas we mixed the pudding until the time came for my father to drop silver threepenny bits into it. We went to the pantomime and the circus, we put up coloured paper chains in the kitchen; and at school, before we broke up for the holidays, we hung decorations and sang carols, the same carols that my mother and I sang in the house. On Christmas Eve Ida and I went to bed excited. We tried to stay awake to catch my father out when he crept into the room but we always fell asleep before he came. At the same time we were able to believe, just for that night, in Father Christmas, as intensely as we believed in stories while they were being told to us.

In the morning we found little net stockings from Woolworth's on our beds, filled with gimcrack toys. Soon my mother and father came in with more substantial presents. We had a goose for Christmas dinner and listened to the King's speech on the wireless.

Then there were our birthdays, when we had kitchen parties with Bob Apple, I-Spy, fairy cakes and lemonade; school terms and holidays; the annual week at the seaside and the fever of getting ready for it; Spring Cleaning in the house while steam rollers rumbled up and. down the street amid a stimulating smell of hot tar, laying new yellow gravel in the road; bath night, the weekly arrival of *The Magnet*, and the tram ride to the East End every Saturday; and innumerable small rituals like shelling sweet-smelling peas and tasting the pods, or my mother's baking days, with samples to taste and more unforgettable aromas.

---

5   Chanukah. An eight-day Jewish festival. Often known as the Festival of Lights. It commemorates the rededication of the Second Temple in Jerusalem. It falls in December.

Chapter 9

The dazzle of electric light changed my life when I was five. My parents took me to wander about the echoing rooms of an empty house; I could not grasp what was happening. I went with my mother to showrooms which enchanted me. Furniture shone, cut glass glittered. Carpets with rich patterns filled the room with their smell. I sat at a table in front of big volumes of wallpaper samples, which to me were simply the best picture books I had ever seen. I cannot remember the move to the house. I know that I was not surprised. For a small child, all is to be taken for granted, since he knows his parents to be omnipotent. My first memory is of myself going down to the cellar, that in itself an adventure, and finding a mouldering volume of *The Boy's Own Paper*. It was forty years old. I read the Victorian tales about explorers in the Dark Continent and heroic subalterns on the North-West Frontier as if they were happenings of my own time.

Foulden Road is in Hackney. It leads into the High Street which is the boundary with Stoke Newington, in those days a more genteel borough. Part of Stoke Newington still looked like a country village, with the New River running through a pretty park. Foulden Road aspired to Stoke Newington gentility. It was a block away from the imposing, domed West Hackney Church which stood in its own grounds and on Sunday mornings many of the Foulden Road families went there in their best clothes.

My father bought 6, Foulden Road, leasehold, on a twenty years' mortgage. He set up a workroom in the basement and, after supper, was down there until late every night doing private jobs to supplement his factory pay. He let two rooms to tenants. He paid off the mortgage in five years, the tenants left and we children were given their rooms. Until then there was a bedroom for my parents, one for Ida and me, a kitchen to live in and a decayed greenhouse which my father rebuilt as a scullery. And the parlour.

This was a Hall of Wonders, with a good carpet on gleaming linoleum, a striking wallpaper and an electric light bowl of hand-painted china. Its principal exhibits were a long table and an imposing sideboard of mahogany polished till they reflected. The sideboard had a canopy supported by twirly pillars, with a mirror at the back. There were a couch and two armchairs of brown leather, with deep cushions, a piano and a gramophone. The fireplace surround was of veined marble. On the mantelpiece were a clock with Westminster chimes and two identical bronze statuettes; classical young men in loincloths restraining rearing steeds. In front of the fireplace was a black bearskin rug on to which was sewn a leopard's skin complete with a glass-eyed head. I wrestled with this leopard and killed it with my bare hands over and over again. Above the fireplace, in mahogany frames, were another large mirror and two big photographs of my grandparents. The photographs now hang in my workroom. My father believed in dazzle. He put in high-powered bulbs that flooded every part of the house with stark white light.

In a year my parents turned a waste of black earth and broken china at the back of the house into a pretty garden, small but, to the eyes of a child used to life in one room, spacious. It had long borders, two flower beds in the centre and fresh gravel paths. The flowers fascinated me – lupins, geraniums, pansies, carnations, roses. I lay at full length with my face close to them, taking in the strong, subtle scents, the bright colours and the patterns of leaves. The garden ended at the blank back wall of a factory which was overgrown with ivy. I flung stones up into the ivy and watched the sparrows scatter. Twenty yards up the street was another factory, where sweets were made. Each day a different smell from the sweet factory flavoured the air we breathed, lemon drops, wine gums, raspberry lumps. We sat down to breakfast every morning to the sound of the factory whistle.

There were three other Jewish families in the street. One lived in the house to our right. They became friends. In the house on the other side lived old Mr. Baker, who had a fringe of beard round his rosy face that made him look like an old farmer in one of the plays that we saw at the Alexandra Theatre down the High Street. No Jew he. Once I listened to him telling my father that the secret of long life was to drink a cup of hot bacon fat every morning. An old man who lived across the road wore an old-fashioned black suit and a square bowler hat. On a piece of paper he traced a circle the size of sixpence for us children and wrote the Lord's Prayer in it.

There were no motor-cars in the street. Once in a while a motor-lorry came past, and some cars were to be seen in the High Street. The tradesmen's carts, the coalman's cart and the dustcart were pulled by horses. I loved and admired horses. Sometimes we saw a fallen cart-horse; a pathetic sight. When I think of what became of this race of patient, peaceful slaves my heart sinks for mankind. The horses all but disappeared in a few decades;

Figure 15 "In a year my parents turned a waste of black earth and broken china at the back of the house into a pretty garden, small but, to the eyes of a child used to life in one room, spacious." Baron aged about thirteen with a friend in the garden at 6, Foulden Road.

only a few remain, to be raced, shown off or petted. Most of the rest went to the knackers' yards to be slaughtered. In my mind this vast unnoticed extermination is an eerie prefiguring of Auschwitz.

I had friends to play with now. The girls were not much in evidence, coming out only to skip in front of their gates or to play hopscotch, in which occasionally we joined them. The boys were forever out in the street, in groups, free of one another's houses, fed by each other's mothers. According to season we gathered caterpillars from the plane trees in our front areas or went collecting conkers. We trooped on to Hackney Downs to play football on a cinder field with teams from other streets. By waiting at horse-troughs and begging rides from carriers we could explore far afield into the countryside, to Enfield, Chingford and Epping Forest, bringing home tadpoles in jars. We shovelled up horse-dung in the streets and sold it at front doors for a penny a bucket as garden manure. Once we picked tulips from the flower-beds of a big house in Amhurst Road and sold them in penny bunches. Once we all stood outside Woolworth's; for dares, boys went in one by one and brought out some trifle they had "nicked". I came out with a pencil for which I had furtively paid a penny. I preferred to go on my own to Woolworth's I stood at the book counter, where I read entire books in daily instalments. The shopgirls came to know me. A test more dangerous than nicking was imposed on us by our little tribe; to dash out into the roadway and leap up to hang on to the tailboard of a big wagon. Sometimes the carter ignored us. Sometimes he turned to lash with his whip. Strange boys on the pavement warned the carters with the cry, "Whip behind you, mister!"

I became tribal story-teller to the boys in the street. Some of my tales were embroidered versions of stories I had read. Others derived from my own fantasies. Often I never knew whether I was telling a story or telling the truth. A couple came to visit us bringing their daughter who was my age, perhaps eight. Earlier that day I had crept lawlessly down to the boiler room at school, a dark dungeon full of great rusting tanks and clusters of fat, red-painted pipes. I had seen a rope hanging from a beam. I told the girl that the caretaker had hanged a little boy by this rope and cut his own throat afterwards. I said that I had seen the huge bloodstain on the floor of the boiler room. She believed this and, while I was telling her, so did I. I was in general a truthful boy. I knew that if I tried to tell a lie I would falter and give myself away. But telling tales like this was different.

My mother did not take me to school any more. We were only three blocks away from the Shacklewell. Waiting at the gate she had become friendly with another mother, who lived in the next street to ours, a

Mrs. Gold. They decided that the two boys could find their way to school together. So, in my sixth year, I began my friendship with Arthur Gold, who one day was to become a championship-class high jumper, then secretary of the Amateur Athletics Association and, eventually, Sir Arthur Gold, a pillar of the British Olympic Committee, a long-time President of the European Athletics Federation and an outstanding world authority in the fight against drugs in athletics.[1]

I was enjoying school. In the playground I belonged to another community of children. I liked the big classrooms with their high windows. I liked the smell of chalk. On the top shelf of each classroom cupboard we had a heap of storybooks to borrow.

My parents often had company in the evenings. The parlour table was laid out with dishes of food. My father served drinks from the sideboard. He played gramophone records. I lay on the leopard skin or under the table listening. Sometimes my father's younger brother Morry came and played jazz on the piano. Morry had started at fourteen as a cabinet-maker's boy, a diminutive creature pushing a barrow all over London with a tower of furniture lashed down to it, for sixpence a load. My father had taken him into the factory and trained him as a furrier, as he did, too, my mother's young brother Alec. My grandfather's earnings were pitiful, as I learned when I helped him in the market, but he had paid for Morry to be tutored in the piano as a boy in Hare Street. My father had been taught the violin. They had musical evenings when my father and mother were courting. My father never played his violin during my childhood. It was on the top shelf of the cupboard in my parents' bedroom. My father would never tell us why he would not play it; a mystery never cleared up, which prompted me to frighten myself with Gothic imaginings, full of strange shapes, shadows and visitations. Daydreaming of these, I took the fiddle down, sawed at it with the bow and waved it about until I broke it. Without a word my father threw it away.

Throughout our childhood my father had a strap next to his place at table. My mother put it there when she laid out the cutlery before each meal. It was a supple leather thong about two feet long, folded over to half that length. During our younger childhood he did not use it or even threaten us with it; but he used it on me when I was twelve. Saturday dinner at one o'clock was sacred. Never had one of us failed to be at the table in time. I was at the house of a boy named Ernie Lyme. We had a plan to bring out a magazine on a jellygraph duplicator, to sell at school for a halfpenny a copy.

---

1   Arthur Gold (1917–2002). Athlete and later Chairman of the British Olympic Association.

The magazine never appeared; we used up the jelly and ran out of funds. One Saturday I was so engrossed with the work that I did not notice the time until I saw that it was four o'clock and ran home. My father was waiting at the parlour window and met me at the door, still white with fear. He threw me to the floor and lashed me with the strap until he was tired out. He went upstairs and did not come down for hours.

Chapter 10

Millie Harris was a sturdy girl with a round face, small eyes and a complexion of mottled pink. She was our maid. Things must have been getting better for my father, the loan nearly paid off, the little attic free for a bedroom. Millie was the first of two maids. The other girl, Edith, was one of thousands who came to service in England from the South Wales valleys to lighten the burdens of their unemployed fathers. The maids did housework from after breakfast until after tea-time. They had a half-day off a week and all their evenings, though they often stayed in to pass the time with us. I do not remember their wearing frilly caps or aprons. My mother paid them five shillings a week. Most of the time they chatted with my mother on equal terms and sat with us around the fire but at meal times the maid sat at the little table in the scullery. My mother, who did all the cooking, served her dish-for-dish with us and the door was open, so that we talked with her at a distance of about eight feet.

Millie was a chatty girl. I was much attached to her. We had not yet exchanged the black iron range in the kitchen for an open grate and she poked the fire through the bars, asking me to tell her what pictures I saw in the glowing coals. She split the skins of chestnuts and put them on the bars to roast. I asked her to tell me about the soldiers. I knew that she went to Woolwich in the evenings; a place on the far side of London as remote as Kamchatka. When I asked why she went to Woolwich, she said, "The soldiers are there."

"What for?"

"They're in the barracks, silly."

"Do they let you in the barracks?"

"Of course not. I wouldn't go in. It's when they go walking-out, see?"

"Are they your friends?"

"Some of them."

"Do you go to the pictures with them?"

"Never mind what I do."

"Tell us, Mill."

"Mind your own business."

I was taken with a fit of kneeling on the floor and trying to look up her skirt. She pulled the skirt to her and told me not to be silly. I did it quite openly, in front of my mother. My mother dragged me out of the room and told me that if I ever did that again my father would give me the strap.

I must have asked from time to time how babies were born; so that one day, when my mother had gone out of the room, Millie said, "My brother knows."

Millie's brother, about whom she had told me many stories, was twelve. I was perhaps eight then. I begged her to tell me and nagged until she said, "All right, it's a word, you mustn't say it, I'll spell it."

When my father was having his supper that evening I said, "I know how babies are born."

"How?"

"It's a word. F-u-c-k."

I cannot remember that my parents made any response. They must have looked at each other and changed the subject. Soon after, Millie's parents came. Her father was a big man like a policeman, her mother a polite woman of the kind my mother would call respectable. I heard the mutter of consultation behind the parlour door. They went away. There was an interval before Millie left. It may not have been because of the word. I walked in on my mother telling a friend and caught the phrase, "in trouble."

My parents' language was prim. Sometimes when my father was angry he muttered "bloody" or "bugger" but we were not supposed to have heard.

We had our set of euphemisms for the body and its functions. "Shit" was a terrible word. "Piss" was only said by the slum boys at school. "Belly" was coarse. If the lower parts of the body or the breaking of wind were referred to at all, it was in oblique or prettified terms.

I asked my parents one evening if they would take me to the British Museum. We did not go. I heard my mother murmur something to my father in Yiddish, the language they only used when they had to say something not for the children's ears. I caught the word *nakt* and guessed that she was warning him that there were naked statues in the Museum. My little sister and I did not see each other naked. I turned my back when she undressed in the bedroom.

We had started to go away on summer holidays, and on one of these I was much disturbed by the first glimpse of something I could not yet comprehend, the depressive side of my father's character. In the train to Margate I had not paid any attention to my parents, my face being glued to the window most of the time; but as we walked out of the station my mother's face went red, she burst into loud, boo-hooing wails and big tears rolled down her cheeks. My father walked on the far side of the station path, looking fiercely to his front. I was shocked and frightened. I had never seen my mother cry before and I only saw her cry once again, a suppressed sniffle, when I was sixteen and the cause of it.

One morning on a later holiday my father suddenly turned away from us when we were walking on the Brighton seafront and walked away into the crowd. We did not see him again until the evening. There were no explanations.

Sometimes, when we had been waiting for a while in a tea shop and his timid hisses to the waitress had been ignored, he stood up and without a word marched out, leaving us to follow. He did not answer if my sister or I asked why, but my mother said, "He thinks it was deliberate."

There were reasons at that time for his sensitivity about antisemitism. Popular novels described Jews as dirty treacherous, alien inferiors. Pages of "To Let" advertisements in *The Hackney and Kingsland Gazette* ended with the words, "no dogs or Jews." We flinched at jokes about Jews in the variety halls and sat in silence when caricatural Jewish comics came on, like Julian Rose, who was billed as Our Hebrew Friend or something like it.[1] I never suffered it among children and hardly noticed if occasionally some strange boys called after me half-heartedly, "Go back to Palestine!" I was depressed when my father told me always to step out of the way of oncomers on the pavement. It did not fit in with my heroic dreams; nor did the implication of not being English. Some Jews respond to all challenges, of whatever sort, by pushing back, or anticipate them by pushing first. I have always stepped out of the way.

Millie Harris came from Sheerness. We remained on good terms with her and her family and went there for our earliest holidays. My memories of Sheerness are scenes from Dickens. The Harrises lived in a clapboard house in an expanse of waste ground, with a tethered goat cropping the sparse, long grass in front of it. Deserted, wind-blown foreshores were out of *Great Expectations*. Sheerness, on the Thames Estuary, did not yet have any of the trappings of a seaside resort. Old concrete pill boxes of the Great War crumbled, exciting to explore. The forts were still manned, grass banks covering casemates from which the guns fired at practice several times a week. At other times we heard the guns from Shoeburyness on

---

1   Julian Rose (1879–1935). Jewish comedian. Often associated with the monologue, "Levinsky's Wedding."

the opposite shore. My father must have still had some of the house loan to pay off; in those first years he took us down one weekend, went back to London to work and came to take us home the next weekend. We rented a room each time in one of the tiny houses near to the dockyard. My mother made our bed and had the use of the kitchen to do her own cooking. When my father hired a boat and rowed us out into the estuary he looked brawny and competent: I felt trusting and secure with him, as I did one year when he and I went to Sheerness on our own for a week. He must have been reading hard at the time and trying to improve his vocabulary. When I wanted to go to the lavatory which was in the yard, he told me that I must first say to the landlady, "Please, madam, may I avail myself of your urinal?"

From the sea wall we saw warships steam into the dockyard; once, a submarine moving on the surface. On a Navy Day we went on board a great battleship, H.M.S. *Nelson*. I was awe-struck. We were proud of the Navy. Everyone was patriotic then. On Empire Day the mothers in poor districts dressed their children in spotless white and bought them little Union Jacks to take to school. Everyone was proud of the Empire. King George and Queen Mary were remote and beloved. Even when things were bad, life was ordered and comprehensible and people felt safe.

When my parents went to visit friends for an evening my mother's sisters Hetty and Annie came to sit with us. My splendid aunt Hetty sang us a song that would have made my parents shrivel. It was called "There Were Three Jews."

The first verse began, "The first one's name was Abraham," and we children had to echo, "Ham, ham, ham!"

The second verse began, "The second one's name was Isaac," and we shouted, "Sick, sick, sick!"

The last verse was climactic. "They all fell over the precipice."

We jumped and somersaulted on our beds and screamed, "Piss, piss, piss?"

*****

I took the unmarried state of these two aunts for granted. They were votaresses, dedicated to me. However, spinsterhood was not permitted among poor Jews of their generation. A sort of bush telegraph or grapevine carried messages to many households connected by blood or marriage. Husbands were found for the two girls. Hetty married a quiet man who worked in a sawmill; motherhood soon gave her fulfilment. A partner for

Annie was transported from South Wales, where he worked as a pithead labourer. A wiry little man, a former Regular Army soldier, he was put to work on George Cohen's Scrap Iron Wharf in the docks and settled down with Annie and my grandfather. He, too, was a man of few words but he made it plain that this was the cushiest billet he had ever known.

Chapter 11

When I was eight my father decreed that we must say "mama" and "papa" instead of "Mummy" and "Daddy". This came as a shock to me. I was angry but I could not persuade my small sister to join me in resistance and we fell into the new way. It was part of the business of betterment as my father saw it. He had picked up the idea at the Marburgs', the German-Jewish family whom he greatly respected as being educated people. They lived in a big house. I liked to go there with him and I admired as much as he did their English (his adjective) drawing-room, all pretty chintzes, flowers, pottery and books of a kind not seen in our family.

I looked on my father as a strong, all-competent protector. I was proud of his smartness; he seemed striking and superior among the people I so far knew. I was aware of his love and enjoyed my closeness to him, especially when we studied together. He was a self-educator. My mother's brothers Izzy the schoolmaster and Harry the clerk lent him books or recommended them. I have an early memory of him sitting at a table bent over an open atlas that Harry had bought for him. I knelt on a chair next to him. We stared at a map of the world and as we saw the meaning of the patchwork of bright colours we explained it to each other. Harry got for him a set of *Cassell's Children's Book of Knowledge*, which became one of the treasures of my childhood. He, too, learned much from it.

I was a docile and admiring pupil of my father in another matter: that of cleanliness. By the time I was six he had drilled me to wash myself down to the waist every morning at the cold tap, hair and all, to clean my teeth with salt and take a salt gargle, and to polish my boots on the scullery step. I performed these tasks with emulative zeal. Until he had a bathroom fitted out, he presided over our Friday night baths in the zinc tub in front of the kitchen range, boiling water in buckets and kettles on top of the range and supplying each of us in turn.

It was only as I grew older that my trusting intimacy with him was eroded. My sister and I both knew that my mother was more intelligent than he was, but he thought her far beneath him, unable to understand the subjects of his reading and his homilies, such as astronomy, politics, the fallacies and contradictions of the Old Testament and the meaning of life. He would sigh with despair or shake his head and exclaim, "Stupid woman!" while she want on placidly with her sewing or ironing. Witnessing such scenes, we children drew away from him and began to see him critically. As I grew older, my own feelings towards him progressed from a vague resentment to anger and then derision.

In his eyes I could do no wrong. I was the son. I would attain the heights he might have reached (so I guess him to have felt) if life had not deprived him of the chance. I am sure he looked forward to the time when he and I would discuss high intellectual matters together, perhaps in front of his uncomprehending and awed wife. This was not to be. In my teens I drifted into courses that were mysterious and frightening to him. Whatever disappointment and alarm he felt he never showed it. He never questioned or criticised me, he did all he could for me and his affection never wavered.

As for my sister, he begrudged her nothing, allowed her to go on to a secondary education, treated her fairly and with a sort of self-conscious kindness, but to him she was only a girl, and daughters were per se a disappointment to a man.

My father's employers were friendly to him, seeing him as not only a superb craftsman but as one who considered himself to be their social equal. They treated him with great respect and paid him well, but on many evenings after supper, when he stretched out in his armchair looking tired and despondent, we listened in silence while he spoke of his great dream, to quit the factory and buy a little shop of his own, selling tobacco and sweets. All this talk filled me with dread and hostility. One winter my parents took me on several expeditions to look at shops for sale in the East End. We must have inspected a dozen little corner shops, ill-lit holes with sunken doorsteps and dirty windows, in remote and decaying corners of Limehouse and Poplar. I was all the more frightened by the silent, lamplit streets of slum houses and the occasional ill-dressed passer-by who looked at us, as I imagined, with suspicion or worse. Luckily my father's timidity, as always, prevailed.

During this phase he appeared blinded to the slavery and penury of a life imprisoned behind a shop counter. He spoke of the pleasure of getting away from the factory, of being free, of being his own master. The truth was that, although he was at ease with his employers, the company of his fellow workers was a constant strain on him. The girl machinists liked him and treated him with respect, there were a couple of older craftsmen with whom he could talk intelligently, but he spoke of the rest of the men as a coarse, foul-mouthed lot, too ignorant to talk of anything other than of which horses to back. And, although he was on the face of it a great dignitary in the factory who, moreover, was forever exerting himself to help others, he must have sensed exaggeration and mockery in their shows of respect, falsity in their smiles and malice in the occasional slap on the back that he was given – some of which I witnessed and understood.

Each year I went with him on the company beano, or coach outing. This was a day trip to one of the seaside resorts near London. He and I kept mostly to ourselves. On these occasions I sometimes felt a pang of sympathy for him but I soon relapsed into the cold and selfish detachment of a child.

He came home from work one evening looking white and shaken. Some of the men had persuaded him to go with them to the Premierland, a boxing hall that was open all day, in which hundreds of East End boys were paired off to batter each other in the hope of making a couple of pounds or in the hope of becoming famous like Kid Berg, the Jewish champion.[1] As soon as my father saw blood flowing, he fainted. This must have enabled his companions to torment him for days with jovial teasing.

When one of the girl machinists was getting married, he gave a party for her at the factory on a Saturday morning, paying for a lavish show of drinks. A teetotaller, he drank only lemonade but, poor innocent man, he did not recognise the taste of gin when tots of it were surreptitiously poured into his glass.

I was playing in the street when he came home. He walked stiffly upright, with a firm but slightly erratic step, his face flushed. He was smiling to himself, and went past me on the pavement apparently without seeing me. Taken aback, I followed him into the house. My mother met him in the hall and, after a brief exchange of words, helped him upstairs. I did not see him again that day.

We were a reading family. My father sat at the table over his improving books and gave me Upton Sinclair's *The Jungle* to read.[2] We all listened raptly every week to the dramatized serials of classic novels on the radio. But my mother and I and my sister, too, as she grew older, were off into a world of imagination that was beyond my father's reach. We had discovered the public library. We brought home our books in a shopping bag every week.

---

1   Jack 'Kid' Berg (1909–1991). Born Judah Bergman. Known by fans as "The Whitechapel Windmill." Boxed at Lightweight and Light Welterweight. See Colin Holmes's review article, "Kings of the Ring, "*International Journey of the History of Sport*, Vol. 8 (1991), pp.429–32.

2   Upton Sinclair (1878–1968) American writer. His novel, *The Jungle* (First English edition, London, 1906), focussed on the harshness of immigrant life in America.

In the next ten years I must have read getting on for two thousand books from the library. When my mother was not busy she sat in her chair by the fireplace reading. One summer's day when the street door was left open, a woman neighbour walked in and caught my mother reading *Pride and Prejudice.* "Ha!" she screamed, "Schoolteacher!"

My parents kept us out in the open air whenever they could. On Sundays my father took us on bus rides to the royal parks or to the river at Richmond. My mother packed chicken sandwiches and flasks of tea. My father stopped at certain street stalls he knew at which the best fruit was sold. He picked out one by one pears and oranges that came up to his exacting standards, huge and delicious fruit such as I have not tasted since. These he would peel for us with the little mother-of-pearl penknife that he always carried,

On Saturdays, after an early lunch, we hurried to the cinema to be in time for the cheap prices; when the super-cinemas were opened after 1930 we enjoyed a long film show, an organist and a stage show amid marble halls and grand staircases. Sometimes we went to one of those other luxurious establishments now provided for the working-class, a Lyons' Corner House; more marble halls, flowers, a band playing and fish and chips, roll and butter and tea for a matter of pence. Barnstorming companies played at the Alexandra, our theatre, Tod Slaughter among them, with *Maria Marten.* Slaughter was the last of the old breed of touring actor-managers, a true descendant of Dickens' Mr. Vincent Crummles in *Nicholas Nickleby.*[3] We queued till the gallery doors clanged open, went up a gloomy stone staircase to buy tickets at the cubby-hole (threepence for children), then raced up to get to the gallery, the children leaping down over the wooden steps, which served for seating, to be at the front. We went for bus rides "up West" to see the sky-signs – "the coloured lights." Ida's girlfriends came in for hilarious dressing-up and theatricals. I played innumerable games of draughts with my father. His depressive streak did not affect our lives, which were lively and happy.

During the week our mother often met us at the school gate with our teas packed for a picnic and took us to eat our meal on Hackney Downs to keep us in the open air. My mother and I sat side by side on the grass looking across the fields at the red brick wall of the Grocers' Company's School

---

3   Tod Slaughter (1885–1956). Actor. Famed for starring in Victorian melodramas. The play *Maria Marten,* or *The Murder in the Red Barn,* based on a true-life murder in Suffolk in the 1820s, existed in several anonymous versions and was widely performed from the mid–19th century onwards. It was made into a well-known film starring Slaughter in 1935.

which ran opposite the entire length of the Downs. The school stood in extensive grounds, a red, Victorian-Gothic building with two wings added, a tower in the centre and wide stone steps with curving balustrades rising to a vaulted oak doorway. It was a grammar school, charging fees, with free places for which scholarship boys competed. Readers of The Magnet, we saw it as Greyfriars School. Sometimes my mother said to me, "That's where you're going one day." I took it for granted that I would.

Chapter 12

Uncle Harry, my mother's brother, was a slim, good-looking young man. From my earliest memory of him he was bald, slightly stooped, always smiling, a shadow of blue stubble on his pale cheeks.

I could not think of anyone nicer than my Uncle Harry in those years. It took no time at all for us to get into a deep, serious conversation; he bent forward when I talked, his eyes gleaming with interest, as if what I had to say mattered to him. He must have been the first who discerned in me an imagination and a passion for words. He lent me a school prize of his, a red volume containing all Shakespeare's plays. He said, "You'll find every word in the English language in this book." On my birthday he always gave me one of the sixpenny Reader's Library books. I still have *Mr. Midshipman Easy* inscribed in his penman's writing; much read, all the pages loose between the covers.

He worked for Blankenberg, a toy importer in Houndsditch. With only a Board School education he was deemed to have "got on" to be doing responsible work in an office. The office was in a front basement, its only daylight coming from a well in the pavement covered by a grating over which passers-by walked all day. I imagined Harry sitting at a high Bob Cratchit desk down there. My mother said that it was no wonder he had a cough.

One day an unexpected, daredevil Harry presented himself to us. Mr. Blankenberg had given him a new job. Now Harry drove a large open touring car to and fro between London and Dusseldorf, bringing back toy samples. He took us for rides and, watching him leaning back at the wheel of the big car, insouciant, wearing a sportsman's check cap, I thought he was like the hero of some high society film. He went to and fro in all weathers, paying no attention to his chronic cough.

Then I became aware of low—toned grown-up conversations taking place, obviously not for the ears of the children. Of course, I found out soon enough. A police sergeant had called at Brune House. He had said to my grandfather, "Levvy, you'll have to come down to the station. We've got your Harry there."

The Customs men had discovered contraband hidden in the car. I did not find out what it was; perhaps industrial diamonds. Harry appeared in court. The sergeant gave evidence for him, saying that he was a young man of good character. The police doctor also gave evidence, and that was when I first heard that Harry had consumption. He was cleared of the charges and dismissed from the case.

From time to time after that he went to a sanatorium at Woburn Sands in Bedfordshire. He sent us picture post-cards and always came back smiling.

At home I lived in the attic now. I had a bookcase and a pigeon-hole desk, made by Jack, one of my younger uncles. The room was called my study. At the age of ten I told my father that I wanted to write for the newspapers. He consulted with Harry and they brought home a Remington typewriter for me, a big machine on a square frame. It cost a pound. I taught myself to type with the help of an instruction manual from the library.

I saw my first article printed in that year. Our teacher at school took us to visit a local newspaper, *The Recorder*. I was fascinated by the clanking flatbed machines, the smell of the ink and the sheets of printed words being everlastingly lifted up in the frames. The teacher sent essays written by another boy and me to the editor of *The Recorder*. These were printed, and a fat man in a raincoat came to take our photograph, which appeared on the front page. He gave us a half-a-crown each. Since then I had read Philip Gibbs' novel about Fleet Street journalism, *The Street of Adventure* and had learned Kipling's poem about the journalist who "has sold his heart to the old Black Art, we call the daily Press."[1]

To me being a journalist meant being a writer. It was the only way I knew to get started. It was romance and adventure. I studied *The Complete Writing For Profit* by Michael Joseph and for the next four years sent off to the newspapers the kind of pieces that Joseph recommended; for instance, in advance of the Easter Parade of hats at Hyde Park, I wrote an article on "Strange Hats Of History", which I sent to the weekly *Tit-Bits*. I never sold an article but the rejection slips were almost as gratifying as publication; they signified that I was in the business of writing.

I last saw Harry by chance when I was on leave from the army. It must have been early in the war for I carried my rifle and full pack, as we had to during the months when a German invasion was expected. I made my way in a cold, penetrating rain from Holborn Hall towards Clerkenwell Road.

---

1   Philip Gibbs, *The Street of Adventure* (London, 1919). Rudyard Kipling's lines appear in his poem, Press (1899).

On the steps of one of the slum tenement buildings on my left I saw Harry. His face lit up as brightly as ever and we greeted each other. I asked him what he was doing here. He said, "Collecting rents."

His face looked wasted, his voice was husky and his coughs were frequent, deep and hollow. He said, "I can't get steady work but it's a living. But tell me," he said, with the old, keen, interested look, "I want to hear all about you."

Not long afterwards my mother wrote to tell me that Harry had died in hospital.

*****

Four doors away from our house lived a kind woman named Mrs. Hammerson who was reputed to be very well-off. Her relations were a family of estate agents named Mendoza. She had a son of about my age, Lewis, a plump boy with pudgy, rosy cheeks and shining black hair brushed flat with a side parting. All the children in the street were invited to his birthday parties which were spectacular occasions.

We sat at a long table with dishes of cakes and tarts down the middle. Clusters of balloons hung from the ceiling. When we went home each of us was given a balloon, a packet of sweets and a small present wrapped in gift paper.

Lewis Hammerson had a child's-size cycle. He rode it up and down the street ringing the bell. It was an ultimate luxury. When I saw it my stomach contracted with envy. He refused my pleas for a ride; until one day he offered me a bargain. If I would push him to Stamford Hill he would let me ride the bicycle back.

He spun the pedals to give himself a start; then I took over and pushed him to the top of Stamford Hill, a distance of about one and a half miles uphill. As we arrived I tottered away from the bike, out of breath. He turned round and pedalled off downhill, leaving me.

A half-hour later I rang the bell of his front door. He appeared in the doorway and I knocked him down. I went home. Soon our doorbell rang. It was Mrs. Hammerson. I listened from the kitchen. She spoke to my mother sounding sorrowful and surprised. My mother's voice in reply was sympathetic, then firmly reassuring, indicative of promised punishment. Mama closed the door and came back to the kitchen. She said, "Why did you hit Lewy Hammerson?"

I told her why. She still looked stern, her lips pursed. Turning her back on me she went out to the scullery, stooped to open the oven door and brought out a tray of her fairy cakes. She straightened up and held out the tray. She said, sternly, "Take two."

The smell of these cakes fresh from the oven was always exquisite. I think she put cinnamon in them. To be given one in its crinkly case of shiny paper was always a big treat.

After the war Lewis Hammerson became a property millionaire and a big philanthropist. His company's HQ was in Park Lane, London, and after his early death he left a bequest to the Lewis W. Hammerson Memorial Hospital.[2]

---

2   Lewis Hammerson (1916–1958) was the founder of the property company, Hammerson plc.

Chapter 13

Also when I was ten, I fell in love with aeroplanes. For the next six years flying was the passion of my life. It occupied my mind more than any of my other concerns, including my studies, until politics made me forget about it.

Aeroplanes were still made of wood and canvas then, even big passenger machines. They were as beautiful to me as sailing ships are to lovers of the sea. I still see the Camel or the SE5a, at the RAF Museum in Hendon, as beautiful.

At Margate, where we spent several holidays, there was a joy-riding aeroplane, one of those taken around the country in those days by barnstorming war veterans. The pilot charged five shillings for a flight, more for such extras as looping the loop. I nagged my parents until they gave in, and they watched, frightened, I am sure, while I went up in the passenger

Figure 16 "For the next six years flying was the passion of my life." Baron in his early teens taking a joy-ride in an Avro 504K piloted by "barnstorming war veterans."

cockpit of a red Avro 504K, one of the classic aeroplanes, first built in 1913. I am pleased even now to have flown in one.

In the years that followed I saved up to have a few more joyrides and once got together a guinea for a trial flying lesson at Broxbourne, a club airfield in Hertfordshire, in an Avro Avian. This lasted for about twenty minutes. The instructor, who sat in a separate cockpit behind me, took off and landed but I kept the Avian's nose on the horizon in a creditable manner and even managed a few turns, although I may have been helped in these by the instructor's discreet pressure on his dual-control joystick and rudder bar. I was convinced that I could fly. I read not infrequently in those days of schoolboys who sneaked on to airfields, took off on their own and flew circuits until they landed safely. Like me, they had practised at home sitting in a chair with a broom between their knees as a control stick and were most skilled and subtle pilots before they ever flew solo.

Whenever I could I went on my own to the aerodromes on the edges of London, at Croydon and at Stag Lane in Edgware, to hang about, watch the 'planes coming and going and (having sneaked past the gate-men) pester mechanics with questions. Every year I spent a day at the Hendon Air Display. I set off on most Saturday mornings with a packet of sandwiches to walk seven miles to Kensington; where I spent the day in the aviation section at the Science Museum, walking seven miles back late in the evening. Eventually I got a reader's ticket to the Science Library and spent hours reading aviation books. I became a great technical expert on aircraft and engines, I had some notion of elementary aerodynamics and I thought I could recognise any type of aeroplane ever built.

My most potent daydreams were about the airmen of the Great War. I knew all about aerial fighting. I bought American magazines, *Wings*, *Aces*, *Battle Aces*, paying sixpence for each and getting threepence back in part exchange; I must have read hundreds of them. In the Reader's Library edition I bought *The Dawn Patrol* by John Monk Saunders.[1] I read it to rags and I saw the film five times, the first version with Richard Barthelmess as the self-sacrificing Captain Courtney. I saw life in terms of a legend of heroes of eighteen led by old men of twenty-five. I could think of nothing to recommend life after the age of eighteen and I aspired to a hero's death in flames at that age.

---

1   John Monk Saunders's novel, *The Dawn Patrol*, first appeared in 1930. Captain Courtney became eclipsed two years later when Biggles (Major James Bigglesworth), the creation of Captain W.E. Johns, made his appearance as a pilot-hero and continued for many years to attract young readers.

My attic room was now decorated with framed pictures of dogfights, a photograph of a German war-time ace, the Baron von Richthofen, and a model propeller over the mantelpiece. In this room I spent weeks building a miniature SE5a out of balsa wood and silk. I painted it and decorated it with red, white and blue insignia. I installed a little pilot in the cockpit. The 'plane was driven by hanks of elastic hooked between the propeller and the tailpost. I launched it from the window of my bedroom, having first lit a stump of candle in the cockpit. It flew out over the garden, an absolutely real SE5a to me, flying over the lines in France. Above the flower beds it burst into flames and dropped plumb. I raced down to the garden, threw myself down on the path, looked through a cluster of lupin stalks that I saw as tree trunks, and contemplated myself in my funeral pyre. This preoccupation with death underlay my enjoyment of the Air Display. Every year I went hoping to see a crash; eventually there was one, but the crew of the Boulton and Paul bomber walked away unhurt.

When I was as the Grocers' School I asked the headmaster if I could get in at Cranwell, the R.A.F. College. He pointed out to me that applicants must have perfect sight and both parents born British. On the second day of the war in 1939 I made a futile attempt to join up in aircrews.

My long walks to and from the Science Museum started a habit of solitary walking which has continued. It was on those walks, too, that daydreams began to get the upper hand in my life. At first they were about flying. Later on, in a sort of serial daydream, I was a famous author. I lived in a manor house, had a mistress, a Frenchwoman named Cécile, kept horses and of course flew my own 'plane. In time these walks took in the Tate Gallery and the National Gallery and I went on my own to Continental films and theatre matinées. Even when I made school friends I kept them on the fringe of my life, for the most part seeing them at school or on the way home; they were not allowed to encroach on a now precious solitude.

In consequence I came to exist at a growing distance from my family. Living with them, I became self-enclosed and uncommunicative. The more I stood back from my parents, the more critically I scrutinised them.

Chapter 14

I started at the Grocers' – Hackney Downs School – in September 1929, on a Junior County Scholarship. I wept when I had to leave the Shacklewell; the last time, as far as I can remember, that I have ever cried.

I had always been happy at the Shacklewell but the last year was the best, when I was in Mr. Jones' class. Mr. Jones was one of those blessed beings endowed with a natural gift for teaching. He was, I guess, still in his thirties. Like all those of my schoolmasters who were between the ages of thirty and fifty when they taught me he had been in the war, but he did not talk about it. Some of the boys claimed to know that he had a wound in his leg that would not heal, although he did not limp. For us this story created an aura of differentness about him, as if the secret wound were the evidence of a secret power that enabled this mild, easy-going man to command, in the most casual and relaxed manner, silent attentiveness from fifty boys among whom were a good many notorious ruffians, the boys from Miller's Terrace, the local slum. One of them, Bert Little, took a real and innocent pride in belonging to a family of burglars.

Mr. Jones gave us points every day, which he chalked on the corners of our desks. He started the day with an inspection for clean hands and nails, giving a point to every boy who passed the test and awarding more throughout the day for other merits, good drawing, it might be, or diligence in tidying the cupboard, or, whimsically, a droll wrong answer or an ingenious mistake at arithmetic. The prize was a penny pastry which was conspicuous all day in a white paper bag on the corner of his table. By the end of the year almost every boy had taken the cake at least once,

I thought I was hopeless at drawing. In the first weeks of the school year the boy who shared a desk with me, Fred Johnson, did a quick drawing for me which was good enough to get a fair mark, after he had finished his own. Fred's father had been killed in the Great War. There were at least one or two such boys in every class, who were looked on with a touch of awe. Mr. Jones soon had me drawing reasonably well and I came to enjoy painting from the flowers, fabrics and wallpapers which he brought to school. We all liked bawling songs from the school song book; he took us in hand and

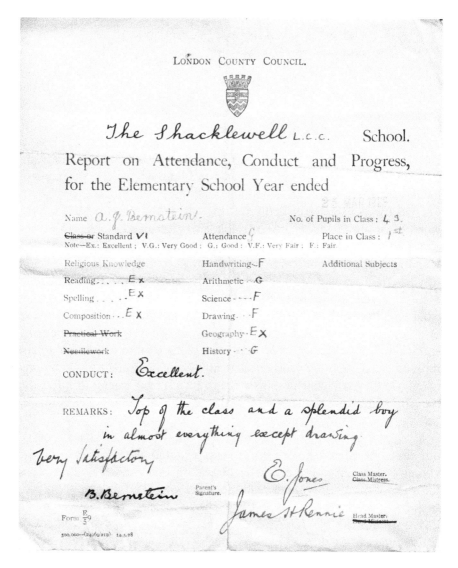

LONDON COUNTY COUNCIL.

The Shacklewell L.C.C. School.

Report on Attendance, Conduct and Progress,
for the Elementary School Year ended

Name *A. P. Bernstein.*   No. of Pupils in Class : 4 3.

Class or Standard **VI**   Attendance *G*   Place in Class : 1st

Note—Ex.: Excellent ; V.G.: Very Good ; G.: Good ; V.F.: Very Fair ; F.: Fair.

Religious Knowledge	Handwriting— F	Additional Subjects
Reading.... E x	Arithmetic — G	
Spelling.... E x	Science ---- F	
Composition... E x	Drawing... F	
Practical Work	Geography— E x	
Needlework	History--- G	

CONDUCT : *Excellent.*

REMARKS : *Top of the class and a splendid boy in almost everything except drawing.*
Very Satisfactory

B. Bernstein   Parent's Signature.

E. Jones   Class Master. Class Mistress.

James H Rennie   Head Master.

Form E/5 9

500,000—(24569/27B) 14.5.28

Figure 17 "I had always been happy at the Shacklewell but the last year was the best, when I was in Mr. Jones' class." Baron's class report, March 1929.

taught us to sing in harmony. Most of the class paid a few pence every week to go to the Isle of Wight for a week in the summer holidays, subsidised by the Children's Country Holiday Fund. We spent the entire summer term compiling a Holiday Book and printing it on a jellygraph; all about the geography, geology, marine life and history of the Isle of Wight. The boys who were going worked themselves up to a high pitch of eagerness. I felt the most poignant envy of them. Mr. Jones based his geography lessons on topical events, the tour of a Test cricket team or a journey by the Prince of Wales. He taught us to swim at the Haggerston Baths and took us on visits to see how the Docks worked, to go over an ocean liner, a power station and half a dozen local factories.

Few boys ever gave trouble but the moment one did he was faced by an implacable Mr. Jones, who sent him for the cane and book. I never heard of a child being beaten in any council school, contrary to what I sometimes read nowadays. There was a short cane provided by the County Council, a register in which details of the offence and punishment had to be entered and a limit of three strokes on the palm of each hand. I dare say Mr. Jones was not a fanatic for corporal punishment, but he knew that boys sometimes bring themselves to a state of intoxication when insolent and are most quickly sobered by this sort of punishment, which does no more than sting.

The Shacklewell was as much a civilising influence as my mother's school had been. The doctor came from time to time. More often, the Nit Nurse appeared to comb our hair and whisk a few boys away for cleansing. Thirty or forty boys in the school paid sixpence a week to buy small violins and attend a violin class. Once we all sat cross-legged in the school hall listening to a grave little boy named Lampard on the dais drawing music from a 'cello as large as he was. He was sent to a music school.

My mother came with me to the Grocers' for an interview. She was dressed in an austere best outfit; a dream was coming true. We sat on an oak bench in the central hall under dark beams, with a long case of trophies on the wall behind us. Masters in black gowns whisked to and fro. It was Greyfriars.

The Grocers' Company is one of the wealthiest of the London livery companies. In the Middle Ages its members, the merchant grocers of London, imported rare spices from the East, brought by camel caravans across deserts. Cloves decorated the school coat of arms and there was a camel in our cap badge. The school was established in 1876, twenty years after the Grocers' Company had founded the great Public School at Oundle. The day school in Hackney was probably thought of as an imitation of it, for the sons of tradesmen, minor professional men and better-paid City clerks. It was taken over by the London County Council in 1907 and became Hackney Downs School but everyone went on calling it the Grocers'.

We waited in a classroom until the Head entered. William Jenkyn Thomas came up to our expectations. He was tall, he had silky white hair, fresh pink cheeks and a gracious manner. He was every inch Doctor Locke of Greyfriars. Something else made his appearance striking. I could not tell what it was until I started at the school and older boys pointed out to me that he had bright ginger eyebrows to go with his white hair. He might well have been a reader of *The Magnet*, so uncannily alike were all his mannerisms to those of a headmaster in a boys' storybook. Like Mr. Jones, he had the gift of teaching, as I was to find later, and he was a kind man. When I was older he put up with my defiant foibles and gave me the freedom of the bookshelves in his study.

A cap, too large for me, was bought at the school outfitters, and a navy blue blazer with the camel badge on its breast pocket. I was stifled with pride to have achieved this uniform. I was taken about to be shown off to the family.

A lot of Grocers' boys attained to eminence of one sort or another. A few became famous. Lord Goodman, Harold Pinter and a former Master of St. Catherine's College, Cambridge, Barry Supple, are products of the school.[1] I have met other prominent academics as well as leading doctors, scientists and administrators who are old Grocers' boys. I have never come across one who spoke other than well of the school. There were, I believe, five such schools in and around East London, Foundation Schools as they were sometimes called. They opened a door of opportunity to poor, clever children and gave society many talented people.

By the end of the Second World War, when the population of Hackney had changed, most of the boys at the school were Jewish. When I started, the Jews were only a minority but their numbers grew each year. The school was burned down in 1963. A comprehensive school that was set up on the site came to a sad end in 1995.

When I started at the Grocers', the fee-paying boys formed a large majority. The few free places were keenly sought after by scholarship boys. The number increased rapidly each year and by the time I left the scholarship boys must have made up half the total of pupils.

*****

---

1   Details relating to the Grocers' School and its prominent alumni appear in Geoffrey Alderman, *Hackney Downs 1876–1995* (London, 2012). Lord Goodman, to whom Baron refers, is Arnold Goodman (1913–1995), leading London lawyer and adviser to the great and the good, including Harold Wilson (qv).

My thirteenth birthday fell at the end of the following year. That was to be the occasion of my barmitzvah.[2] In this ceremony the boy shows that he is now a man by going up to the minister's platform during the Sabbath synagogue service and reading a portion of the Law; in effect conducting the service for a little while. A celebration follows, sometimes ostentatious.

My parents took it for granted that I would be barmitzvahed. Religion or Free Thought had nothing to do with it in their eyes. It was a social duty for them to give hospitality and a tribal duty for me to perform. I cannot believe that they would have put on a showy celebration but I was never to know.

*****

Early in the year my father had his first heart attack. He was thirty-six. He was treated at home, as patients were then. Tall, imposing Doctor Maltby came morning and evening. One day he brought a specialist with him, a great man named Hoskins who was humbly shown up to the bedroom by my mother. Two porters followed him, carrying an immense cabinet of some ebony material, at least four feet long; the electro-cardiograph machine of the time.

After several months at home, most of them in bed, my father was well enough to convalesce. In the summer he went away to a quiet boarding-house at Boscombe, taking my sister Ida with him. It was agreed that in the autumn I should start to prepare for my barmitzvah.

School broke up for the summer holidays and my mother took me to Margate for a week. We stayed in Cliftonville, the better-off part of Margate, in a Jewish boarding-house. My mother took a room for us and another for my grandmother Levinson and my youngest aunt, Doris.

Cliftonville was an enchanting place to me. I fancied it to be just like the Continent, another Deauville or Le Touquet. The open-air swimming pool was floodlit at night, crowded with bathers whose cries mingled with music of the Palm Court kind. Excitingly, couples were to be seen scampering away from the poolside to the dark beach. Another band played in a piazza lit by chains of coloured lamps, people sat at café tables and waiters in white jackets hurried to and fro.

One day Doris and I came out of the water after a swim, picked up our towels and clothes and went back to the boarding-house to dress. We ran up the stairs, into the room I shared with my mother; Doris had forgotten

---

2   Barmitzvah. Coming of age ceremony for Jewish boys of thirteen.

Figure 18 "Cliftonville was an enchanting place to me." Baron, aged about twelve, with his sister Ida while on holiday in "the better-off part of Margate."

to ask for the key to her own room. She went to the far side of the bed, I stayed by the wardrobe. I pulled down my costume and began to towel myself. I was self-conscious and proud of our daring behaviour, although after I glimpsed Doris in the wardrobe mirror I took care not to look at the glass again. I did not have time to dwell on my excitement, for there was a confusion of heavy, hurried footsteps coming up the stairs and the sound of my grandmother's loud panting. She burst into the room, red in the face and out of breath, with my mother close behind her.

She cried, "Dry yourselves, children, you'll catch cold," and waddled hastily to envelop Doris in her towel and hustle her out of the room.

My mother closed the door behind them and said, "Give me your wet costume. I'll hang it out."

For a few moments I was capable of nothing but astonishment. When I calmed down, I had things to reflect upon. I saw my grandmother in a new character; that of an old peasant woman, in appearance and mind, who did not trust either her beloved *Dvorele* or her adored twelve-year-old grandson to undress together in a room. Later still I wondered about my mother's part in the affair. Had she been compelled to follow when my grandmother rushed from the beach, or had she shared her panic?

*****

My father went back to the factory in the autumn. I started to study my barmitzvah portion. An instructor came to the house, a Mr. Joseph. I had learned some Hebrew already; for a couple of years at synagogue Hebrew classes, run like a Sunday School, before that at an old-fashioned *cheder* conducted by an aged rabbi in a dirty basement room. Here, in the manner of *der Heim*, a dozen boys lounged around a long table, reading or whispering, while the old man took them one by one for fifteen minutes each of tuition with a stick and a huge prayer book.[3] He fascinated me by blowing his nose without a handkerchief, into a box of sand at a range of about four feet. Mr. Joseph, my new instructor, had been in the war. A deep scar puckered one side of his neck. He told me that it was from a bayonet wound. I insisted on hearing the story of his hand-to-hand fight for life. It dominated his imagination as much as it did mine. One memory led to another. At every lesson there was more reminiscing and less teaching.

---

3   *Cheder*. A school where Jewish children can learn Hebrew and acquire religious knowledge; *der Heim*, or *alte haym*, is a reference to the old home or homeland.

One day in a sudden aggressive outburst I told my parents that I was not going to be barmitzvahed. I said that if they forced me to go to the synagogue I would take a ham sandwich in my pocket and lay it down on the Scroll of the Law, an unspeakable sacrilege.[4]

My parents showed no sign of the consternation they must have felt. I had appeared docile and resigned until then; for myself, I cannot remember any building up of hostility and resolve in me before this rebellion. They looked at each other. My mother sighed. She broke a silence by telling me that my tea was on the kitchen table.

They were alone together in the parlour for a half-hour, then they came to the kitchen. They did no more than try to persuade me with reasonable arguments. They did not raise their voices. In the interval I had worked myself up into a fury, to justify myself. I reminded my father of all his lectures about the hypocrisy of religion. I told him that he had been hypocritical himself, never going to synagogue but sending me there on certain High Festivals. I spoke about the men in their black best suits standing outside the synagogue on Yom Kippur, all round me, talking business. I meant all this but behind it all, what had brought me to make this stand was my shyness, which had become an agony. I could not face the ordeal.

My parents must have been utterly taken aback. I had always been a good, obedient boy but they knew what a serious creature I was and when they saw me pale and determined, they, gentle people, simply desisted. Nothing more was said. My lessons were stopped. Many years later my mother told me that they gave up because my father was still weak after his heart attack. Not a thought of this entered my mind when I confronted them nor of the predicament I had left them in with family and friends. Once it was over, I hardly thought of the matter again.

I went unbarmitzvahed. I do not know if I am still a Jew in the eyes of the religious. None of the family ever spoke on the subject in my hearing. They were all as affectionate as ever. My father's parents could not have cared tuppence about it but my dear grandmother Levinson must have been reduced by the news to a state of utter incomprehension and grief. This did not even occur to me when I visited her, still fierce and full of myself. She received me with the smile and the kiss that I was used to and she gave me the present she had already bought, a blue velvet bag with a Star of David embroidered on it in gold braid, and with a prayer shawl and a prayer book inside it.

---

4   The Scroll. A handwritten copy of the Torah, the holiest book in Judaism. It contains the five books of Moses. It is kept in the Ark of each synagogue.

Not long ago one of my cousins, a visitor from the United States where he settled many years ago, was reminiscing about our childhood days. He said, "We were all frightened of you then." My sister Ida laughed and agreed.

Were my parents frightened of me? And the rest of the family? What was there in a quiet, polite, well-behaved child to intimidate them? Perhaps a sensed intensity. Perhaps I was set apart as the clever one.

As the years went on I myself became oppressed by the notion that I was set apart from people around me. I puzzled to understand their goings-on. They often seemed to look upon me as, in the words of one friend of long acquaintance, a dark horse.

In the last months of the year the weather became worse I heard that *buba* Levinson had her usual winter bronchitis; then, suddenly, that she was dead, of pneumonia. She was sixty.

At Brune House, among the weeping women, I saw my mother sitting upright and silent, her face stony, her lips closed. I felt proud of her stoicism and of my own lack of any emotion.

After the Second World War, when I was nearly thirty, I was walking one day along Stoke Newington High Street, on a stretch which had been on my way to school when I was small. I do not recall what I was thinking about, certainly not my grandmother, when a great shock of grief for her suddenly smote me. I stopped in my tracks and felt for a few moments like rocking myself as the old men did in synagogues. When I went on my way, the desolation inside me persisted.

This was before I had ever read Proust. In *À La Recherche*, Marcel finds himself to be indifferent when his beloved grandmother dies. Much later, during his second visit to Balbec, he stoops to take off his boots. "I shook with sobs, tears streamed from my eyes ... I had just perceived in my memory ... the tender, preoccupied and dejected face of my grandmother ... the troubles of memory are closely associated with the heart's intermissions."

Chapter 15

I had entered my new school in a spirit of reverential awe at my surroundings, mingled with eagerness. I soon acquired the swagger of an initiate. Two new subjects of study fascinated me, English grammar and the French language. It took me a little time to see the point of grammar. Then I realised that it showed me how to say exactly what I wanted to say. Our French lessons for the first few weeks consisted only of phonetic training. We bunched up our lips, put our tongues in unfamiliar positions, whistled the French 'u', oo-ed and aah-ed. In the evenings, as I listened to French radio announcers, the purpose of these exercises dawned on me and I was on the way to getting a tolerable French accent. No such light came to show me the precision and economy of Latin or the logic of mathematics, and I took little interest in these subjects throughout my school career.

I got high marks in everything during the first year, but I learned at the end of the first week that I was not the cleverest boy in the world, as I had been led to believe at the Shacklewell School and at home. In our weekly report cards I took turns in the first three places with two quiet and modest boys named Snellgrove and Citron, and there were several others at our heels. I met Citron after the war. He had fought in tanks in North Africa and had lost his right hand.

Competition added both tension and zest to life. It is a boon to clever children. It unites them. Not only does it spur them on but they learn from each other, they recommend reading out of eagerness to share and discuss a pleasure with children of their own calibre, and they gladly help each other to master knotty points, perhaps partly out of conceit. Discovered affinities led me to the cementing of friendships, some of which have lasted to the present day. The time of long walks in company, long and earnest conversations and grandiloquent pronouncements had begun. Arthur Gold had come from the Shacklewell a year before me. We were already familiar presences in each other's houses. He took up athletics seriously at the Grocers', laying the foundations of his remarkable career. He trained on the running track at Victoria Park. I often accompanied him and galloped loyally round the track at an ever-increasing distance behind him.

Figure 19 "The time of long walks in company, long and earnest conversations and grandiloquent pronouncements had begun." Baron aged about fifteen with Arthur Gold.

School displaced home as the centre of my life. It was the place where I at last fitted in. In time our family home became only an annexe to it, a place where I was little more than a lodger. School was also a realisation of the fantasy life I had lived in earlier childhood as a reader of *The Magnet*. Since to scholarship boys like me the school was our own Greyfriars, we accepted whacking as a symbol of our elevation. It was administered only by the Head, and entailed a visit to his study, at the top of a flight of stone steps, in the school tower. It was a sobering experience and no worse than that.

Robert Fenson the porter, Bobs, who was with us until he retired in 1934 after fifty-two years of service, to be replaced by a symbolically dull and dour council porter, was beloved by all of us. He wore a top hat and a frock coat bordered with gold braid, and addressed us benevolently as young gentlemen. We had the obligatory fearsome and comical sergeant-major in Mr. Marley, an astonishing gymnast with a body hard as teak, although he must have been in his early sixties, and a profiteer in his stores such as only the army can produce. We had a farcical parody of the Officers' Training Corps, with wooden rifles and no uniforms, but we marched with zest behind a zealous and cacophonous drum-and-bugle band. We had an indoor swimming pool to which we resorted whenever permitted, although it was unfiltered and foul to an almost viscid degree. We had a tuck shop under the gloomy imitation cloisters, fives courts that were always in use and a playing field at Lower Edmonton to which we went by an exciting train journey on our free Wednesday afternoons. There was a school boathouse on the bank of the River Lea. It was pleasant to wander down there on a light evening to watch our own boats, Fours, practising or racing.

The School Theatre was not used in those days for plays but after the war, when a brilliant teacher, Mr. Brierley, introduced drama, I went back to the school to see several fine productions, in the programmes for which the name of H. Pinter is to be found. It was an amphitheatre, in which every morning the school, except for the Jews, assembled for prayers. In the evenings boys could go into the theatre to practise music, and in my last two years I played the piano in a small jazz band there. A school Social Club that met in the dining-hall in the evenings was much enjoyed and was the scene of hilarious concerts. Most of the boys took school for granted as the centre of their lives. I do not remember coming across anyone who hated it as English Public Schools of that time appeared to be hated by some of their inmates.

On the last day of the school year the Head presided over a great sing-song in the theatre, a ritual letting-off of steam. It culminated with the School Song, "The Elephant Battery", the choruses of which brought us to a frenzy of bawled, throat-hurting song and thunderous stamping feet.

During my first term I was filled with awe and veneration by the masters in their black gowns. Even more awesome was the Principal of McGill University in Canada, an Old Boy of the school, who was on a visit and taught my form for a week, I suppose for the fun of it. For us it was an experience to arouse not only wonder but (like the list of old Grocers' achievements and distinctions in every issue of the School magazine) a sense of what was possible, something transforming to children from homes in which the outlook was narrow and ambitions small.

Later on we got to know more about the masters and we looked upon a couple of them as comic figures but I cannot remember any who were disliked. They were nearly all, I believe, Oxford or Cambridge men, and some of them in this backwater must have led disappointed lives. One, a man with ruined good looks and a brilliant mind, was said by the boys to have been brought down by drink. Every one of them except the Head, who was too old, had fought in the War. One had a fearful scar in his skull. Another had lungs damaged by poison gas. Not one of them was a misfit or a dullard. All of them taught well. I remember them all with gratitude and some with affection.

We were addicted to sports with fervour, at times with hysteria. The great sporting event of the year was the annual soccer match between our First Eleven and the Casuals, one of the best amateur clubs in the country. One year, unbelievably, the School team won. An army of us marched back from the sports ground to the railway station, almost weeping with joy, singing to the tune of "Marching Through Georgia": "Now we've beat the Casuals, wasn't it a spree?" – a song which I had composed and taught them, capering in front of them with clenched, waving fists.

*****

Scholastically my second year at school was a comedown from my first. I lost interest in getting marks and top places and sometimes fell back to about the middle of the field. This did not worry me. Now that I was at home in the school, I no longer needed to compete. Without giving any thought to the matter I tended more and more to follow my own interests, often to the detriment of formal studies.

I plunged into an orgy of reading, reading in bed, in the playground, during lessons, in the evenings after scamping my official homework, reading that was quite indiscriminate, an exploration in all directions. Out of reading there bred a sort of ferment (it seems to me in memory) which soon made itself manifest as the need to write.[1]

My parents knew nothing of this new turn. All that they could see were the indifferent class reports. They must have been surprised and troubled by these, for I had seen the glow of exultation in their faces in the previous

---

1   See Figure 4 in the Introduction above for an illustration of Baron's self-image at this time.

year as they scanned the reports, my father sometimes triumphantly reading them aloud. However, they made no comment. They listened smiling to my chatter about school and always displayed an air of quiet if slightly anxious encouragement.

Since flying – perhaps flying and death – still occupied a great part of my fantasy life, it inevitably provided the material for my first purposeful efforts to become a writer of fiction. These began in the autumn of my twelfth year. I wrote a short story, "The Long Dive". Two young men, brothers, have invested all their hopes and money in the design and building of a new type of sports 'plane. (I wrote at a time when most aeroplanes were still made of wood and canvas and were often built by enthusiasts in small workshops or garages). After some episodes in which their relationship is revealed as a mixture of love and, on the part of the younger brother, jealousy, the day of a crucial test flight arrives. Potential backers have come to watch. The older brother is supposed to fly the single-seater machine but his junior tricks him and takes off. Now the pilot puts the machine through a series of aerobatics, each manoeuvre more exacting than its predecessors. He exalts (as I so often did in imagination) in his freedom of the skies. Then comes the culminating test, to demonstrate the strength of the airframe, a long steep dive. The dive begins. As the pilot holds the machine to it, he sees dangerous symptoms. He dives even more steeply. The wings are straining at their roots. He continues. They are going to yield. He carries on. The wings rip away. The pilot has a parachute but he does not use it. Through the eyes of his distraught brother we see the suicide accomplish itself.

I followed this with a novel, which filled a thick exercise book and which was mostly written during lessons, while a teacher's voice lectured on in the remote background. The title, "A Lightning Before Death", was taken from *Romeo and Juliet*:

"How oft when men are at the point of death
Have they been merry! which their keepers call
A lightning before death."

The story takes place during the Great War, in 1918. Freiherr the Baron Lothar von Kleist is the reigning air ace on the Western Front. He is the hero of the German Press, which dubs him the Black Knight, or *der Korsar*, the Corsair, because of the black triplane that he flies, which is decorated with a skull-and-crossbones emblem. He leads a crack fighter squadron which British fliers call the Kleist Circus. Like his model in real life, the

Baron Manfred von Richthofen, who flew a red triplane, he has shot down eighty-two Allied aircraft.

His antagonist in the story is a lieutenant in the British Royal Flying Corps. Roy Smith is such a mediocre pilot and so poor a shot that his Squadron commander has more than once threatened to have him transferred to the trenches. Smith's first encounter with von Kleist takes place. He loses his nerve, tries to get away and is shot down. He escapes unhurt but is humiliated by the contempt of his fellow pilots. Now he goes after von Kleist, and in a second encounter is again shot down. This time he is wounded. He returns from hospital. It is only because of the desperate shortage of pilots that he is once again allowed to fly. He goes on patrols, all the time looking out for von Kleist. One day the squadron sights the Circus and attacks. Now obsessed, Smith engages von Kleist but for the third time is hopelessly outfought. At last, with von Kleist on his tail and about to administer the *coup de grace*, he deliberately rams the German's triplane. The machines fall, locked together. Both pilots perish in the flames.

*****

In September 1931, Great Britain went off the Gold Standard. To everyone I knew, the pound sterling was a financial Rock of Gibraltar, or Holy of Holies. We all believed that we could go to the Bank of England and exchange a pound note for a sovereign coin of solid gold. Most families had a few gold sovereigns, kept as souvenirs of rosy days before the black chasm of the 1914 war opened up.

But now the unbelievable seemed to be happening every day. A month before, the government, a Labour government, had broken up in disagreement when told that savage economic cuts were the only way to avoid bankruptcy. The Prime Minister, Ramsay MacDonald, and a few of his colleagues had joined with the Tories and some Liberals to form a National Government. The pay cuts were put in force. Incredibly, they provoked a mutiny in that other Holy of Holies in the national mind, the Royal Navy. Pawnbrokers put up posters offering to pay five pounds for a gold sovereign. No one had ever heard of devaluation before.

The Slump – people began to speak that word as they might have said, the Plague – had been devastating lives throughout Europe and North America since 1929. In this country, mills, pits, factories and shipyards had closed down. Whole areas had come to a standstill. The number of unemployed climbed every month, reaching undreamed-of figures. Yet to most people in Britain life had seemed to jog on serenely, until the autumn shocks.

The same September I was starting my third year at the Grocers' three months before my fourteenth birthday. I read the daily newspaper minutely and every week went to the reading room at the public library to keep up with the *New Statesman* but I had no partisan interest in politics , nor did my parents consider themselves to be party supporters, although my father judged all events by considering how they would affect the *arbeiter*, the working man, his newspaper was the Labour *Daily Herald* and at the recent elections he and my mother had, as always, voted Labour.

I soon became aware that my parents were deeply worried by events. I overheard their low-toned, anxious conversations and broke into them with questions. My father knew what five pound notes offered for a gold sovereign meant. He was a Jew of an immigrant generation, alert to events in foreign countries which the true-born majority in those islands ignored, and he reminded me of the German inflation of 1923, when a postage stamp cost ten million marks. He asked what was going to happen to the savings which he had earned by working till all those midnights. Then I learned that his factory had closed down. I was seized with fright. In a few weeks' time – this was in October or November – I would be fourteen and legally old enough to work. Ought I to leave school? How could I hope to get a job?

But my father continued to go out at seven o'clock every morning, dressed as impeccably as ever, and there was no sign that money was short in our home. I assumed that there had been a false alarm and returned to the comfort of books and daydreams.

In fact, my father went every day to pass the time away in an empty factory. Sooner than lose his services when business picked up in the future, his employers were paying him a small weekly wage to act as little more than a caretaker. This was a lifeline to him. He would never – even if we were starving – he could never have stood in a queue to draw the dole. Eventually, as I have related earlier, he was inspired to design an article, apparently of a modest price appropriate to bad times, which sold well and put the firm back to work.

I recall another episode which, although trivial, brings back to me with particular sharpness the nature of these times. Acquaintances of my parents often came to them for advice. My mother in particular was a wise and calming counsellor to tearful wives who came with tales about their husbands' transgressions. Anyone who was in need of money, food or clothing, as well as advice, never went away unsatisfied. My parents were busy now exerting themselves for numerous out-of-work friends.

Every Sunday morning a flea market was held on Kingsland Waste, a stretch of wide pavement on which all comers were free to lay out their wares on the ground. One of my father's acquaintances, Ruby, was out of work and proposed (perhaps on my father's suggestion) to try his luck there. My parents scoured the house for unwanted articles and enlisted other friends to do the same. My father also, without asking me – could I possibly stand in the way of a good deed? – lent Ruby my gramophone, so that he could play it and attract customers to his display.

This was a gramophone that my grandfather Levinson had made for me when I was a little boy. It was not a child's toy but a small replica of his own magnificent machine. I thought I had outgrown childish things but I still treasured the gramophone as the work of my grandfather's hands and I was furious with my father for taking it. I never saw it again. Ruby had sold few of his wares but someone had offered him a paltry sum for the gramophone and it was gone. I sulked over this for some time.

*****

Perhaps these events did in the end lead me to think about the world outside my head. Perhaps the tendency was encouraged by a friendship I struck up with a boy named Clarke. I cannot remember his first name; I doubt if I ever knew it. Boys in those days usually referred to or addressed all but their closest friends by their surnames. He was a clever and serious boy, and we got to conducting some long conversations together with the upshot that in a form debate we both spoke in favour of the League of Nations, which was generally considered a daring thing to do. Then Clarke brought to school a book of ghastly photographs of dead soldiers and of others with facial wounds and we both became pacifists. We declared ourselves to be conscientious objectors and dropped out of the school battalion. During every parade we had to stand in line with some other Reds, as we were dubbed, on the edge of the parade-ground. Walking past me once, Mr. Fowler, the master with the deep cleft of a wound in his skull, paused for a moment to stare at me and say, "You belong to the army that marches on its belly."

Chapter 16

I was to sit for the Matriculation exam in the summer of my fifteenth year. The Matric. was the forerunner of the modern O-Levels, themselves now superseded. Boys who were leaving school looked upon it as a valuable passport to a job. Officially, as its name indicated, it was the key requirement for the few who wanted to go on to a university.

For the last two years I had been begging my parents to buy me a bicycle and had been told that I was too young. Now they promised to let me have one when I passed the Matric.

At the beginning of that year, 1933, Hitler came to power in Germany. The English newspapers carried stories of beatings-up and concentration camps and published photographs of elderly Jews scrubbing the streets while storm-troopers stood over them with whips. I was little moved by all this, my mind being too much taken up with other matters – the English and French poetry I was reading for Matric, for example, and the prospect of owning the bicycle I had picked out for myself and which I was eventually to own, a B.S.A. Silver Wing. My father, however, was visibly agitated. He took me to a protest meeting at the Scala Theatre.

Then it dawned on me that I was myself affected. The Marburgs' two sons, both in their twenties, went every summer on a cycling tour in Germany, joining the army of young people who wandered about that land, sleeping in youth hostels and barns and (the soldiers of 1939!) pledging eternal friendship. They had promised to take me with them this summer since we were all confident that I would get my bike. I had listened to their tales of beautiful landscapes and castles perched above the Rhine and had looked forward passionately to the adventure. Now I realised that we, as Jews, would not be able to go. Thus, for a second time, my concern at great and tragic events was only selfish, aroused by a trivial cause.

However, this disappointment had a lasting and beneficial effect. My schoolbooks now included *The Oxford Book of French Verse* and my liking for the French language became a passion which extended itself to everything French. I read every French book and newspaper I could get and worked on my accent with the help of French radio announcers. Among other things, I studied *Muirhead's Blue Guide to Paris* so intently and memorised the sectional street maps of that city so effectively that when at last, at the age of sixteen, I set foot in Paris I walked the streets as knowingly and confidently as if I had been there before.

*****

British people in general paid little attention to the accession of a Nazi government in Germany. There was, if anything, a vague sentiment of goodwill. It was probably formed out of the experience of the millions of Britons who had fought in France in the Great War, most of whom had come back with an abiding hatred of their French allies and some affection for the German soldier, whom they referred to as "old Jerry". Few people went abroad, but those who travelled to Germany on cheap tours came back enthusiastic at what they had seen. The prevalent feeling was that Germany had got a new broom, something we could do with here. As to the persecution of Reds and Jews, it was mostly a case of, "Between you and me, old man—" and a raised eyebrow. The Left were an unregarded minority.

There was not even this much interest in the school, which never took notice of anything outside the walls of its grounds, except for cricket and football scores. A small group of Fascists made its presence known and there was a mild stir at one of the popular evening lectures which we had from time to time. One of our distinguished Old Boys, a historian, H.A. Jones, who had written the official history of the air warfare between 1914 and 1918, came to speak about his recent tour of Germany.[1] He described to a crowded audience the renascence of that country in the usual glowing terms. The so-called atrocities were only some excesses committed by over-enthusiastic followers. He had gone to Germany as a guest of the new German government and, having met some of the men at the top, he could assure us that they were pretty decent and responsible fellows who would soon put a stop to this sort of thing.

The Fascists numbered five. They belonged to the Imperial Fascist League, a small organization, long established, which was so fanatical that when Oswald Mosley's much more powerful British Union of Fascists came

---

1   Henry Albert Jones (1893–1945). Took over from Sir Walter Raleigh as the official historian of *The War in the Air*, the official history of the RAF in the Great War.

into being, the IFL denounced it as a tool of the Jews.[2] Two of the Fascists were in my form, amiable fellows with whom I argued in a good-humoured way. One of them joined the police force at the end of that year. I next met him a few years later, on the fringe of a communist meeting in Hyde Park. He was a detective in the Special Branch at Scotland Yard, on the hunt for enemies of the State.

The other three were all notorious duds, fee-payers who were stuck in one of those forms to which the hopelessly brainless were consigned. One of these was a thin, intense boy almost trembling with bitterness. He would not speak to any Jew and I had no wish to speak to him. The others were cheerful oafs who were probably trying to act like Public School hearties. They were friendly enough to me, hailing me jovially as "the Red" until, I suppose, I began to take it for granted that I was one. In any case it was inevitable that a boy like me would come to socialism. The events of that year must have played a part in it. My conversations with Clarke must already have tended that way, so must my talks with a new classmate, Edwin Fairchild. Unlike most of the boys, who lived in the neighbourhood of the school, Fairchild had a long journey to make, his home being in Hampstead Garden Suburb. His father had once been a prominent member of the Fabian Society and is mentioned in some works on Labour history. Oddly, Fairchild liked to go about with the Fascist hearties. He had a wild side which they suited. In the Second World War he became a Royal Air Force pilot and was killed when his bomber was shot down over Germany.

I read all the books I could find that had any approximation to my new interest – books on twentieth-century history, on Germany and on Soviet Russia, George Bernard Shaw's *Intelligent Woman's Guide to Socialism*, William Morris's *News From Nowhere* – more books than I can remember.[3] As my excitement about my great discovery waxed, so my studies for Matric became more and more perfunctory. In the Easter holiday and the first weeks of the summer term, when I should have been revising hard for the examination, I tackled Karl Marx's *Capital* – Volume One, that is, the

---

2　　Oswald Ernald Mosley (1896–1980). Leading British politician. Member of Parliament. Later formed the British Union of Fascists in 1932. Interned as a threat to national security between 1940 and 1943. Resumed his political life after the Second World War in the Union Movement. He produced an exculpatory autobiography, *My Life* (London, 1968).

3　　George Bernard Shaw's *Intelligent Woman's Guide to Socialism* appeared in 1929. William Morris's *News from Nowhere* was published in 1891. Karl Marx's *Das Kapital*, Vol. 1, came out in English translation in 1867.

essential work; Volumes Two and Three being only collections of material mined after Marx's death from a mountain of notes and drafts by his comrade Friedrich Engels. I toiled at this long and densely-argued work and achieved a fair understanding of it.

I sat for the Matric after some desperate night-before revisions and answered the papers in an absent, almost flippant spirit. Afterwards I was stricken with shame. It came upon me that failure would destroy my belief in my abilities; but the real shame was at the blow it would be to my kind, trusting parents.

One day towards the end of the term the Head walked into our form room, giving the usual whisk to the tail of his gown as he appeared. He read out our results. When I heard that I had passed I muttered, "Thank God!" he paused and directed a keen look at me and later, encountering me in a corridor, he said to me, "You could have done better." Of the set of distinctions he had expected of me I had been awarded only one, in Oral French.

*****

In the autumn I went into the Sixth Form. By the beginning of the next year, 1934, I was completely rehabilitated in the eyes of the masters, having, for reasons of my own of which they knew nothing and which will be touched on later, rejoined the battalion. I was at once made a platoon commander, then a House Prefect, then a School Monitor, becoming one of a small set of aristocrats who wore a silver badge on the peaks of their caps and who had a Common Room of their own.

There were three Sixth Forms, Arts, Science and Commercial. Mr. Moody, the master of the Arts Form, which I joined, was a Cambridge man and a historian. I was to sit for the Higher Schools examination in two years' time, taking papers in English, French, Latin and History. In my English syllabus I had Hazlitt, Scott and the Romantic poets. In French, the Romantics and Balzac. History covered the eighteenth century and the Napoleonic era. This was all agreeable to me. I lapped it up, but in a serendipitous way, never working hard at it; I was embarking on a wider education of my own.

Though I did not know it, I and the other five or six boys in the Arts Sixth were treated like Oxford or Cambridge students. We met masters for what were in effect tutorials, were set reading and essays and were then left to ourselves for most of the school day. Our preferred haunt was the school library, a long room well-lit by tall windows, with tables and chairs in bays between the book stacks. There was a large and catholic stock of books.

I had lived until now without a thought of what I was going to do when I left school. As the two years of the Sixth Form course went by, I became increasingly aware of a taste for the serious study of history. The awareness was vague enough, for I never thought about it practically and had no idea

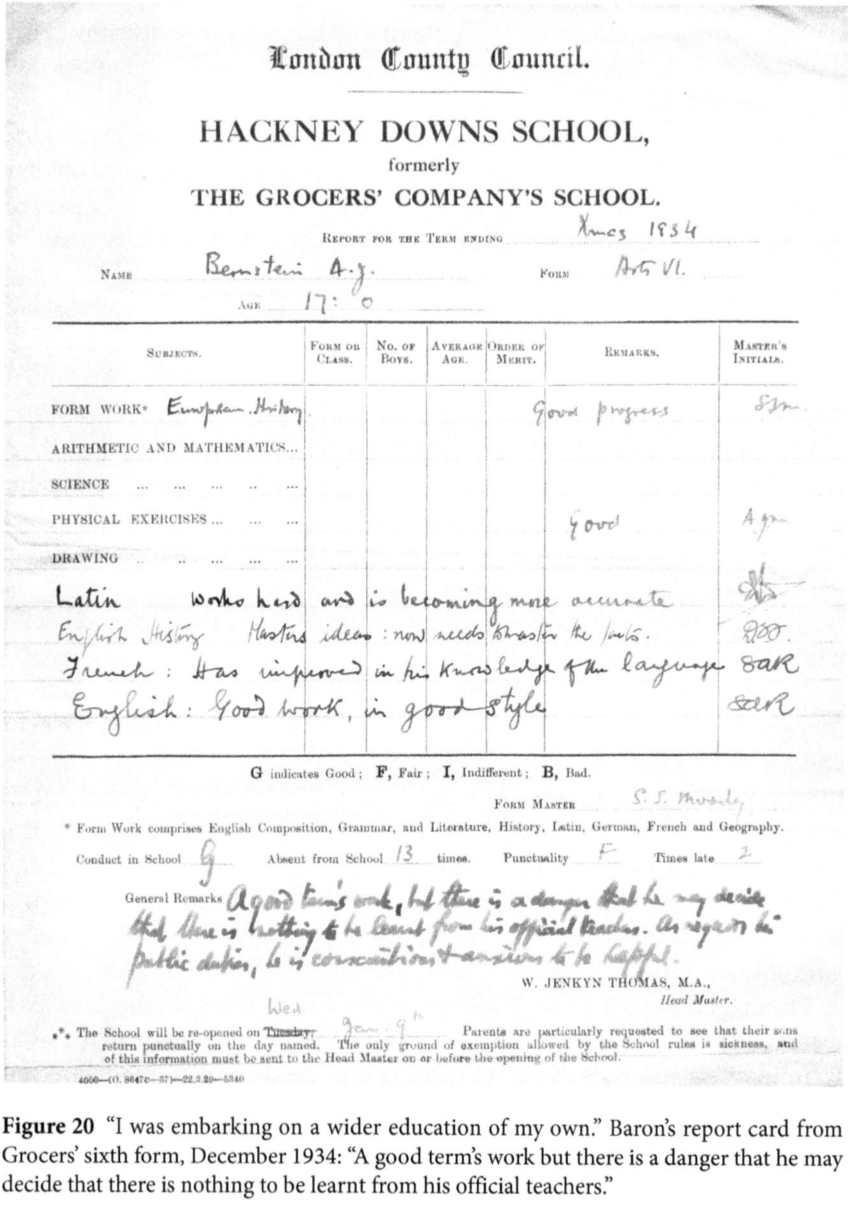

Figure 20 "I was embarking on a wider education of my own." Baron's report card from Grocers' sixth form, December 1934: "A good term's work but there is a danger that he may decide that there is nothing to be learnt from his official teachers."

what it entailed. Indeed, I had no idea what a university was like, although as time went on I conceived a determination to get into Cambridge. For at least the first part of my Sixth Form years I did not know that every student who graduated got a degree. I imagined, as my family did, that Bachelor of Arts was an uncommon distinction. I never found out about postgraduate studies or about the ladder of lectureships, readerships, Fellowships and professorial chairs that one had to climb or how at all one became a historian. Nobody spoke to me about these matters. It did not occur to any of my Oxbridge masters to do so, or to me to ask them.

My bicycle, the reward for my Matric certificate, was a sports model with dropped handlebars, all blue and white enamel and gleaming chrome. Out of curiosity about Cambridge and some hope of learning more about it, I set off one day on the fifty-mile ride there. I fell in love with it and went there three more times. It was a place to dream about, ancient, beautiful, swarming with black-gowned students and bicycles. I mooned about King's Parade and haunted the Backs. Once I stayed overnight, in a room over a teashop somewhere behind King's Parade, All the waitresses were French and strikingly pretty. I decided that this must be a brothel for rich young gentlemen students. It was a long time before I fell asleep. The girls tip-toed up and down the stairs whispering to one another but I heard no male footsteps and no girl tapped at my door. So, with one thing and another, my passion for Cambridge waxed, but I learned nothing about university life.

With no lessons to speak of and most of the day my own, I was carried away by freedom. Essays had to be handed in but I could turn off an essay in no time. I scribbled my essays with great conceit, more concerned to enjoy sport with words than to show knowledge or judgement. I handed in an essay in which I wrote about Murat's cavalry all in white pouring over the crest of a hill. The tolerant Mr. Moody, who had great hopes of me for Cambridge, gave me an 'A' but appended a note, "Which battle, by the way?" Essays were the only writing I did during these two years, except for verse, of which I wrote a good deal. Only three poems survive, in the school magazine.

I was soon deep in my own private explorations. After dabbling in Spanish for a term, I started to teach myself German. I trawled the Public Library for books on politics and economics. In the school library I read Fielding, Smollett and Sterne, essays and novels by D.H. Lawrence and Aldous Huxley, Clive Bell and Roger Fry on art, Voltaire, Montesquieu, Rousseau and whatever else took my fancy – Hakluyt, Anson's Voyages – everything but my set books.

A couple of diligent boys in the school library bent over tables all day working at their essays. The rest of us in Arts constituted ourselves as a little clique of intellectuals. We chatted the time away, enthusing about Freud, Van Gogh, T.S. Eliot and Continental films. We considered ourselves to be advanced people, discoverers, members of the Bohemian vanguard, readers as we were of the Liberal *News Chronicle*, the *New Statesman* and *John O'London's Weekly*.[4]

Our literary idol was Richard Aldington, whom we worshipped for his novel *Death of a Hero*.[5] It is the story of a writer, George Winterbourne, who is presented as a doomed child of his time, from his birth in the late nineteenth century to his death on the Western Front. It is written in a wild, splenetic style, attacking with savagery every character and every institution mentioned, apart from the hero. Its most violent fury is provoked by Victorianism, which is Aldington's label for everything conventional, and its arch-villains are parents. Its treatment of sex was considered to be daring at the time. Nowadays it would be thought of as arch. The edition we read was censored, asterisks replacing the forbidden words. This gave us a great thrill. What could **** mean? We were carried away by the novel's charge of anger. We were all George Winterbournes.

---

4   *News Chronicle*. 1930–1960, a leading liberal newspaper published between 1930 and 1960. *John O'London's Weekly* was a weekly literary magazine, published between 1919 and 1954.

5   Richard Aldington, born Edward Godfree Aldington (1891–1962). Writer and poet. His *Death of a Hero* (London, 1929), is regarded as a major work.

Chapter 17

On days when I should have been studying I roamed the streets, my head full of my new preoccupations. I went on my own to the Tate Gallery and took back to school a postcard of Van Gogh's "Landscape with Cypresses". Perhaps it was already decorating the walls of ten thousand bedsitters but I knew nothing of that. It was my own discovery. I was light-headed with excitement. At school even my tolerant teachers thought it was "pretty eccentric" and my few supporters looked upon it as real advanced stuff. The master in charge of the library, a Catholic and my friendly adviser on reading, remarked in the nicest of ways that the Steins were trying to overturn civilization – Einstein, Epstein and Gertrude, and now they had been joined by Bernstein.

I went to other galleries and discovered such things as Objective Abstractionism. I saw "Poil de Carotte" and "Liebelei" at the Academy Cinema and, still under the ecstatic shock of reading *Crime and Punishment*, saw Gaston Baty's Théâtre de Montparnasse present their version of it at the New Theatre.[1] From the gallery the low set, like a corridor of scenes or a series of cinema frames, looked like so many cubes of light in which was enacted, oh, such a drama!

"*C'est moi qui ai tué Alyena Ivanovna, la vieille, à coups de hache, pour la voler!*" – the last words of the kneeling Raskolnikov. I sat frozen while the gallery emptied.

At the Sadler's Wells I saw Jules Romain's "Doctor Knock".[2] I did not know until fifty—five years later that I had seen Louis Jouvet on the stage.[3] On Sunday nights I went to performances of the Left Theatre, a group of professionals who put on revolutionary plays. I saw "The Sailors of Cattero" by

---

1   "Poil de Carotte" (dir. Julien Duvivier, 1932): "Liebelei" (dir. Max Ophüls, 1933).
2   Jules Romains, Knock. A 1923 satirical play on modern medicine.
3   Louis Jouvet (1887–1951), was a French actor and director.

Friedrich Wolff and a play by Ernst Toller.[4] I had been much affected by the reading of a volume of Toller's plays.

Always on the prowl to find the intellectuals I had read so much about, I joined the New London Film Society. The "highbrows" were much caricatured by the daily press. The she-intellectual was supposed to wear her hair in a straight fringe on the forehead, with a long peasanty gown and a string of beads. The he-intellectual had a beard and wore an open-necked shirt. Both sexes wore sandals. Many of the people I saw at the Film Society and the Left Theatre really did look like that. One-colour sports shirts with short sleeves were a novelty then; rather advanced, I thought. I bought one, dark green. It was the first item of clothing I had ever bought for myself. I always carried a book when I went to "advanced" performances. I thought it helped me to look the part. My hope was that someone would speak to me. I would be invited home to coffee at a Bloomsbury flat. "Bloomsbury" always went with "intellectual" as a term of abuse. I would show my poems and then—. But nobody noticed a boy hanging about at the back of the gallery.

*****

I spent most of my evenings roaming the borough from one Speakers' Corner to another, listening to the political orators.

On the wide roadway at the corner of Ridley Road, after the market stalls had been packed away, a dozen revolutionary sects put up their platforms. The tinier the group the more fire its orators breathed. I soon learned not to expect enlightenment at these meetings. Most of the listeners who gathered about the platforms were there to be entertained and showed it noisily. It was a form of street theatre, as we say nowadays. Each man (the speakers were all men) stood on a high narrow platform with a front like a lectern, which he clutched with both hands. Raising his tortured face to the sky he threw his shouts into the general babble and clamour, sometimes leaning forward to glare down at us, as from a very high place, jabbing a long forefinger which seemed to accuse each one of us. The cries of the

---

4   Friedrich Wolf, *The Sailors of Cattaro*. Written in 1930. It dwelt on the Austro-Hungarian navy mutiny in 1918. Ernst Toller (1898–1938). Playwright and politician. Exiled from Germany in 1933. His play *The Machine Wreckers* (London, 1923) is based largely on the Luddites of the early nineteenth century fighting against the introduction of textile machinery in the Nottingham area.

orators competed, some hoarse, flagging but dogged, others like snarls that ripped the air and went on at undiminished volume, bouncing back in echo from the tall blank wall of Woolworth's.

I went with some hopes to the meetings of the Hackney Independent Labour Party; its militants were the attraction. They were all Jews of the pugnacious kind, with red angry faces that sprouted either stubble or bushy beards, great mops of uncombed hair and lumbermen's shirts unbuttoned to the waists to show hirsute chests and hanging over crumpled grey flannel trousers. The women stay in my mind as all sallow and skinny, with long, tarnished fair hair and shapeless dresses. I do not remember any of these as Jewish and I put them all down as daughters of aristocratic families who had fled from their mansions to marry into the Cause; in Free Love, of course. Men and women wore the final mark of bohemianism, sandals. The trouble was that they were all so dirty. Sandals were all very well but I discovered that they revealed monstrous feet; excrescences of hard yellow skin grained with lines of dirt, huge discoloured toenails. And they were all so old! Not one of them looked under thirty. I did not want to read my poems to any of them.

I took more seriously the meetings of the Friends of the Soviet Union, at the corner of the next turning to ours, opposite the West Hackney Church. On Tuesday evenings the FSU put up a platform there and sold their magazine at the street corner. A handful of supporters clustered round the platform. I went regularly and listened from the other side of the street, sitting on the edge of the horses' drinking-trough at which I had used to wait for lifts from carters when I was a child.

I believed everything the FSU speakers told me. I wanted to believe what the gospel preachers call Good News. Nobody was out of work in Russia. Nobody was on the Means Test. Just imagine, millions of men and women who had once been enemies of the people had now volunteered, actually volunteered, to build a great canal in the Arctic, a work which showed their repentance and gave them new pride in themselves. This was the White Sea Canal, one of the worst atrocities of the Gulag.[5] But then, I had the word of the great Maxim Gorky that this was the greatest enterprise of moral

---

5   The White Sea Canal. Stalinist project to link the Arctic to the Baltic. It took Gulag workers twenty-one months to complete. Opened in 1933 and until 1961 called the *Stalin White Sea Canal*. See S. Kotkin, Stalin. Waiting for Hitler. 1928–1941 (London, 2017), pp.133–4; and N. Baron, *Soviet Karelia: Politics, Planning and Terror in Stalin's Russia, 1920–1939* (London, 2007), pp.129–35.

redemption in history.[6] The political show trials just beginning were absolutely fair. The accused confessed with such zeal because they were thoroughly ashamed of themselves and, whatever the verdicts read out in court, I might be sure that they would all be treated with forgiveness. And why should I not believe this, when the great Liberal journalist of the time, A.J. Cummings, in our own *News Chronicle*, swore by the fairness of the trials and the genuineness of the confessions?[7] There was a great troop of famous writers, journalists, scientists, clergymen and other celebrities, treated in those days as Wise Men by the Press which published their pronouncements under bold headlines, who acted as the bellwethers of the Left. Who was I, one of their innocent and gullible flock, to disbelieve what the great Professor Haldane told me, or the great Bernard Shaw or the great Paul Robeson or the great Henri Barbusse or the great Romain Rolland?[8]

I approached the young man who sold the magazine *Russia Today* at the street corner and asked him a question. "Oh, yes," he replied. "They've got Free Love all over the place there."

*****

---

6   Maxim Gorky (1868–1926). Writer. Returned to the Soviet Union in 1926 after a period in exile. Experienced an uneasy relationship with the ruling authorities there.

7   A.J. Cummings (1882–1957). A leading Liberal journalist. Served as political editor of the *News Chronicle*, a paper taken by Baron's family. He is now something of a forgotten public figure. See H.C.G. Matthew and Brian Harrison, eds, *Oxford Dictionary of National Biography*, Vol. 14 (Oxford, 2004) pp.638–9 [cited hereafter as ODNB].

8   J.B.S. Haldane (1892–1964). Leading British scientist and Marxist. He became an Indian citizen in 1961. See *ODNB*., Vol. 24, pp.507–9 and G. Werksey, *The Visible College* (London, 1978). George Bernard Shaw (1856–1950). Playwright and political activist. Key figure in the Fabian Society and later an enthusiast for the Soviet system. Paul Robeson (1898–1976). American bass baritone. His sympathies with the Soviet Union led to his blacklisting in the McCarthy era. Much influenced in his politics by the Spanish Civil War. Robeson sang "Joe Hill," and "England arise! " at the funeral of Harry Pollitt. (qv). Henri Barbusse (1873–1935). French novelist and Communist. Best known in Britain for his novel, *Under Fire*, a translation of *Le Feu*, which appeared in 1916. Romain Rolland (1866–1944). French dramatist, novelist and essayist. Awarded the Nobel Prize for Literature in 1915.

In the summer of my sixteenth year I brought a friendly band of boys and girls into the house and my parents learned that these were young members of the Labour Party which I had joined. This was harmless enough. The young people were nicely dressed and polite and my parents were glad to see me making friends.

But I had told them nothing. At this time, something more drastic than a flirtation with labour had befallen me, as I shall relate in the next chapter. In the coming years, when my activities must have become more and more mysterious to my parents, causing them anxiety and alarm, I did not say a word to them about what I was doing and it never occurred to me to consider their feelings. This was the time that my father must have looked forward to in my childhood, when he and his clever son would have much to talk about. Instead, I became a stranger. I did not speak about my new political life to my companions at school, either, although I was now going about with Labour Party girls and this should have been a matter for boasting among my schoolfellows, to whom girls were the subject of much talk but remained a matter for theoretical speculation.

*****

In my two years in the Sixth I became friendly with Georges Leboucher, the French assistant, and with Hellmuth Steger, the German assistant. Leboucher was a man of the Left; in that decade a French *instituteur* could be nothing else. Steger took me out for tea and buns after school and was keen to know what I had read in pamphlets about the doings of the German Communist Party, now driven underground by the Nazis. When he had gone back to Germany he sent me a postcard, signing it, "Hellmuth Steger, an ardent Nazi". I met Leboucher in Paris after the war. He had been taken ill while he was a prisoner-of-war and was probably dying when Steger, in the uniform of a German army officer, arrived at the camp, arranged for him to be transferred to a good hospital where he was well cared for, and so saved his life.

In the summer of 1935 my second Day of Reckoning came, the beginning of the Higher Schools Examination. The English, French and History papers turned out to be easy, although I gained no distinctions. The problem was Latin, a pass in which was then still required for the Intermediate degree qualification. The Latin language papers presented no difficulty. The fourth book of the *Aeneid*, in particular, had taken my fancy; I knew pages of it by heart and loved to chant the verse aloud. The trouble lay in the Roman History paper. Our set topic was the war with the Numidian king Jugurtha.

It was a complicated affair, its antecedents and consequences even more so, and as recounted by Sallust the story was repellently boring. I had decided not to have anything to do with it, and set down nothing on my Roman History paper but a few sentences.

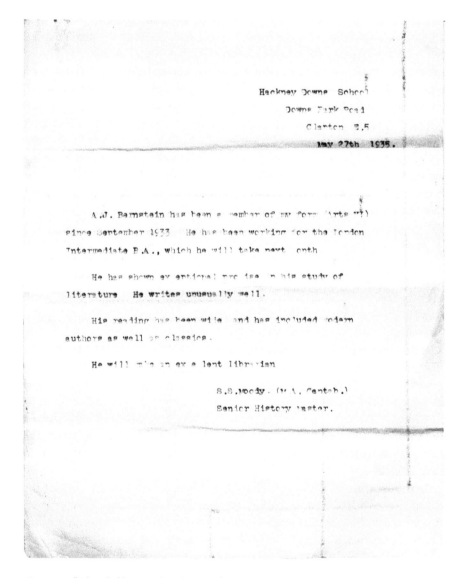

Figure 21 "I dreaded leaving this pleasant, familiar scene." An employment reference written by Mr Moody a month before Baron left Grocers', 27 May 1935: "He has shown exceptional promise in his study of literature. He writes unusually well."

I passed the certificate examination in all subjects and was in due course offered places at London University, in King's College and University College; but the Intermediate B.A. qualification in Latin was withheld. To get it I would have to sit a Latin examination again at the end of my first university year.

Now should have come the history scholarship at Cambridge, to which Mr. Moody had urged me. I did not sit for it and I did not take up either of the London University places.

On the last day of term I went up the steps in the tower and said goodbye to the Head in his study. At the top of the front steps of the school I lingered in front of the sham-Gothic doorway. Before me there was a wide expanse of gravel then a big carriage gateway set in red brick walls. Across the road from this were the fields of Hackney Downs. I dreaded leaving this pleasant, familiar scene. For six years the School had given me a haven, happy occupations, friends and esteem. For the last two of these years I had been leading a secretive and very different life, to which I was supposedly dedicated and to which I should have been eager to hasten. On the contrary, I felt only fear at going out.

I had no idea what the scholarly life was like, which I was now rejecting, but I must have felt the tug of it. I do not regret the course my life has taken since but still, in my late years, I reflect how happy I would have been to pass from one secure, satisfying life to another, in the halls of learning.

PART TWO:
A Political Education

Chapter 18

One morning in February 1934, I sat in the school hall, on the oak bench on which I had sat with my mother nearly five years before. I had a history tutorial with Mr. Moody in five minutes' time. Waiting, I picked up a *Daily Express* and glanced at it.

I was not an emotional boy and the emotion that seized me after a few minutes of reading was something new; tears in my eyes and a lump in the chest that made it hard to breathe. What had this effect on me was a dispatch from Vienna by Sefton Delmer, one of the great foreign correspondents of the time.[1] Government troops in that city, after they had thrown out the socialist city council, had bombarded the blocks of workers' flats with artillery at point-blank range. The socialist workers, trapped with their women and children, held out with rifles against the heavy weapons of the *Heimwehr*. It took three days of hand-to-hand fighting to crush them. Nine of their leaders were hanged, one of them being carried to the gallows on a stretcher after he had been disembowelled by bullets.

I could not have been very attentive during my forty-five minutes with Mr. Moody. Afterwards I slipped out of the school and went to the Stoke Newington Public Library to read all the other newspapers.

On my way back along Church Street, the old village street of Stoke Newington, I paused at the sight of a poster on the front railings of a house. The house was the headquarters of the local Labour Party, its front door and window surrounds painted red. On the poster, handwritten in thick blue pencil was:

---

1   Sefton Delmer (1904–1979). Well known journalist. Often called "Der Chef." Employed on black propaganda for the Allies during the Second World War. Often associated with his work for the *Daily Express*.

THE STRUGGLE
IN
AUSTRIA

Tonight: 8 p.m.
Speaker: Dorothy Woodman

*****

Two rooms had been knocked into one to make a small meeting-hall, with the usual table and rows of bentwood chairs. There were posters on the walls. A poster pinned to the front of the table advertised the youth section of the Labour Party, the League of Youth.

I sat in a row near the back, at the end near the door in case I decided to slip off. Thirty or forty young people gathered. They looked a pleasant enough lot, in respectable after-work clothes. They were all older than me. The girls had the air of typists or shop assistants, which most of them turned out to be. The young men were of a kind who might be clerks or storemen or skilled workers; as I learned later, they for the most part were. The well-spoken chairman was an estate agent. I was to find out that many of them were the children of Labour Party members. The Labour League of Youth, or LLY, was mainly a social club for them. The leaders of the organization were solidly moderate. Militancy was still, though not far, in the future. The members turned out as a matter of family loyalty to organize fund-raising events or help at election times but most of them knew little about politics.

Dorothy Woodman was obviously an Intellectual.[2] She had a round face and hair bobbed in a straight fringe. I do not remember her speech. There was applause, a vote of thanks, more clapping and she went away.

Among the latecomers who had slipped in during her speech was a young man wearing shorts and a red sports shirt, with a bicycle which he leaned against the wall. He went to the table and conferred with the Chairman, He had dramatic good looks, with black, glossy hair and a gypsy complexion. The chairman told us that a comrade from South Tottenham had something to say to us. I did not take notice of the visitor's name that night, but I was to hear it again; it was Willis.

---

2   Dorothy Woodman (1902–1970). Socialist and journalist. She reported on fascism in Britain and Germany in the 1930s. She was considered by MI5 to be a 'near-communist', but suspected by the Communist Party leadership of being an agent. See TNA, KV2/1607.

He asked us to support some girls at a Tottenham clothing factory who had walked out on strike. He sat down. There was a lethargic silence in the room while the chairman conferred with other people at the table. Timid and shy all my life, I cannot say what agitation seized me then so that I stood up and shouted, in some inarticulate fashion, something like, "Look they're on strike!" and sat down.

The chairman said something to soothe me. There was a collection. A resolution of support was passed. The comrade from South Tottenham left. Any Other Business was concluded and the meeting broke up. I stood up to leave.

A woman was sitting on her own in the back row. She stood up as I did, turned towards me and said, "Bravo!" I was taken aback. She said, "For speaking up like that."

She was small and swarthy, with eyes like bright black beads. She wore a swagger coat in some thick, light brown material with a big collar turned up. It gave her a military look; and her hair was bobbed in a straight fringe.

Whatever she went on to say, it must have unlocked my tongue, for after a little while she said, "Well, if you want to be a writer you ought to meet my husband. He's a writer." She invited me back with her for a coffee.

This was a momentous invitation. As far as I can recollect she was the first grown-up with whom I had ever had a conversation outside of the family and school. (She was, it turned out, twenty-three years old.) Her flat was not in Bloomsbury, but Stamford Hill would do. Her husband was as small as she was, a wiry man with a combative, gamecock manner and hair upspringing in a quiff. Nothing was said about writing until I dared to ask him about it.

"Ah, yes," he said. "I'll give you a copy of something I've just done."

This was a twelve-page pamphlet with a green cover published by the Young Communist League of Great Britain. The title was: "FIGHT THE WARMONGERS NOW!"

The author did not talk to me any more about politics but he asked me questions: what did I do? Why had I come to the meeting? and so on. I answered volubly. I had a lot to pour out. Very likely I told him about my poems. He said that I must come again and I did so, several times in the next few weeks.

During this time I joined the Labour Youth. I understood by now that my new friends at the flat were communists. I had decided to be Labour. At the flat I had lively arguments about it. I stood up for my point of view and was overjoyed to have found my tongue. My friends were no less welcoming than before and I was proud to know them; grown-ups, intellectuals, communists. They told me that they had a friend staying with them who wanted to meet me. This was flattering. I met him the next night.

He was John Gollan, a Scot.[3] Gollan was an engaging fellow. He was slight and bony with hollow cheeks and bad teeth which he often showed in an odd open-mouthed grin. The skin of his face was waxen and faintly tawny. His characteristic expression was patient and slightly smiling. He spoke all the time in a mild, reasonable voice and I was flattered by the air of intent consideration with which he listened to everything I said. I was flattered to know him. He, too, looked forward to more meetings and I was soon having regular discussions with him.

I learned at our first meeting that he was the national secretary of the Young Communist League. I was no match for him in argument and came completely under his spell. It was obvious to me, as he pointed out, that the LLY needed gingering-up. I was dismayed at his suggestion that I could do something about it, but I felt so flattered and grown-up among these adults who took me seriously, and Gollan was so helpful in suggesting to me what steps I could take, that I began to stand up at branch meetings of the LLY to put forward ideas, his ideas, for more militant activities.

I had usually in the past, whatever my evening activities, got home by eleven o'clock or so; but at my friends' flat I stayed talking until well after midnight. One night I let myself in to the house and saw that the kitchen light was still on. My parents, normally in bed before eleven, were there, my father in his corner armchair, my mother sitting upright on a wooden chair by the table. My mother said, "Where have you been?"

I was dumbfounded by this. They had never asked such questions before. She said, "You come in late every night. And wearing that shirt."

"What shirt?"

She pointed to my dark green shirt and said, "All these coloured shirts. You'll get into trouble wearing that shirt."

"No I won't. I'm not a Greenshirt."

There was such an organisation. They preached something called Social Credit. I said, "I've been to see friends."

---

3   John Gollan (1911–1977). Lifelong Communist. His papers are to be found in the People's History Museum, Manchester. Intelligence files on him are in the National Archives (TNA KV2/1772–8). In 1956 Gollan succeeded Harry Pollitt as General Secretary of the Communist Party of Great Britain. See Matthew and Harrison (eds), *ODNB.*, Vol. 22, pp.706–7. There is file on him in the Comintern archives, held in the Russian State Archive of Socio-Political History in Moscow (the former Soviet party archive, hereafter RGASPI), f. 495, op.198, d. 22.

"Do they stay out late, too?"

"They're grown-ups. It's a man I know and his wife. They're clever people. Intellectuals. I go to their flat."

"Where is this flat?"

"Up the Hill."

"Oh," she said. "Clever people."

"Yes."

"Intellectuals."

"Yes."

She sat thinking. She sniffed hard and I did not realise at first what was happening. Then a big tear welled up on one side end rolled down next to her nose. She dabbed it away with her little handkerchief and said, in a thick voice, "I bet they're not even married."

This was the only protest either of them ever made at my new activities and no other question was ever asked. After that they were anxious and silent witnesses of my life.

It was inevitable that Gollan would bring about my conversion.[4] I had always remembered this as having happened swiftly, given my youth and his persuasive powers. However, I now recall an incident which establishes that I must have held out for at least three months, although during that time I was already virtually doing his bidding. In June of that year Oswald Mosley, the leader of the British Union of Fascists, held a meeting at Olympia, a big hall in West London.[5] The Fascists were very much in the news and were recruiting fast, with energetic support from one of the most popular newspapers in the country, the *Daily Mail*. Communists with forged tickets were at the meeting in some numbers and tried to break it up. The uniformed Blackshirt stewards used spectacular brutality in throwing them out. There were cracked skulls, broken bones, ambulances racing to and fro. This event caused a great deal of public debate. It was quite unlike British politics heretofore. Our family newspaper, now the *News Chronicle*, was staunchly against the fascists but it also condemned the communists. I echoed it in my argument with Gollan; we did not want Nazi storm-troop

---

4   For an account of Baron's career in the CPGB, see Andrew Whitehead, "Very heaven it was to be a Young Communist," in Susie Thomas, Andrew Whitehead and Ken Worpole (eds), *So We Live: The Novels of Alexander Baron* (Nottingham, 2019), pp.55–82.

5   The Olympia meeting, organised by the British Union of Fascists to showcase its political programme took place in June 1934. On this event and its significance of the meeting, see M. Pugh, "The British Union of Fascists and the Olympia Meeting," *Historical Journal*, Vol. 41 (1998), pp.529–42.

behaviour in London but neither did we want communists also resorting to force and denying free speech. Gollan leaned forward, jabbed a bony forefinger at me and said, quietly and intensely, "Our people there were bloody heroes. And they were fighting for you!"

Did he, I wondered, mean because I was a Jew?

It must have been very soon after this that I recognised that I was now a communist, one of Gollan's entourage. I was not formally recruited. In the fourteen years of work for the Young Communist League and the Communist Party that followed I never officially joined either organization or paid a week's dues, although I became a leader of the YCL and an apparatchik (a member of the apparatus or core of full-time professionals) of some standing in the Party.

I learned early on that my writer acquaintance, John Douglas (his real name was Urquhart) had until recently worked in Moscow as a leading official of the Communist Youth International (KIM), a sub-section of the Communist International or Comintern.[6] He had been sent back to London for a reason of which I learned in time: he had been denounced. Perhaps London was a healthier place for him to be. A resolution appeared in Moscow publications condemning him as a politically bankrupt deviationist. His wife, who had brought me to the flat, had worked in the Comintern or the KIM as a secretary. After a couple of years they went back to Moscow.[7]

Douglas's flat seemed to be a point of arrival for visitors from Moscow, "the other side" or "over bye" as it was always called. One of them

---

6   The Comintern, known also as the Third International, was established in 1919. Stalin dissolved it in 1943. See K. McDermott and J. Agnew, *The Comintern. A History of International Communism from Lenin to Stalin* (New York, 1997).

7   John Douglas (Urquhart). Born 1906–7. Joined the Young Communist League in 1926 and served later as its National Secretary. Attended the Lenin School in Moscow in 1930–31 (see p.148, footnote 5, below). Fluent Russian speaker. He might be the Douglas mentioned in a KIM Executive Committee document in the Comintern archive, RGASPI, Moscow, f. 533, op.4, d.317. He resigned from the CPGB in 1939 following the Nazi-Soviet Pact. Worked later in John Brown's shipyard on the Clyde before becoming a tutor-organiser for the WEA. Married Annabel (Bunty) Urquhart. Since they met only in 1939, she could not have been the woman who took Baron to the flat in Stamford Hill. (Baron's giving Douglas the name of Urquhart confuses the situation.) Douglas died in 1996.

was Alex Massie, who at that time was very high up in the International.[8] At our first meeting he sat down with me and engaged me in earnest talk. I still remember his mild, encouraging voice. A Party courier who travelled between London and Moscow also appeared often, sleeping on the spare divan for a night or two before he disappeared again. Julie, the Party member who had led the factory girls' strike which had sparked off my blurted appeal at the Labour Youth meeting, lived nearby: I met her at the flat. She looked like one of the Sweater Girls who were soon to become popular in the cinema, stars like Ann Sheridan and Lana Turner. She had a mop of black, curly hair and she wore a high-necked white jersey with a swishing black skirt and a shiny red belt. She was now a rising star in the Party and inspired awe in me. She once gave me an armful of books, several volumes of Lenin and works by Stalin, whose tedious texts I faithfully read.

Douglas's wife was active in the local YCL and took to bringing members to the flat. One evening while they were talking, Douglas walked into the room with Gollan behind him. He listened to a few murmured words from Gollan, then shouted, "Out, you lot!"' As they started to go out he said, "I don't want to see any of you here again." I had got up to leave. He put out a hand to stop me and said, "Not you." I sat down, proud to be one of an inner circle.

In all my years in the movement I never had any experience of life in a local branch. I had only a view-from-above of the rank-and-file. The only communists I had much to do with were leaders, first of the YCL and, very soon, of the Party. My mother, I suppose, would have had better reason to weep if she had known that at the age of sixteen I had tumbled, entirely by accident, into becoming an apprentice to communist leaders and men from Moscow.

---

8   Alex Massie. Leading activist in Young Communist League. Author of numerous books and pamphlets, including *The Chartist Youth Response* (London, 1930) and Labour's Case for Ownership and Control (London, 1945). Associated with the Marx Memorial Library and Workers' School. Died 1948. There appears not to be a personal file in the Comintern archives but some of his communications to the KIM Executive Committee can be found in RGASPI f. 533, op.10, d. 341 (letters from J. Gollan, A. Massie, 1938); f. 533, op.10, d. 366 (letters from Massie and Povey).

Chapter 19

The Communist Party of Great Britain was a small organization at that time, barely five thousand strong. It professed to be a purely British body but by its statutes it was a section of a single world party, the Communist International, the declared aim of which was to bring into being a world soviet republic. Armed revolution was to be the means.[1]

The Communist International ("Comintern" is a Russian-language form of abbreviation) was founded in 1919 by Lenin and the Russian Communist Party. By 1934 communist parties existed in most countries of the world. All were minutely controlled by the Comintern in Moscow which, although its machine was staffed by people of many nationalities, was in its turn minutely controlled by the Russians. Stalin gave a great deal of his time to it. British communists in Moscow sometimes encountered him at committee meetings. During my days at Douglas's flat I saw a report of a meeting of a sub-committee, or commission, held in Moscow to discuss the finances of the Hamburg organization of the German Communist Party. Comrade Stalin was present and took part in the discussion.

Stalin and his underlings saw to it that all the national communist parties were blindly and fanatically Stalinist. In every party expulsion was the penalty for any member who uttered a word out of line. From time to time a mass purge took place in one communist party or another. No commands from above were needed (although they were often sent) to instigate these purges. The loyal Party members carried them out with religious zeal. Such is the state of mind of people whose need is to surrender themselves completely to a messianic faith.

---

1   The history of the CPGB has resulted in a vast forest of literature. See Francis Beckett, *Enemy Within. The Rise and Fall of the British Communist Party* (London, 1995), for an accessible account. For biographical details on some Party members, many of whom might otherwise be lost to history, see Graham Stevenson's website: https://graham-stevenson.me.uk. For the official history of the period when Baron was active, see Noreen Branson's *History of the Communist Party of Great Britain 1927–1941* (London, 1985) and her *History of the Communist Party of Great Britain 1941–1951* (London, 1997).

The Young Communist League was very different from the LLY. It only numbered two or three thousand and most of its members were already dedicated revolutionaries Some of them were the children of communists. Many others worked in big factories and had been recruited in the course of class struggles by their seniors in the trade unions. They regarded themselves as cadets in training, members of a young guard or shock troop, on their honour to show themselves worthy of graduating into the Communist Party, in whose mystique they were steeped. Just as the Communist Youth International was the most important adjunct of the Comintern, so the British YCL was fully involved with the parent party, its leaders ranking as equals among the Party leadership.

I had joined dazedly, as it were, ignorant of what I was going in to. What led me into it? My head was ringing with the magic word, socialism. Here were the elite, I thought, who had discovered the one and only way, the infallible and speedy way, to bestow a paradisal life upon the human race.

As I became used to YCL and Party ways, I learned nothing that repelled me. On the contrary, I was thrilled and proud. The Party was not fettered by a "bourgeois" democracy. Its command system was military. Excellent: my dreams were military. I wanted to become a good soldier.

*****

The account, then, that I have given earlier of my relations with Gollan should not leave the impression that I joined as an innocent young victim. At first I was truly confused as to what I did and did not belong to, and in what relation the Communists stood to the Labour Party. I soon cleared this up and played the game knowingly, like the girl who is secretly willing to be seduced.

What I learned was that the Communists were excluded from the Labour Party: more, they were under anathema. Labour's relations with the other British parties were gentlemanly enough but the entire official Labour movement, leaders and rank-and-file alike, looked upon communism and revolution with loathing. Anyone who belonged either to an open communist body or to any one of a long list of proscribed Communist front organizations, some of them with innocent-sounding names, was at once expelled from the Labour Party and debarred from office in some trade unions. The small Communist Party, on its side, needed to tie up alongside the huge official movement, like a tug alongside an ocean liner, to draw the mass of organized workers into militant action. This was the tactic of the united front, the achievement of which, I was taught, would be followed by the rapid radicalization of the masses who would come to recognise that the Communist Party was their true leader.

It was made plain to me that, so far from trying to win me away from the Labour League of Youth, my mentors wanted me to stay in it, to advance myself within it and to help draw it into a united front with the Young Communists. I had, of course, to keep my membership of the YCL a secret.[2]

At first I was careless about this and took part in some activities of the local YCL, a practice to which Douglas soon put a stop. As early as this in my communist career I discovered that there was a stranger dwelling inside me who remained a sceptical observer of much that I did, who perceived that, far from being the vanguard of the masses as our textbooks taught us, we were a futile handful and that some of our proceedings were merely absurd.

For instance, I took part in what the local YCL termed an anti-war parade. About a dozen-and-a-half of us, in YCL uniform (khaki shirts and red ties) and wearing First World War army gas masks, marched in column of threes from Stamford Hill to Dalston Junction on a Saturday afternoon. Crowds of shoppers were on the pavements and the heavy traffic –trams, cars and horse-drawn carts – forced us to straggle along close to the kerb. To win over the respectable workers of Hackney and Stoke Newington, we lustily sang the marching song of the Soviet Air Force, which proclaimed that the Red airmen would drop only leaflets on the workers "while we bomb your bosses", or we chanted such slogans as:

> *Hitler and Mosley,*
> *What are they for?*
> *Thuggery, buggery,*
> *Hunger and war.*

As we approached the corner of Foulden Road, where my home was, I saw Mrs. Susie Bates, who lived two doors away from my family. She was a tall lady, very big at the top and narrowing down like a huge pear to balance on small feet in high-heeled shoes. She looked at us with distaste and raised her gold-rimmed glasses to her eyes. Feeling sure that she recognised me, I

---

2   For analysis of this policy, see Alan Campbell and John McIlroy, "'The Trojan Horse': Communist Entrism in the British Labour Party, 1933–43," *Labor History*, 2018, DOI: 10.1080/0023656X.2018.1436938.

was consumed with shame. The whole proceeding seemed to me ludicrous and repellent.

I felt much the same in the demonstrations on which we marched almost every weekend to Trafalgar Square or Hyde Park. I got used to such things in time but, now that I look back, I believe that the sceptical outsider in me was not killed but only went into hiding daring my subsequent communist years. Even while I believed passionately, with all my heart and mind, he was there, observing, listening and making notes for future use.

*****

I cannot remember the occasion on which Ted Willis and I were introduced to each other at the Douglases' flat.[3] I only retain a mental snapshot of the two of us waiting together on the doorstep. I must have realised as soon as we spoke that he, too, was a recent recruit, and it soon became clear that he, too, had been coming to the flat for some time to meet Gollan, who must have calculated that we were better dealt with separately. Now Gollan had brought us together to send us forth on a mission to win over the entire Labour youth movement to a revolutionary course.

This did not strike me as a large task for two isolated individuals, one of them a twenty-year-old factory worker and the other a schoolboy of sixteen. I was full of faith, pride and innocent confidence.

The next mental snapshot is of my first visit to Ted's home in Tottenham. Mrs. Willis, a striking woman with looks like her son's, who was to become an additional aunt to me, opened the door. Ted had appeared on the first floor landing, with an open book in one hand and the other hand raised like John the Baptist's in a painting, declaiming:

"Loveliest of trees, the cherry now
Is hung with bloom along the bough,
And stands about the woodland ride
Wearing white for Eastertide."

---

3   Edward Henry Willis, Baron Willis (1914–1992). Playwright, novelist and scriptwriter. Political activist. Ted Willis is probably best known to the general public as writer of the television series, "Dixon of Dock Green" which ran for more than twenty years. See his Whatever happened to *Tom Mix? The Story of one of my lives* (London, 1970) and *Evening All: fifty years over a hot typewriter* (London, 1991). There is a file on him in the Comintern archive, RGASPI, Moscow, f. 495, op.198, d. 1273.

This was to be the first of a series of meetings at which we were to bring together likely people from LLY branches to take park in our work. A few were YCL members who had been sent into the LLY. fed and I, each cycling from one branch meeting to another, had singled out other people who might be recruited.

While we waited for others to arrive, however, it was not of politics that Ted and I talked. I spoke the name of Housman as a password and we went at it about poetry. It was of poetry that we talked eagerly when we met before the next few meetings until the pace and scale of our work ruled out such distractions.

After this first exhilarating period I deliberately banished literature from my life, poetry and prose alike. Gollan despised the arts and I believed that he must be utterly right about everything. For the next six years, until I joined the army in war-time, I did not read a line of poetry and I read little more than half-a-dozen novels (I am sure of this) and these only books of which the Party approved.

Ted, who was more mature by four years and much experience, kept a mind of his own and never put aside his interest in such things. I was not surprised when, during the war, he revealed his talent as a writer. Our partnership soon took the shape that it was to retain. He, bold, full of initiative and new ideas and a compelling platform speaker, became a sort of Camille Desmoulins, a popular public figure in the Labour movement.[4] I, limited by my shyness, tried to keep in the background, speaking only at internal meetings and doing the office work. Once, later on, when we had both in our different ways became known, Alex Massie showed me a galley proof, an extract from a report by some security organization, that a Party printer had handed in. An entry for Ted described him as an excellent type of young Englishman who had fallen into bad company, not an unfair description of him at that time. I was described as a Jew of foreign origin who always kept behind the scenes, being perhaps the bad influence behind Willis.

As time went on we recruited more people to our work and made contacts all over the country until we had built up a national organization of Young Communists working inside the LLY. It would not be accurate to call this infiltration. As far as I know, all of our members after the intro-duction of a first few were genuine members of the League of Youth whose minds had moved further to the left, who were prepared to go over to the

---

4   Camille Desmoulins (1760–1794). Political ally of Georges Danton in the French Revolution and executed along with other Dantonists.

Communists but who were persuaded to stay and work for the good cause, that of working-class unity, inside the Labour Party.

The whole Labour movement was by now becoming affected by the grim events in Nazi Germany and by the growth of a fascist movement in this country which threatened to bring horrors of the same sort here. Militancy was in the air. We began to get a hearing in the LLY branches. We did not see our activities as underhand, any more than children do who conceal their forbidden doings from their parents. As our numbers increased we felt ourselves more and more to be genuine and zealous members of the Labour Party. We believed that we were acting to save its soul. There were several left-wing ginger groups in the Labour Party, tolerated because they were not communist. We believed that we saw further than they did, being members of a movement which had already created a socialist paradise on one-sixth of the earth's surface. It was a pity that we had to work clandestinely, but that was the fault of misguided or wicked Labour leaders.

For a year or so I continued to spend a good deal of my time in the LLY branch that I had joined in Stoke Newington. It was one of the happy years of my life. Indeed I now look back on it as the only time in my political life when I was genuinely happy. The members were an ordinary decent lot. I was as much at ease among them as I had been at school, young men and women who were of an age with me, who came from the same background, who accepted the conventions of respectable working-class life even in the ways they broke them and who were open and unguarded in their speech.

It was a contrast to the Communist Party milieu in which I came more and more to spend a parallel life. There, to start with, I was always among people much older. Still a schoolboy, I was, perhaps unconsciously, out of my depth among them. It is odd to recall how, in spite of a fanatical devotion to the Party, I always felt ill at ease among Party people and in some undefinable human way, in a milieu in which comradeship was supposed to be supreme, disconsolate and excluded. But this didn't spell itself out in my mind. I supposed myself to be supremely proud and happy.

In the League of Youth we went out canvassing for the Labour Party, addressed envelopes, pushed leaflets through letter-boxes, helped the women's section to run bazaars and jumble sales for the funds and held a street-corner meeting every week. I was too shy to speak at these, but I was given the job of heckling our own speaker to draw a crowd, which I enjoyed. We listened to visiting speakers, with discussions afterwards, and at some meetings we debated policy. The branch, like most others, was run by moderates and was contented to be so. We argued with vigour but we were all good friends. My bicycle came into its own now; every summer weekend a covey of us swooped along the Old Cambridge Road to camp at a Socialist Youth Hostel and swim in the River Lea. There were frequent social evenings in the Party rooms and occasional Town Hall dances. I learned to quick-step and waltz. After the meetings we gathered for hours in an Italian café over penny cups of tea, arguing and joking. The major blessing for me was to be with girls after nine years of a boys' school.

I now led my life on tracks which did not meet. Home and school were in one, politics in another. Politics in turn divided into two tracks, Labour and Communist. Gollan was our constant and attentive mentor but we also met leaders of the Communist Party itself to whom we were important contacts. I came under the wing of D.F. Springhall, who at that time was London District Organizer.[5] He was a big man with a gleaming bullet head. He looked like an old-fashioned bruiser. In a leather coat with a pistol on a belt he could have passed for a Tartar political commissar in Soviet Russia, This brutish appearance was contradicted by small eyes looking out of fatty surrounds in a pinkish face and by a high, quacking voice. He was one of the inner ring of the Party leaders. Seven years later he was sent to prison as a Soviet spy.

He put me in the care of one of his officials, Ray Matlock, a man for whom I felt an instant disgust. Matlock was a pudgy fellow with a slack, unhealthy face. He had a stooping walk and wore enormous boots which slapped along like snowshoes. Springhall referred to him as Kipper Feet. I had an appointment with him one evening at the dingy District Office in one of the old streets behind the Bishopsgate rail yards. I sat on a chair in the downstairs passage from eight to ten o'clock and no Matlock appeared. Springhall came downstairs from a meeting. He asked me what I was doing there. I told him. Springhall was an old Royal Navy man and he let loose a string of Navy obscenities that was worth hearing. He promised to sort Matlock out.

Not long afterwards Matlock was sent to Moscow where he was given a humble job in the Comintern offices. After a while he returned to London

---

5   D.F. Springhall (1901–1953). British Communist. "Springy," sometimes known as "Dave Miller," studied at the International Lenin School (1928–1931). During the Spanish Civil War, acted as Political Commissar of the British Batallion, then Assistant Political Commissar of the 15th International Brigade. Wounded in the face and recalled to England. Editor of the *Daily Worker* (1938). Imprisoned for spying on behalf of the Soviets (1943), and then expelled from the CPGB. Worked towards the end of his life in China. He died in a Moscow hospital but lies buried in Chinese soil. See TNA KV2/1594–1598.

and invited me to lunch. We met at a workman's café in the little market opposite Mount Pleasant Post Office. I tucked into a sausage toad-in-the-hole. He talked to me about the delights of Moscow. He leaned across the table, his nasty eyes gleaming, and said, "I expect you'll go before long."

I said, "I hope so."

"You'll have a grand time," he said. "Take plenty of women's stockings with you."

"What for?"

"For the women, of course."

"What women?"

"Listen, boy, you can have any girl in Moscow for a pair of stockings. They don't ask for silk. Take the cheapest you can get."

I took this in for a moment or two, then I got up and hurried out into the street. I stood in the gutter between two market stalls and spewed my meal up. This time I went to 16, King Street, the Party headquarters, and told Gollan. I was still choking over it and nearly in tears. Gollan thanked me for telling him. A couple of weeks later he told me that Matlock had been sent back to production. This was Party jargon. It meant that Matlock had been sent to work in a factory.

This affair deepened my faith in the Party. I was thrilled and flattered to be on close terms with its leaders. To me they were men (there were at the time no women in the top stratum) rendered powerful and rather mysterious by their association with the Comintern, in the shadow of whose power they stood. I saw them as examples of the "people of a new type" that Stalin had called for. I was to spend the next few years trying to be one of the people of a new type. As for Matlock, the word for him in Party language was bureaucrat. Bureaucrats were a sort of vermin that threatened to infest a revolutionary Party and must be hunted out. Not for nothing had Stalin called them "office rats."

From now on, when I was in my Party character (all the while I rode on my bike to weekend camp with my LLY friends) I took myself with great seriousness, trying to imitate the leaders' idiom, their taciturn manner and their sober dress. I studied the theological texts of Communism to acquire some fraction of their familiarity with Scripture; and whenever I could I carried a briefcase like them. This briefcase was another reward from my parents, this one for having passed the Higher Schools. How could I have been so uncommunicative to them? I had been a guileless boy, unable to keep back my thoughts. My aunt Hetty had said to me, "What's in your lung is on your tongue." My life was now a mystery to them although I was still at school.

I was not yet rid of my notions about becoming a writer, and I must have confided them to a YCL friend of my own age, Oscar Lewenstein, who years later became a well-known impresario in both theatre and cinema.[6] He told me to call on the editor of a communist weekly, the *Young Worker*, who might have something for me to do.

This paper was produced in another of the old Shoreditch streets near the railway. I waited in a bare room which had tall windows along one side grimed with railway soot and which had only a few chairs for furniture. A long ledge under the window served for a desk. On it were a big, old-fashioned typewriter and a litter of copy pads and thick pencils. Box files with scribbled labels stood on the shelf on the opposite wall and the bare wooden floor was littered with scrap paper, old galley proofs, discarded newspapers and cigarette ends. Through an open doorway I heard the thump and churn of printing presses. The air reeked with the smell of printer's ink. Both sound and smell were exciting.

The editor came into the room. He was a muscular young man with a matting of black hair on his arms and bared chest. Later on he was one of Hugh Cudlipp's *Daily Mirror* team in that newspaper's finest years.[7] His first words were, "I understand you're a poet."

I managed a "Yes."

He pushed a high stool up to the ledge. "Sit yourself down."

I did so. He gave me a copy pad and a pencil. He said, "Write me a poem about Thaelmann."

Thaelmann was the leader of the German Communist Party.[8] He was in a concentration camp. There was a campaign all over the world to get him released. I said, "O.K."

He went back to the printshop. I laboured for a long time. When he came back I gave him a poem in free verse. He stood in the middle of the room

---

6   Silvion Oscar Lewenstein (1917–1997). British theatre and film producer and Communist. He wrote an autobiography, *Kicking Against the Pricks* (London, 1994). A transcript of an interview he had with Margot Kettle on 9 January 1984 can be found in the People's History Museum, Manchester, (CP/1ND/KETT/03/25). See also TNA KV2/3991.

7   Hugh Cudlipp (1913–1998). Journalist and newspaper editor.

8   Ernst Thaelmann (1886–1944). Leader of the Communist Party of Germany for much of the Weimar period and a revered figure in Marxist circles. Executed by the Nazis in Buchenwald concentration camp. See B. Lazitch and M.M. Drachkovitch, *Biographical Dictionary of the Comintern* (Stanford, CA., 1973), pp.402–3 (later Lazitch and Drachkovitch, *Biographical Dictionary*).

looking at it, sniffing a couple of times. "This is no good," he said. "I want something for the young workers to sing on a demo."

Next time he came back I gave him a song, set to the tune of "Hearts of Oak". He printed this in the next issue. I cut it out to keep in my wallet.

I had taken Matlock seriously when he had said that I might soon be going to Moscow. I was so used to going to the flat, seeing people arrive from Moscow and hearing talk of how things were "over bye" that I thought of the British Communist Party as only an outlying branch. Moscow was the place that mattered. I knew that potential leaders were sent there to be trained for up to three years at the Lenin School.[9] I assumed that if I showed my worth I might well be sent to it. I was encouraged in this ambition by Alex Massie. Talking to me once about Moscow, he said, "But I expect you'll see it for yourself before long."

When I first met Massie at the flat, just after he had arrived from Russia, he was wearing what I eventually came to recognise as the standard Soviet outfit, a flat-brimmed trilby hat and a heavy black overcoat. A huge black brief-case, also a part of the Moscow outfit, bulged with books, papers and travel necessities.

Alex looked like a Russian. He had a square face with small eyes, a somewhat snub nose and a dense upright brush of black hair. He was a Scot, a former steel worker, born in Aberdeen. His wife, Maggie Jordan, was a plump little Yorkshire woman who had once worked in the woollen mills.[10] Alex was an executive member of the Communist Youth International. He and Maggie had worked for the International in many countries, including

9   The International Lenin School was run by the Communist International from 1926 to 1938. An estimated 150 students from Britain trained there. See G. Cohen and K. Morgan, "Stalin's Sausage Machine. British Students at the International Lenin School," *Twentieth Century British History*, Vol. 13 (2002), pp.327–55. See also J. McIlroy, A Campbell, B. McLoughlin and J. Halstead, "Forging the Faithful. The British at the International Lenin School," *Labour History Review*, Vol. 68 (2003), pp.99–128.

10   Maggie Jordan. A mill worker from Shipley in Yorkshire, involved in Young Communist League activities from 1923. Studied at the International Lenin School between 1927 and 1930. Employed by the international broadcasting service of Radio Moscow from 1933 until 1939. Author of *How the Soviet People Live and Work* (London, 1940); *Soviet Women at War* (Leicester, 1942) and *Women in Soviet Society* (London, 1944). She remained active in Communist politics at least until the 1970s. Described by Geoff Hodgson in the Communist Party of Great Britain Biographical Project (British Library) as "a tremendous woman." His assessment of her tallies with Baron's. See, finally, her personal file in the Comintern archive, RGASPI, Moscow, f. 495, op.198, d. 494.

China, in which a Nationalist Party led by Chiang Kai-shek exercised a savage dictatorship. Torture and execution awaited captured communists. Dozens at a time were beheaded in public places, often with foreign tourists among the onlookers. I had read André Malraux's great novel of the Chinese revolutionary movement, *La Condition Humaine*, and I revered Alex and Maggie for the perils they must have endured.

Unless we had some immediate problem to discuss Alex did not talk politics to me. Nor did Gollan. They were two new, wise uncles, who chatted illuminatingly about life. Alex was a modest, self-educated man, who spoke about books with a fresh enthusiasm. He once named to me the greatest book he had ever read. It was not Marx's *Capital* but *The Decline and Fall of the Roman Empire*.[11] I at once set about reading it.

I do not think that he or Maggie owned anything but the bare necessities. When Alex came to London on his own he sometimes took a bed at a Salvation Army hostel or a Rowton doss-house.

I still remember his quiet voice and the slight smile that rarely left his face. Recently a friend, recalling Alex and Maggie, called them saints. Of a sort, they were. I loved them and still do. Alex died suddenly in 1948. I had quit the Party by then. It was a time when people who left the Party were reviled as renegades. Leading Party members spared me this treatment and continued to be friendly. An old Moscow associate of Alex and two other leading people were going to visit Maggie; they asked me to go with them. She sat as if made of stone, on a bentwood chair, her hands clasped in her lap. The room was small, poor, scarcely furnished. It was how they had always lived.

With my head and my time so filled with politics, I gave little thought to my school responsibilities during my last eighteen months there. The Higher Schools exam was to have been a climax in my life and the determinant of my future. It can be imagined how little I prepared for it and how little I cared. When I nevertheless managed to pass, Gollan asked me what I was going to do when I left school. I told him that I had to choose between the two colleges of London University which had offered me places. I do not know if I mentioned the possibility of Cambridge.

He said, "You don't want to be a bloody student, do you?"

"I don't know."

"What will you work at afterwards?"

"Teaching history, I suppose."

---

11   Edward Gibbon's long-acclaimed *Decline and Fall of the Roman Empire* appeared in six
     volumes between 1776 and 1789.

"Did you know," he said, "that there are thirty-seven applications for every job teaching history?"

"No."

"Do you think they'll give a job to a Jew?"

"I don't know."

We went on to talk about other things but I came away brooding upon what he had said to me. It had reminded me of another experience.

I had already been up for my interview at University College, London. The Chairman of the interviewing committee was a Professor Jeaffreson, a great man whose name I had seen on examination papers. I was leaving the room when he called after me, "By the way —"

I turned round, at the door. "Sir?"

"What is your religion?"

I said that I was Jewish. He thanked me and I went out.

The next day at school I told Mr. Moody that the interview seemed to have gone well. I mentioned that Jeaffreson was one of the interviewers. As I was about to go, he said, "By the way —." I turned round. He said, "Did Professor Jeaffreson ask you about your religion?"

"Yes, sir."

He said, "I'm sure you'll be all right," and went into a classroom. The college offered me a deferred place, not unreasonably at my age. But Gollan had lit a fuse in my mind. I decided not to go to college. From now on I took it for granted that I would one day become a professional revolutionary, employed full-time by the Party.

Gollan wanted me to get some experience among the proletariat by going to work in a factory. I would have liked to but I shrank from dealing one more blow to my father. The driving purpose in many a working man's life is to ensure that his child, or one of his children at least, will not have to work "at the bench". I knew how deeply this was true of my father.

I sat for an examination and was accepted by the London County Council for a place as a general grade clerk.

Chapter 20

In the autumn of 1935 I started work at County Hall, an imposing building on the south bank of the Thames, opposite the Houses of Parliament. Ted Willis was still in his job at the Chiswick bus works. He did not become a full-time political worker till 1937. My turn came in 1938.

Politics, however, was by now my main occupation, my hours at the Council offices a frustrating interruption; consequently I was an indifferent public servant. My day began at five a.m. when old Mr. Humphries, the crippled newspaper seller, pushed our *News Chronicle* and my *Daily Worker* through the letter-box.[1] My father got up at the same time. I washed, read the papers and had breakfast with my father, then settled down to read, politics of course. I went to County Hall in a series of jolting rides on crowded trams which at that hour were filled with the smells of bodies, working clothes and cheap shag tobacco.

My job, for most of my time with the Council, was to pay the grants of technical scholarship holders. Each grant had to be separately calculated term by term according to the number of days attended by the student. Poor at figures, bored by them and already tired by the late hours I had kept the night before, with my mind on far different matters, I miscalculated hundreds of grants and got almost every page total wrong in the big register of payments that I kept. My seniors in the office went over all my figures end corrected them without ever complaining.

This was not all they had to put up with. All day long the telephone bell rang for me, as I gave the office number to comrades who needed to keep in touch with me. I spent hours on the 'phone conducting my political business but I was never reprimanded. Everyone at County Hall was tolerant toward me. When in the end I gave notice to leave, the Establishment Officer astonished me by asking if there was anything he could do to induce me to stay. I left the office at five o'clock each day and set off for my true work. I was so tired by the succession of such days that I often fell asleep in

---

1   *The Daily Worker*, the newspaper of the British Communist Party. It began to appear in 1930 and continued publication until 1966 when it was renamed the *Morning Star*.

the tram. Then the real slog began; writing articles, getting out letters and circulars, attending meetings and travelling all over London to meet people or conduct study groups. I never got home before midnight. My mother had left sandwiches for me on the kitchen table. I had my supper and settled down to more political reading until the small hours.

*****

This frantic daily round was dictated by the growing success of our work in the LLY. Before a year had passed, lively debates about policy were taking place in almost all the branches, many of which were now committed to the Left. The impetus for this accelerating swing came from the events of the day. There was a growing public unease at the futile attempts of the Chamberlain government to appease Hitler.[2] And there was the matter of the Blackshirts, whose Nazi-type uniformed detachments and whose Nazi propaganda brought fascism into the streets of British towns.

The leaders of the Labour Party made speeches opposing Mr. Chamberlain but did nothing more. They called on their members to ignore the Mosley Blackshirts. All the natural qualities of youth provoked rebellion against such poor fare. Labour and Communist youth took part together in protest marches and meetings against appeasement and were prominent in the crowds who opposed the Blackshirts, in many places closing down their meetings and chasing them away.

Until I became too busy with national work I took part with members of my own LLY branch in many local actions and escapades. Once I was out with another comrade; we decided, for the hell of it, to paste some anti-Fascist posters on the door of a Fascist headquarters near Hackney Downs while a meeting was going on inside. A latecomer to the meeting raised the alarm and we fled with a hallooing pack of Blackshirts in pursuit. They wore army boots and wide leather belts with big buckles of steel plate; it was no joke to go down under a mob of them. They chased us on to Hackney Downs where we separated. The other comrade ran on until he met a group of hefty Jewish boys coming away from a gym. The Fascists gave them a wide berth and continued after me. I was running across a field littered with recumbent couples. Several of these lay under a stand of oak trees in the middle of the field. I ran into the thicker darkness among the trees, threw

---

2   Arthur Neville Chamberlain (1869–1940). One of the Chamberlain political family with
     a power base in Birmingham. British Prime Minister (1937–1940). Widely associated
     with the policy of appeasement towards Nazi Germany.

myself down close to the foot of one of them, lay with my face towards it and hugged myself in a loving embrace, hoping to look like a copulating couple. Perhaps I did, for the pack of pursuers ran past.

Ted was less lucky on one occasion. He went with a group of comrades to an indoor meeting at one of the Fascists' local headquarters, in Kentish Town. it was in a disused warehouse, the top floor of which had been turned into a meeting hall. Ted was the first to stand up and interrupt the speaker with a shouted, repeated question. The rest of the comrades were to follow his example and, one by one, to receive the same treatment. Uniformed stewards stationed in the aisles closed in on him and dragged him out of the hall. More stewards were posted from top to bottom of the stairway. Ted was thrown and kicked down flight after flight of stone steps. He was spectacularly bruised when he met us next evening and had a broken arm in a sling.

*****

Quite early in my LLY career it was the stir of anti-fascist activity that led to my first step into prominence. Another one of my accidents played a part in it. At one of our branch meetings the chairman read out a letter inviting us to send a delegate to a conference of North London branches to set up an action committee against Fascism. As usual (the apathy of others is often how the Left gets its opportunities) no-one else wanted to go. I volunteered.

The meeting was in the Labour Hall at Southgate. I sat in a back corner, by a piano. On the platform was the inspirer of the meeting, the same Dorothy Woodman I had gone to hear at the start of my political career. I knew by now that this prominent Labour Party intellectual was secretly "one of us."

She lived with Kingsley Martin, the editor of the *New Statesman*.[3] This weekly journal was at the peak of its influence in the years that led up to the Second World War, not only in left-wing political circles but as a beacon to many thousands all over the country who, like me in my school years, had to go to the public libraries to read it. Ted Willis came to know the couple well and one day explained to me that they had a sado-masochistic relationship, the robust Dorothy being in command. As time went on the *Statesman* fell completely into step with the Communist Party. Kingsley

---

3   Basil Kingsley Martin (1897–1969). Journalist and editor of the New Statesman between
     1930 and 1960. See his memoirs, *Father Figures* (London, 1966) and *Editor* (London,
     1968).

refused to publish articles critical of Soviet actions. I happily thought of this as the work of Dorothy, and imagined her wielding her corrective cane upon the gentle, grey-haired editor.

She briskly took command of the meeting. The first step, she told us, was to elect a chairman for the meeting. She asked for nominations. There must have been a hundred people in the hall but no-one spoke up. I was sitting at the side, with my elbow on the end board of a piano. The piano lid was up. My elbow slipped and a jangle of keys broke the silence. Heads turned. Dorothy Woodman called out, "I nominate the comrade by the piano!"

Thunderstruck, I heard a shout of "Agreed!" and in a daze I went up to the platform. I had no idea what to do. Dorothy Woodman must have guided me through the proceedings. Massie was much amused by my account of the meeting. He gave me a copy of Walter Citrine's book *The Labour Chairman*.[4] I had it off by heart at the next meeting and was, as always afterwards, a stern chairman.

I was still afraid to speak at public meetings. Gollan decided to break me of this. The socialist students at the London School of Economics had invited all the left-wing youth organizations to send speakers to explain their policies in a symposium at the college. Gollan sent me to represent the Labour League of Youth. He saw nothing odd in this.

The large hall was full. My turn came to speak. I stood up and advanced to the front of the platform, looking at the upturned faces and nerving myself. I threw out my left arm, forefinger pointing, as I had seen Gollan do. "Comrades, we in the Labour League of Youth…" Encouraged by the sound of my own voice I took a pace forward, "…know that the only way forward is through unity…" On the last word I took another step forward and fell off the front of the platform, which was about four feet high. I hit the floor amid a general surprised silence, then there was a great surge of laughter. I picked myself up as the laughter continued on a not unsympathetic note, went up the steps on to the platform, stepped forward, bowed like a little boy after his violin solo and retreated to my seat, now to prolonged applause.

After this not even Gollan could induce me to speak in public. I often spoke at internal meetings and conferences but even at these I sometimes had to bottle up fright. In one big conference hall a girl comrade who was sitting well back in the public gallery told me that while I was speaking she could see my hand shaking as it held my notes.

---

4   Walter Citrine, *The Labour Chairman* (London, 1921). In Socialist circles it became regarded as a bible on chairmanship.

Ever since Lenin and two associates founded a journal *Iskra* (*The Spark*), in 1900 it became the unvarying practice of communists everywhere to establish a newspaper or journal as the moving force of every organization and campaign. Accordingly we started a monthly journal, *Advance*. At first we produced it on a duplicating machine, then we printed it in a magazine format and later on as a broadsheet, a popular paper designed for young people which we sold in great numbers on the streets. We did not bring it out as the organ of a faction, internal LLY matters being kept to a minimum, but as a propaganda and recruiting paper for the benefit of the LLY. As a result, so far from being a handful of plotters, the YCL group, ever growing in size, stood out as the best members of the organisation, more and more of them being elected on to its area and national committees. The sales of *Advance* reached thirty thousand an issue, climbing to fifty thousand for special numbers.

I found an outlet in the paper for my desire to write. I soon became its editor. Professional journalists, designers and illustrators gave time to help me. I received a good professional training at their hands. In time *Advance* was adopted as the official paper of the League of Youth.[5]

I was elected on to the London area committee of the LLY and then on to its national committee. The area committee appointed me as its representative on the Executive Committee of the London Labour Party. Behind the scenes, of course, and simultaneously, I had become a member of the national council of the Young Communist League and was sometimes invited to meetings of the Party's district executive. Fat envelopes full of memoranda and agendas poured in on me. There were not enough hours in the day for my work and certainly no time at all for anything else. It seems to me in recollection that I was at the same time always tired and never tired. But it meant that I no longer had time to go to my local branch except when I wanted them to pass a resolution for me. The friendships I had made there faded away. The happy days were over.

*****

Until the end of the Second World War, when a dispersal of local populations was seen to have taken place in London, a large part of the East End of the capital, near to the docks at which so many refugees from

---

5   On Baron and Willis's involvement with *Advance*, see Christine Collette, *The International Faith. Labour's Attitudes to European Socialism, 1918–39* (Aldershot, 1998), pp.171–9 and passim.

the Tsarist Empire had landed between 1880 and 1914, was mostly peopled by Jews, whose way of life reigned in the streets as it had in *stetl* and ghetto. They lived on good terms with some of their Christian neighbours, so that a symbiotic mingling of idiom and vocabularies occurred in the speech of both. Others around the Jews hated them. It was not, then, surprising to learn that Mosley's British Union of Fascists had recruited heavily among the workers in areas on the fringes of the Jewish settlement, Limehouse, Bethnal Green and Shoreditch. But when Mosley announced that he was going to lead a great march of his uniformed storm troops through the heart of the Jewish quarter on 4 October 1936, consternation and rage swept this area.

This was the occasion of the event now celebrated in left-wing histories as the Battle of Cable Street.[6] The leaders of the Communist Party in London were slow to take notice of Mosley's intention and were only roused to plan steps against it by desperate pleas from the East End leadership. It was they, the East Enders, who planned the action in Cable Street and carried it out alone.

The Party membership in the East End was of course mainly Jewish but the proportion of Jews in the Communist Party throughout the country was small. A few Jews were to be found in the middle grades of leadership and in the central committee but none ever penetrated into the inner controlling core. The Party leaders were mostly hard men raised in poverty among the factory chimneys. They looked on Jews with, at the least, reserve, seeing them as soft people, not real proletarians even if they were workers born in destitution; too clever to be altogether trusted. If I had told my seniors that I had read *Capital* when I was fifteen they would have thought it typically Jewish.

The East End Jewish communists were to me a type apart from other Party people.[7] When I went on an errand to the East End, perhaps to meet a comrade in a tumbledown shop in some narrow, cobbled old ghetto street, I felt a touch of the excitement of my childhood visits. It was a different world from that of my everyday political round. I liked the warmth and

---

6   The battle of Cable Street, 4 October 1936, remains alive in historical folklore. For one version of events see "Hidden London. The Real Battle of Cable Street," You Tube, 26 September 2012. See also Tony Kushner and Nadia Valman (eds), *Remembering Cable Street* (Elstree, 1999).

7   The best general account of London Jews in the CPGB during the 1930s and '40s is: H.F. Srebrnik. *London Jews and British Communism 1935–1945* (London, 1995).

animation of the comrades I met and the excitement with which they spoke. In my grandfathers' earlier days there had flourished in the East End a Jewish, Yiddish-speaking labour movement of great ardour and idealism and I felt something of the same spirit in the Jewish comrades I met, cutters, pressers and girl machinists from the workshops, cabbies, market traders, shopkeepers, typists, warehousemen, doctors and lawyers and not a few prosperous self-made businessmen.[8] Elsewhere in the Party the complicated theories of Marxism had to be drummed into the members who bore the instruction doggedly like schoolchildren. These fell upon it hungrily, in noisy, talmudical disputations.

I should not idealise them. There were repulsive revolutionary windbags and people on the make among them and some whose ugly fanaticism was of the sort that provides recruits for the secret police of communist regimes. However, it was they who threw up barricades in Cable Street to stop the Fascists, joined, it is said, by dockers who came down into the street from their tenements. I still applaud what they did. As to the principle of free speech, which I had invoked during my earlier acquaintance with John Gollan, this is a luxury which in time of war has to be rationed. Indeed, one can look back at the event as a tiny skirmish before the coming war, with partisans of the enemy. A successful Fascist march through the East End could have ignited a murderous race war in the area.

Six weeks after 4 October an Act of Parliament was introduced banning political uniforms and giving the police powers to stop provocative marches or meetings. After that the Fascist movement fizzled out in Britain, a nine days' wonder. It dwindled all the more rapidly in East London thanks to an inspired initiative by the local Communist Party , which organized a wave of rent strikes, long overdue, that swept through the tenements, uniting the Jewish and Christian workers, many former Fascists being among the latter.

My aunty Hetty was married now, with a small child. She lived in one of the old tenement blocks in a street leading into Brick Lane and she took part in the strike. She told me, "The Communists came to us and said we should stand sentries out in front in case the bailiffs came. Sentries? What did we know about sentries? We told Sophie the old *beigel*-woman to sit by the gate with her sack of *beigels* and if she saw strange men coming she should give a *schrei*."

When I went down to the East End on 4 October my tram came to a stop in Commercial Street at the end of a line of halted tramcars. I got

---

8   On businessmen and the CPGB, see TNA HO 45/22575/196.

down and walked up the street towards Gardiner's Corner. This big open space, formed by the junction of five thoroughfares, is at the entrance to Whitechapel High Street, a wide boulevard that strikes through the middle of the quarter. It was packed to all its walls by a vast crowd, a dark mass that extended well into the converging streets. In the Press reports next day the size of this crowd was generally estimated at half a million. Red banners tossed here and there above the heads but the chanting of slogans – the Party's watchword for that day was, "They shall not pass!" – broke out only from groups that seemed lost among the mass, from whom there rose only a remarkably muted buzz and clamour of exchanged comment, out of which individual, indignant shouts continually broke. The press of bodies around me was so dense that when at last I reached Gardiner's Corner I could go no further. Here and there I saw the figures of mounted police and the heads of their horses bobbing futilely at the edges of the crowd, as unable to advance as I was. Some of the faces around me were angry, others questioning and querulous. All these people were passive, having come to protest only by standing there. But they had made of themselves an immense, solid barrier of human flesh, impassable without slaughter.

This was the real phenomenon that day. Narrow Cable Street was only a back entry into the East End which the fighting minority blocked up. The intended triumph of the Fascists had been to march along Whitechapel High Street behind their military bands. It was the way of Gandhi that defeated them.

I gave up my vain attempts to penetrate into the crowd and slipped away through Wentworth Street to Brune House, only a couple of hundred yards away. My grandfather Levinson opened the door to me. He growled, "My boy! Come in!" and at once went off into the kitchen in a sort of elated trot to pour a mug of his usual thick brown tea. Busy at the gas stove, he said to me, "I have been waiting for you. You are just the man I want."

We went into the parlour. In the distance the noise of the crowd rose and fell like that of surf on a pebble beach. He pointed to a chair and uttered his customary, peremptory, "Sit!" I obeyed. He was busy at his gramophone, winding it up, fitting the needle, handling records lovingly; the old ceremony. He said, "Here are three sopranos. They will sing the same aria. Tell me the best one."

It was *"Una voce poco fa"*. I sat and listened, fearful of failing, until the last of the three records came to an end. "Well?" he growled.

Heart in mouth, I said. "Number three."

His look was as stern as ever. "And who was it?"

I had recognised in one voice a warmth as well as a purity that I thought I knew. I took the plunge. "Galli-Curci."[9]

He showed brown teeth under his moustache in an approving grin. "Ha! Good! Good! Good boy!"

Sitting with him in that old familiar room, I could hear the faraway noise of the crowd, but it was the music, no longer politics that stirred emotions in me.

*****

By this time, like my grandfather Levinson, I had shaken hands with Mr. Tom Mann, the old trade union pioneer. Gollan had introduced me to him and told him something about me. True to his Victorian origins — he had taught in a chapel Sunday School when he was young — the old man clasped my hand and told me, in the words of the Christian hymn, to fight the good fight with all my might. I had not shaken hands with that other heroic veteran, Mr. Ben Tillett but I had seen him many times at the National Trade Union Club in Holborn. He always sat on a high stool at the end of the bar near the door, looking sad or pensive. His black wideawake hat lay on the counter next to him. After he had done much to build up the biggest trade union in the country, the Transport and General Workers', he was thrust aside by a colleague who had the physique and drive of a charging bull, Ernest Bevin, and he was now a forgotten man.[10] I never saw anyone talking to him and to my discredit I could not summon up the nerve to do so, although I had every reason to as the editor of a youth movement journal.

Mann was small and bent when I met him, but he looked hale, with a leathery, unblemished skin, sprouting moustache and clear, merry eyes. When he cracked a joke he skipped in a little three-step dance to celebrate

---

9   Amelita Galli-Curci (1882–1963). Popular Italian soprano. 'Una voce poco fa' ('A voice a little while ago') is an aria from Rossini's 1816 opera buffa *Il barbiere di Siviglia* (*The Barber of Seville*). In one of Baron's notes for revisions, he wondered whether the aria that his grandfather played him was in fact 'Visi d'arte' ('I have lived from love') from Puccini's opera *Tosca*.

10   Ernest Bevin (1881–1951). Prominent trade union leader and MP. Co-founded the Transport and General Workers' Union and served as its General Secretary between 1922 and 1940. Later held office as Minister of Labour (1940–1945) and Foreign Secretary (1945–1951). See Alan Bullock, *Ernest Bevin: A Biography* (London, 2002) and, more recently, Andrew Adonis, *Ernest Bevin. Labour's Churchill* (London, 2020).

it. I revered him for the great deeds of his younger days and he still seems to me to have been one of the few early socialists who remained pure souls to the end. He had belonged to the Communist Party since its foundation, seeing it as the home for a revolutionary trade unionist. I believe that he lived insulated by his own goodness from knowledge of the dark side of communism and that to the end of his life in 1941 he cherished the same innocent dreams and illusions that my friends and I had when we were sixteen.

Chapter 21

To understand the background of the next two chapters of my account a little explanation of history is necessary. 1936 and 1937 were the years in which the attempt was made to create a People's Front (in English political parlance, Popular Front) in Europe.[1]

The idea of the People's Front was launched by the Communist International at its Seventh World Congress in the summer of 1935. It was put forward by the new general Secretary of the Comintern, the Bulgarian Georgi Dimitrov, a lion-hearted man who only a year before had stood in the dock in Nazi Germany, under the threat, as a communist, of execution by the axe.[2] He had confounded the Nazis by his aggressive defence of himself and his beliefs; and in a confrontation with Marshal Goering which made headlines all over the world he had reduced the Nazi leader to gibbering fury.[3] Astonishingly Dimitrov was acquitted (perhaps as part of a subtle exchange of diplomatic hints between Germany and Russia, which was to lead up to the German-Soviet Pact of August,1939). He became a hero to liberal-minded people all over the world as well as to communists and now stood at Stalin's right hand, encouraging Stalin's inclination to seek an alliance with Western governments against the rapidly growing military power of Germany.

---

1   The policy of the People's Front or Popular Front was announced in *Pravda* in May 1934. See A. Brown, *The Rise and Fall of Communism* (London, 2010), pp.88–180; D. Priestland, *The Red Flag. A History of Communism* (London, 2010), pp.188–233; on France, where Baron became especially enthused by and involved in events, see J. Jackson, *The Popular Front in France. Defending Democracy 1934–38* (Cambridge, 1990).

2   Georgi Dimitrov (1882–1949). Bulgarian Communist. Leading figure in the Comintern between 1929 and 1943. Accused by the Nazis in 1933 of being the perpetrator of the Reichstag fire. Prime Minister of Bulgaria, 1946–1949. See Lazitch and Drachkovitch, *Biographical Dictionary*, pp.77–9.

3   Hermann Wilhelm Goering (1883–1946). First World War fighter ace. Later a key figure in Hitler's Germany. Tried as a war criminal at Nuremberg and sentenced to death but committed suicide before his planned execution.

This called for a change in the policies of the communist parties. Hitherto they had all worked to bring about Soviet revolution in their countries. Their bitterest enmity had been reserved for parties of the Labour or social-democratic type, their successful rivals, whom they vilified as social-fascists.

Now the calls for revolution were silenced. The Socialists were no longer social-fascists. The Communists appealed not only to Socialists but to the leaders of Liberal and other centre parties to join them in People's Fronts which would fight for a military alliance with Russia against Hitler and in their own countries defend democracy against the Fascists.

The People's Front was a tactic, of course. It was meant to lead, after Hitler had been overthrown or defeated in war, to a situation in which the Communists would have attained such a commanding position that the final revolution would be inevitable and comparatively easy. It was a tactic but it was not, in the short term, a deception. Certainly it was not seen as one by the Party members, who everywhere threw themselves with exemplary devotion and often with self-sacrifice into the fight for demo-cracy, as witness the rank-and-file communists (this is not the place to study the manoeuvres of their leaders) who fought in the International Brigades in the Spanish Civil War. People's Front governments came briefly into power in France and Spain. The membership of the communist parties soared. The French party, which was fifty thousand strong in early 1934, rapidly reached a membership of three hundred thousand. The Spanish party, with only fifteen hundred members in 1931, had a hundred thousand in June, 1936, on the eve of the civil war and numbered more than half a million at the height of that struggle. Even the little British Communist Party trebled its numbers from five thousand to fifteen thousand. Nor was it dismissed as a tactic by vast numbers of people of liberal inclination in the Western countries. Indeed, the communists came to be widely accepted and respected as doughty and resourceful democrats, particularly by intellectuals. There began a sort of golden age of Western communism, which would be rudely ended in 1939 by the thunderbolt announcement of the Soviet-German Pact.

This mood ran high in Britain. It was not shared by the Labour Party leaders who dismissed the Popular Front idea with contempt. The Labour League of Youth members saw it otherwise. To them it was simple common sense. Within a year or so we swept to power inside the organization.

As for me, bliss was it then, indeed. And very heaven it was, to be a Young Communist at this time. I gained immensely in confidence and the inner critic ceased to whisper his disparagements. All the more glorious was it that the most triumphant and colourful enactment of the drama (the spotlight was soon to shift to Spain) was at the moment in my beloved France.

*****

The summer days were brilliant in Paris in June, 1936. On the hot Saturday nights couples danced in the streets to accordion music outside cafes in the working-class quarters. By day immense processions surged on the boulevards raising thickets of red banners. Oratory rang through loud speakers. Women lifted up ecstatic faces at the sight of *not' Maurice* – Thorez, the Communist Party leader, not Chevalier.[4] A *Front Fopulaire* government had taken office early in the month with the Socialist Léon Blum as Prime Minister.[5] Hundreds of thousands of workers were on strike, occupying their places of work, a new tactic and one laden with revolutionary symbolism. Even the Paris *midinettes* and the shop assistants in the great department stores were on strike.[6] The Party kept the movement strictly within bounds in order not to scare off the middle-class. The discipline was strict. At the Galeries Lafayette, it was said, the sales people in the bedding department slept on the floor leaving the display of beds in immaculate condition. The atmosphere was festive. Relatives of the strikers flocked to the workplaces with hot food and clean clothing. Sympathetic stage and film stars, artists and other celebrities, concert parties, theatre troupes and orators went from one strike location to another. The strikers claimed to be backing up the new government, and encouraging it so that it would be able to secure for them higher wages, better conditions and holidays with pay.

The Communist Party had refused to join the new government, preferring, it explained, to support it from the outside. How typical, I thought approvingly, how modest of the comrades to shun the trappings of office and stay in the background. (The Party, of course, had instigated the "spontaneous" strikes. They were a first taste of a strategy designed to

---

4   *Not' Maurice.* The reference is to Maurice Thorez (1900–1964), leading French Communist and, towards the end of his life, General-Secretary of the French Communist Party (PCF). See Lazitch and Drahkovitch, *Biographical Dictionary*, pp.404–5. The other Maurice here is Maurice Chevalier (1888–1972), the French entertainer.
5   Léon Blum (1872–1950). French Socialist politician. Three times Prime Minister of the French Republic.
6   *Midinettes.* Seamstresses.

dominate the government from the outside while avoiding responsibility for its failures and reactionary backsliding until the time came when the Party could supplant it.)

As soon as I arrived in Paris I felt as if I had been transported into the joyful and fraternal future. The city, from the eastern suburbs to the Place de la Concorde (beyond that was foreign territory) was the Party's. I saw familiar badges everywhere, on the lapels of jackets and the bosoms of frocks, worn by people in the throngs of passers-by or in the Métro or at café tables. I talked with strangers as if they were old friends. Some Party leaders took me for lunch to a Party restaurant where the Party *patron* and his family and all the Party waitresses crowded round our table to ask us how we liked each dish and each wine that they brought.

I sat with an exiled German socialist leader on a café *terrasse* in the Boulevard Saint Michel. He was a middle-aged man with gold-rimmed glasses, the leader of the German socialist youth movement, which was now no more than a name. While he talked I was looking at a girl who stood at the edge of the pavement nearby selling *L'Humanité*, the French Communist Party newspaper. She was tall, with a pleasant tranquil face and a clear gaze in which I read the nobility of a communist. At that time there were raids upon the Latin Quarter by right-wing and fascist militants armed with their favoured weapon, the walking-stick with a handle loaded with lead. There she stood, her head up, smiling, fearless, I thought. I despised the man at the table with me, the ineffectual bourgeois democrat maundering on. She was one of us (a phrase I now used often), united with me in the ultimate and greatest Holy Order in history. Now beautiful Paris was ours. I was transported with pride at being there, at being one with the masters of it all. I was intoxicated with the legend of Dimitrov, just think, a communist like me, by the Long March of the Chinese communists, by the tale of German communists who shouted defiance at the Nazis before the headsman's axe fell on their necks, by the Asturian *dinamiteros* of the 1934 uprising, the miners who threw themselves with their explosives under the tracks of tanks.[7]

---

7   The Long March of the Chinese Communists. The military retreat in 1934–35 by the Red Army of the Chinese Communist Party to escape from the Kuomintang, Chinese nationalist army; the Asturian miners' strike took place between 4–19 October1934. The *dinamiteros* were miners who specialised in the use of explosives. The strike developed into a violent revolutionary revolt, and was crushed by General Franco, at that time a senior general of the Spanish republican army, at the cost of over three thousand lives.

The Young Communist League at this time called itself a school for heroes. My ambition was to be a hero. I was impelled by the notion of honour. I had to uphold the honour of a communist. In Paris I saw nothing wrong with the headline in a Party newspaper: STALINE, NOTRE SOLEIL![8] Of course I well understood that the People's Front was to lead eventually to a revolutionary situation, as the government would be driven by necessity to clamp down on the strikes that the communists had secretly orchestrated. But I did not see the Party's new-found devotion to electoral democracy as deception. It was (I had been well trained by now) all explained by the dialectic of history. We meant what we said in the present historical situation, but we were the agents of history and must act on its behalf to bring about a new historical situation which would dictate new measures to us. We were the midwives of an inevitable utopia.

My love for France found many satisfactions in the YCL and this bound me even more closely to the cause. I read French publications, acted as interpreter and guide for visitors from France and at the very beginning of my YCL career, while I was still a schoolboy of sixteen, I was sent to France for the first time. It was a journey which I had long yearned to make and for which I had ardently prepared myself with guide-book and maps. But I had entertained little hope of going there until I was older.

All the greater was my astonishment and joy on an autumn Saturday in 1934 when, at home on my own, reading, I went to answer a ring at the front door and found Ted Willis on the doorstep. His bicycle was propped by a pedal against the pavement kerb behind him. He gave me a five-pound note and a piece of paper on which Gollan had written an address, and told me to go to Paris. It was, of all days, Yom Kippur, the supreme Jewish fast. My parents had taken my sister to the East End to visit my grandparents. I left a note on the kitchen table, "Gone to Paris. Back Monday". The reader would have to understand the nature of the times, the *moeurs* of a working-class Jewish family and the particular character of my parents to appreciate what a bombshell this was going to be for them, how incredulous they would be. I was incredulous myself as I set off for Victoria Station, bound for experiences of which I could not have dared to dream.

I crossed the Channel by the night boat to Dieppe and entered into the world of a Marcel Carné film: narrow cobbled streets lit only by splashes of yellow lights, tall buildings with immense blue posters on their side walls, dockers and railwaymen, who at that time still wore the traditional blue

---

8   "Staline. Notre Soleil!" A slogan, apparently originating in the Soviet Union, which might be translated as: "Stalin. Our Shining Light!"

blouse of the worker, and a café outside which I sat while the train was about to leave for Paris to order a café-crême, speaking French in France for the first time.[9]

In Paris, at the address Gollan had given to me I met a mysterious man named Paul, who wore thick glimmering glasses and who told me that I was to go to a conference of French youth organisations where I was to tell the delegates that I was sent by the Labour League of Youth (I was not) and that the LLY supported the united front (it did not). A comrade told me later that he had seen Paul in the Comintern building in Moscow. He was obviously a big shot.[10]

At the conference I was led up to the *président d'honneur* and was stunned to recognise a hero of mine, André Malraux. I had read his novel *La Condition Humaine* in a state of ecstasy.[11] I knew passages of it almost by heart. Several well-dressed young men clustered around his chair like courtiers. Filled with awe and terror I could only utter, "Enchanté, monsieur."

I backed away but two of the courtiers seized me, one by each arm. One of them hissed in my ear, "Mais c'est un grand homme. Il faut faire hommage."

---

9   Marcel Carné (1906–1996). French film director. Most acclaimed for *Quai des brumes* (1938), *Le Jour Se Leve* (1939) and *Les Enfants du paradis* (shot in Vichy in 1945).

10   Who was 'Paul'? Baron's notes for revision include an elliptical comment, prompted by reading a review of *Le Livre Noir du Communisme* in the *Times Literary Supplement*, 27 March 1998: "Who was Comrade Paul (1934)? Fried (1, Cité *Paradis*)." Eugen Fried was the Comintern official appointed to oversee the French Communist Party leadership in the 1930s. His alias, however, was Clément. He was murdered by the Gestapo in 1943. See Annie Kriegel, S. Courtois, *Eugen Fried. Le grand sécret du PCF* (Paris, 1997). The address in Paris that Baron names was occupied by two of Willi Münzenberg's organisations, the World Student Association (RME) and the International Committee for Aid to the Spanish People, and was also one of Otto Katz's private addresses. See Geoff Andrews, *The Shadow Man: At the Heart of the Cambridge Spy Circle* (London, 2015), p.77. Baron mentions Otto Katz in another of his notes, implying that he met, or at least saw, him in person at some point, see pp.344–5, endnote to p.71. Otto Katz (André Simone) was condemned to death in 1952 in the Slánský trial in Czechoslovakia, alongside Otto Schling, with whom Baron was later acquainted in London (c.f. Chapter 31). One of Katz's close associates was German Communist leader Paul Merker (but in 1934 he was still operating underground in Germany). On Katz, see Jonathan Miles, *The Dangerous Otto Katz. The Many Lives of a Soviet Spy* (London, 2010).

11   André Malraux (1901–1976). French novelist and political figure. His best- known work is: *La Condition Humaine* (Paris, 1933).

They pushed me forward. I had caught a snatch of someone else's *hommage* and started off, "*Cher maître, à la part de la jeunesse d'Angleterre …*"

Malraux said, in English, "It's all right. I know. Come and sit here." I sat down next to him. From time to time during the morning he addressed asides to me, to which I could only croak inarticulate replies. On his insistence I delivered my fraternal greetings in English and he interpreted. At the close of the session he called a journalist up from the Press table and told him to take me to lunch. I ate this meal outdoors, on a street facing the cathedral of Notre Dame, in a state of trance.

In the afternoon I sat on the *tribune d'honneur* at a meeting which packed the Buffalo football stadium. I was now in the care of Paul Vaillant-Couturier, a Party leader and an intellectual, who was at this time much concerned with the youth movement. On this or on a later occasion he gave me a copy of his recent book *La Malheur d'être Jeune*.[12] The great men of the Left were all round me: Louis Aragon, the scientist Paul Langevin, the novelist Jean-Richard Bloch, and famous politicians of the day.[13] I returned to school on Monday and told my tale. My classmates listened to it with disbelieving grins. My parents only asked me if I had had a nice time.

In July the following year, 1935, Gollan sent me to France again, this time to Toulouse, where an international meeting of socialist youth leaders was to take place. The Spanish socialist and communist youth movements, which were already in a united front, were discussing a full merger. Massie, back from Moscow, told me that the Spanish delegate would put forward a resolution recommending all socialist youth organizations to move in that direction. I was once more to pass myself off as a representative of the Labour League of Youth and back up the Spaniard.[14]

---

12   Paul Vaillant-Couturier (1892–1937). Leading member of the French Communist Party. Journalist and one-time editor-in-chief of *L'Humanité*. See Lazitch and Drachkovitch, *Biographical Dictionary*, pp.423–4. His *La Malheur d'être Jeune* appeared in Paris in 1935 and dwells on youth shaken by the contemporary crisis in capitalism.

13   Louis Aragon (1897–1972). French poet and novelist. Lifelong Communist. Paul Langevin (1872–1946). Leading French scientist. Opponent of fascism; Jean-Richard Bloch (184–1947). Critic, novelist, playwright and Communist.

14   For discussion of the Toulouse meeting, and the *Advance* group's involvement, see Christine Collette's *The International Faith*, p.171.

Although it was to be only six months before a People's Front government was elected in Spain, the Spanish revolutionary Left was still underground and the meeting was held in Toulouse for the convenience of Cabello, a leader of the Spanish socialist youth movement, who was coming over the Pyrenees.[15] Massie told me that Raymond Guyot, the former French YCL leader who was now Secretary of the Communist Youth International, would be in Toulouse to see me, although he was at the time wanted by the police in France on some past charge concerning anti-militarist propaganda among the armed forces.[16] Gollan added another conspiratorial touch by asking me to give him a copy of my passport photograph, which he put in his wallet.

I passed through Paris, where a girl in Guyot's office told me where to go to be put in touch with him in Toulouse. At the conference Cabello and I hammered away for the idea of a merger. He spoke as a leader of the Spanish socialists but he was almost as bogus as I was, being one of the undercover communists who had colonized his organization and were steering it towards a merger in which it would be swallowed by the communists. Cabello and I duly presented a resolution proposing a single youth movement for socialists and communists in each country but it was defeated.

Afterwards I found the café which the girl in Paris had named as a rendezvous. After a while a man in a black beret and a long black leather coat walked in, came straight to my table, no doubt with the benefit of my passport photograph, and said, simply, "*Tu viens?*" We followed a river embankment to a tiny hotel between two shops. A guard lounged in the doorway and another sat on the stairs inside. I was shown into a room. Guyot was sitting on the edge of the bed. I gave him my impression of the conference. He told me to write a report and leave it with the girl in Paris. I did this and I went back to London.

---

15   Most likely Alfredo Cabello, a senior official of the Spanish socialist youth organisation from the early 1930s, and ally of socialist youth leader Santiago Carrillo. Both were clandestine communists. In September 1936 (fourteen months after the Toulouse meeting) Cabello is listed as the member of the Executive Committee of the newly-formed *Juventudes Socialistas Unificadas* (JSU, Unified Socialist Youth) responsible for international affairs, but in reality he remained loyal to the communists. See Helen Graham, *Socialism and War. The Spanish socialist party in power and crisis 1936–1939* (Cambridge, 1991), p.247 and Paul Heywood, *Marxism and the Failure of Organised Socialism in Spain, 1879–1936* (Cambridge, 1991), pp.138–9.

16   Raymond Guyot (1903–1986). Leading French Communist from 1921. Involved in Comintern activities. Member of the French National Assembly between 1946 and 1958.

Figure 22 In 1937 Baron took his parents and sister on holiday to Paris. Here he shows his mother Fanny the view from the Arc de Triomphe.

A few weeks later Massie returned to London from another spell in Moscow. He showed me a copy of my report typed in violet ink on that extraordinarily thin Comintern paper which was supposed to dissolve in the mouth if need arose. He told me that Guyot had been pleased with the report and again prophesied that they would soon be having me over there.

My passport photograph must have gone into the huge set of files on cadres which were kept in the Comintern HQ. All photographs in these files had to be renewed every three years (so I learned years later from the memoirs of a defector). This may have explained an incident that occurred three years on, in 1938. I discovered by chance that an older colleague had taken a photo of me in the street without telling me. He had done it from some distance away and had blown up the head and shoulders to make the simulacrum of a passport photograph. I puzzled about this but it did not occur to me to ask him about it.

*****

I was not uniquely credulous in accepting STALINE, NOTRE SOLEIL. Several million people did so at that time. All the same, I was of a particular extreme naivety which was sometimes ludicrous. During a visit which Guyot made to Britain, I had the job one day of escorting him about the city of Glasgow. He made his own way there and when I met him I asked if he had had a good journey. He replied, "Yes, except for some trouble with the frontier police."

"What frontier?"

"The Scottish frontier. They emptied my bag and frisked me."

I cried out, "There is no Scottish frontier! This is a scandal! I'll get Gallacher to raise it in Parliament."[17]

Then I saw him smiling and I obediently laughed with him.

Had Gollan or Massie talked about me? Had Guyot formed an impression of me at previous meetings? If there is a file on me in the Comintern archives, I should like to see it. I might find, in the course of a character assessment, the words, "A naive, gullible comrade."[18]

---

17 Willie Gallacher (1881–1965). Founder member of the British Communist Party. Elected MP for West Fife and represented it until 1950. Author of *Revolt on the Clyde* (sl. 1936); *The Case for Communism* (sl. 1949) and The Last Memoirs of William Gallacher (London, 1966). The Humboldt University in East Berlin published a *festschrift* in his honour. See P.M. Kemp-Ashraf and J. Mitchell (eds), *Essays in Honour of William Gallacher* (Berlin, 1966). He remained an important figure in the Party until his death.

18 Baron, remarkably, is not far off the mark. For Max Weiss' characterisation of Baron in the Comintern archives, see footnote to p.205.

Chapter 22

It was simply not possible for the faith of a young communist to flag in the climactic years before the Second World War when the general drama was heightened by that of the Spanish Civil War, which burned on before our eyes like some mesmeric conflagration.[1]

Three months after it broke out, in October 1936, I was at home when the front door bell rang. I went and opened the door. Sidney Avner stood there. He was a member of the Young Communist League, a student, so tall that he seemed to fill the porch, a handsome boy with curly hair.[2] His cheeks were flushed pink. He said, without preliminaries, "Oh, Alec, I'm so happy. I must tell someone. I've been to bed with Julie … And I'm going to Spain."

At Christmas that year, on the morning after a party, I went out and bought a newspaper. On its front page was the first list of British volunteers killed in Spain. Avner was one of them.

He belonged to a squad of fourteen British in a German battalion of the International Brigade. Another of them was Esmond Romilly, a nephew of Winston Churchill who was headline news at the time, both for going to fight in Spain and for eloping with one of the daughters of the pro-fascist

---

1   On events in Spain, see Paul Preston, *The Spanish Civil War* (First ed., London, 1974). For biographical details on British volunteers in the Republican cause, see: www.international-brigades.org.uk/ and https://internationalbrigadesinspain.weebly.com/british-battalion.html (accessed 26 March 2021). See also Tom Buchanan, *Britain and the Spanish Civil War* (Cambridge, 1997); James K. Hopkins, *Into the Heat and the Fire. The British in the Spanish Civil War* (Stanford, CA., 1998) and Richard Baxell, *Unlikely Warriors: the British in the Spanish Civil War and the fight against fascism* (London, 2012), with the author's website: www.richardbaxell.info (accessed 26 November 2021). TNA KV5/112 provides a list of volunteers compiled by the security services which, however, is incomplete.

2   Sidney Avner, an activist in the Young Communist League, lived in Clapham. Attached to the British Unit in the German Thaelmann Battalion in the Spanish Civil War and died in action near Boadilla in December 1936.

Lord Redesdale.[3] Romilly tells the story of the squad in a book, *Boadilla*. Most of them were killed. Avner is referred to as Big Sid in Romilly's account.

I knew Romilly. One of the Red bookshops that I haunted was in Parton Street in Holborn. Romilly and another boy who had run away from school with him, lived in a room over the shop. They had run away from Wellington, one of the great Public Schools, and were bringing out a left-wing magazine for schoolboys, "Out of Bounds". In the Second World War Romilly joined the Fleet Air Arm as a pilot and was killed in action.

The history of the Spanish Civil War is a tangled skein which there is no need to pick at here. The main thrust of communist policy on Spain during the war is clear. It was determined by Soviet strategic interests.

To serve his purposes, Stalin sent aid to the Spanish Republic and ordered the Comintern to establish the International Brigade. When, two years later, he feared that this course might leave him to face Germany and Italy in isolation he withdrew his support and the Republic collapsed.

In May 1936, two months before the outbreak of the war, and just after the electoral victory of the People's Front, the British communist leader Harry Pollitt visited Spain with a Comintern commission which reported to Moscow that the country was ripe for a take-over.[4] The establishment of "Soviet power" was of course to be orchestrated behind the facade of the democratic republic. I have not seen any reference to this secret decision in the histories of the war; Pollitt told a few of his inner circle about it on his return to London and it was passed on to me. It is an example of the revolution by stealth which the communists intended to bring about under the cover of People's Front regimes. During the Civil War in Spain the communists were well on the way to power, controlling the secret police and attaining a preponderant position in the army, thanks largely to the

---

3   Esmond Romilly (1918–1941). A nephew of Winston Churchill, at the age of eighteen he joined the International Brigades in Spain. Invalided out. His book *Boadilla* (London, 1937) draws on his personal experiences of the Battle of Boadilla del Monte on the Madrid Front. Later married Jessica Mitford, daughter of Lord Redesdale. He joined the Royal Canadian Airforce in the Second World War and was killed during a bombing raid over Germany.

4   Harry Pollitt (1890–1960). He joined the British Communist Party on its formation. Elected General Secretary of the Party in 1929 and held this office until 1956. He then became the Party's Chairman. See Kevin Morgan, *Harry Pollitt* (Manchester, 1993). As might be expected there are numerous MI5 files. See TNA KV2/1034–1047, for example.

valour of the communist rank-and-file who formed most of the shock troops and to the skill of Party commanders who had received advanced military training in Russia. Only military defeat frustrated their plans.

In the same month the veteran Spanish Socialist Party leader Largo Caballero came to London.[5] I was taken to meet him. Afterwards I said to Gollan that Caballero had not impressed me. He looked like a sleepy old tortoise. Gollan lowered an eyelid in a slow wink and said nothing. I said, "Is that the Spanish Lenin?"

"Ay," Gollan said. "With a little help from us."

The Comintern had decided that Caballero could be relied on as an obedient front man for them and were promoting him as leader of the prospective communist take-over. Claud Cockburn has written about the propaganda factory which he and a Czech communist ran in Paris putting this and other stories out to the world press.[6] In due course, during the war, Caballero became Prime Minister of the Republic. He did not turn out to be the puppet the communists had hoped for and after a campaign of intrigue, defamation and Soviet blackmail they brought about his downfall.

I had planned to go to Madrid on 18 July 1936. This was the date on which the communist and socialist youth organizations were to ratify their merger into a single body at a congress. My colleagues in the YCL leadership were going on the same day to another meeting at Geneva which was considered to be more important, the Madrid congress only being a ceremonial affair. I was about to set off when I received a telegram from Spain cancelling the congress. An army revolt had broken out in Spanish Morocco, The Civil War had begun.

I was ready once more to set off for Madrid in December of that year. I was to accompany a cargo of food to Spain on board a converted trawler, the "Mino", which was owned by the Earl of Kinnoull.[7] I put a few things into a fibre suitcase, said a casual "Cheerio" to my mother and father, who only smiled and wished me a safe journey, and went to Party headquarters

---

5   Largo Caballero (1869–1946). Spanish Socialist. Served as Prime Minister of the Second Spanish Republic. With the defeat of the Republicans he fled to France. The Nazis subsequently interned him in Sachsenhausen concentration camp. Died in Paris.

6   Claud Cockburn (1904–1981). Journalist. Under the name Frank Pitcairn he wrote for the *Daily Worker* and at the request of Harry Pollitt covered the Spanish Civil War for that paper. See *I Claud. Autobiography* (Harmondsworth, 1967), for reflections on his life. He features in Matthew and Harrison (eds), ODNB., Vol. 12, pp.333–4. MI5 took a keen interest in his activities. See TNA KV2/1546–1555.

7   Kinnoull. A hereditary Scottish peer.

to say goodbye to Gollan. I did not expect to come back soon. The siege of Madrid had become a world drama. Everyone in the Party wanted to get there. The International Brigade had been fighting there for the past month. At 16, King Street, Gollan told me that the "Mino"'s voyage was cancelled. The Spanish Embassy had 'phoned to warn that one of Franco's cruisers, the "Canaries", was waiting off Brest to intercept her. Later, the food was sent as commercial freight to Bilbao.

The Labour League of Youth had a warehouse full of food, collected since July by the boys and girls of its branches. They toured the streets in open trucks, ringing handbells and knocking at doors to beg food for the Republic. I went on several of these expeditions. It was touching to see the housewives coming out of the poorest houses and tenements, each holding out her contribution, a tin of condensed milk from the pantry perhaps, or just a sixpenny piece. I sat on the platform at a town hall meeting while the crates of food were wheeled forward on porters' trolleys and piled in stacks that grew all round us. A Youth Foodship Committee was set up, promoted of course by the YCL. Other youth organizations, Christian or liberal, supported it. It was a small effort towards our goal, the Popular Front. By the end of the year it was sending out regular consignments. Ted Willis left his factory job to become its full-time organizer.

Almost all the men who went out to the International Brigade were Party members. Propaganda pretended otherwise, to present the Brigade as an image of "the united democratic forces." Functionaries of the Party were not allowed to volunteer. They were in too short supply to be spared.

It was not for want of courage that Party officials stayed at home. Four of them had been sent to Spain to see the British Battalion through its first few months in action. All of them did their jobs well under fire. One, Walter Tapsell, was killed and my old mentor D. F. Springhall was wounded.[8] One of the others, the excellent George Aitken, who was a political commissar, told me, years later, a story about the Battle of Jarama which I found

8   Walter Tapsell (1904–1938). Born in East London. Executive member and National Organiser for the YCL Executive Committee of YCL 1928–1929. Executive Committee of CPGB 1926–1929. Attended the Lenin School in Moscow. Executive Political Commissar for the British Battalion in the Spanish Civil War. Killed in action at Calaceite. See TNA KV2/1192–1194.

affecting.[9] The British Battalion was newly-formed and barely trained when in February 1937 it was thrown into the line to stop the enemy from cutting the road between Madrid and Valencia. The Battalion held fast but lost two-thirds of its men. On the night before the battle one of the volunteers, the writer Christopher Caudwell, came to Aitken and confessed that he could not go on.[10] He said that he would be of more use in his Party branch. Aitken said, "Come and see me again tomorrow evening," but by then poor Caudwell (his real name was St. John Sprigg) was among the dead. Much is made of the so-called writers-in-arms, of whom Caudwell was one. I do not tell this story to belittle the poor fellow. On the contrary, having taken part in a war, I consider it to be more sympathetic to him than any drum-beating propaganda story.

None of the YCL leaders went. Ted Willis and I were reaping a harvest of success in the Labour Party and were certainly not to be spared.[11] Also, I was under age (and was still under age in 1938 when the International Brigades were disbanded); after some scandals and the threat of prosecution the Party had instituted a lower age-limit of twenty-one for recruits.

We had a first-class comrade at the head of the YCL contingent in the British Battalion. Monty Rosenfield, from Lancashire, was a tall and handsome boy, always merry, women adored him.[12] In the Second World War he fought as an infantryman, was awarded a Military Medal for bravery, was badly wounded, returned to the front before his wound was healed and was killed by a mortar burst.

Monty was the same age as I was, so I assumed that he had been allowed to stay on in Spain by special dispensation; after all, he had been withdrawn

---

9   George Aitken (born 1894). A First World War veteran, wounded at Loos. Leading Communist Party activist. Attended the Lenin School in 1927. Worked for the Comintern. Replaced Springhall as Political Commissar of the British Battalion. Later Political Commissar of the 15th Brigade, holding this position through the Battles of Jarama and Brunete. Resigned from the CPGB in 1940. He later became involved in the Labour Party. See TNA KV2/ 2493-2495 for Intelligence files on him.

10 Christopher Caudwell (1907–1937), the penname of Christopher St John Sprigg. He wrote criticism, poetry, short stories and novels. Killed in Spain during the Battle of Jarama Valley in February 1937.

11 For the Soviet prohibition on sending cadres to Spain, see the Introduction to this volume, p.15.

12 Monty Rosenfield (1917–1944). In the Second World War, participated in the battle of the Anzio beachhead where he sustained wounds. His actions there resulted in his being awarded the Military Medal. He soon returned to the fighting before being killed on the Italian front.

from his rifle company and posted to Battalion HQ. Forty years later a former senior officer of the Battalion told me that Monty had stayed on to work for the SIM (Servicio de Información Militar), the secret police of the Republican armed forces. The men, among whom he was popular, were told that the Battalion commander had appointed him to oversee their welfare. When he went among them with his notebook they poured out their grievances and their often furious criticisms of the Party.[13] I am sure that he saw himself as occupying a post of honour, a spiritual guardian of the men, plucking out hidden enemies from their midst.

If I had gone I should only, as a leading comrade, have been employed in political work. It might well have been the same as Monty's. If so, would I have spied and denounced zealously, proud of my important responsibility, feeling that I had been put upon my honour, the honour of a communist?

Many YCL members fought in Spain but only a handful went from the Labour League of Youth. They were of a different sort from the intense young communists. They were ordinary British youth, amiably willing to help in a good cause as they would be nowadays for Band Aid or Sport Relief, but Spain was to most of them a faraway country of which they knew little.

On each of the several occasions when the British Battalion suffered heavy casualties the Party combed its ranks to raise new drafts of volunteers. At one of these times Gollan called on us to bring in a batch of recruits from the LLY and asked me to find ten of them. Once faced with the job I realised that I had no heart for it, but I decided to make a start late one night after a meeting, when I was alone with another League of Youth comrade on a deserted Underground platform. He was a big, strapping boy, a good cricketer. I asked him if he would go. He remained silent for a few moments, during which I was in a state of misery. He could only be wondering why I had not volunteered. Then he answered, "I'm terribly sorry. My mum and dad would be awfully upset. I couldn't do it to them." I was deeply relieved. This boy became an officer in the Royal Navy during the war. He commanded a small fighting ship and was, I believe, decorated. I did not ask anyone else to go and I have for years felt grateful to him for refusing. I am thankful that I did not send anyone out to fight.

---

13 However, the International Brigade Memorial Trust online biography states that Rosenfield was: "one of four teenage Jewish volunteers who arrived in Spain in Febuary 1938. They were all found to be underage and, it appears, were kept at the base until it could be arranged to send them home. It is not clear if the four saw any action. All were reptriated at the end of May 1938." See: www.international-brigades.org.uk/the-volunteers (accessed 24 November 2021).

I was never questioned about my failure to provide a single recruit. Gollan must have taken my tender years into account and perhaps my shyness, as he did in other matters.

*****

Bill Featherstone was a member of the Paddington branch of the LLY. He was one of several hundred whom we had secretly recruited as YCL-ers. He was a big, red-headed young man with a wild streak that sometimes overmastered him when he was provoked. In 1938 he joined the British Battalion in Spain. After a while he ceased to write home. No news could be got of him. His father, his girlfriend and the local comrades repeated enquiries in vain.

After the International Brigades had been disbanded and the remnant of the British Battalion had come home, it fell to me to accompany Bill's father when he went to interview thirty or forty men at Victoria Station. They had been brought home in a special railway coach, still suffering from severe internal wounds. Ambulances waited to take them to hospitals in London. None of them recalled Bill. He never returned. In time his name sank out of sight in my mind.

In the 1990s, with some Soviet archives now open, I was studying a collection of documents of the Comintern and came across one which in 1938 had been sent to Moscow from some unnamed source in the International Brigades. It was a "list of suspicious individuals" in the Fifteenth Brigade, which included the British, Canadian and American Battalions.[14] It was a surprising enough document for the number of names on it, a hundred and twenty-five of the three nationalities, twenty per cent at least, perhaps more, of the dwindling number who remained in an otherwise Spanish Brigade. I knew that this list was crazy, maniacal; but that, I realised, was the state of mind of the secret police officers or senior commissars who alone could have compiled it, and of the Soviet NKVD men who stood behind them.

From the words on the page came a whiff of the sulphur and brimstone of Stalin's Great Terror which was at its height in 1938 and which raged across Republican Spain. As if the heartbreaking odds against which the Internationals fought, their terrible losses and their manifold sufferings were

---

14   Baron is referring to Document 48, 'List of Suspicious Individuals and Deserters from the XV Brigade', July-August 1938, in Harvey Klehr, John Earl Haynes, Fridrikh Igorevich Firsov, eds, *The Secret World of American Communism* (New Haven, 1995).

not enough, they had to live under the threat of the Comintern's watchdogs. A former officer of the British Battalion, who served bravely from the first days to the end, told me, "We were watched all the time. How we were watched!"

And there, of course, was the name which I had almost forgotten: "Wm. Henry Featherstone. Wrote home calumnious letters." He was sent to the International Brigade prison at Castelldefels, a place I have since visited, thirteen miles south of Barcelona. An American communist was in charge there, a secret police officer who took prisoners out into the grounds at night and shot them. Castelldefels is where Bill Featherstone's trail ends, with a second entry in the list, "Bad individual. Intercepted letter."[15]

Because he was militant he had followed Ted and me but he was not yet a real communist. He had gone to Spain to fight for democracy, not for the Comintern. I can imagine the kind of angry letter he had tried to send home, as he had a right to do. What happened in the prison to earn him a bullet? Had the fiery, red-headed young Londoner refused to sign some monstrous "confession"? Was he shot to silence him after what he had seen? Whatever happened, I have no doubt of his fate.

I am an old man now but I am ridden by the memory of these distant events, of him and of Monty, the one murdered by the secret police, the other in their ranks, both brave, honourable in intent and so alike; and I am all the more fervently relieved that I did not send Bill Featherstone or anyone else to fight where I did not go myself.

*****

15   For many years, William Henry (Bill) Featherstone's death in the Spanish Civil War was not listed. He now appears at www.international-brigades.org.uk/content/roll-honour (accessed 26 November 2021) as dying in the Military Hospital at Vich (Catalonia) in November 1938. Baron's account implies otherwise. The Comintern archives in Moscow contain further data on Featherstone's final months, but not definitive information on his death. It includes a report by the American communist Tony de Maio (presumably the SIM officer to whom Baron refers) stating: "a mistake was made by me here, [Featherstone] shouldn't have been released. He is a bad egg." There is also a letter from 'André' (presumably 'Mad André' Marty, also mentioned in the memoir, pl. 191) to Harry Pollitt and others, dated 13 July 1938, informing them about the intercepted letter and urging care in handling letters home, so that "some of our friends do not believe all the lies of some demoralized elements." Feathstone's letter had been intercepted and reported by Bill Rust, editor of *The Daily Worker*, who also features frequently in the memoir. See RGASPI, f. 545, op.6, d. 132, ll. 7–10. We are grateful to Richard Baxell for pointing us to this source.

Ted ran his Youth Foodship Committee from a depot and office in Islington. With his instinct for the telling slogan he appealed for funds to save the children and money poured in from thousands of people far outside the ranks of the Left. Bulk consignments of tinned milk were packed in crates which were sent to Republican Spain as ships' cargoes. On every crate the words LECHE PARA NIÑOS were stencilled: MILK FOR CHILDREN.

At some time towards the end of 1938 Ted borrowed my right-hand assistant at *Advance*, our business manager Frank Brown, to help him at the Foodship office. Frank had been a member of my LLY branch in Stoke Newington; in 1934 he had been my first secret recruit to the YCL. Since then, he had worked for Ted or me in one capacity or another and was a close friend to both of us.

Of what followed I knew nothing until forty-six years later. In 1984 I received a telephone call from Frank, then a letter, then another long telephone call. He was seriously ill (fatally so, although he did not yet know it) and he poured out to me secrets and feelings that had been pent up in him since 1938.

At the Foodship office Frank, at Ted's request, had drawn a series of cash cheques and handed the money to Ted. He had "half realised that something was going on," to quote his letter, but he had obeyed instructions. He was in no doubt that Ted, also acting under instructions, had been "draining the funds" and passing the money on to Gollan. Frank did not blame Ted: looking back, he saw all three of us as dupes. But he had conceived and nursed for the rest of his life a hatred of Gollan which I remembered having noticed at times over the years. He wrote in his letter, "I must have been deliberately set up as the fall guy." This had obviously been the hardest aspect of the affair for him to live with ever since.

If I had known of the episode at the time it took place I would not have been troubled; if I had been in Ted's shoes I would have obeyed Gollan with a light heart. I knew that everything we did was for the highest good. Thus, money taken from a children's fund for the YCL or Party meant that it would be used to bring nearer the time when there would be no wars and no children without milk. It was not that I would have paused to think about such a matter. I took for granted that we raised money by means which the unenlightened would consider shady: I had chuckled when Gollan had told me how one of our staff had got a large sum of money for us from a Jewish business man by telling him that it was needed to smuggle Jews out of Germany.

When we trained our YCL members we devoted a special lesson to the subject of morality. We took as our text the dicta of Lenin on communist morality, which, significantly, he had enunciated in an address to a congress of the All-Russian Young Communist League, in 1920.

"Is there such a thing as communist ethics?" he asked. "Of course there is." He went on to repeat several times the single proposition that morality stemmed from the interests of the class struggle of the proletariat. "We say, morality is what serves to destroy the old exploiting society ... communist morality is that which serves the struggle and unites the working people against all exploitation ..." This, again and again.

It meant, of course, that anything we chose to do was moral. It imbued us with a proud feeling of virtue to know that we were moral beings, more moral than anyone else, in fact, since we alone served the highest of all ends.

Ted, however, did not treat the matter as lightly as I would have. While we were waiting to go in to a meeting, I heard him softly whistling to himself a jaunty tune that I knew. It was "Goodbye-ee", a soldier's song of the 1914–1918 war. I had always remembered its poignant last line, "Bong swahr, old thing, cheerio, chin-chin, napoo, toodle-oo, goodbye-ee."

On an impulse I said to him, "Are you going to the Battalion?"

He said, "Soon. They're letting me go for six months to do political work." Political work did not include fighting but to us it was the next best thing.

In the event he never went. Years later I told him what I had learned from Frank Brown and asked him if that was why he had applied to go to Spain. He said, "Yes. I had quite a set-to with Pollitt about going. He agreed, but wriggled out of it later.

As for Gollan, he was a tough veteran with a clear conscience. He may have known that, about this time, Harry Pollitt had also tried to raid a Spanish relief fund. This was the International Brigade Dependants' Aid fund. It was administered by Fred Copeman, a former commander of the Battalion who had been invalided home suffering from illness and wounds. Copeman was a brave, good man. He had served in the Royal Navy and always spoke of it with affection. He had destitute families to support and disabled men who could not work; some of them had no legs. He resisted Pollitt angrily. I do not know how that affair ended. In the following year Copeman left the Party.[16]

---

16 Fred Copeman (1907–1983). Joined Royal Navy aged 14, and led the strike committee during the 1931 Invergordon Naval Mutiny. Joined CPGB in 1934. Fought in the Spanish Civil War and sustained wounds at the 1937 Battle of Jarama. Commanded British Batallion from March to July and November to December 1937. Repatriated in May 1938 on grounds of illness. He left the Party in the late 1930s. His autobiography is: *Reason in Revolt* (London, 1948). See also TNA KV2/2322≠2323.

Chapter 23

By 1937 the Young Communist League was in full control of the Labour Party's youth movement. The national committee of the LLY consisted of eleven elected members and a paid organizer provided by the Labour Party. Ten of the eleven were secret YCL-ers.

The organizer came as part of a deal we had struck with the Labour Party. We had put forward ambitious plans to build up the youth movement. These coincided with the natural desire of the adult party to have a large reservoir of new blood. Our plans were accepted. *Advance* was now recognised as the official organ of the LLY. No other official Labour Party publication was as attractive or had as healthy a sale.

Whatever the Labour Party leaders knew about communists in the youth movement, they chose to turn a blind eye. They were probably influenced in part by the climate of the times. The country was now waking up to the threat of war with Nazi Germany. Anger against the cowardice and inertia of Neville Chamberlain and his government was widespread. The Labour leaders had caught this mood and were becoming more vigorous in their opposition. They were ready to show more indulgence to hotheaded youth.

Our motive for building up the LLY was to activate more young people to turn out and fight against Chamberlain; and since we were becoming ever more confident in a victory for the Left in the Labour movement, we saw ourselves one day contributing tens of thousands of members to the merged Labour-Communist youth organization that we aimed at, under Communist control.

I now had to work at a furious pace, sometimes twenty-one hours a day. The London County Council office was now little more than a base for me. I spent hours on the office telephone with comrades, met them during long lunch hours and at the end of the afternoon once more slipped away early to further meetings. Sometimes, I absented myself from work for days. I spent the evenings at meetings, often hurrying from one to another; the LLY was running a campaign of street corner meetings which we tried to make attractive by touches of pageantry and by putting singers up onto the platforms.

For my most important work, getting out the paper (for which I, sometimes with Ted Willis, wrote each month thousands of words under different names) I had to treat night as my working day. For most of the hours of darkness I was at the *Advance* office in Holborn. There was a workman's coffee stall at the corner of the street where I refreshed myself with a saveloy sandwich and a hot mug of Camp coffee. There were all-night trams, one every hour, to take me home towards morning. During my time at County Hall two paid summer holidays, each of fourteen days, were due to me. I spent the first of these working on the paper. As the second approached, I promised myself that I would go to France, of which I had seen little outside Paris, cycle alone to Burgundy, dip crusty bread into big bowls of coffee and drink rough wine in country *estaminets*.[1] Then Frank Brown, our business manager, collapsed through overwork, and I took his place while he was packed off to a farmhouse in the Yorkshire dales for a fortnight.

*****

Ted and I were now a good deal in the company of the Labour Party leaders. As chairman of the LLY Ted was *ex officio* a member of the Labour Party National Executive Committee. I was named as representative of the London membership of the LLY on the Executive Committee of the London Labour Party.

This brought me to the notice of Herbert Morrison, the Labour Party leader in London.[2] He was a short, stocky man with a quiff of hair combed up from his forehead, which the cartoonists always exaggerated. He wore horn-rimmed glasses behind which the lid of one eye was closed: an infection had destroyed the eye soon after he was born. He was the son of working-class parents in Brixton, in south London, and his speech, though correct, always had a Cockney intonation. He was a brilliant municipal leader and under his command the London County Council had introduced a unified and efficient transport service, replaced the slums with good housing on a grand scale, built new schools, reformed the poor-relief system and established a Green Belt around the capital. The committee on which I

---

1   Estaminet. Small café also offering alcohol
2   Herbert Morrison, Baron Morrison of Lambeth (1888–1965). Labour politician. Leader of the London County Council in the 1930s. Deputy Prime Minister 1945–1951. See B. Donoughue and G.W. Jones, *Herbert Morrison. Portrait of a Politician* (London, 1973 and 2001).

now sat drafted policies for the County Council and ran the party machine in the twenty-eight boroughs of London.

I was eager to make my presence known on the committee. In my visits to the East End I had been outraged at what I had learned of the corruption in certain boroughs that were run by Labour. Long-serving local leaders and their hangers-on, both councillors and officials, took bribes and sold favours as a matter of course; these had become accepted as normal procedure by people who had business with the councils.

At the close of my first Executive Committee meeting I raised this matter under the heading of Any Other Business and demanded a committee of enquiry to clean up the boroughs concerned. Morrison ruled me out of order and sent me a note summoning me to his office the next day. I worked as a clerk on the fourth floor at County Hall. The grand suite provided for the Leader of the Council was on the first floor, in a carpeted and oak-panelled corridor. I went down next day by the back stairs to avoid being seen by any of the uniformed office messengers who might recognise me. Morrison spoke to me in a reasonable and earnest way: older heads than mine were at work upon this problem, it had to be handled with care, and so on. He wanted me to drop it. I agreed. The youth movement were not out to make trouble at this time, and besides, I rather liked him.

I talked with him a number of times in his office. He laughed one day when I told him that I worked as a clerk upstairs: he joked that I would get him the sack. He struck up a friendship with Ted, too, on the National Executive, He intimated to each of us, separately, that there could be great careers ahead of us in the Labour Party if we would only sober up.

During the Second World War and in the two Labour governments that followed Morrison occupied high ministerial posts; at one time he was in the running to become the party leader. But when he died in 1965 after a long illness, with the sight of his one eye failing, he was a solitary man, deserted by all his former colleagues. I heard of this after his death and remarked to Ted that it was sad. "Yes," Ted said, "I used to go to his place sometime and sit with him of an evening."

Stafford Cripps was another of the so-called Big Four among the leaders of the Labour Party.[3] (The others were Morrison, Hugh Dalton end Clement

---

3   Stafford Cripps (1889–1952). Labour politician. Elected MP in 1931. Expelled in 1939. British Ambassador to Moscow 1940–42. Member of the War Cabinet (1942). He rejoined the Labour Party in 1945. Served as President of the Board of Trade and later as Chancellor of the Exchequer (1949–1950). See P.F. Clarke, *The Cripps Version* (London, 2002).

Attlee.)[4] He had for some years been mildly inclined to the Left; he now became a patron of the youth movement and a friend to several of its leaders. As a guest of his wife Isobel I had two first experiences, of dining at a Soho restaurant and of sitting in the dress circle of a West End theatre.

Ted and I went to supper one night in March 1937 with Cripps at his London house. We arrived soon after the news had come through that Hitler's army had invaded Austria. Cripps was a vegetarian. We feasted on exiguous salads and a jug of water. Victor Gollancz arrived late. This shrewd and successful publisher, the founder of the influential Left Book Club, was an emotional and at times hysterical person.[5] His usually florid face was patched with pallor and he was out of breath. He cried in a squeaky voice, "That man" – he meant Chamberlain – "will do nothing. We shall have the Nazis here. We shall all be in a concentration camp, you will see! It is the end, the end!" I had no sympathy for him. Close ally of the Communist Party though he was, I despised him as a bourgeois coward. Yet when in the next year Chamberlain postponed the outbreak of war by signing the Munich agreement with Hitler, after a crisis that had terrified the country, I felt a great, secret relief. This did not stop me from writing an article denouncing the Munich Sell-Out. Many people on the Left later confessed to having had the same conflict of feelings.[6]

I interviewed Hugh Dalton in September 1938, the week before Munich. When I went to see him the Territorial Army had been mobilized. I saw air raid shelters being dug in the parks and sandbags being built up around

---

4   Hugh Dalton (1887–1962). Labour Politician. Served in the War Cabinet as Minister of Economic Warfare, Established Special Operations Executive (1940). Chancellor of the Exchequer between 1949 and 1950. See Ben Pimlott, *Hugh Dalton* (London, 1985); Clement Attlee (1883–1967). Labour politician. Elected Leader of the Labour Party in 1935. Deputy Prime Minister in the War Cabinet from 1942. Prime Minister 1945-51. See Francis Beckett, *Clem Attlee* (London, 2007). Beckett's play on Attlee, "A Modest Little Man," played in London in 2019.

5   Victor Gollancz (1893–1967). British publisher. Launched the Left Book Club in 1936. See Ruth Dudley Edwards, *Victor Gollancz. A Biography* (London, 1987).

6   Munich. Refers to the infamous Munich agreement of 29 September 1938 involving Germany, Britain, France and Italy which ceded the Sudetenland, a mainly German-speaking western part of Czechoslovakia, to Germany. Viewed as part of the policy to appease Hitler's political ambitions. See David Faber, *Munich 1938. Appeasement and World War II* (London, 2008); Tim Bouverie, *Appeasing Hitler: Chamberlain, Churchill and the Road to War* (London, 2019); and Robert Harris's novel, *Munich* (London, 2017).

public buildings as blast protection. Dalton was a big man, over six feet tall and broad of shoulder, with a great domed bald head. He had a big, booming voice, on which Queen Victoria had remarked when he was four years old, saying that "it was just like his father's." His father was tutor to the royal children.

I had gone to see him because he was just back from Paris, where he had been having confidential talks with members of the French General Staff. He loomed over me, almost steaming with self-importance as he spoke. "Don't you worry," he said. "It will be a short, sharp war. The French will knock over the Siegfried Line like a row of jampots." Dalton boomed his way through an illustrious ministerial career until 1947, when he was Chancellor of the Exchequer and presided over a stock market crash, a coal supply crisis during which the nation froze, a balance of payments crisis and a run on sterling. Finally, perhaps driven out of his wits, he unwittingly leaked some of his Budget proposals to a journalist who published them. Although he occupied some lesser posts after his resignation this was effectively the end of his career.

I was still interested in aviation and had taken note of a series of Royal Air Force 'plane crashes during 1937 and early 1938, all of them involving the same aircraft, the Hawker Fury fighter. In early summer 1938, I went to see Clem Attlee, the leader of the parliamentary Labour Party, in his room at the House of Commons. Attlee, the future Prime Minister in two Labour governments, was the only one of the Big Four who had fought in the Great War. He had seen action at Gallipoli and in France, where he had been badly wounded. For years after the war he called himself Major Attlee and his constituents in Limehouse, in the East End of London, still called him the Major. I asked him if he thought that the design of the Hawker Fury was faulty. Was it not something we should take up? Sitting upright in a high-backed chair, looking very military, he took the pipe from between his teeth, barked, "Rubbish!" and put the pipe back in place.

I said that there was another question. The Fury was a biplane. Weren't biplanes out of date? The Germans were flying a marvellous fighter in Spain, the Messerschmitt 109. It was a monoplane. Biplanes could never match monoplanes as fighters. Attlee removed the pipe again long enough to rap out, "You leave the RAF alone. D'you hear?" I stood up, said I had nothing more to ask and thanked him for seeing me. From Attlee, a sharp. "Sit down!" I did so. He said, "There's going to be a war." I replied that was what I'd come here about. He repeated, "There's going to be a war. We've got a jolly good Air Force. We shall need it. Off you go now." I did not know that the Spitfires and Hurricanes were coming along.

I dare say that he did.

*****

When we had begun our work inside the LLY the membership had been rising rapidly and had reached thirty thousand. Since then the League had been in decline. By 1938, in spite of our colourful recruiting campaigns, all efforts to build it up had failed. At this time, it could not have had much more than a third of its peak membership.

We communists were to blame for this. In 1934 the LLY had been just the sort of organization we now wanted, one to which young people could come for their social enjoyments, with some popularly presented political education and the chance to take part in political campaigns. We had torn it apart with our own politics, the kind of doctrinaire, jargon-ridden, bloody-minded politics that British youngsters could not understand and which repelled them.

This was inevitable, for we ourselves were products of a movement that was born and bred in Russia, but it was also a result of the war in the LLY that had raged for three years between us and the Trotskyists. Various small groups of extreme, dissident communists who saw the exiled Russian leader Leon Trotsky as their Moses, had busily colonised the LLY.[7] At branch meetings and at every conference the Trotskyists and the Stalinists went for each other's throats. We shouted at each other about Lenin's Testament, the Canton Commune, Radek, Bukharin, Preobrazhensky and Vyshinsky.[8] We were two lots of inflamed young sectarians exactly alike.

---

7   Leon Trotsky (1879–1940). Born Lev Bronstein. Revolutionary and theorist. Founder of the Red Army. Lost out to Stalin in the struggle to determine the future of Soviet socialism. Murdered in Mexico on Stalin's orders.

8   Lenin's Testament. The document believed to have been dictated by Lenin in 1922–23 proposing changes to Soviet governing bodies. Critical of leading Bolsheviks, especially Stalin; Canton Commune. Failed Communist uprising in in 1927 in Guangzhou; Karl Radek (1885–1939). Leading Bolshevik. Active in the Comintern. Later fell foul of Stalin. Executed while in a penal colony. Nikolai Bukharin (1888–1938). Prominent Bolshevik politician, theorist and writer. Editor of *Pravda*, 1918–29. Associated with the strategy of Socialism in one Country. In disagreement with Stalin over the pace of industrialisation. Executed March 1938; E.A. Preobrazhensky (1883–1937). Bolshevik economist. In favour of rapid industrialisation at the expense of the peasantry. With Bukharin he wrote *The ABC of Communism* (Harmondsworth, 1969; first published in Russian in 1919); Andrei Vyshinsky (1883–1954). Soviet jurist. Best known as prosecuting counsel at the Moscow purge trials of the 1930s. Prepared the Soviet case against the Nazi war criminals at Nuremberg. Soviet Foreign Minister, 1949–1953.

It was obligatory for all Party and YCL members to believe utterly, without the minutest spot of reservation, every word of the mad gibberish of denunciation poured out in Moscow by the State Prosecutor during the macabre trials of so-called Trotskyists at which a procession of Soviet leaders had been condemned to death. In this matter we were expected to cease being rational British people and to think like Russian fanatics who might have been conceived in the mind of Dostoevsky. The Soviet prosecutor had called his victims poisonous reptiles, crocodiles, hyenas, jackals, vermin, degenerates, fiends, beasts of prey and political syphilitics, and we had been conditioned to see our own Trotskyists as such. For the ordinary members of the LLY the ordeal of listening to excited, jargon-ridden, incomprehensible disputations fraught with such hatred became too much of an ordeal and they drifted away in thousands.

I was vehemently engaged in this war. I wrote articles against the Trotskyists, taught classes on the menace of Trotskyist fascism and ranted against them at conferences. To better refute the devil's scriptures I read through the works of Leon Trotsky, coming at last to his *History of the Russian Revolution*. Alas, I was enraptured by this masterpiece of romantic historical writing, only becoming a Stalinist again when I had finished it.[9] Weakness again peeped out when I was attracted by a Trotskyist girl. She was small, with a pastel face that looked out from a cloud of misty red hair. At the entrance to a conference hall I hovered close to her, struggling with the notion of buying a newspaper from her. A hand shot out and took me by the throat. This hand belonged to the Trotskyist leader Gerry Healy, the same whose death a few years ago was the occasion for long obituaries in the newspapers.[10] Most of these concentrated on his expulsion from the Workers' Revolutionary Party when he was well past the age of seventy, for having had affairs with twenty-six young female members of the party. He was, at the time he was busy strangling me, in his middle twenties I remember him as short, with broad, powerful shoulders and long dangling arms with the large hands of a labourer at the end of them. He had a pale, bony, fanatical face with lank red hair plastered down above it. He accused me of having jostled the girl; perhaps his anger was proprietorial. I swung my fists without reaching him until we were separated.

---

9   Trotsky's *History of the Russian Revolution* appeared in three volumes. The first English translation became available in 1932.

10 Gerry Healy (1913–1989). Political activist. Co-founder of the International Committee of the Fourth International. Leader of the Socialist Labour League and then the Workers Revolutionary Party.

I heard more about this girl a little later. We had a spy in the Trotskyist organization. I dare say they had spies in ours. Our spy had got into their political bureau. In one of his reports he informed us that a prominent Trotskyist had complained to their leadership that his work was suffering for want of sex. The red-headed girl had been detailed to sleep with him. I envied him.

*****

I took a day off and cycled to Oxford to visit Denis Hoyland; an interlude, a glimpse of the life upon which, at Gollan's behest, I had turned my back when I was seventeen.

Denis was an undergraduate at Balliol College. He was going out with one of our girls. He was a son of one of the Quaker families in Birmingham which had made fortunes out of cocoa and chocolate. He was a big fellow, with a kind, strong, Saxon face and a tumble of fairish hair.

I spent a couple of hours wandering among the Oxford colleges. It stirred me to look at places that I thought of as the halls of learning. They still awaken longings in me. But the sight of the dreaming spires did not then provoke any regrets in my mind. I was borne up by the conviction that I had chosen a higher calling.

Denis had rooms at Holywell Manor. We sat in a splendid, spacious room which was full of sunlight admitted by tall pointed windows. While we talked I could not take my eyes off the bookshelves. They were of light, polished wood, round three walls of the room, running beneath the windows. There must have been at least fifty feet of them, packed from the floor up with books, many of which looked new and expensive.

An elderly man in a black suit came in. His bearing was respectful. He called Denis "Sir", setting down in front of us a tray on which were a jug of fresh orange juice and one of cream. I thought (as H.G. Wells had cried out to a student audience when, already a great man, he visited Cambridge to speak), no wonder rich men's sons are so big and strong.

I went to the windows and looked out. I saw a garden bounded by perfectly-clipped hedges, with flowerbeds around a small paved court in the centre of which stood a sundial. A student sprawled on a garden bench reading a book. I reflected that he had three years with nothing to do but that.

The picture of the student reading in the garden probably went out of my mind when I cycled back to London but it came back to me in later times, again and again.

****

Early in 1938 the opportunity came for me to give up my job at County Hall and to work full-time in politics. The weekly *Tribune* was about to lose its editor and its assistant editor.[11] On Communist Party instructions, I applied for the editor's job.

Tribune was at that time an important organ of political opinion, selling thirty thousand copies a week. It was a mouthpiece for the more active and Left-inclined elements in the Labour and trade union movement. Its standing in Labour circles was high. It was accepted by Right and Left alike as a legitimate platform for debate.

It was run by an editorial board on which Stafford Cripps sat with Aneurin Bevan, Victor Gollancz and George Strauss, a millionaire Labour MP who put up the money for the paper.[12] This group had now declared itself in favour of a Popular Front. The editor of *Tribune* was William Mellor, a veteran Labour journalist of considerable repute. His assistant was Michael Foot.[13] Both of them were among the large body of left-wing Labourites who were ready to join in a united front with the Communists but could not stomach the company of the Liberals. Labour had fought so long and so hard to supplant the Liberals as an alternative party of government that many socialists would not agree to anything that might revive Liberal fortunes. Mellor refused to advocate the Popular Front and was dismissed. Michael Foot resigned in sympathy.

Harry Pollitt, the Communist Party leader, had established a considerable influence over Stafford Cripps and was having private talks with him at the time. He was looking forward to the Labour Party Conference in the coming autumn at which Right and Left alike were determined to settle once and for all the matter of the Popular Front. He must have seen the conference as crucial for his policies, a last chance, since everyone in politics took for granted now that a war was looming.

When I obediently applied for the editorship of *Tribune* I did not know that I was only one of several pieces being played on the board by Pollitt,

---

11   *Tribune* began to appear in 1937 as an organ of democratic socialism. It continues to be published.

12   Aneurin 'Nye' Bevan (1897–1963). Labour politician. Minister of Health (1945–1951); George Strauss, Baron Strauss (1901–1993). Labour politician. Served as an MP for forty-six years. Created a life peer in 1979.

13   William Mellor (1888–1942). CPGB member 1920–1924. Editor of the *Daily Herald* (1926–1930); Michael Foot (1913–2010). Labour politician. Journalist. Author. Leader of the Labour Party (1980–1983). Foot became Bevan's biographer. See *Aneurin Bevan*, 2 vols (London, 2011) On Gollancz and Cripps, see above.

who wanted to control the paper as his voice inside the Labour Party during the run-up to the conference. I did not learn until years afterwards that others, Fleet Street journalists, highly-qualified men and secret Communist Party members, had also been entered. Not surprisingly, two of these constituted the short list. Then one of them withdrew on instructions from the Communist Party. That left the CP's preferred candidate in place. He was H.J. Hartshorn, a foreign sub-editor on the *Manchester Guardian*, who was duly appointed.

George Strauss invited me to come and see him at the House of Commons. He explained to me that the editorial board would in future take over the political direction of the paper and that instead of appointing an editor of political standing they had chosen a purely professional journalist, of course a man of Labour sympathies. A new assistant editor, chosen simply as a technician, had the Fleet Street experience which I lacked. Strauss expressed his regret that there was no post for me.

It only took Hartshorn a fortnight to get rid of the new assistant editor and to send for me to replace him. At the same time, Ted Willis proposed himself to Stafford Cripps as a new member of the editorial board and was co-opted. Also attending the board at the time was Konni Zilliacus, a rather mysterious figure who had recently become prominent in the Labour Party as an expert on foreign affairs.[14] Zilly, as everybody called him, was a sort of walking cosmopolitan cocktail, apparently able to speak all the languages of mankind. He was born in Japan of a Finnish-Swedish father and a Scottish-American mother. In the 1914–1918 war he had worked for British Intelligence and some believed that he was now a Soviet agent. By view is that he was nothing so petty but that he was a willing mouthpiece for the Soviet ambassador and for other senior personages in the Soviet Foreign Ministry with whom he was intimate. A big man like Dalton, with a bald head, buck teeth and a silly-ass smile which rarely left his face, he exercised a powerful enough spell over the members of the editorial board to ensure, in co-operation with Ted, that the Communist Party now had *Tribune* in its pocket.

In the event the editorial board exercised little control over the paper. Hartshorn went to meet them once a week. He wanted me to go with him but I pleaded pressure of work. After all, Ted was there. In the office

14 Konni Zilliacus (1894–1967). Labour MP, first elected for Gateshead and then for Manchester Gorton. He had an extensive knowledge of foreign affairs. See Matthew and Harrison (eds), *ODNB.*, Vol. 60, pp.992–3 and, for more detail, Archie Potts, *Zilliacus. A Life for Peace and Socialism* (London, 2002).

Hartshorn, as an ordinary Party member, yielded place to me and I decided on most of the contents week by week. It was I who held regular meetings with Emile Burns, the member of the Communist Party leadership who was responsible for affairs inside the Labour Party, where a number of Communist Party members operated, some of them in prominent positions. I suspect that I carried things with too high a hand in the office but whatever Hartshorn felt he remained good-natured and simply took to announcing frequently that he was going off for a drink.

I recently looked through a file of *Tribune* to see what I had made of the paper. In this matter, too, I lacked tact and discretion, for too many numbers looked like imitations of the communist *Daily Worker*. However, the members of the editorial board were pleased enough with it. Hartshorn only bought back one message of disapproval, after I had written a book review rubbishing the work of the Italian writer Ignazio Silone.[15] Once eminent in the Communist Party, he had left it and now denounced all dictatorships, declaring fascism and communist to be alike. Obviously, I knew, a man to be reviled.

After the war, when I began my career as a novelist, I was much influenced by Silone's great trilogy, *Fontamara, Bread and Wine* and *The Seed beneath the Snow,* works now sadly forgotten in this country. I told the actress Beatrix Lehmann, who was a Party member, how much I regretted my review.[16] She replied, "Not at all. When a famous man is our enemy we must defame him. De-fame. Strip him of it." So I had thought in 1938.

*****

Emile Burns was a scholar of distinction and a translator of important works from French, German and Russian.[17] His wife Elinor was also a scholar and writer.[18] They were both tall, thin and gentle-looking. He, the taller of the

---

15   Ignazio Silone (1900–1978). The pseudonym of Secondino Tranquilli. Communist, then socialist. Author of powerful anti-fascist novels. He retired from political activity after the Second World War. See Lazitch and Drachkovitch, *Biographical Dictionary*, pp.369–70.
16   Beatrix Lehmann (1903–1979). British actress, theatre director, novelist and communist.
17   Emile Burns (1889–1972). Joined the Communist Party in 1921. From 1921–29 acted as secretary of the Labour Research Department. He served on the CPGB Executive Committee. A prolific writer for the Party. See also MI5 files in TNA KV2/1759–1764.
18   Elinor Burns (1887–1978). Joined the CPGB in 1923 and served on the CPGB Executive from 1943 until 1956. Closely involved after the Second World War with the People's Publishing Society.

two, walked with a stoop, always with an abstracted expression. They looked like two figures in a cartoon by Max Beerbohm.[19] Their lives were said to be saintly. Both of them were experts in showing the worst excesses of Stalin in the most innocent and reasonable light, echoing his blood-thirsty maledictions against his victims with the well-bred, well-spoken calm of a pair of old-fashioned members of the Fabian society advocating the merits of vegetarianism. Emile laid his plans against adversaries in the Labour Party with a gleam of boyish guile in his eyes.

I had occasionally met Krishna Menon in the previous couple of years. He ran the India League, an organization which worked in the cause of Indian independence and gained a good deal of support in this country. He was a member of the Labour Party and a councillor in the London Borough of Saint Pancras. He was much respected in the Labour Party and was on close terms with most of its leaders as a friend of Jawaharlal Nehru and his representative in this country.[20]

Now, when I met him on my visits to Emile Burns' flat in Hampstead, I learned that he was an undercover Communist Party member. Ted confirmed this. At the Labour Party Conference every year, Harry Pollitt was present and watched the proceedings from the public gallery. In the evenings, Ted and Krishna met him at secret back-street rendezvous. They discussed the next days' tactics with him; Ted conveyed these to other delegates who were undercover Communist Party members or, as open communists, were present as trade union representatives.

While I was at *Tribune* I saw Krishna often. Our office was just off the Strand end of Fleet Street. His was at the Fleet Street end of the Strand, on the other side of the road. Sometimes he came into the office, to hand me a press statement or talk about events. More often we saw each other across the street. He would hail me with a raised umbrella and come across, weaving among the cars and buses, his long legs working like struts jointed at the knees, to lead me off to a tea-room.

After the war, when India was independent, he became a great man in world politics. Nehru was the Prime Minister and Krishna was acknow-

---

19 Max Beerbohm (1872–1956). British essayist and caricaturist. See particularly his *Fifty Caricatures* (London, 1913). One of the better know is Number 47, which carries the title, "Are we as welcome as ever?" and depicts the Court Jews of Edwardian England wondering whether they would carry as much weight under George V.

20 Krishna Menon (1896–1974). Indian nationalist, diplomat and politician. Collaborated with Allen Lane in establishing Penguin Books; Jawaharlal Nehru (1889–1964). Leading Indian nationalist. The first Prime Minister of India, 1947–1964.

ledged to be his closest adviser. In 1947 he came to London as the Indian High Commissioner.

One night in 1948 I left a party in Maida Vale and waited at a bus stop on my way home. It was a little before midnight. A bus stopped for me. The lower deck was empty except for the conductor and one passenger. This was Krishna. He sat huddled in a threadbare brown raglan overcoat with its collar turned up as if to hide his face. Surprised to see him as I came along the aisle behind him, and pleased, for I had liked him, I paused for a moment, about to greet him. He glanced up at me, turned his head away from me and looked out of the window. Taking the hint, I went on to a front seat and sat down, not looking back.

The bus stopped at the next stage. I was aware that he was getting off. When I locked round I saw him on the pavement, hurrying away in the opposite direction to ours, with the old, unmistakeable long-legged stride.

I mentioned this the next evening to Ted, who had known Krishna much better than I had. Ted pointed out that Harry Pollitt's home was on the same bus route, further out. "That was Krishna," he said. "He'd been to see Harry."

After Menon returned to India he became that country's Foreign Minister and later on was appointed Defence Minister. I do not know if I was right to assume that all this time he was still an undercover communist.

Chapter 24

Early in 1939 all our enterprises crashed in an abrupt defeat. At the Labour Party Conference in the preceding autumn the resolutions of the Left had been thrown out. The party leadership decided to finish off once and for all the Popular Front agitation. With the Conference decisions as their authority, they issued ultimatums. When these were ignored they expelled Stafford Cripps and his associates from the Labour Party. Local Labour Parties which continued to voice their support for a Popular Front were disaffiliated. The League of Youth was wrenched out of our hands, its national committee being disbanded and its annual conference cancelled. The pro-communist Left in the Labour Party was at a dead end.

The Communist Party and YCL leaders met to assess this defeat. With war now plainly almost upon us, very likely to come in the summer, their first concern was to strengthen and prepare their own organization. Members could not be allowed to linger uselessly in the Labour Party and the LLY. The Communists in both organizations were instructed to withdraw.

The move was made publicly. We declared that we were honest Labour people who had been victimised and who had been left no alternative but to join the Communist Party or YCL in order to continue to fight against the country's enemies. We appealed to all Labour Party and LLY members who had the same aims to follow us.

The YCL assured the LLY members that it would not ask them to embrace the communist creed but would offer itself as a school in which they could learn more about communism and give it fair consideration. All office-holders in the LLY would be given corresponding offices in the YCL. Ted and I were invited to join the inner executive of the YCL (to which we both of course already belonged). Ted was to become London District Organizer. As the former editor of *Advance*, I was invited to take over the editorship of the YCL weekly, *Challenge*.

I wrote to Stafford Cripps telling him that I had been invited to transform *Challenge* into a popular youth journal open to all. He replied that he approved of my decision and wished me luck.

We were confident that we would bring over the bulk of the LLY members to the Young Communist League. Even the ten or twelve thousand or so who remained would multiply by four or five the membership of the YCL, which had scarcely increased its numbers at all in the years of the Popular Front, although the Communist Party had grown rapidly.

I moved into my new office. We waited for the flood of recruits from the League of Youth. The four hundred or so who had already worked for the YCL inside the LLY came over to us. Few others followed them. Gollan became grim and impatient. He sent half-a-dozen former leaders of the LLY out to the provinces to end the puzzling delay and start the expected stream of newcomers. My assignment was in Bristol. I got hold of a list of LLY members and canvassed them, tackling the members of branch committees first. If these came perhaps they would induce the others to follow them. I spent hours pleading and arguing with them on the doorsteps of their homes. Not one agreed to join us. When it came to the point they were obdurately Labour like their parents. It was all very well being militant but they were militant Labour. Communism was something they didn't hold with.

Some were embarrassed. Most apologised for turning me down. They were sorry, they said, but they'd just never thought of being communists. When I returned to London I found that none of the other missionaries had fared any better. The YCL had to be satisfied with its four hundred recalled members.

*****

I produced *Challenge* in a small attic office at the top of a building in East Road, Hoxton. The business manager occupied the basement. There were only the two of us. The rooms in between were taken up by the YCL staff. A corps of volunteers distributed the paper each week, some taking parcels to the railway stations, others delivering the London orders on bicycles. I lent my bicycle for this purpose and never saw it again.

Pay had not been mentioned before I started. No-one brought me any pay for the first four weeks end I did not ask for any, thinking that the YCL must be in some financial crisis about which I had better not enquire, although nothing was said about a crisis at the meetings of the executive which at this time consisted of Gollan, Mick Bennett, Ted Willis and me.

In my early days in the movement I had become aware of Mick Bennett as one of the people who appeared intermittently from foreign parts.[1] From time to time I would see him standing in Gollan's office, a fair-haired young man of medium height, with a fresh, cheerful face. He always wore the same raincoat, a garment stained by travel but to me of a dashing military cut, foreign, perhaps Russian.

He was back in London now. He did not talk of his past — none of those who had worked abroad ever did — but I had heard his wife Ada in the typists' room talking with pride of his time in Moscow as an associate of the great men of the Comintern. He had, in fact, been a member of the Executive Committee of the Communist Youth International; to me, invested thereby with glamour.

His speech was always calm and deliberate, lightened by his gift for amiable repartee. He was the quickest and most resourceful of us in matters of action. He was always kind and helpful to me.

I was not likely to pipe up about my problems in committee with my three impressive seniors. In the end, ashamed of living on my parents, I went downstairs to Gollan and asked him if I could have a bit of money to see me through.

He said, rather curtly, "Why? Aren't you getting enough?"

I told him that I was not getting anything.

He looked me over for a moment, then he said, "You're in charge up there. Tell Fred" — the business manager — "what you need."

I told Fred to pay me two pounds ten shillings a week. I gave a pound of this to my mother.

The work was hard. It was not easy to get out a twelve-page newspaper every week on my own. It was a communist principle that a large part of the contents of a workers' paper must be contributed by the workers who read it. Some of our readers came to the office to tell me their stories. I spent a lot of time during office hours and in the evenings going out to meet others, sometimes waiting for them at the factory gate and going to a café to have supper with them. Going to press with the paper occupied a full day.

In addition to this work, I had many responsibilities to the YCL, internal discussions, public meetings and classes to take. A sixty-strong

---

1 Mick Bennett (Max Ravden) (1913–1997). Leading activist in the Young Communist League. Attended the Lenin School. After the Second World War he became a full-time worker for the CPGB in Yorkshire. Later assistant editor of the *Daily Worker*. MI5 took a keen interest in his political career. See TNA KV2/2013–2020. For his Comintern personal file, see RGASPI, Moscow, f. 495, op.198, d. 226.

Party group at Elliott's, a big engineering factory in South London, was split into two, those of its members who were aged under twenty-five, some two dozen of them, being constituted as a YCL group. I took charge of them and went to their weekly meetings, which I greatly enjoyed. Some were apprentices, some were already skilled; all of them were intelligent, energetic, serious, sporting and fun-loving. The first half of each meeting was an education class; the second half was spent discussing their YCL activity in the factory.

All four of the YCL leaders were treated by the senior Communist Party as members of its own leadership and were routinely given important Party responsibilities. For the London District Communist Party Committee, I went to oversee the work of a large East London branch in Shoreditch. Later, a small class of picked people was formed to be trained for possible underground work in the future; I taught the class, which met in Hackney. I had to swallow my shyness and speak at factory-gate meetings. I never formally joined the Party and until the end of my time as a communist I was totally unknown to the Party membership but that did not weaken my authority. The local leaders and the rank-and-file welcomed and obeyed anyone who came to them in the guise of "a comrade from the Centre," or from the District.

Once Jimmy Shields, an official at Party headquarters, sent me to the Midlands to bring about the removal of a Party organizer.[2] This had to be done, for some reason unknown to me, without the intervention of King Street becoming known. I called on the four trustworthy people whose addresses Shields had given me, set up a little conspiracy to bring about the resignation of the organizer "by democratic means" (which came to pass) and departed. To all these four comrades I was only an anonymous "comrade from the Centre" but they did what I asked them to do.

As if all this were not enough I studied more than ever at nights. So did Gollan, Mick Bennett and Ted. It was another communist principle that the answers to all one's current problems were to be found in the works of Lenin and Stalin, and we turned to these texts as indeed did the most veteran and experienced leaders of the Party. In much the same way had Cromwell opened his Bible to seek guidance on the eve of a battle or at some new political juncture, like him, we always found what suited us.

---

2   Jimmy Shields (1900–1949). Joined the CPGB in 1921. Worked in South Africa. Editor of the *Daily Worker* (1936–37). Deeply involved in international work. Another Party figure kept under close surveillance by the security service. See TNA KV2/2801-2805. See also next footnote.

That I now spoke in public was Gollan's doing. He was determined at last to break my resistance. One evening he invited me to come to our habitual café for a cup of tea. There he told me that he was due to speak in two hours' time at an indoor meeting in Reading. I was to take his place. He handed me his notes, some headings on a postcard, gave me some tips on the art of oratory and sent me off to Paddington Station. I survived this meeting and went on to speak at others. It never became easier; all were occasions of concealed misery to me, with one exception.

At Gollan's demand the Party embarked on a campaign to attack the last remnants of fascist influence in the East End. It began with a show of strength, a march of several thousand members and sympathisers, led by Gollan, through the so-called "fascist areas." This went unchallenged. There followed a series of outdoor meetings in these areas. I was sent to speak at one of these in Bethnal Green. It was in a street not far from the pub which was the Fascists' rallying-point, "The Salmon and Ball".

I mounted a high, precariously-narrow platform at the end of the street and looked down at the crowd. It packed the sheet from wall to wall all the way to the far end. The street was narrow, lined by tall blackened buildings all the windows of which were open and crammed with staring faces. I was fascinated by the sight. My opening sentences were laboured but I was soon exulting in the silence of the crowd, the upturned faces in the street and the faces in the windows. They were listening to me. The sound of my voice ringing against the high walls filled me with elation. I forgot myself, almost unaware of what I was saying until I was interrupted by a tugging at the turn-up of one of my trouser legs. It was the next speaker, the local Communist leader Phil Piratin, who hissed at me that he had been waiting for an hour and that I had left him nothing to say.[3]

*****

The YCL, unlike *Challenge*, was well-staffed, suspiciously so for a tiny organization. Every week Gollan went to 16, King Street and came back with a subsidy from the Party, out of which wages were paid. The Party also

---

3   Phil Piratin (1907–1995). Communist activist in the 1930s and '40s. Elected MP for Mile End in Stepney in 1945 and represented it until 1950. He then became circulation manager for the *Daily Worker*. After the Soviet invasion of Hungary in 1956 ceased to work full-time for the Party and later made a career for himself in business. He wrote *Our Flag Stays Red* (London, 1948), an account of East End politics in the 1930s and '40s. British intelligence files can be found at TNA KV2/2033–2034.

had a much greater corps of full-time organizers all over the country than its own resources could maintain. It was of course in turn subsidised by the Communist International. I knew nothing to substantiate this and thought little about it but I took it for granted. If challenged I would have said that it was as natural and right for the Soviet workers to make voluntary contributions to help their comrades in still-unliberated countries, as it was for British people to subscribe to international solidarity funds.

In return for its money the Comintern demanded an utter subservience from its member parties. They had to obey every instruction to the last letter, and watch every word that every member spoke or wrote for the most minute implication of heresy. Now that I was at the centre of things I saw evidences of this from time to time. I regarded these only as instances of the vigilant care with which our international leaders watched over and protected us.

In those months, as summer approached, I felt the air to be electric with danger. Hitler sent his army to seize the whole of Czechoslovakia, in breach of the agreement he had only recently signed at Munich. Dangerous incidents flared up on the German-Polish border. The Führer's screaming voice was forever to be heard on the radio, uttering new threats and demands. We were soldiers ready to go; the military analogy was always in our minds. Our discipline was our strength; we should treasure it.

I took it as a matter of course, then, when in May the Party performed an about-turn on a major political matter, that of conscription. Two weeks earlier the Government had introduced a Conscription Bill in Parliament. We should have welcomed it. We were the most fire-breathing advocates of a firm stand against Hitler. Instead, the Party and the YCL at once lashed out with a fierce campaign of opposition. We were not alone in opposing the measure. In accordance with a long-standing tradition of the Left, the Labour Party and the Trades Union Congress had also opposed the Conscription Bill. Later they saw sense, but the point about our change of tune was that it was instant, carried out in obedience to orders from abroad.[4]

I was at the *Daily Worker* printing plant on the morning of 17 May, seeing the next issue of *Challenge* through the press, when I was called to the telephone. Gollan spoke to me from Party headquarters. He told me to kill

---

4   For debates on the extent of CPGB 'autonomy' from Moscow's direction, see *Labour History Review*, 2003–2004; and for further discussion, John Mcilroy and Alan Campbell, 'A peripheral vision: Communist historiography in Britain', *American Communist History*, 4:2, 2005, 125–157, DOI: 10.1080/14743890500389900, and comments by Keith Laybourn and Bryan D. Palmer.

everything about conscription in the paper and to meet him for lunch. I scrapped the front page and scribbled a vague and temporising article which stormed against both Chamberlain and Hitler and did not mention conscription. The news editor of the *Daily Worker* was busy at the same task, having received an enigmatic 'phone call from Harry Pollitt.

At lunch Gollan told me that André Marty had walked unexpectedly into Pollitt's office, shouted abuse at him, thumped the table and demanded a reversal of our policy, bellowing that the French and Soviet conscript armies would not shed their blood for us.[5] Pollitt complied at once. So did those members of the political bureau who were close at hand, hastily assembled.

Marty, a veteran leader of the French Communist Party and the Comintern, was the subject of heroic legends in the movement. In 1919, as a petty officer in the French navy, he had led a mutiny against French support for the anti-Bolshevik armies in the Russian Civil War. During the war in Spain he was Inspector-General of the International Brigades.

Gollan spoke bluntly about this venerated man, making plain that he regarded him as a dangerous brute. It was the first intimation to me that any of my demi-gods could be imperfect or worse. Gollan knew (as I realised in later years when I learned the facts) that Marty was notorious in the Communist International for his brutishness and that in the International Brigades he had been a maniacal witch-hunter who had ordered the execution of at least hundreds of innocent soldiers. I have only lately read once-secret reports sent to Pollitt from Spain during the Civil War, which refer to Marty as "mad André." Gollan must have seen these reports when they were received. When the French Communist Party eventually expelled Marty in December 1952, it described him as clinically insane.

Only a handful of us ever knew the truth about this change of policy. The Party and YCL members were summoned to branch and area meetings during the next three weeks at which they were invited to reconsider our policy freely and democratically. Of course they all came to the same conclusion and were strengthened in their belief that they belonged to a free and democratic party.

*****

---

5   Andre Marty (1886–1956). Leading French Communist. Long-serving secretary of the Comintern. Involved in the Spanish Civil War and is the inspiration for a vicious, paranoid character who makes a fleeting appearance in Ernest Hemingway's *For Whom the Bell Tolls*. He had first come to political prominence in 1919 when leading a French naval revolt in the Black Sea.

Even when, in that tense but to me exciting summer, I suddenly learned that I — myself, none other — was the target of a bolt from the blue, a denunciation from the Comintern, the shock was only mild and momentary. A communication had come from Moscow accusing the editor of *Challenge* of being an *agent-provocateur*. I did not see it; it was apparently for Gollan's eyes only. He seemed unconcerned by it, even amused. I always took my cue from him and felt reassured.

Moscow had given no explanation of the charge. Before Gollan spoke to me he had already gone through every issue of *Challenge* that I had edited and had not detected a single deviationist word. Nor had that old Moscow hand, Alex Massie. Finally, a comrade who had recently returned after a stint of several years in Russia was called in, as being possibly more attuned to the current state of mind in the Comintern. He at last pointed out two causes of offence. In an article praising the Soviet Union I had, for the sake of what grammarians have called elegant variation, referred at one point to that state as Russia. A week later I had reproduced a cartoon from the French satirical journal *Le Canard Enchaîné* advocating a military alliance against Hitler, in which Britain, France and the Soviet Union were represented by the traditional figures of John Bull, Marianne and a Russian Bear, the last wearing a Red Army helmet. He explained that the use of the word "Russia" would be interpreted in Moscow as a cunning innuendo that the Soviet Union was only the old Russian imperialism under a new name. The cartoon would have been seen by the Moscow invigilators as conveying the message more blatantly, a clinching proof that I was conducting a deliberate anti-Soviet campaign. He added that they might already have been angered by my reply to a telegram from the editor of the Soviet Communist Youth newspaper *Komsomolskaya Pravda* which had asked for five thousand words on the plight of the peasantry in Great Britain.[6] I had wired back "No peasantry in Great Britain."

I heard no more about the affair. A reply was sent to Moscow, either by Gollan or Pollitt, no doubt clearing me as an excellent but new comrade, young and fresh from the Labour Party, who would learn to do better. Gollan spoke as if the matter was closed. He underestimated the tenacity of our Comintern guardians. Nearly a year later, in wartime, a tall American appeared in our offices and was at once closeted with Gollan. Others joined in their discussions; I was not called in. I heard the American referred to as Mac. From other snatches of talk I learned that he had come from Moscow. Civilian travel to and from Britain had all but ended; I heard that he had

---

6   *Komsomolskaya Pravda*. Began life in 1925 as the official organ of the Communist Union of Youth.

travelled by way of Oslo, a capital still briefly neutral. I was outside the room when he had a final meeting with my colleagues. He emerged, dropped a hand on my shoulder, and told me quite pleasantly not to make such mistakes again, and left.

That was the last of it as far as I know. Recently, in yet another document that came my way from the Moscow archives, "Mac" is identified as Max Weiss. The date on which he left New York for Russia is given, 10 January 1939. His duties in Moscow cannot have taken long. Soon after his visit to us he was once more active in the USA, as a leader of the American YCL and later in the political bureau of the Party.[7]

Perhaps the Comintern overseers lost interest in an affair as trivial as mine. The storm of war was soon to sweep over Russia; and in 1943 the Comintern was dissolved. If the Cadres Department, which kept an eye on personnel, had in mind a sterner treatment for me than the mild reprimand accorded to me by Mac, I shall never know, unless more papers come to light. Until they do, I shall continue to believe that the affair fizzled out.[8] It

---

7   Max ('Mac') Weiss. Prominent American communist activist. As student, joined US YCL in 1928 and from mid-1930s one of the YCL leadership. Prolific author of books and pamphlets. For an older Weiss in a mellower mood, see Richard Wormser's oral history video "Max Gordon, Sid Stein, Max Weiss" in *Communist Party Oral Histories*, Tamiment Library and Robert F. Wager Archive (http://digitaltamiment.hosting.nyu.edu/s/digtam/item/3683).

8   In fact, Max Weiss wrote the following report on Baron to the Comintern, retained in Baron's file in Moscow (RGASPI, Moscow, f. 495, op.198, d. 1275; translated from Russian by Nick Baron):

> Communication from member of IKKIM comrade Weiss, Max, 15.11.1939, after trip to England

ALEC BERNSTEIN

   Editor of 'Challenge'. Previously he was editor of the newspaper of the Labour League of Youth. He is a good journalist rather than a well-developed political leader. Thanks to his insufficient political development, and also his working methods acquired in the Labour League of Youth, he has absolutely no sense of political vigilance. When I asked him about the counter-revolutionary material printed in 'Challenge', he told me that he had read through the material before it was printed, but at that time hadn't seen anything incorrect in it. He doesn't give me the impression of having sufficient political preparation to be editor of the central publication of the KSM [YCL in Russian – Ed.]. His good qualifications as a journalist could be useful if he worked alongside a politically developed comrade, who would be the senior editor; on no account should he serve as the sole editor of the newspaper.

did not worry me at the time. Afterwards I was, if anything, gratified that notice had been taken of me in Moscow, and that the comrades there had been so vigilant and in the conclusion so benign — an example to us all.

*****

2 1

Сообщение члена ИККИМ тов.Вейс Макса 15.IX.1939 г. после командировки в Англию.

АЛЕК БЕРНШТЕЙН.

Редактор "Челлендж".Прежде он был редактором газеты Лейбаристской Лиги Молодежи. Он скорее хороший журналист чем хорошо развитый политический руководитель. Благодаря своему недостаточному политическому развитию, а также методов работы,приобретенным в Лейбористской Лиге Молодежи,у него нет никого чувства политической бдительности Когда я спросил его о контр-революционном материале, напечатанном в "Челлендж", то он сказал мне, что он прочел материал до того, как был напечатан но что в то время он не увидел в этом ничего неверного. Он не производит на меня впечателения достаточно политически подготовленного для того, чтобы быть редактором центрального органа КСМ. Его хорошая квалификация журналиста могла бы быть полезной если бы он работал с политически развитым товарищем,который был бы ответственным редактором; он ни в коем случае не должен быть редактором газеты один.

Figure 23 Max Weiss' report on Baron to the Comintern, 15 November 1939, preserved in the Russian archives (see footnote on p.205 for translation).

The members of the YCL who believed what *Challenge* told them, that we were a thoroughly British organization calling the country to arms to defend its democratic heritage against Hitler, did not hold back from translating our words into their deeds, as other YCL-ers before them had done by going out to fight in Spain. Many boys in the YCL joined the Territorial Army to train for war in their spare time and some of them distinguished themselves in action when the war came. In general the members were young people of an excellent sort, often capable of great initiative and devotion. A handful of them, working only in their evening time after a day's work and possessed of no funds except what they could whip up from their friends, would organize a big political pageant or a season of summer holiday camps or a great Bank Holiday fête which brought in thousands of pounds for the YCL. Lenin wrote that under communism "every cook will learn to govern" and we saw our young people as examples of the way in which the Party and its preparatory school, the YCL, brought out the creative abilities of the people.

Continually tired by my round of work, I was as continually refreshed by my encounters with them. I was proud of them and a trifle awed by the responsibility of being one of their leaders, although they numbered not quite three thousand. Of course they were dupes and I was a dupe and our membership never increased, in spite of all our efforts, because a majority of young people, quite as intelligent as we were and as public-spirited as we professed to be, were attracted by no phantasm of Utopia and were too sensible to give up their right to think for themselves.

It was in order to get at this majority that we stage managed the setting up of organizations like a British Youth Peace Assembly and a Youth Parliament. A great variety of religious and social service organizations with a total membership that must have run into a million or two, sent representatives to these bodies.

Behind the scenes we drew up resolutions which, for instance, committed the BYPA to support for a military alliance with Russia, and the Youth Parliament to drawing up a Youth Charter of demands for the better social and economic treatment of young people. These resolutions were put forward by representatives of non-political organizations and adopted with acclaim at Conferences. We then pretended to believe that we had gained the support of one or two million organized young people for our policies, although we were well aware that the young people concerned did not even know that the BYPA and the Youth Parliament existed. However, there was a by-product of these activities. It speaks much for the atmosphere of those days and for the glamour that communists had acquired in the eyes of many, particularly middle-class people of intellectual and liberal leanings, that several leaders of other youth movements secretly joined the YCL or the Party. They came from church organizations, League of Nations Union youth groups and other respectable bodies. Thanks to them the committees of the Youth Peace Assembly and the Youth Parliament became two more of the numerous puppet shows dominated by the communists. Most of these conversions were made by one man, John Gollan.

Gollan, who since 1934 had been my own principal mentor, or Mephistopheles, was a remarkable man. He had grown up as one of a family of eight children in an Edinburgh slum tenement. Childhood malnutrition was probably the cause of his emaciated appearance, which was not improved by the yellow teeth and fingers of a chain smoker. He was an unyielding puritan in political matters but he was the supreme example of the communist ability to show a fair face in any company, displaying charm, patience, reasonableness and willingness to listen, and a persuasiveness that proved irresistible to many.

Within the Party he combined fanatical orthodoxy with flexibility and a tolerant attitude to error. We took it for granted that he would one day lead the Party although there were several people before him in precedence, yet he was utterly lacking in the prevailing servility towards the Comintern and Stalin, and showed a prickly independence in his dealings with Moscow, often being sarcastic or scathing about the bureaucracy there. For all that, the Russians evidently knew their man. During this pre-war period he went to the Soviet Union for six weeks' rest. The Russians treated him like a visiting prince. He stayed at a palatial sanatorium and was treated by the best doctors. In Moscow, at a time when Soviet secrecy was almost maniacal, the military conducted him round the headquarters of their anti-aircraft defences. When he came back he told me that German bombers would never get through these defences, and in 1941 this turned out to be true.

He had never ceased to educate himself and was at this time teaching himself mathematics. To further his studies he wrote a book on youth in British industry which was well reviewed in the press. He was particularly interested in military matters. He had discussions with Basil Liddell Hart, the unorthodox military theorist whose doctrines fell on deaf ears in this country but were studied by the German panzer generals.[9]

There were certain other aspects of his chameleon nature of which I only heard years later from Ted, with whom he had been on confidential terms. He had confessed to Ted that he detested Jews, also that until his marriage

---

9   Basil Liddell Hart (1896–1970). Soldier, historian, journalist and well-known military theorist.

he slept with a woman only once a month, doing so as a hygienic act. His partner was a Jewish girl; and to me he was never anything but kind and encouraging. Later, he married an excellent girl, one of the "bourgeois" youth leaders he had won over to communism in the British Youth Peace Assembly. Thanks to her, his way of life was transformed.

I was by now an accomplished apprentice to the chameleon, many-faced mode of life. I was with Gollan when he received a deputation of left-wing writers. He was the soul of concern for their problems and of interest in their work, for which he was full of praise. He listened to them with an air of respect, made a few suggestions modestly and offered them warm thanks before they went off. We listened to them going down the bare wooden staircase. When they had passed the lower landing, he said, "Bastards!" expressing my thoughts as well as his; for he had trained me.[10]

---

10 Echoes of Gollan's views were heard elsewhere in the Party. See Neal Wood, *Communism and the British Intellectuals* (London, 1959), pp.28–9.

Chapter 25

On Sunday morning, 3 September 1939, Fred Heath, our business manager, and I were alone at the office. He had brought a small radio set with him. We listened to Big Ben booming out the time, eleven o'clock, then Neville Chamberlain, the sad old Prime Minister, spoke.

Twelve months before, during the Munich crisis, I had been secretly frightened. I was quite serene now as we listened to Chamberlain: "...and consequently this country is now at war with Germany."

Soon afterwards the air raid sirens began their ululations. I was not surprised, except at the brevity of the interval we had been allowed after the broadcast. I had grown up in the belief that as soon as a new war broke out we would hear the noise of an approaching fleet of bombers swell to thunder as the aircraft flew over London dropping poison gas and killing tens of thousands with their first blow. This was the belief of the authorities, too, who had made preparations to cope with a holocaust. But it was a false alarm. Within a few minutes we heard the steady note of the "All Clear". By this time Fred and I were in the basement room, which was filled with stacks of back numbers. We eyed these as possible protection and hung about, grinning at each other. It all seemed too foolish for words.

Many people must have felt as I did on that morning. We had been through too many crises, warnings and false alarms to be frightened any more. Fred got on with his accounts and I went back to my editing.

As to what the population at large felt about the war I could only guess. I and my comrades had lived for the past three years in a world of manifestoes, huge protest demonstrations and meetings and the shared assumption that war was approaching. We imagined ourselves to be part of a nation that like us expected war and was both aroused and resolved.

I found that this was not so on my first day in the army, ten months later. I was in a hut with eleven other recruits. They were still incredulous at this war which had dropped upon them out of the blue. I asked, "But didn't you know it was coming?" "No!" they all shouted and one of them said, "You could have knocked me down with a feather." Crises had come and gone. People carried on in their own small private worlds, uneasy at times when things looked especially bad but forgetting the crises as things that always blew over. "It was only politics," another of the recruits said, "You don't take any notice." The big black headlines were on the front page of the newspaper but they always turned over to the sports pages at the back.

Next morning, 4 September, before I went to the office I made my way to the Royal Air Force headquarters building in Kingsway. A throng of young men already waited outside to volunteer for flying duties. I joined them. After a time we filed into the lobby of the building. One by one the young men were turned away or were sent on to the RAF recruiting centre in Edgware. I came up to the sergeant who sat behind a small table. He glanced up at my glasses and said, "Run along, son. Don't waste your time."

My attempt to join the RAF was of course a breach of YCL discipline. It was not for me to decide my part in the war effort. I did not tell my colleagues at the office about this episode.

It may not have been out of political fervour that I had tried to volunteer, but because an impulse had surged up to fulfil my boyhood desire to get up into the sky, perhaps to pursue the death in flames of which I had begun to dream when I was ten or eleven years old. I cannot decide if a certain streak in me then should be described as self-destructive or simply romantic.

Certainly, though, after all my political training I was not of one piece. Another self was always there, waiting its time.

I entered into the Second World War, then, in good spirits, the more so since I took it to be absolutely certain that I would not come out of it alive, another belief that hinted at the self-destructive. In any case, everything was simple. Our first job was to fight the Germans. However, I was to learn in a few weeks' time that life for a communist was never as simple as that.

*****

Of all the infamies committed by the Communist Party of Great Britain, its about-turn at the beginning of the Second World War is the most widely known, the most disgraceful and the most ludicrous. On 3 September the Party was engaged, heart and soul, in what it referred to as the fight against Fascism. A month later it was clamorously opposed to the war, on orders from a foreign dictator. My colleagues and I were parties to this.[1]

---

1   On the political cartwheel performed by the CPGB on the correct response to the War, see K. Morgan, *Against Fascism and War: Ruptures and Continuities in British Communist Politics 1935–41* (Manchester, 1989); F. King and G. Matthews (eds), *About Turn: The British Communist Party and the Second World War* (London, 1990); and A. Thorpe, *The British Communist Party and Moscow 1920–43* (Manchester, 2000), pp.256–73.

The process began eleven days before this country went to war, on 23 August 1939, when the Nazi-Soviet Non-Aggression Pact was announced. This was so clearly a green light for Hitler to strike wherever else he wanted to and the photographs of Stalin hobnobbing cordially with the Nazis were so revolting, that some rebellion at least might have been expected from communists. Few members left or protested either then or when, a few weeks later, the Party was turned like a wooden doll on a spindle to oppose the war. Only one of its leaders protested and left the Party. This was George Aitken, who by his act refused to betray the dead of the International Brigade whom he had led in Spain. Only one YCL member rang up on 23 August, audibly in tears, to tell me that he had torn up his membership card. I said, "Good riddance," and put down the receiver.

The signature of the pact by the Soviet leaders was no more than an act of *Realpolitik*. Judgement on such a deal is a waste of breath, since all diplomacy is guided by self-interest, no matter what claims of high principle may sometimes be made for it. In a speech on 10 March 1939 Stalin had given what should have been seen in London and Paris as a plain forewarning, setting out the grounds for a possible negotiation with the Germans, cautioning Britain and France that he was not going to pull other peoples' chestnuts out of the fire and adding the blunt comments that "it would be naive to preach morality" and "politics is politics." British Communist Party leaders had listened to the speech in Moscow. On their return to London they had advised some of their immediate subordinates to think hard about this passage. We in the YCL leadership had several times discussed it. We may have raised eyebrows when we read about the signing of the Non-Aggression Pact that morning but we were not shocked and we came into the office in high good humour, saying, "So that's what the old bugger meant!" – the old bugger being Stalin.

In the first issue of *Challenge* after the declaration of war we continued to beat the anti-fascist drum. Our front page headline, in big letters, was: THIS IS THE WAY TO VICTORY!

Twenty-eight days later we told our young readers that "the war can and must be ended. Negotiations should be opened up without delay for the establishment of peace in Europe."

The members were given to understand that the Party leaders had been divided from the start, had failed to respond to a new situation and were now correcting their error. The truth was, as I and my friends knew, that the about-turn had been carried out in obedience to instructions from the Comintern which my old patron D.F. Springhall had brought back from Moscow. Only three of the national committee had opposed it, Pollitt, J.R.

Campbell and Willie Gallacher.[2] They had done so fiercely, resigning from their posts. Rajani Palme Dutt replaced Pollitt as Party leader.[3] But all three of them recanted and returned to Party duties within seven weeks. It did not take long to brainwash the members. The Party leaders arranged the usual period during which a pretence was maintained that the Party was democratically reconsidering its policy, holding hundreds of meetings at which under the guise of discussion an intense indoctrination was conducted. It was not difficult to convince the rank-and-file.

The view that Britain and France had been trying to push Russia alone into a war with Germany was perfectly tenable and was widely held on the Left. Therefore, the argument ran, Stalin had been forced to protect his country in the only way possible. When the Red Army occupied eastern Poland as part of the bargain with Hitler, we claimed that it had saved eleven million Poles from the Nazis. I printed a front-page article by Alex Massie telling our readers that the German people were on the verge of a revolution; a peace offer from us would encourage them to overthrow Hitler. Why, then, should we be at war?

Of course, twenty months later, on 22 June 1941, when the German army invaded Russia, the British Communist Party, like every other one of the eighty-five communist parties in the world, executed yet another about-turn and declared its passionate support for the war.

It may be asked how I could have described as young people of an excellent sort those members of ours who swallowed all this and stayed with us.

Most Party and YCL members had joined since 1935 as anti-fascists. They were mostly ignorant of more long-range communist intentions, knew little about the Comintern and believed that they belonged to a party which was

---

2   J.R. Campbell (1894–1969). Founder-member of the British Communist Party, in which he became a key figure. With Harry Pollitt he opposed the early Moscow line on the Second World War. Assistant editor of the *Daily Worker* from 1942 and editor between 1949 and 1959. Under constant MI5 surveillance. He appears in virtually all histories of British Communism. See his entry in Matthew and Harrison (eds), *ODNB.*, Vol. 9, pp.841–2. An obituary appeared in The Times, 20 September 1969. See also TNA KV2/1186–1188 on his various activities. He features prominently in Alison Macleod, *The Death of Uncle Joe* (Woodbridge, 1997). Cited later as *Uncle Joe*. On Springhall, Pollitt and Gallacher, see above.

3   Rajani Palme Dutt (1896–1974). Founder-member of the CPGB. Founded and then edited *Labour Monthly* between 1921 and 1974. Prolific author. Comintern worker. Key influence for many years on CPGB policy making. His inflexible Marxism led to his losing influence in the Party in the 1950s and 1960s. See J. Callaghan, *Rajani Palme Dutt: A Study in British Stalinism* (London, 1993).

an independent, purely British body. They forsook their dedication to fight against fascism because the Party worked cleverly upon their anti-fascist sentiments, playing up to their loathing of the Chamberlain government which was still in office and to an underlying pacifism that had been widespread in this country since the last war. They were persuaded that the defeat of fascism could be brought about in a nice, peaceful way. In any case, they had been saturated by our propaganda and convinced by our lies for the last four years. So had we, their leaders, of course. We who had been brought to believe in the justice of the monstrous Moscow Show Trials were ready to believe anything. Many people who have acquired blind faith cannot continue without it, so unfailingly does it enable them to carry on through the chaos and besetting fears of life. Reason is quenched, too, by the capacity of many people to take a joyful pride in being loyal to no matter what, against all the evidence.

One day in 1944 I lay in a grassy dip in Normandy next to a heap of dead German soldiers. Their faces were chalky white, their mouths grinned open and fair hair stuck out in untidy fringes under the rims of helmets, but I reflected that they must have been a fine-looking lot. I was still a communist and, I do not suppose that my thoughts ran any further than this. But later, in retrospect, I saw them as also, very likely, young people of an excellent sort, misled like us by blind faith and like us poisoned by wicked lies.

*****

The winter of 1939 was a grim time. We had to get used to the blackout, dark empty streets at night, and the Phoney War, that period of eerie silence and stalemate at the front in France, punctuated by daily news of ships torpedoed by German submarines. The Press Censors took over the Senate House of London University. Two or three times a week I went to the great, bare amphitheatre, handed in a batch of galley proofs and waited for them to come back stamped and perhaps blue-pencilled. From time to time the news of another sinking at sea boomed over loudspeakers. Once, the Chief Censor sent for me. He was a naval officer of some senior rank. He said, genially, "Showing the tip of the red flag, eh? I just wanted to have a look at you."

We tasted unpopularity for the first time in several years. People seemed apathetic about the war but at our open-air meetings they looked sullenly at us, and when the Soviet Union attacked Finland we faced noisily hostile audiences.

Opposition to a war being a negative and, perforce, purely verbal affair, we concentrated on the positive side of our new policy, which was to defend the rights and living conditions of the people, including the conscript soldiers, against the capitalist class which, we claimed, had landed us all in an unnecessary conflict.

Challenge carried such headlines as UP WITH WAGES, DOWN WITH OVERTIME! and SHAM AIR RAID SHELTERS EXPOSED! We printed letters which spoke for themselves. From a soldier's wife: "I don't know how to manage on my allowance." From the mother of an evacuated child: "They want me to pay towards my child's keep. I can't afford it." From an evacuated mother: "My babies are ill. I can't get them into hospital." From a soldier: "Most of my pay goes on grub." From another, that he had to drive his truck through floods and then had his money docked to pay for damage to the engine. From a boy with TB, that an army medical board had passed him as fit. Youngsters wrote to tell us that they had been thrown out of work by the war. Some of them explained that they had been refused relief. A group of soldiers who had been served with bad food left it on the table and walked out of the dining hall. From a factory, a letter about a boy of sixteen who was working fifty-one hours a week for twelve shillings, of which he had to spend six shillings on fares. Another factory letter was about a boy of fourteen whose arm had been torn off in a machine which had no guard. Girl cleaning-workers had been told by their boss that they were not allowed to strike because there was a war on. We told them that they had a right to strike and not to be afraid to do so.

All this was a sort of sniping or harassment from the flanks against the war. It was only a preliminary policy. The Comintern had labelled the war as imperialist. The policy of communists towards an imperialist war had been laid down by Lenin in November 1914 and was still binding upon us, sacred, not a single one of its words to be changed. The crucial words were "revolutionary defeatism," which would, in Lenin's own phrase, eventually "turn the imperialist war into a civil war."

We did not talk of such dangerous things; it would have been an invitation to the government to crush us. A few of us at the headquarters talked guardedly of "turning" the war — even among ourselves we dared not use more than this one code word: and perhaps in the country some old Party hands speculated among themselves as to whether the Leninist policy now operated. We were not ready, in fact, to face up to the logic (in Party terms) of our opposition to the war. One prominent comrade did scribble a sheaf of parodies which he wanted to circulate as "Songs for Soldiers", I remember one, to the tune of "Run, Rabbit, Run":

> *Run, Tommy, run, Tommy, run, run, run,*
> *Don't show the Germans your gun, gun, gun.*
> *Live and laugh,*
> *Be like the General Staff,*
> *And run, Tommy, run, Tommy, run, run, run.*

This was revolutionary defeatism, but the song book was never published. The author was probably told to put a match to it.

We know now, from documentary evidence, that when Stalin had ordered the Comintern leader Dimitrov to enforce the policy of opposition to an imperialist war, he, Stalin, had insisted that for the time being communists must nowhere in the world go beyond the preliminary stage. Springhall had passed on this instruction when he arrived in London.

For all our self-imposed restraint, we waited in the first days of 1940 for the police raids that would announce a government attack upon the Party and YCL. The state papers for that time are now open and reveal that after the start of the war the Cabinet was resolved to reduce the influence of both the Fascists and the CPGB. Many leaders and activists of the British Union of Fascists were arrested during spring 1940 and interned on the Isle of Man.[4] The *Daily Worker* was eventually banned in January 1941, but otherwise the government took no measures against the communists beyond surveillance.[5]

Opposite our building was the showroom of a funeral arson, with his range of tombstones on display. From early 1940, Scotland Yard detectives took over the showroom and crouched behind the tombstones watching our front entrance. Sometimes we stood in the street and contemplated this comic sight. Others followed us when we went to and fro. I was told of ways to give them the slip by a colleague who had worked in foreign countries and had no doubt been trained in such matters but I never bothered to carry out the prescribed manoeuvres, since there was nothing secret about my daily round.

---

4   On internment during the Second World War, see A, W.B. Simpson. *In the Highest Degree Odious. Detention without trial in wartime Britain* (Oxford, 1992)

5   For discussion of the government's decision not to ban the CPGB, but to closely monitor its activities, see Kevin Morgan, 'Within and beyond the law? British communist history and the archives of state surveillance', Political Extremism and Radicalism in the Twentieth Century, Cengage Learning (EMEA) Ltd, 2018: www.gale.com/binaries/content/assets/gale-us-en/primary-sources/intl-gps/intl-gps-essays/full-ghn-contextual-essays/gps_essay_plex_morgan1_website.pdf (accessed 26 January 2022).

Throughout 1940 the Party, which seemed to know of the government's secret discussions about suppressing the communists, perhaps from some informant in the higher civil service, continued to insist that the attack was still pending and undertook a series of counter-measures.

Jimmy Shields, a quiet man of whose responsibilities I had known nothing, although he had an office at 16, King Street, was in charge of these measures. In 1937–38, Shields had worked in Moscow as a member of the Comintern's Cadre Department. In the British Communist Party, he led the Control Commission, effectively its security section. He was thin and grey, with a skull-like face which was frequently softened by a ghost of humour. He had joined the British Communist Party in 1921, within a year of its foundation, and had worked for the Comintern all over the world, having for a time been General Secretary of the South African Communist Party.[6]

Shield's first concern was to preserve the Party's top officials from arrest. It was decided that the YCL leadership should be included. Gollan had left us to work at Party headquarters. That left a triumvirate in charge of the YCL – Mick Bennett, Ted Willis and me – who were to go underground. Shields seemed to be an expert at his work, judging by the arrangements he made for me. (I and my two YCL colleagues did not confide in each other, so I shall write here only of plans made for me.)

A cache of money was put away for my use and a hideout was found. It was in a big psychiatric hospital in South London. When the Party gave me the word I was at once to go into the hospital as the private patient of a senior consultant who was an undercover Party member. I would have a room to myself, with a telephone. I would be able to go out and to receive visitors. In any case, a courier would keep me in touch with the outside world. A girl was to do this job. I met her in the evenings in Regent's Park to train her for her duties while we walked round the lake like a courting couple. The Party leaders at King Street were put on a rota system, only one at a time going into the office while the others worked from their hideouts. We arranged to do the same but were lax about it.

The YCL was determined to maintain groups in certain of the biggest defence factories in the country. We picked a number of comrades whom

---

6   For Shields' work in Moscow, see Peter Huber, "The Cadre Department, the OMS and the 'Dimitrov' and 'Manuilsky' Secretariats during the phase of the *Terror*," in Mikhail Narinsky and Jurgen Rojahn, eds., *Centre and Periphery: The History of the Comintern in the Light of New Documents* (Amsterdam: International Institute of Social History, 1996), p.148. See also 'Jimmy Shields', *Encyclopedia of Communist Biographies* https://grahamstevenson.me.uk/2009/07/31/jimmy-shields/ (accessed 26 March 2020).

we judged not to be known to the police and sent them to get jobs in these factories. Their instructions were to lie low, and not to make themselves known to the YCL-ers already in place. If our groups were wiped out these comrades would start new ones.

Challenge was to be printed illegally, if it became necessary, in a miniature format. A small platen printing press was located by Shields' people. It was the property of an unemployed Party member, a Jewish tailor who lived in a side street in Spitalfields and who had agreed to give it up. I went to collect it, in a tiny Austin car driven by a comrade.

The tailor's home was not ideally situated for a supposedly secret mission. The day was fine and a small army of women sat in the street on home-made wooden benches as my grandmother had done. Across the way were tenements with crowded balconies from which mothers screamed down to their children, swarms of whom played in the courtyard and in the street, setting up a deafening noise. When we pulled up outside the tailor's house they swarmed around the car. My comrade and I inspected the printing machine in a back scullery, then started to manhandle it along a narrow passage to the street. While we were doing this the owner's wife came down a staircase and paused to watch us. She did not speak to us but her eyes burned with fury. Her husband followed us and she followed him, muttering to him. I was at the back end of the machine and caught enough of her complaints to gather that we were taking away her dowry. We got out to the pavement and became the object of interest to the neighbouring women at their front doors as well as to those on the balconies opposite, while the horde of children was still assembled round the car. Everyone watched and commented while we worked the machine one way and the other in a series of attempts to get it aboard. We drove off at last. There was a crisis in Clerkenwell, where the weight of the machine on the back axle brought the little car to a stop, but we were able to get under way again and in time we reached our destination. This was a house in a commuter village in Hertfordshire. The owner was an undercover Party member, a scientist. We drove into a lean-to garage, closed the doors so that we were unobserved, unloaded the machine and laboured to get it up staircases to the top of the house, eventually installing it on the rafters in a loft that was hidden behind panelling.

So far from feeling a furtive, potential outlaw, I was filled with confidence and pride at these activities. I trusted the Party, which always knew what to do and seemed to have its eyes and ears everywhere. I was imbued with the feeling that I belonged to a fellowship of courageous and unselfish people in all walks of life on whom (I left out of account the tailor's angry wife) I could always rely.

We had chosen the location for the press because it was near to Watford, which was a big centre of the printing industry. I met a group of Party printers there, splendid fellows, who promised to set up type for me and who took me along the Grand Union Canal to see the great paper mills there, our comrades in which, they promised me, would easily be able to smuggle out stocks of paper if I needed them. In London I conferred with another group of Party printing workers who also promised to set type for me, compositors employed by the Labour *Daily Herald*. There was a vigorous Printers' Anti-Fascist Movement and the Party had strong groups among the printing staffs of all the big newspapers, a fine, intelligent lot. A wholesale stationer got a stock of suitable paper for us, which we stored in a cellar, already cut to size. For transport we relied on Charlie, a freelance lorry driver who, into the bargain, suffered from some invisible disability that made him unfit for military service. I expected perilous times to come, but I wanted to be put to the test, and I felt strengthened by the support of all this good company, a real cross-section, it seemed, of the better sort.

There is a postscript to all this. A year later I came on leave from the army and learned that the printing press was back with the tailor, his wife having made his life a misery until we returned it. We could not in any case have used it because a squad of soldiers had been billeted upon the scientist, taking up their quarters in the attic next to the secret loft. Our stack of printing paper had been ruined by damp. Charlie, the driver, had been put out of business by petrol rationing, had sold his truck and was working in a defence factory.

*****

Summers before disasters are always described in clichés as golden. The summer of 1940 really was golden. The sunlight gilded every day, the parks were full of strollers, picnickers and tennis players. Multitudes were busy in their gardens. Everyone was summery, casual and uncaring. On 10 May the German army attacked in the Low Countries and within days the entire allied front had collapsed. The sun continued to blaze, the parks were still full, the gardeners still busy, radio sets gave out terrifying news through the open windows of summertime and nobody appeared to be taking any notice. Everyone seemed to go on being as summery, casual and uncaring as before.

I had travelled up north on one of those strange days, to see a printer in a small town in Lincolnshire. Shields had passed his name to me. My errand was to arrange for the printer to do a job for us, producing some harmless-looking catalogue covers which could one day be used to conceal political pamphlets. Things had happened during the day which had made me suspicious. The printer had called in a friend as if, I thought, he wanted a witness. The friend had taken me home, supplied me with sandwiches and newspapers, and then had disappeared for an hour without explanation. Had he been to the police? I had carried on, telling myself that Shields knew what he was doing and that I must trust his instructions. I caught a train back to London and never heard any more of the affair.

On the journey home that evening I was stranded on a deserted railway platform at Retford, a dismal-looking town in Nottinghamshire, waiting for a train to London. It was a brilliant evening. I was reflecting on the chances that I would have to take when the Party really was illegal. I listened to a BBC radio news bulletin through the open window of the stationmaster's office. In the same calm neutral manner as if he was giving the day's cricket score or the shipping forecasts, the news-reader announced that Arras had fallen to the Germans, whose vanguards were continuing towards Paris. I listened idly; it was too incredible to make an impression. It came into my mind, as I strolled up and down the platform, that all this was happening in that same northern plain of France through which I had walked in 1936, stealing a day or two on my way to a conference in Paris. When the Germans reached Calais they would be only twenty-one miles from England. I took it for granted that they would invade us and occupy the country.

It then occurred to me, only randomly, that I was a Jew. I would be underground, of course, and I would work against the Germans; I took this for granted in spite of the neutralist stance of the Party. My imagination did not go any farther and I did not worry. I did wonder what would become of my family. I would not be able to do anything for them. I thought of all this with detachment until my mind went back to my own immediate tasks.

Several days after my return to London I stood on a bridge and looked down at a train creeping into one of the city's big railway stations. Soldiers crowded at the windows. They were bare-headed, with tousled hair and tanned faces. Some appeared to be half-dressed. A few were bandaged. I realised that I was looking at men who had been saved from the beaches at Dunkirk. I felt obscurely stirred, with a touch of distress. I am sure that this was the other self in me awakened again. My eyes did not see them as victims of an imperialist war; instead I was aware of the wish that I could have been one of them. There was something going on around me that I did not want to be left out of any more.

While all this was happening I fell in love. I mention this because it added to the dream-like character that the time has since assumed for me. It was all part of a fantastic film entitled "Summer, 1940". I was given the name and telephone number of one of our girls who was doing excellent work for us in a big electrical factory in North London. I met her one evening to get a story for the paper. She had a strong body and a white face that was set off by a thick mass of black hair. She had just finished a long shift and looked tired – sulky, I thought, and ugly.

I hardly slept that night and telephoned her early next morning to catch her before she left for the factory. After that I had to contrive intervals in the rush of my own work in order to meet her. In what were, in fact, my last four weeks as a civilian, Nelly and I were only able to see each other a few times, meeting late in the evening.

*****

My life at this time ran in two streams. Beneath my fanatical belief which was beyond question and despite the elation, happiness and optimism that I felt, all deepened by pride in the responsibilities which the Party had entrusted to me, another stream ran underground, as it were, one of depression. This I refused to acknowledge but it rose up in me sometimes at two o'clock in the morning when I was alone at my desk in an empty building or when I was walking home through dark silent streets.

My YCL colleagues Mick Bennett and Ted Willis were much older than I was, the younger of them, Ted, by four years. I saw little of them outside work and had no time to see anyone else except on matters of duty, Nelly being the exception. They were married men with homes of their own; both, too, even busier than I was and often absent from London. They were kind to me, occasionally asking me home to supper or to go out with them and their wives for a day's walk in the country, but I felt more and more that to them I was still a schoolboy for all my twenty-two years. When I uttered some naive remark, which happened not infrequently, I thought I saw them exchanging smiles. I felt in some way excluded from full comradeship; in short I was, without realising it, lonely.

*****

One more episode completes the tale of that summer.

One morning, in the mid-June 1940, a couple of weeks after the last soldiers had been brought back from Dunkirk, I answered the telephone and heard the polite voice of a middle-class young man informing me that he was an officer of the Special Branch speaking from New Scotland Yard. He wondered if I would be kind enough to give him a little of my time.

We made an appointment. I told my colleagues that he was coming and when he arrived I left the door of my room wide open. It was so easy for a seed of suspicion to be planted, and to germinate at some future date.

He was a neatly-dressed young man. He thanked me for seeing him. He said that he knew how busy I was. He came to the point and asked me if I could explain why I had not yet been called up for military service.

I was nonplussed by this. I had registered a year ago. After the medical examination (which had taken place in Islington on 8 December 1939), I had been classed as Grade Three (Vision). I said that perhaps they didn't want me because I wore glasses. He said he shouldn't think that was the case.

I cannot remember how much we knew at that time about the activities of MI5. It was probably a shot in the dark when I suggested that perhaps this was a case of the left hand not knowing what the right hand was doing. He considered this for a few moments, then he stood up, thanked me and left.

A week or two later I arrived home one night and saw a small buff envelope propped up on the mantelpiece, I knew what it was and felt a great drench of pleasure.

I went to the office next morning in a triumphant mood to tell my two colleagues, Ted and Mick, that I had my call-up notice for the army. Their call-up notices, also for the army, arrived that day. They were both plainly as pleased as I was. Since we were of different ages and had registered at different times, it was hard to believe that this simultaneous call to the colours was a coincidence. I assumed that the Special Branch man had been our benefactor.

On 25 July 1940 I enlisted at Islington in the British Army. At the YCL we appointed our successors, leaving its affairs in good order. On the evening before my departure I went with Mick Bennett to say some goodbyes. In accordance with the Party's security measures, the Party leader Palme Dutt was at his hide-out, a flat above a butcher's shop in Bloomsbury. Rajani Palme Dutt was the son of an Indian father and a Swedish mother, his origins privileged and distinguished (Perse School and a Classical First at Balliol College, Oxford). The Party rank-and-file venerated him as the intellectual giant of the Political Bureau but we, like his colleagues in the PB, treated "old Rajani" as a bit of a joke for his jargon-ridden verbosity both in speech and print. He sat in the kitchen looking glum and gave us as cheerful a send-off as a professional mourner shaking hands with the relatives after a funeral.

We went on to 16, King Street, where Harry Pollitt chatted and wished us luck. Then we went upstairs to have a final talk with Robert Robson, who looked after military matters for the Party.[7] Robbie was a quiet, amiable man who had fought at Passchendaele. I felt a good deal of affection for him. He told us to forget politics for six months and to concentrate on becoming good soldiers. He came out onto the landing and as we started down the stairs called after us, "Enjoy yourselves!"

I set out the next morning as eagerly as a boy released from school for the long summer holidays. I was still full of resolve, looking forward to the army as a new field of work, the most challenging yet, but this did not account for the feeling of sheer escape that buoyed me up, escape perhaps from the ghost of depression that had been haunting me, or even, unknown to me, from the life that I had been leading.

---

7   Robert William Robson, 'Robbie.' Founder-member of the British Communist Party. Contributor to *Labour Monthly*. Recruiter for the Spanish Civil War. The Party contact for members engaged on military service in the Second World War. Of interest to MI5. See TNA KV/2/1176–1179.

PART THREE:
Days of Youth and Blood

Chapter 26

Because I wore glasses I had been called up into the Pioneer Corps. This had been a disappointment. I wanted to be an infantryman. I hoped that I would be able to do something about it. In the meantime I enjoyed my first holiday since my schooldays.

The training centre was in a requisitioned holiday camp on the cliffs at Westward Ho in Devon. I was there for three weeks. The summer weather was resplendent. We seem in memory to have passed our days sunbathing on the grass under an incandescent sky, looking down at a sea that was a sparkling sheet of pale blue; but these idyllic hours were in reality only intervals interrupted by innumerable calls to get on parade. An unready country was scrambling to kit out a huge new army and all the things that were to make us look like soldiers were doled out to us in bits and pieces. On other parades we had our genitals examined by doctors, who lifted the parts concerned daintily with the ends of their swagger sticks, we were inoculated and we were lectured on a diversity of subjects.

When we started to train, the theme of most of our drills was saluting. We marched up and down like stiff, clockwork toys, saluting to the front, to the right and to the left; saluting obviously being the first and by far the principal duty of a soldier. We also learned to form up in squads, to dismiss ceremoniously, to turn, about-turn and wheel. We did not see a rifle for two weeks. At last a group of us sat on the grass around a Regular Army corporal who showed us a Lee-Enfield rifle, named the parts for us and passed it round for each of us to hold.

I suppose some recruits feel uprooted or lost for a time. It all seemed a natural continuation of life for me, and from the general atmosphere of young male jollity that prevailed I assumed that most of the others felt the same. I was in a holiday campers' chalet with eleven other men. From the first night they applied themselves with passion to the task of getting a high polish on their boots. This called for a great deal of work. First the thick grease of storage had to be scraped off the boots, then the residue of grease had to be worked out of the leather, this being done painstakingly with the bone handles of toothbrushes. Nobody taught us how to do this. It was lore

Figure 24 "Because I wore glasses I had been called up into the Pioneer Corps." Baron as a fresh recruit to 172 Company (middle row, second from right).

handed down by fathers who had been soldiers in the Great War. Then we went on for night after night brushing the boots, not ordered by anyone to do so, while we brought the toecaps to a liquid gloss.

I must say more about this enthusiasm. It may be hard for the modern reader to understand it but it was of the time. Soon afterwards, when we had been formed into a company, we had to mount daily guards over our new quarters. Guard-mounting was performed with ceremony, each barrack-room taking over the duty for twenty-four hours. The smartest guard each week was given an award. The award was an officer's swagger stick, to be retained until lost to another barrack-room. The men competed fanatically for this prize. Soldiers about to parade for guard duty were dressed, tidied, brushed and critically inspected by their comrades who then, in case the ground might be wet or dusty, carried them in chairlifts and set them down carefully on the parade square. They enjoyed drill and when they were allowed out they paraded the streets with a swagger. None of this, of course, had anything to do with zeal for the war.

Later, when experience had taught me to think about all this, I saw how conceited men are, especially young men, how like children they are in wanting to dress up, look showy and adorn themselves with tribal clothing and badges. They want to show off to the girls but there is also, I am sure, an instinct for unison in most men, so that they are willing to be led anywhere, unthinking, by nothing more than the steady tap of a drum.

The one thing that the men did reject with a high contempt was the army food. Later in the war the army supplied well-cooked and nutritious food, having put a large proportion of the British catering profession into uniform to do the job, but in 1940 there was only improvisation, with patches of chaos. The thieving cook was a traditional figure in the British army. Many a cookhouse was run by a twentieth-century Bardolph who conducted a lucrative business on the side, selling off the soldiers' food to civilians. Most of his staff might well be shirkers who had never boiled an egg but wanted a soft job and no parades. On the first night at the holiday camp an orderly brought a large bucket into the chalet. It was full of stew left over from the day. The recruits sniffed at it and told him to take his pig-swill away. Before he did so I filled my mess-tins with stew which I ate heartily. I was following the advice given to me a week before by a YCL comrade or leave from the Fusiliers. He said, "Eat everything. Shut your eyes and think of something else but get it down you. It'll keep you going." The next morning in the dining-hall I filed past a succession of trestle tables and was given a bowl of porridge, then a kipper which was dropped in the porridge, then a spoonful of jam dropped on to the kipper, then two thick slices of bread with sooty fingerprints on them, a lump of butter and a mug of tea. I got all this down me and continued on the same principle as long as I was in the army.

When I arrived at the camp I was apprehensive about something quite different, the business of using a common latrine. It had always made me sick to go into a WC too soon after someone else. I feared that the latrines would be too much for me. In the event there was no problem. The latrines were pervaded by no smell except that of chloride of lime. They had comfortable seats made by the regimental carpenters and they were always scrubbed white. They were resorts of sociability in which soldiers sat and communed like the patricians of ancient Rome.

*****

On my third or fourth day in the army I tackled the business of getting into the infantry. I reported sick on some pretext and was sent to Bideford to see an army doctor. When my turn came to see him I told him that there had been a mistake in my medical grading. I wanted to be upgraded to A1. He said, "That's a simple matter," took my soldier's service book, and made an entry on the medical record page, "Re-examined. A1"

In the street afterwards I came face-to-face with a huge poster. It had a striking border of red, white and blue and was headed by the word FRANCAIS! in large letters. It suited my triumphant mood to stand there and read aloud to myself de Gaulle's proclamation of 18 June 1940 summoning the French to fight on, enjoying the feel of the French words in my mouth.[1] It could not have occurred to me, at least for these few moments, that my French comrades were against fighting on, and that I, too, was supposed to be against the war. As soon as I was back in camp I wrote out an application to be transferred to the infantry and handed it in at the office. In honour of my birthplace I asked to go to the Royal Berkshire Regiment.

I looked upon it as a simple matter of duty to make this application; duty to the Party. All sorts of people belonged to the Party and communists in the army behaved in different ways according to their characters. But among those of the trained and dedicated inner core it was taken for granted that a Party man must equip himself to become a future leader of masses, and that included the mass of soldiers. I wanted to get used to battle and to best my courage under fire. One day, I thought, we would need the support of the fighting soldiers, the best of them, and they would only listen to and follow those whom they respected as brave men and capable military leaders.[2]

*****

Our company, just formed, arrived at Southampton during a daylight air raid. We split into single files, one on each side of the street, and made our way through the town amid a din of gunfire and exploding bombs. One formation after another of Heinkels moved steadily across a blue sky that had not a cloud in it. They were low enough for me to recognise them by

---

1   De Gaulle is Charles de Gaulle (1890–1970). French military officer. Leader of the French government-in-exile in London. Later President of the French Republic (1959–1969). See J. Jackson, *A Certain Idea of France. The Life of Charles de Gaulle* (London, 2018).

2   See Hugh Purcell's *The Last English Revolutionary. Tom Wintringham 1898–1949* (Stroud, 2004), for Wintringham's views on the potentially important role of a citizens' army in securing and defending social change.

their plexiglass fronts and the round tips of their wings, which seemed transparent. Clusters of gleaming dots higher up were British fighters, each at the head of a vapour trail. In one part of the sky 'planes fought like a swarm of gnats and I saw a parachute going down.

These raids continued day and night while we were in Southampton. I counted nineteen in one period of twenty-four hours. We were quartered in a school building near to the power station. The concrete playground was our barrack square. About eight hundred yards beyond the playground wall, the power station stood in an area of waste land.

We now had drill parades and weapon training all day long and took pride in our progress. While we marched and counter-marched, or threw dummy grenades, German 'planes came again and again to attack the power station. We watched the bombs exploding on the waste ground, feeling no more than a detached wonderment at so many near misses. Our training was never interrupted. We slept at nights in two-decker bunk beds and during the regular night raids, which were longer and much heavier than those by day, we stayed in our beds listening to the noise. I took note of my own reaction to the raids; they did not disturb my serenity and I felt reassured about myself.

One night a bomb blew off a top corner of our school, laying open an unused part of the upper floor. Nobody was hurt but an old corporal who had been in the Great War started to howl and thrash about. He was carried to the guardroom where the off-duty sentries held him down until after the All Clear when he fell into an exhausted sleep. He was taken away next day.

I enjoyed sentry duty at night during the raids. I have published a short story about it.[3] There was a spacious sentry-box at the gates which was protected by banked sandbags. Stacked in it, to keep them away from the building, were crates of petrol bottles, known as Molotov cocktails, which we were supposed to throw at the German tanks when they arrived. During off-duty spells we liked to stay there, where we were not disturbed by the comings and goings of the guardroom; we stretched out on top of the crates and slept soundly through the uproar of explosions.

Items of kit continued to arrive piecemeal. We jemmied open long crates and took out our rifles, heavy P14's, packed in grease since 1918. Later we exchanged these for Lee-Enfields. These were small and light and to us they looked beautiful.

---

3   Baron's essay on sentry duty appears as: "The Sentry," in Alexander Baron, *The Human Kind* (London, 2011 ed.), pp.11–15.

Figure 25 "Later we exchanged these for Lee-Enfields. These were small and light and to us they looked beautiful." Baron cleaning his rife during training.

We all took it for granted, with the utmost complacency, that the Germans were soon going to invade Britain. I can only imagine (since I cannot remember) that our minds did not run to considering what would then happen. Certainly we could not have imagined that we would beat them off, for amount of muddle in an army still sorting itself out was phenomenal. Fred Karno's Army, the name of a comic stage troupe of the past, was what we called it.

We were sent to dig slit trenches along a ridge that ran inland of the town. We looked down into a valley in which the Saunders-Roe aircraft factory stood. One day a neat formation of Heinkels passed over our heads. Bombs fell away as it continued sedately over the factory, which disappeared in great clouds of smoke. Our men shouted with something near to approval as if they had seen a goal scored. Early in September – I think it was on the 7th – there took place a stand-to on the South Coast which was afterwards referred to as the Great Invasion Scare. I was in a party told off to defend a road junction. We lay in a ditch with rifles for which we had been given ten bullets each. We also had a beer crate with a dozen Molotov cocktails in it. Inevitably one of the men had a pack of cards and we played pontoon all day.

*****

Most of the men in the company were Londoners and there were seven or eight other Jews in it. These were all of the sort that my grandfathers, the cobbler and the mechanic, used to call *grobbe yidden*, coarse Jews. One of them was a barber, another was a cabbie and the rest were probably street hucksters of one sort or another. On Saturday mornings, according to army custom, there was always a very smart company parade, often gruelling, with the sergeant-major in charge. Saturday is the Jewish Sabbath. The cabbie accosted me and asked if I would join in a request for the Jews to have Saturday morning off to go to synagogue. I refused.

The company paraded on Saturday morning. As soon as we were all aligned in perfect ranks, the sergeant-major commanded silence, waited till it was absolute, then announced, "I have a request from the Israelites among us to hold their own church parade — Very well — " Then in a bark of command, "One Israelite — right — marker!"

When soldiers fall in, one man is called forward first to act as a human post on which they align themselves. He is the marker. Silence returned. No-one moved. The sergeant-major looked up and down the ranks in what I thought was a significant way, then gave vent, in a prolonged and rising scream, to the cry, "Right — markah-ah!" Still none of the Jews moved. I marched out of the ranks in the prescribed ceremonious manner, swinging my arms stiffly to shoulder height, fists lightly clenched, and came to a halt in front of the sergeant-major with the skip-and-jump rat-rat of my boots that was required. I was now stiffly at attention. He eyed me for a moment, then gave the command, "Fall in, the Israelites!"

The Jews fell in. He inspected us all for neatness, stopped in front of me and said, "You—. Senior soldier—. March them off!"

I filled my lungs and enjoyed a moment I had waited for, the giving of my first order. I discovered that I had an NCO's voice, as I called the series of commands that brought the party to attention, turned them to the left and marched them off in front of the silent company. As we went out through the gates the sentry, a friend of mine, stiffened up and smartly swung his free hand to smack the butt of his rifle in salute. We marched up the street. From the rear I called the step and gave the customary injunctions, "Eyes to your front, don't look at the girls, they'll look at you, swing your arms, come on, let's have bags of swank," and so on. We turned into the main street. The cabbie turned his head and informed all that the caff was just ahead on our right. I summoned up a sergeant-major's scream, "Eyes to your front! Quiet in the ranks or I'll march you back. Left, right, left, right." Only a handful of old men were present at the service when we filed into the synagogue. They looked at us in surprise. The other Jews were given prayer shawls and joined in the service. I sat alone in a row of empty pews at the back.

I heard nothing about my transfer. I put the delay down to the general muddle. I treated the first few months as a holiday, as Robson had advised, but I learned a good deal about the men during this time and knew the odd soldier here and there who declared himself to be a bit of a Red, or spoke about past fights with the Fascists or referred to his trade union. In time I enlisted some of them, one in each barrack room, to sell *Challenge* every week. From time to time we took collections among the men, always for causes to which no exception could be taken, for example, to help disabled veterans of the International Brigade and later on for Mrs. Churchill's Aid Russia Fund.

I got out an occasional issue of a company magazine on an office duplicating machine, the usual jokey affair, with news, cartoons and some mildly satirical verse about such things as the stinginess of our coal ration in the winter. For a short time, for the fun of it, I devised a more outspoken newspaper which consisted of items stuck to the roller blind of a window. Men came into the room and pulled the blind down to read, then let it roll up again on its spring. An Orderly Officer inspected the room every day but he did not touch the blind, being only on the lookout for dirty window-panes. The Army Council had authorized the setting up of Men's Messing Committees as a channel for complaints about the food. My *Challenge* sellers and I held a series of election meetings in the barrack-rooms and six of us constituted the resulting committee. We tried to strike only a sober note and always to make positive suggestions and we got some improvements made.

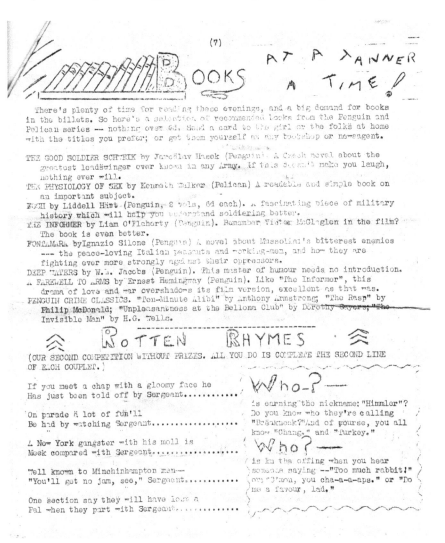

Figure 26 "I got out an occasional issue of a company magazine on an office duplicating machine, the usual jokey affair." The Books and Poetry sections of "Pioneer Parade. The Monthly Paper of 172 Company, Pioneer Corps," Volume 1, No. 2, Editor J.A. Bernstein.

The matter of revolutionary politics was not on the agenda and it never came up. Nor was there any hint of defeatism in our activities. I was as much heartened as any of the soldiers by British victories in the North African desert and as depressed by set-backs. I guess that this was true of most communist soldiers. They were young men who had wanted for years to get to grips with the Nazis and in the army they were preparing to do this. Thus, certainly in my case, the army gradually replaced the Party as the object of loyalty.

Yet it was to take seven years to bring me to a final break with communism. In *Gulliver's Travels* the sleeping Gulliver is tied down by the Lilliputians with hundreds of threads which together are so strong that he can only slowly free himself. During the coming years my threads were to snap one by one, sometimes for trivial reasons. One incident at this time perhaps snapped a thread. We were billeted in the bare rooms of a rather grand house, with fine ceilings and panelling. A wag in my room remarked that even the mice here had mink coats. It was, however, cold and damp in the winter. I sent a humorous piece about it to *Challenge*. I was furious a week or two later when I saw that the new editor had rewritten it and invented some additions to turn it into a bitter attack on the authorities. When I next met him I went at him angrily, telling him that he had saddled me with a lot of lies. He heard me out in a puzzled silence. He protested that he had only touched it up a bit, to give it an agitational edge. He might well have asked, what were a few lies between comrades? I am not suggesting that my fanatical faith was in the least impaired by such an incident; but I believe that from now on, unnoticed by me, the threads were being snapped one by one by such episodes.

I had time for reading during these months and applied myself to various works of Marxist theory. Among them was Engels's *The Origin of the Family* which had just for the first time come out in an English translation.[4] I was struck by what this book had to say about the position of women in society. I had formed a generally high opinion of the men around me; perhaps the soldiers and the civilians whom I met in different countries during the war

---

4   Friedrich Engels (1820–1895). Communist, businessman, journalist and social scientist. He helped to fund Marx's activities. Engels wrote *Die Lage der arbeiten Klasse in England* (Leipzig, 1845). It appeared in England as *The Condition of the Working Class in England in 1844* (London, 1891). With Marx he wrote the call to arms in the shape of the Communist Manifesto [*Manifest der Kommunistischen Partei*] which first appeared in 1848. The first English translation was printed in 1850. Engels's book The Origin of the Family. *Private Property and the State* came out in 1884.

were more congenial to me than the "people of a new type" among whom I had felt so isolated during my last year with the Party. But my juvenile and puritan soul was grieved at the to-me insulting way in which they spoke about women. I bought a school exercise book and wrote by hand a pamphlet on the Woman Question. I started by asking if it was right to refer to a woman as a piece of cunt. Men who had read it accosted me to talk about it. Some came into my room to have an argument; all these discussions were serious.

This was the first piece of independent writing that I did in the army.[5] Although I regarded it as a political exercise it may have indicated the first slight melting of the lump of fanatical conformity that my brain had become. Beside the Marxist works I read all the military literature that I could get hold of, from army training manuals to works on strategy in which I pored over the campaigns of Belisarius and Stonewall Jackson's exploits in the Shenandoah Valley.[6] The picture of a Pioneer private solemnly engaged in such studies may have been as comic as in retrospect it now appears; but I knew that one of the leaders of the Spanish YCL, a student comrade, had risen to become a corps commander in the Spanish Civil War, and had I been less hidebound I might have thought of that other one, a bespectacled Jew like me, who had led armies to victory, Leon Trotsky.

I read, but I did not yet make use of my relative liberty to read freely. The hunger to do so was still too securely buried. The only novel that I read in my first year in the army was *David Copperfield*. Like my homily, this was borrowed by a number of the men. Later, I was to write another short story about the discussions that this book provoked.[7]

Late in 1941 I read *War and Peace*, in an ancient three-volume edition. This probably seemed permissible because the Soviet Union had come into the war. After that I read every novel or book of stories that I could lay my hands on.

*****

---

5   Soon after he entered the Army Baron could not resist his journalistic itch. See *Pioneer Parade*, Vol. 1, December 1940, Vol. 2, January 1941, Vol. 3, February 1941, and Vol. 4, March–April 1941, for a cyclostyled publication he edited. See Figure 26, p.235.

6   Belisarius (500–565AD). Byzantine general involved in Emperor Justinian's plan to reconquer the former Western Empire. Stonewall Jackson (1824–1863). Confederate General from Virginia. Died of wounds during the American Civil War.

7   Baron's fictional account of the discussion among his army colleagues of Dickens's *David Copperfield* appears in Alexander Baron, "Copperfield and the 'Erbs," in his *The Human Kind* (London, 2011) pp.16–19.

I was by now well known to the officers. The company commander, an old Regular, was nonplussed by me. Sometimes for instance when I was giving him a critical report on the dirty state of the cookhouse (the Messing Committee had conducted a solemn inspection, ushered by an officer), I could see a mixture of outrage and bewilderment in his expression but he remained polite. The Officers' Mess waiters were among my supporters and told me that he argued about me with his second-in-command, Captain Morden, who maintained that I was a keen soldier and that the best course was to give me a lance-corporal's stripe. On one occasion the captain spoke a few encouraging words to me, hinting at this and advising me to keep my nose clean.

From friendly sergeants I learned that the sergeant-major had been denouncing me as a Red and a fifth-columnist and saying that he would settle my hash. For four days running he put me on fatigue duty cleaning out the cook-house sumps. This was the filthiest job in our daily round. Even defaulters were supposed only to get it once. At the end of a day I had to scrub myself and my clothes to get rid of the stinking sludge. I thought it proper to do the job without complaining. But on the fourth morning my sergeant, plainly in a fury, told me to ignore the order. He ran across to the office. I saw him at the door talking to Captain Morden. I never had to do the job again.

A new sergeant joined the company. He was a supernumerary, apparently with no fixed duties. This time it was the quartermaster sergeant who warned me that the newcomer was from the Field Security Police. He had been sent to keep an eye on me. At my suggestion, my *Challenge* sellers passed the news round the company. Wherever the new sergeant went after that he was accosted by soldiers who invited him to put their names down as Reds and who shouted rudely after him when he continued on his way. He soon left us.

I could have learned more about this surveillance. One day the company commander went out and left the key of his metal Secrets Box in the pocket of a discarded tunic. His batman, or servant, took my security file from the box and brought it to my barrack room. I thanked him for bringing it but I refused to open it, calling on all the men present to be witnesses, and told him to put it back in the box at once.

All through these months London was enduring the Blitz. Thousands were killed. A large part of the East End was laid waste. A telegram came for a boy in my room. All his family were dead. A few days after this I was called to the Orderly Room. Captain Morden told me that the police had telephoned from London. Our house had been hit. My family were unhurt but I was to go. He gave me a pass for forty-eight hours.

I went at night. The train stopped several times in South London. From a high embankment I could see explosions. Fires were burning. The raid was still going on when I reached Waterloo Station. I could not get across London before morning; I set off on foot for Dolphin Square, where someone I knew had a flat. Bombs were falling in the neighbourhood, whistling loudly. I was walking with two other soldiers and we dropped flat on the pavement just before a great explosion close by. We were on the opposite side of the street to Saint Thomas' Hospital and we thought that it had been hit. At Dolphin Square someone let me into the flat. I walked into the living room. Several people sat drinking tea at a long table. Gollan sat in an armchair at the head of the table, looking at his ease. He greeted me with his customary, open-mouthed smile, one which always appeared to show great delight. He went on telling us amusing anecdotes until the All Clear sounded.

Next morning I saw the daily scene of the Blitz: mounds of rubble, rescue workers still busy, flooded roadways covered with apparent tangles of limp fire hose and tired people going home from the shelters with their bundles of bedding. Ambulance bells still sounded from all directions. As I approached my mother's house I met an air raid warden who told me that a landmine had dropped nearby. A few nights earlier, several people from the street had been drowned when a burst water-main flooded a shelter. The door of our house stood open. The front window bay was damaged. At the back, the long wall which went down to a basement yard was leaning away from the roof. My family had been evacuated. I found a note from my mother on a mantelpiece to let me know where they had gone.

I traced them to a house on the western outskirts of London. It was in an area of big factories; of course, a target area. There was no spare room in the house; my parents and my sister were camped on the upstairs landing. I spent a night with them there, sleeping soundly on the floor, through an air raid which kept them awake. In the morning I stood in the street looking at the houses opposite. All the roof slates had been stripped off them by blast during the night. Overhead a big formation of Heinkels crawled across the sky in the first raid of the day.

*****

Not long afterwards I had a letter from Nelly, who was now living in Lancashire. She wrote that she was utterly miserable and asked me to come. Because of the invasion threat there was no army leave except on compassionate grounds. I had had one compassionate leave to see my family and I could not hope to get another. I told my room-mates that I had to get up north to see a girl and they took the matter in hand. The clerks at company headquarters had their own stock of stolen passes and railway warrants and provided me with one of each, both properly stamped and with forged signatures. My sergeant told me that he could cover up for me for three days but not a moment longer. When the time came to set out, I found the company driver waiting at the door in the major's car. It had been decided that I might be seen by one of our officers on my way to the local railway station and I was driven to a station further up the line.

All the railway stations swarmed with Military Police. Redcaps stopped me at Waterloo and Euston and again at London Road station in Manchester. I crossed Manchester, caught a local train to Rochdale and spent the day with Nelly. She must have got over her depression. She did not say a word about her letter and I did not ask her.

It was getting dark that evening when she saw me off at the station. The little train crawled towards Manchester. The only other person in the compartment was a woman in the opposite corner. She was middle-aged and plain and she looked tired out. She sat looking out of her window. After a while she turned her face to me and spoke abruptly. She said that it was a rotten life.

I said, "Yes."

She said that her husband was away in the army. She paused, then added, "He's a rotten bugger. It's a relief really."

There was nothing for me to say. She asked if I wanted a bed for the night. I thanked her and said that I had a train to catch. She looked out of her window and neither of us spoke again.

The train stopped for a long time on the outskirts of Manchester. We could see and hear an air raid in progress. I had to catch a train at eleven o'clock to get back to my quarters in time. I could only hope that it would be held up by the raid as we were.

The All Clear was still sounding when I left the local station with only a few minutes to spare. I ran across the town burdened with my greatcoat, pack, gas-mask and rifle. On my way, far down a side street, I saw red-brick cotton warehouses in the glare of a fire still burning.

I ran to the London platform at the other railway station just as my train started to move. It was packed with troops. Soldiers crowded in the open doorways of the coaches as I ran alongside. The train gathered speed. I threw my rifle and a soldier in the train caught it. I had to go after it. Full pack on my back, hung about with gear, I leaped. Hands caught me and hauled me aboard.

Chapter 27

An officer told me that the infantry had been over-recruited after Dunkirk. Forty battalions were being disbanded; the men were being sent to other arms of the service. I thought this must be the reason why my transfer had not come through. I had been at the tank gunnery school in Dorset for a spell and was excited by tanks. I put in another application, this one for the Royal Armoured Corps.

In the meantime I was enjoying my present life. I learned to lay barbed wire entanglements and to construct various defensive works. I stacked shells and laid cables for the gunners. I loaded and unloaded trucks, mixed cement as a bricklayer's labourer and went up and down a ladder with a hod of bricks on my shoulders. Still eating everything, I became fit. My pioneer duties were intermitted with military training. We went on exercises, threw live grenades and at the rifle range we fired the course required to qualify us for proficiency pay. All these activities took place in the English countryside. Except for an occasional day's ramble or a spin on my bike I had seen nothing of country landscapes before now; to live among them was a joyful experience.

A leave roster was introduced and there was sometimes a weekend pass to be had. I went up to London occasionally. Most of my old colleagues were in the army or were working for the Party in the provinces. I felt a stranger at the YCL office but I liked going to 16, King Street, to chat with Robson. My mother and sister had been evacuated to Newbury. My father still worked at the factory and joined them at weekends. I sometimes hitch-hiked up to Newbury to visit them. Petrol was now scarce and there was hardly any civilian traffic. I enjoyed tramping along empty roads among the lovely Berkshire Downs, occasionally getting a lift in an army truck or joining the swarm of soldiers and army girls perched all over a huge tank transporter.

My family lodged with a spinster lady, Miss Hyde, a tiny woman with a sharp nose and gold-rimmed spectacles. She was always about me in a flutter in case I kicked the legs of her parlour table with my big boots. Once a detective called to question her about my visits. She told him that there must be some mistake; I was a nice young man. My parents smiled when they told me this but they must have been horror-struck to learn that detectives were interested in me. The company commander, I was told by my friends in the office, had to notify the authorities of my destination every time I was given a pass; thus, when I went by train, using an army railway warrant, there was always a detective waiting for me at Newbury Station.

*****

Robson was arranging for civilians living near army camps to give hospitality to communist service men and to help them keep in touch with Party life. He asked me to visit a Party member in Salisbury, who was in touch with a number of soldiers from the many huge training camps on Salisbury Plain.

I met the man, a young scientist. He told me that he was in contact with twenty-six soldiers. I gave him my address and asked him to let me know how he got on. Soon afterwards I had a note from him inviting me to meet a few friends in a room over a pub in Salisbury. This worried me. Robson had gone to great lengths to avoid what he called provocations. The Party now forbade members in the armed forces from paying their membership subscriptions (though many of them disregarded this, being quite unable to comprehend it); they were not allowed to recruit; and it was a childish folly to assemble them in meetings, for obvious reasons of security. But there was no time for me to do anything on this occasion except go along.

I was delayed on the way and found the meeting in full swing. Almost all the twenty-six were present. The scientist sat at a small table writing in an exercise book. He had all our addresses in it and he had been taking orders from everyone for Party literature, of which he would be their future supplier.

I sat next to a man from the Armoured Corps. I asked him what did. He said that he was in the camp office. His job was to make up drafts of replacements for the Eighth Army tanks in North Africa. He said, "They're dying like flies out there."

I said, "You're a fit chap. Why don't you go?"

He looked incredulous, laughed and said, "Go? You don't see any green in my eye, comrade."

After the meeting we all went down to the pub. The scientist had left his bicycle in the yard. He came to me looking anxious and told me that his exercise book had been stolen from the saddlebag. He said, "Some drunk, I expect. He'll only chuck it away."

I thought otherwise and so did Robson when I told him. But some time later Robson told me that the scientist had been given a job at a secret military establishment and was now an army captain.

Perhaps it was a drunk.

The climactic event of this period for Party members was the People's Convention, a conference that was organised from behind the scenes by the Party to cater for every kind of pacifist and anti-war sentiment.[1] The organizers claimed to have the support of two million people. This was the usual communist self-deception. The support was only on paper, secured by Party members getting resolutions passed by committees, mostly in trade unions. The two million people knew nothing about the Convention. Nor did anyone else in the country except, as it turned out, for the military authorities.

I went as a delegate, so called after I had told the *Challenge* readers in the company that I would go and see what it was all about. The venue was a large assembly room in a London hotel, close to one of the Bloomsbury squares. I entered the hall. The conference had not yet opened. People stood talking in groups. I was chatting with an acquaintance when I saw my old mentor D.F. Springhall pushing through the throng towards me, holding a hand up to attract my attention. Delighted to see him, I just had time to say, "Hallo," when be gripped my arm, said, "You'll have to blow. You'd better get your skates on," and steered me to a fire door. I went down a fire escape, crossed the central courtyard and made my way out through another building to a back street. Military trucks passed me and drew up in the square at the far end of the street. Army and Air Force police got down from them and were sent off at the double in different directions. I crossed the street unchallenged end watched while they surrounded the block.

Two soldiers were kept at the conference to make a show of military representation. One of them was Ted Willis. He was put up as a sacrificial lamb to provide a touch of revolutionary drama. He obliged with a fiery anti-war speech that aroused the desired roars of applause and surge of resolve. Some days later he was abruptly discharged from the army. He was called to his company office and told to pack his personal possessions and leave at once. His papers were marked, "Services no longer required." He told me that he went to a friend's house, sat down alone in a room and wept.

---

1   The People's Convention (1940–41), an anti-war Communist-inspired initiative, designed, inter alia, to attack the old appeasers of Hitler, some of who were now waxing fat on profits from the War.

Mick Bennett, who was not at the Convention, was the next to be discharged. Nothing happened to me.

Then came the German attack on Russia in June 1941. At once the Party performed its second turnabout. Now it not merely supported the war but surpassed all others in warlike fervour and proclaimed patriotism. All the zeal and energy of the Party was now put into exhorting the workers in the factories to produce more war materials and to support the repeated Soviet appeals for its allies to attack in the west and so draw German troops away from Russia. The cry, "Open a Second Front now!" gained a great deal of public support. It is still a matter of contention whether a second front was practicable between 1941 and the Normandy landings of 1944. I knew or cared nothing then about the pros and cons. I drew up a letter asking our company commander to prolong our working day by an extra training period to enable us to prepare for a second front. Nearly all the men signed it. Nothing came of it.

*****

Ferguson, in my billet, was a Scot, with a red, brutal face and a brush of black hair, a heavily-built man with a lot of loose fat on him. He kept to himself a good deal, sitting on his bed and forever blancoing or polishing his equipment. When approached he showed a sullen, menacing face, which became less so when he opened his mouth, for he liked to take his false teeth out, to give them a rest, as he explained. Bare gums changed him, giving him a pathetic, babylike look. Once, seeing me reading, he surprised me by pausing at my bed and remarking that he liked a good read himself. He went to his pack and produced from it a volume of Robert Burns' poems. I never saw him again with this or any other book in his hands.

One night he went to a village dance with a local girl who was known to the men as Black Bess. He and Bess left the dance early; he came in to the billet sometime after lights out. We heard him blundering about, plainly unsteadied by drink.

Men quizzed him out of the darkness with coy shouts of "Where have you been, Jim?"

Without thinking and in all innocence I called, "He's been riding bonny Black Bess."

He came to my bed, pulled my blankets off and demanded that I get up and fight. I stood up, expostulating, trying to push him off and then to fend off his punches. The corporal separated us and told us that anyone who wanted to fight in his section was going to do it in a ring with gloves on. He named a day in the following week. We were to fight five rounds.

Everyone but me showed great enthusiasm for such an entertainment. From the next bed to mine Bob Chappell assured me that he would train me. He was a big man with a bony face and slightly buck teeth. He had hair like dirty straw which would never lie down; he was sometimes told on parade to get his hair cut but nothing short of cropping to the skull would have tamed it and he said that he refused to look like a gorilla. He came from Deptford and had an old-fashioned Cockney accent.

At every meal he took his place behind me in the queue. As soon as anything appetising was put on my plate he reached forward over my shoulder with a fork and transferred the portion to his own plate, saying, "You're in training, son."

He took me out for a run every evening. As we jogged past one of the two pubs in the village he would shout, "He's in there boozing, son," and a few minutes later lead the way into the other pub.

In the billet he gave me boxing lessons. Between the two rows of beds he pranced in front of me with his gloves up, yelping, "Come on, 'it me, 'it me!" I came on obediently and he knocked me down, then danced around me, milling his fists and shouting, "Come on, come on, 'it me!"

Beds were moved on the evening of the fight, men formed a ring und seconds appeared with towels end buckets of water. We set to. I spent the best part of three rounds going backwards round the ring and trying, not always successfully, to keep out of Ferguson's reach. I stood up to him during the last two rounds. He was sweating by now and breathing hard. I got a few not very effective punches past his guard. The corporal called time and announced a draw, a decision either diplomatic or sentimental, which elicited a clamour of approval. I had no more dealings with Ferguson after this but he did not appear to be unfriendly.

*****

A telegram came for me: "Come at once, Mother ill. Uncle Ted." I took it to Captain Morden and asked for a compassionate leave. The proper procedure was for the captain to telephone to my mother's local police station to ask for confirmation. Instead he turned at once to the sergeant-major end told him to give me a pass for seven days.

Ted needed me to write a pamphlet for him. He was now running the YCL on his own – Mick had not yet been discharged – and had moved the headquarters to a small suite of offices in Southampton Row in Central London. Funds were low, the Party's subsidy had dried up, perhaps because the Party was cut off from the Comintern, and, after the air raids, rents in the central area were now affordable.

He had help from a few girls, some of them unpaid volunteers; most of the young men were now in uniform. He got out *Challenge* single-handed every week, ran the headquarters, spoke at public meetings, attended committees, conducted education classes and travelled all over the country. Besides this YCL work he had duties heaped on him by the Communist Party, which was itself short of staff. He lived at the office, going in the small hours every night to a nearby Turkish baths to snatch a few hours' sleep. Years before, when we were two youngsters on bicycles, he had once enthused to me about a marvellous book he had just read, by Arnold Bennett, *How to Live On Twenty-Four Hours A Day*.[2] He was trying to do that now. What he did not tell me was that he had begun to write short stories and plays, secretly spending hours of the night at it.

During my week of leave, the two of us carried on with our tasks and saw little of each other, except when we had an occasional tea-break together. In the evenings he went off on his round of meetings. I worked late every day, and as everyone else I knew was out of town, I walked the streets afterwards or went to a cinema, before I want to my bed at Ted's mother's house.

I returned to the company on a golden summer evening. Walking from the station, I could see the back of our billet on a hill across the fields. The French windows were open and men lay sunning themselves on the sloping lawn. I came along the lane beneath the hill, past the pond in which an old carter whom I knew was watering his horse. I was calmed by the peace of it all. Two of the men on the lawn got up and came down the hill to meet me, my recent second Bob Chappell and the corporal. They fell in on each side of me, one of them taking my rifle and the other taking my pack. I had gone off without telling my section anything about the telegram: the corporal asked if I had had a good time.

I said, "Fucking horrible."

Bob said, "Did you get any of the other?"

I said, "Don't make me laugh."

At the billet I unpacked my kit. The cook came in with a mug of tea and a steak sandwich for me. Later on I went down to the pub with the corporal at his invitation. All the evening men sent pints along the bar for me. I was no beer drinker but I kept putting it down, feeling more and more exhilarated, and, as it seemed, not at all drunk, although the floor felt unusually springy beneath my feet.

---

2   See Arnold Bennett *How to Live on Twenty-Four Hours A Day* (2nd ed., London 1908).

It was still dusk when I left in company with the corporal. The girl called Black Bess was standing at the end of the lane. She was a small, shapely girl with a clear brown skin, bright eyes and the helmet of glossy black hair for which she was nicknamed. I had not spoken to her before. The corporal introduced us and after a little while went on his way. Bess turned out to be an intelligent, shrewd, good-natured and thoroughly independent girl. She was a hard worker, helping on a smallholding and looking after four smaller brothers and sisters. She was five years younger than I was but far more worldly. I had come into the army knowing nothing about people except what I had got from literature, that is, from literature approved by the Party as "correct", having been isolated by my age in that closed world since I was a schoolboy. My call-up was truly a release. No wonder that the threads were breaking. I remained friendly with Bess until the company moved.

*****

We moved to one of the army's big permanent camps. It was at Warminster in Wiltshire. I believe it is now the home of the School of Infantry. The company was mobilised to go overseas. I was delighted; it was almost as good as an infantry transfer. After an embarkation leave we went into training. Bales of tropical kit were delivered to the stores. I hoped that this meant the desert and the Eighth Army.

One day the company paraded for a route-march. We waited to set off when the sergeant-major called my name. I marched out and halted in front of him. He told me to go back to my hut. As I went I heard the orders shouted and the tramp of the company marching off.

I waited for a long time in the hut. The camp was silent except for a clatter of buckets or a snatch of talk when some fatigue men went by the hut. At last the door opened and Captain Morden came in. He said, "Pack your kit. You're leaving us." Going out he turned in the doorway and said, "I'm sorry about this."

I was stunned. I felt humiliated, near to tears, and angry like a small boy who resents a punishment that he believes to be unjust. I was desolated at being taken away from my friends.

I packed. An orderly came to the hut for me. I went to a small, open truck that was standing outside the office, Captain Morden was waiting by it. He said again that he was sorry, wished me luck and shook hands with me. He went back into the office and I got into the back of the truck. As we drove out of the camp gate we passed a group of fatigue men and clerks who had gathered there to see me off with waves and friendly shouts.

Chapter 28

I was delivered to another company in a camp of Nissen huts on the edge of Salisbury Plain. An orderly sergeant of monstrous obesity waddled at my side to a hut. On the way he told me that if I slipped him a bob or two he would get me a day pass any time I wanted one.

There was a row of home-made beds in the hut, knocked together out of timbers and sandbags. The men were friendly. They helped me to repair a broken bed and took me to the canteen. I cheered up quickly. In bed that night I summed up my position. I was a good soldier and now that Russia was an ally and the Party was all for the war I need not feel any guilt at my enthusiasm for the army. I decided that I would try to come to an honourable compact with the High Command.

I went in front of my new commanding officer the next day and handed to him a letter addressed to the security authorities. In it I said that from now on I would refrain from any political talk and activity as long as I was in the army. I pointed out that in doing so I was giving up the normal rights of a soldier. I asked only that in return I should be given any promotion that I earned and that I should not be again kept back from going overseas. I felt justified as a communist in making this offer, since I believed that the paramount political duty of a Party member in the army was to fight.

The officer read my letter. He told me that he would see that it got into the right hands. I thanked him and waited for the order to dismiss; he said, "Look here, you're obviously an educated fellow. You can't be happy with the pick-and-shovel lot. Would you like to come into the office? Shall I look out for some other employment for you, where you can use your brains?"

I said that he was very kind, but that I was happy enough for the time being.

I never received any acknowledgement of my letter but within a few months, after this company had undergone a transformation, I was promoted to lance-corporal then to full corporal; and in time I went overseas with them.

This letter, which I never mentioned to anyone in the Party, was a turning-point in my life, for I honoured it to the letter – at least, according to my lights – until the end of the war. Consequently I came to feel less and less like a communist among soldiers, more and more like a soldier among all the rest.

I have qualified "to the letter" because I went to see Robson whenever I was on leave and met whichever of my old Party colleagues were in London, discussing army affairs with them. I once received a note urging me to come up to London for something special. It turned out to be a grand reception at the Free French headquarters in Kensington to welcome a leader of the French Communist Party, Fernand Grenier, who had arrived to join de Gaulle's Committee of National Liberation.[1]

In 1942 I wrote a series of articles in *Challenge* under a pen name. I did not consider them to be a breach of my undertaking because they were all intended to help the war effort. If I look back at them with some distaste it is because I took my cue from the Soviet journalist Ilya Ehrenburg who had published some fiery articles calling for utter hatred of the Germans; mine, too, were "hate" articles.[2] It was in order for a Russian to write in this way while the Germans were committing every kind of atrocity in his country, but not for a journalist in England, even if he was in uniform. Bloodthirsty exhortations from those who are at a safe distance behind the front line are one of the nastier aspects of war.

I met Robson for the last time in the summer of 1942. When I went on that occasion to see him he told me that he had closed down the organization he had built up to keep in touch with communists in the armed forces. It was not safe for me to come to King Street anymore; the PB was in a panic about a recent incident. He told me about it. (The PB, of course, was the Political Bureau. It had been renamed the Political Committee as part of the cosmetic changes introduced since 1935. To us it was the same old PB, the Comintern's command post in the Party).

A short while previously Robson had walked into Springhall's office at King Street and seen a soldier, a well-known Party member with whom of course I was acquainted, emptying a pile of unused army service books onto Springhall's desk. This book, the AB64 Part One, was carried by every soldier as his identity document and pass. No-one else but the Russians could want these books. It was obvious that Springhall was working for them. The Party leaders were furious at him for compromising them and above all for carrying on his activities at Party headquarters.

---

1 Fernand Grenier (1901–1992). Leading French Communist
2 Ilya Ehrenberg (1891–1967), Soviet novelist, journalist and historian. He reported on the First World War, the Spanish Civil War and the Second World War. With Vassily Grossmann he detailed Nazi genocidal policies towards Soviet Jewry.

Not long after this I met Springhall by chance while I was on a pub crawl with Mick Bennett. We were in "The Lamb" on Lamb's Conduit Street in Bloomsbury, when Springhall came in with Peter Zinkin.[3] Zinkin was the industrial organizer. The National Shop Stewards' Council had an office a few doors from the pub. This was the front through which hundreds of Party shop stewards exercised a commanding influence in the factories. The Party's strongest groups were in the big defence plants. Springhall and Zinkin had just come from a meeting of the shop stewards and it was now obvious to me why Springy was involved with them.

He asked me where I was stationed. I told him that I was in a camp near Portsmouth. He said, "Ah, good old Pompey. I was there in my Navy days. They got lovely 'ores in Pompey."

Mick Bennett knew me well enough to take me aside and murmur, "Old Springy's a rough diamond. Don't take any notice."

In the autumn Springhall was arrested for espionage and was sentenced to seven years in prison. The court heard evidence of his transactions with men in the services. Some of them were in the dock with him but the soldier Robson had seen with him in King Street was not among them.

*****

The transformation of the company came about suddenly. One day the waddling orderly sergeant disappeared. He was followed by batches of older men and of those who were in lower medical grades. In their place came drafts of fit men, some from infantry depots, a tough young sergeant-major from the Black Watch and new young officers. A new commanding officer took over, a fit man in early middle age with a no-nonsense look about him. We moved quarters to a camp in Hampshire which we shared with a battalion of Royal Warwicks. We undertook one more pioneer task, the excavation of an underground headquarters for Combined Operations at Fort Southwick, working with a tunnelling company of sappers. Then we commenced infantry training which lasted for nearly a year.

The Pioneer Corps was being reorganized. It had been formed early in the war as a labour corps, with pioneer duties at the front being performed

---

3   Peter Zinkin (1904–1983). Active in the Independent Labour Party before joining the Communist party in 1926. Sent to Moscow in 1931. Later worked as Industrial Organiser for the Party. In 1945 appointed political correspondent for the *Daily Worker*. Remained active in the Party until his death. A damning portrait of him appears scattered in Alison Macleod, *Uncle Joe*.

by separate pioneer battalions of the infantry as in the 1914-1918 war. Now many Pioneer Corps companies were being knocked into shape as forward troops. During 1942 the succession of Allied defeats and retreats was ended by the victories at Alamein and Stalingrad. After that the Allies took the offensive on all fronts.[4] Pioneer companies spent up to two years in training as infantry and took part in all the great battles later on, often performing specialist assault roles. Pioneers took part in many Commando landings from the sea. There was a Pioneer company on the strength of the First Airborne Division. According to the official history of the Pioneer Corps, nearly ten thousand Pioneers were reported killed or missing in the war.

I now had the matter of the infantry to consider. Everything was now changing for the better. I liked the new commanding officer and he appeared to like me. I went before him and told him that I wished to apply for an officer's commission in the infantry. He said that he would be glad to support me and the application was sent off.

The ensuing events took place over many months. After a time I was called to a War Office Selection Board. I spent three days at a country house near Winchester, one of about sixty candidates. We were put through psychological tests and a number of practical exercises to test us for initiative, resourcefulness and ability to lead.

We were divided into groups of twelve called syndicates. An officer supervised each syndicate and stayed with it all day. We took all our meals at table with him. We were supposed to engage in intelligent and gentlemanly conversation after dinner. I suspected at the time that we were being scrutinised for social acceptability, with the etiquette of the Officers' Mess in mind, but I may have been too suspicious, for many of the candidates were keen young infantry sergeants whom the supervising officers obviously and rightly made welcome. There were two caricatural Silly Asses in our syndicate who tried to show their leadership by ordering the rest of us about but we ignored them.

Our officer was a Greenjacket major who had come back from the Western Desert with a leg wound. One morning he set us an exercise. The twelve of us were to be prisoners of war. The major and two armed guards

---

4   El Alamein, North Africa. This battle in October-November 1942, and the vanquishing of Rommel's Afrika Corps, proved the decisive turning point in the so-called Desert War. Stalingrad (now renamed Volgograd). The surrender here to the Soviets of the German Sixth Army under Paulus, in late January, early February 1943, ended one of the fiercest battles of the Second World War and marked a turning point in the European theatre of operations.

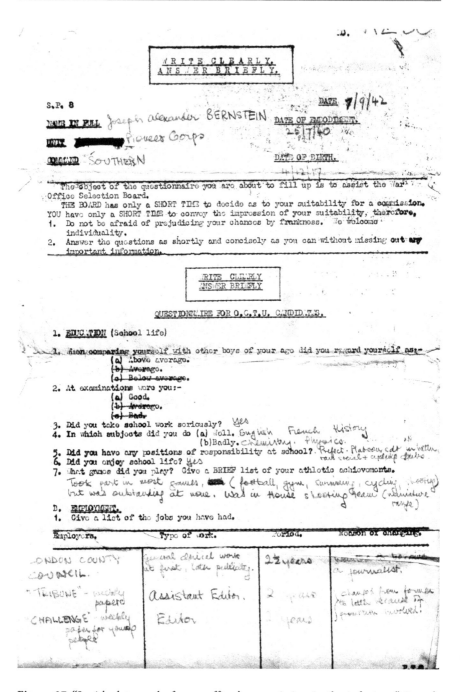

Figure 27 "I wished to apply for an officer's commission in the infantry..." Baron's application for a commission. Note that Baron carefully avoids mention of his communist associations. He describes "Challenge" as a "weekly paper for young people" (p.1) and

B. **EMPLOYMENT.** (contd)

2. What were your ambitions on leaving school? *To become a journalist*
3. How did you got your first job? *Took an examination*
4. Did you consider your civil job a suitable one? *Yes*
5. What do you propose to do after the war? *Get a job with a national daily paper*
6. Have you ever been definitely in charge of men:
   If so how many (a) in civil life? (b) in the Army?
   Yes. As assistant editor & later editor, in charge of office staffs of about two dozen people. In army, as lance-corporal; in charge of party of 12-15 men.

C. **INTERESTS.**

1. What experience have you had of the following? If you have had NONE write 'NONE'.

   DRIVING CARS. *Been taught, but had no opportunity to drive for 2½ year (since joining army).*

   RIDING MOTOR CYCLES. *None.*

   HANDLING MACHINERY. *None*

   WIRELESS *None.*

   HANDLING ELECTRICAL EQUIPMENT. *None.*

   CONSTRUCTIONAL WORK. *Building Nissen Huts. Trenching. (In army).*

   ORGANISING. *(a) in my journalistic jobs (b) as member of: Labour Party's youth advisory committee, organising clubs for young people.*

   INSTRUCTING. *Lecturing to above-mentioned clubs on history & economics.*

   TRAVEL. *Visited France a number of times on business.*

   CAMPING. *Spent ... took ... camping between ... on ...*

   ART. *None.*

2. What active games or sport have you kept up since you left school? *Cycling, camping, walking*
3. What sort of books do you read? *Novels. History. Used to read a lot about flying, but had little chance since joining army. Recently have been reading several books on mathematics & popular science + warfare.*
4. What other hobbies and interests have you? *None.*
5. Where and how have most of your holidays been spent.
   (a) camping & cycling (b) in France - mainly in Paris, but twice walking in Normandy.

6. What are your views on foreign service?
   Look on it as the main object of my being in the army. At the moment my main ambition is to be among men who set foot in Western Europe again — it will mean taking part in one of the great turning-points of history.

mentions organisational experience as a "member of Labour Party's Youth Advisory Committee" (p.2). In answer to Question 6 "What are your views on foreign service", Baron writes: "Look on it as the main object of my being in the Army. At the moment, my main ambition is to be among the men who set foot in Western Europe again – it will mean taking part in one of the great turning-points of history."

were to march us to the cage. We were to make a break for it. He named me as leader of the prisoners.

We tramped off at the side of the main Southampton road. The major and the guards marched alongside and behind the party. I placed myself in the outside rank just behind the major. We went on for the best part of a mile; then, in what I hoped was a rugby tackle, I dived at the major from behind, clasping his legs and bringing him down. Two other prisoners whom I had instructed went for the two guards. The other nine prisoners got away. While they dashed off I fought to keep the major pinned down, using one hand to stop him getting at his pistol and the other to grasp him by the hair. The other two pairs were rolling about on the roadway. The major called the exercise off and the party gathered again. He limped to the roadside and sat down on the bank. I followed, expecting praise. He said, "Congratulations! You've opened my wound."

On the last afternoon I took my turn in front of the Selection Board. Afterwards the major told me that I had been accepted for training as an officer, to be commissioned into a line regiment of infantry.

I assumed that the next step was for me to be sent for a six months course at an Officer Cadet Training Unit (OCTU). Instead, after a wait long enough to arouse a few impulses of anxiety in me, I received a summons to an interview with the commander of 47 Division, Major-General Sir Gerald Templer.[5]

I waited outside a glass conservatory at the back of a country house. A captain opened the door and I marched in ceremoniously, the iron studs on my boots making a great clatter on a tiled floor. Templer sat behind a small table at the end of the empty room. He was a tall, lean man with a bleak, hollow-cheeked face and a piercing look. He ordered me to stand at ease (this is a stiff, formal position) and at once began to fire questions at me so rapidly that I took it to be a test. I fielded them, trying to retain every one of them but to answer the most important first. He spoke in a quiet, curt voice. Without warning, he said, "Now tell me about communism."

I gave him an equivocal account of my career in the Labour Party and the YCL; truthful as a description of the surface of my life, dishonest in that I left out the underground part of it. He interrupted with more questions, his voice remaining neutral. I told him that what had driven me into politics so young was a hatred of Nazi Germany. Everyone had seemed indifferent

---

5 Major-General, later Field Marshal Sir Gerald Templer (1898–1979). Soldier. Best known to the public for his defeat of nationalist forces in Malaya. Chief of the Imperial General Staff, 1955–58.

to the threat. Only the communists had offered me a chance to have a go. Row the army gave me a much better chance to do that. I spoke from the heart; but also from a split mind. I looked at his level, intent gaze, and I thought, this fellow's got my number.

After the war Templer became a Field Marshal and Chief of the Imperial General Staff. Two famous journalists who knew him, James Cameron and Louis Heren, have written of him as a bitter anti-communist.[6] He stood up, came round the table, shook hands with me and said, "You'll make an officer. Try to be a good one."

Two years of frustration were over. So I thought.

*****

I enjoyed living under canvas. The Hampshire countryside was lovely. Some friends and I found a waterhole in the middle of a meadow. The water was icy. However deep we plunged we could not find the bottom. We went there in the evenings when we were still hot and sweaty after an arduous day. The shock of the cold water revived us. Afterwards we lay on the grass, the evening sunshine still warm enough to dry us.

A young soldier who had just come into the company attached himself to our bathing party. He had been one of the latest intake from the infantry, boys from a Young Soldiers' Battalion who had joined up as volunteers and were now old enough for active service. He was a country boy, small, with flat fair hair cut in front with a pudding-basin fringe; the classical ploughboy who had taken the King's Shilling. We took little notice of him but he forced himself on us like an affectionate puppy, which was all I took him for, frisking about us, clinging on to us in the water and climbing over us on the grass. At last the one of the men pushed him off and told him savagely to get out of our way. He did not come with us again.

Perhaps the other men knew more than I did, for I was surprised some time later when the boy disappeared from the company and my sergeant, when I asked him what had become of young Fred, said, "He's gone. It's just as well. Sergeant Macey found LeFevre and Mayfield buggering him behind the ablutions. They're lucky. They could have got ten years for it. But anyone could see the boy was a poof."

---

6   James Cameron (1911–1985). Well-known British journalist. Worked towards the end of his life for *The Guardian*; Louis Heron (1919–1995) Born and raised in the East End, Heron became a journalist, spending his entire career working at *The Times*.

LeFevre (pronounced Lefeaver) and Mayfield were miners from the North-East. I cannot guess how a possibly Huguenot name became implanted in that region. Fred's case was a revelation to me. So was that of the two miners. I had thought of proletarians as members of an ideal caste, incapable of what I thought of then as beastly and perverted acts. This was the only instance I came across of homosexuality in my six years' service.

I had come into the army as ignorant of human nature and full of illusions as a schoolboy, having been preserved as one by my years in the Party machine. Since then both my ignorance and my attachment to the Party had diminished, but only slowly, for I clung to them, being reluctant to acknowledge that people lived largely for the satisfaction of simple brute instincts. I was still repeatedly taken aback by what I saw of sexual behaviour which was like that of dogs trotting about in the street. I remember one occasion when we picked up an Air Force girl while we were travelling in the back of a covered truck. She was fair and pretty. I took her to be the kind of girl toward whom one ought to be protective. Soon she was lying on the floor at the back of the truck with her legs up, giggling and gasping pleasurably. Among the men who went to her were some whom I had thought to be faithful husbands. She dropped from the tailboard outside an Air Force camp and walked off, as bright as ever, while the men waved and called cheerful goodbyes after her.

I thought, how do they know? Why are they so sure of each other? How can all these transactions take place so instantly and confidently without a word being spoken? I decided that I lacked some kind of psychic antennae which other people possessed.

Chapter 29

We moved to Barton Stacey in Hampshire, another old-established army camp. It was a neat, miniature town of the military with an immense parade ground. Our huts, well-built with good amenities, lined one side of the square; on the others were all the other quarters of an army base as well as stores, hospital, transport park and canteens. Wherever we were all day long the faint, clear ring of orders and the tramp of boots came to us from the square. Smart columns of men swung past.

We shared the camp with the Royal Ulster Rifles, an Air Landing battalion. There were parachute battalions in the neighbourhood, the same which we were to see in Sicily. On the night before the invasion of Sicily the Ulsters were towed in gliders towards the coast by inexperienced American pilots who dropped them all into the sea.

They were smart and spry at Barton Stacey. Everyone had to be smart. The camp was spick and span. Not a scrap of paper was to be seen on the ground. Outside the guardroom by the gate there was a long mirror in which we were to check our appearance. The guards would not let any man out who was not dressed correctly to the last button.

All the more remarkable was the toleration accorded to a newcomer to the company, Corporal Fylde, like myself an officer candidate waiting to go to a cadet unit. He was a tall young man, educated, with a courteous and quizzical manner which persuaded officers to treat him as one of their own, an eccentric, and guard commanders let him pass as an obvious officer in. disguise, in spite of the fact that his attire was flamboyantly incorrect. He wore riding breeches with leather gaiters and at the criminally-unbuttoned neck of his blouse a variety of coloured foulards.

Fylde and I played the piano every night in the corporals' club. Sometimes we took turns but we were most applauded when we sat side by side and knocked out swing or jazz together. The corporals of three regiments, the Paras, the Ulsters and the Pioneers, sat at their small tables talking and drinking, apparently taking no notice of us, but their boots thundered rhythmically on the floor in time with "Nobody's Sweetheart Now" or "Somebody Stole My Gal".

Figure 28 "They were smart and spry at Barton Stacey. Everyone had to be smart." Undated photograph of Corporal Bernstein.

Fylde left us and was commissioned as a Pioneer officer. I can only tell the rest of his story in the roundabout way in which news travels among the common soldiers. During the Sicilian campaign one of our corporals was transferred as a patient to an Algiers base hospital. There he came across another corporal whom we had both known. This man had been wounded by a shell during the Salerno landings in September 1943 and had suffered a particularly grievous mutilation, having lost an arm and a leg on the same side. He said that Fylde had been an officer in his company. The Germans had put in a big counter-attack at the start of the operation which had driven the British back almost into the sea, and Fylde had been killed in hand-to-hand fighting. We heard this news when we were already on the Italian mainland, soon before we were to be shipped home.

At the end of the year we moved to Plymouth. We took over a fine building in the Devonport area. It was a former naval hospital, easily turned into a barracks. There was a big parade ground at the front. At the rear its grounds, with plenty of room for training, sloped down to a wide inlet of the sea, opposite to the great Devonport naval base.

Our period of hard training began. While the company was being brought up to a creditable standard as infantry, officers and NCO's were sent away on courses to acquire different skills. A young officer returned to teach a group of us the use of high explosives in the field. I went on a course at which I learned how to root up mines safely with a bayonet, to deal with trip wires and to neutralize other kinds of booby-traps. I was fascinated by the subject. I taught it to the NCO's who taught it to the men and from now on I became the company specialist in this kind of work. The gamble built into it was that the clever German pioneers sometimes reversed the mechanisms of their devices so that to use the safety switch or to cut the trip wire would set off the explosive.

A small group of the keenest NCO's formed, who in the course of the year became a group of friends. We thought and talked a lot about how best to train soldiers for war because we considered it to be a matter of life or death for the men in our charge. We became known as the 'Ginger Group'. Others often gathered around us to discuss these matters. One dictum of ours was that an NCO was no good unless a third of his men referred to him as "that bastard". This proposition is not as unpleasant as it looks. I coined it to catch the attention of my listeners. It should be reversed. In a good unit the NCO ought to be able to convince most of his men that they will be safer and more effective if they become a good team. In any human group it is realistic to assume that some will remain anti-social but in war most of these will be carried on by the will and tempo of the majority, and

Figures 29 and 30 "A small group of the keenest NCO's formed, who in the course of the year became a group of friends." Two photographs of Baron with the "Ginger Group" of NCOs in 172 Company, Pioneer Corps, 1941–42. Baron mentions the names of two of these close army friends in his memoir: Billy Strachan and Eric Gray (see also Figures 6 and 36).

by the need to survive. NCO's had to learn that they would now be doing their men a bad turn if during a training period they took them behind the sheds to pass the time with a quiet smoke. The corporal who kept his men trotting in a circle and dropping flat every time he shouted, "Down!" was not a sadist but was teaching them how to save their lives.

The entire British army was transforming itself. A great part in this transformation was played by the new battle schools, at which leaders were trained in realistic war conditions. The idea spread. By the time we went into training, it seemed as if every division and area Command had its school for the new, tough methods. I went to one of these schools. It was on Dartmoor, which had become a big training area. One day an instructor, Sergeant Mansfield, called me out of a ring of students and invited me to take his rifle off him. I went for him. He had an iron grip on the rifle and we both went down. We thumped over and over on the ground until the rifle snapped in two at the small of the butt. At the end of the course I was kept on for a time as a weapons instructor. I had by now found that I could leave off my glasses when I was on duty and still see well at a distance, so that I was always up to scratch on the firing ranges.

Later on I was sent to another school, which was for NCO's from throughout the Southern Command. The aim of this school was to weed out those who were not fit to lead men in the field; these were to be stripped of their rank. The course lasted a month. It soon became apparent that the commandant was mad. He heard two men grumbling while they were being taught to avoid offering themselves as targets by rolling down a hill. He stood over them for a half-hour ordering them to roll up the hill from the bottom and goading them on. He waited to catch the stragglers at the end of a cross-country run and sent them to run three times round the assault course. Of the hundred and twenty students more than twenty dropped out with injuries. At the end of the course it was rumoured that another twenty were reduced to the ranks. Ten were recommended for commissions, of whom I was one. I was pleased by this. The delay in my posting to an Officer Cadet Training Unit had started to puzzle me a little, although I had been too busy with the training to think much about it.

When I returned to my company the delay was explained. The major sent for me and showed me a letter from the War Office. It rejected my application for a commission. No explanation was given. At the foot was the stamp of the Adjutant-General's Department and a Military Intelligence reference number.

*****

ARMY FORM B.2617

J. 904

RECOMMENDATION FORM FOR CANDIDATES FOR
OFFICER CADET TRAINING UNITS.

PART I.   (To be completed by the Candidate.)

1. Surname BERNSTEIN   2. Army Number 13042620

3. Christian names JOSEPH ALEXANDER

4. Rank LANCE-CORPORAL   5. Date of Promotion 30/6/42

6. Unit ▓▓ COMPANY, PIONEER CORPS

7. Date of joining present unit 13/12/1941

8. Date of enlistment 25/7/1940

NOT ACCEPTED
A.M.D./J/1219/A8/E
1.8/4/42

9. Date of birth* 4/12/1917   11. Civil Identity No.

10. Place of birth* MAIDENHEAD, BERKS.   12. Religion JEWISH

13. Nationality at birth BRITISH

14. Name and nationality at birth of father BARNETT BERNSTEIN. RUSSIAN. (British Subject by Naturalisation)

15. Name and nationality at birth of mother FANNY LEVINSON. BRITISH.

16. Married or single SINGLE

17. Nationality at birth of wife

18. Number of children

19. Next of kin and Permanent Address of next of kin BARNETT BERNSTEIN (Father), 4, KING'S RD., NEWBURY, BERKS.

20. School or other Educational Establishments (with dates) ELEMENTARY SCHOOL 1923-1929. HACKNEY DOWNS (Secondary) SCHOOL 1929-1935

21. Educational certificates (with dates) GENERAL SCHOOLS CERTIFICATE (with Matriculation) 1933. HIGHER SCHOOLS CERTIFICATE. 1935.

22. Languages (state if written or spoken) FRENCH (WRITTEN AND SPOKEN)

23. Civil occupation JOURNALIST

24. Name of last employer Challenge Publications, Premier House, 150 Southampton Row, London, W.C.1.

Figure 31 "No explanation was given." Although first accepted for infantry officer training, Baron was then unexpectedly rejected. Form stamped by Adjutant-General's Department and marked 'Not Accepted', 10 November 1942. Baron's father's nationality at birth has been double-ringed in blue pencil.

While we were at Plymouth the city underwent the series of night raids which laid waste a good part of it. While these were going on I was relaxed in my bed, tired and satisfied after the day's training, indifferent to the throb of engines in the sky and the explosions that shook the windows. The other men seemed to care no more than I did. At midday on Saturdays, after we had made our barrack rooms spotless and trim and turned out for a smart parade, we were allowed out. Union Street was the busiest street in Devonport. It was by tradition the street of sailors ashore. Now it was thronged by uniforms of every kind and by the women who went with them. We saw no hint of the air raids in the faces of the people who streamed past us. Noisy torrents of sailors, soldiers and women poured past pubs and bars crowded to their open doorways, every one sending a different bray of music out to the street.

Religious canteens invited us to come in and also drew crowds. Young prostitutes sauntered up and down in front of the shop windows. The best-known place of assignation, a slot-machine arcade known as the Snake Pit, was so crammed that we had to force our wary into the crush. A little beyond the end of the street Plymouth Hoe was a prospect of calm. The sea sparkled. Sunderland flying boats landed sedately under our gaze.

Before our little group of corporals left barracks we always, on principle, ate the midday meal. In town we went from one canteen to another. Eggs, chips, sausages, baked beans, toast, buns and cakes disappeared down our maws as if our insides were fathomless. Late in the afternoon, regularly, we swept in through the double doors of a big, communal restaurant and our waitress friends hurried from all directions to greet us. Leaving their customers unattended they ushered us to a table, hurried to and fro with dishes for us, lingered to chat, ignored pleas from other tables and when we left, wrote out derisory bills for us.

None of my friends had ever been to a smart restaurant before and I had only gone, in Soho, as a guest, but we found one, French or Italian, near to the bottom of Union Street and we took to going there to dine well with a bottle or two of wine. After that, those of us who had not left to keep dates joined the immense queues outside the cinemas. As often as not a couple of our officers were in the queue, perhaps with girls; and as often as not one of them, a bit of a scamp, came down the line to touch one of us for a fiver. It was a court martial offence for an officer to borrow money from the Other Ranks. I was well off. I had never in my life had as much money in my pocket as I had now on a corporal's pay.

I had another interview with the major. He told me that my recommendation from the battle-school commandant had been of no avail and that he could do no more for me. He gave me the file on my case, probably doing so against regulations. I thought of using it to fight the case publicly. I knew Members of Parliament and other prominent people who would support me. But by now the company was buzzing with rumours that we were soon to go overseas. The Quartermaster confirmed that he had bales of desert kit in the stores. I wondered what theatre of war it could be meant for; the fighting in North Africa was all but over. I knew, however, that I wanted to go; and I did not intend to give the authorities a pretext to keep me back in England once again.

Embarkation leave followed. I went to London and had supper with Mick Bennett and his wife. I do not recall that I bothered to see any other Party people. I went to the East End to see my grandparents. The two little households had survived in the midst of ruins. My father's parents sat looking me over in wonderment. I was touched by the affection and solicitude in their voices. My mother's father had not changed by a hair of his bristling whiskers. All of them filled mugs of sweet brown tea for me and offered me tasty tit-bits.

I spent the rest of my leave in Newbury. My family now had a place of their own. It was in one of those slum courts common in English country towns. Four habitations gave on to a flagstoned passage which one entered from the street beneath a square archway. The dwellings had flimsy plank front doors like those of sheds. My parents were cheerful but very quiet. When it was time for me to leave I told them not to come to the station and they said goodbye to me, quietly, at the door.

*****

A gruelling week followed this leave. Every morning we were taken out for a hard physical test. Of these I can only remember the forced march and the cross-country run. Each day the men who dropped out were told to pack their kit and parade outside the company office. A truck took them away and returned in the afternoon with an equal number of replacements, beefy lads from the infantry.

The men were on their toes. They vied with one another to do well. It was not because they wanted to go overseas. Many might have preferred to stay at home if they had been asked in privacy and after being given time to cool off. But they were carried along by the mass. Each was bound in a web of friendships which he did not want to betray. It was in the nature of young men to want to pass physical tests, to endure as much and run as fast as their comrades. Many must have looked no farther than that. Besides, training had conditioned them to war as a natural activity and imbued them with the idea that they knew how to get through it. There was an ingredient of real resolve in their feelings. The war had to be won. There was also the question of manhood, there was curiosity about strange lands and new experiences, and an indefinable vibration of excitement.

There were two other Jews in the company, *grobbe yidden* whom I knew only by name. One day, after the forced march, I walked past the company office and saw them standing with their piled kit ready to leave. One of them called to me and I approached him. He said, "You ought to be ashamed of yourself, a yiddisher boy!" I was so astonished by this and it has come back into my thoughts so obstinately that I must explain why I have told the story, although it may give pain to some and nourish the prejudices of others.

The war was not fought for the Jews, though many British soldiers thought it was. It was (in the last resort) one more war of states at each other's throats to extend or to defend their power.

Others fought against the Germans for their freedom. Jews had to fight against extermination. The number of distinctions that they won for bravery in all the allied armies was far beyond the proportion of Jews to their compatriots. In that fortress of antisemitism, the Soviet Army, a hundred Jews rose to the rank of general during the war. They were as disproportionately prominent in the Resistance movements and had their own heartbreakingly brave Resistance movements even in the Nazi ghettos and camps.

Many periods of persecution in many countries have produced many kinds of Jew, most of whom display some admirable characteristics. But adversity is not to be recommended as an improving experience; it also makes people selfish, cowardly and sharp-witted to exploit or sacrifice others for their own survival. At the time I simply detested these two men. Later, I realised that the utter righteousness, the tone of moral authority in which I was addressed, came from minds which had been mutilated by past mistreatments and had shrunk into tiny organs of self-preservation, fit for nothing else. What I saw as shame they would only see as virtue. I suppose it can be said that wretches of this sort are victims, by descent, of the past.

*****

There was no doubt now that we were going. A wave of drunkenness swept through the company on the nights when the men spent their pay. The NCO's remained immune from this. They were all busy and I remember them as a quiet, pre-occupied lot during these days. Every night, long after

Lights Out, men came clattering up the stone staircases, singing, hallooing and quarrelling and reeling aggressively around the barrack rooms. NCO's treated these men kindly, only enlisting them in the mornings to clean up the puddles of urine and vomit that made the building stink.

"The bells are ringing, for me and my gal." Whenever I hear this tune I think of our departure. My friends and I went one evening to see Gene Kelly in the film.[1] We strode back from the cinema whistling the tune in empty streets, our boots ringing on the pavement. When we walked in through the gates the guard commander told us that the company was confined to barracks from now on.

The next day was all activity. We packed our kit. Quarters always had to be left bare and spotless by a departing unit; a fever of toil gave the men no time to brood. Every bit of furniture was taken down and carried to the stores. Paillasses were emptied and the straw burned. Floors and staircases were swept and scrubbed. Outside the stores trucks were being loaded. Men scribbled forbidden letters. A few slipped away over the wall to post letters or to say goodbye to girls. The atmosphere was cheerful enough.

We sat on the floor with our kit and talked. It was after midnight when we were called out on parade. The major told us to be quiet, the sergeant-major gave us the left-turn, and without ceremony, in silence, we marched out. We tramped a long way through dark, empty streets. The only sound was the tramp of our boots. We marched across waste ground into a rail yard. We halted and endured one of those long, long, army waits, until we were taken to the train, a dozen of us at a time, and seen into compartments.

As soon as the train was on its way the NCO's left their men and made off down the train to some empty coaches. Two to a compartment we stretched out on the seats and slept soundly.

It was daylight when I was awakened by clanking, the screech of brakes and the feel of the train slowing down. We crawled between streets of shabby little houses, over and under bridges. The NCO's went back to their men. A Liverpool man shouted to me, "Look, corporal, that's Scottie Road, that's where I live!"

We slowed to a stop under a structure of red-painted girders. The side of a ship rose like a wall on our left. On our right there was a brick wall with doors in it and a line of Military Police in front of it. Our officers got down from the train and conferred with officers on the quay. A whole morning

---

1   Baron's reference is to the 1942 film "For Me and My Gal", starring Gene Kelly and Judy Garland.

seemed to go by while we waited inertly in the train. The carriage doors were opened by Redcaps who shouted to us to get out.

We formed a line in front of the coaches and once more waited for a long time. Across the quay gangways went up steeply to entries in the side of the ship. We could see nothing of the ship but the wall of riveted, black steel plates. Once more we were told off in parties and we went up the gangways into the ship. Seamen led us along passages and down companion ways, one flight of stairs after another, deep into the ship, to the floor of a hold which had been turned into a troop deck. Long tables and benches were bolted to the floor. Steel hammock lockers and storage compartments for our kit lined the bulkheads at each end of the hold. Electric lights were on all the time, dimmed at night, under thick glass in cages.

Army and Navy officers came and went, teaching us the routine. Seamen showed us how to sling and stow hammocks. We could either sleep on the tables or in hammocks. The corporals decided on hammocks. I found it easy to get in and out of a hammock and deeply comfortable to sleep in one. Shipboard food was ample and good; our first meal came down to us, a supper of tasty corned beef-hash in huge tins.

There were no send-offs in the Second World War when a British troopship sailed. We were not allowed out of the hold until late the next morning. We knew nothing of the departure. When we went on deck the next day we were at sea north of Ireland, out of sight of land. A cold breeze blew. The sea was choppy. No other ship was to be seen. Late in the day we saw the first signs of our convoy, two or three small stains of smoke in the sky, ships appearing like little toys in the distance.

Chapter 30

I went through two campaigns between July 1943 and December 1944. I have written three books about the lives of men and women in the war. I made use in these books of my own experiences as well as of scenes that I witnessed and stories that others told me. Now that I have to write about myself during this period I shall not go over the same ground by writing a narrative of wartime experiences. I shall describe a few occasions which remain as landmarks in my life. Otherwise I shall confine myself to happenings that affected my character and outlook, the crucial matters in my life being my relations with the Party and the re-emergence of my resolve to become a writer.

I have to make clear that I thought very little about the Communist Party during this time but the changes in me must have prepared me, without my knowing it, for a future break with it. As for writing, I was now, in July 1943, about to be presented with the greatest gift that an aspirant writer can enjoy, that of a profound, determining experience in which I would eventually come to see a way to express all that I then had to say about life. Perhaps it was the hunger for such an experience that had urged all my earlier efforts to get into the infantry.

*****

The troopship was a converted liner with at least a couple of thousand men on board, most of them Canadians. Getting them out of the ship to land on an open shore was a complicated business. Our hold was crammed with soldiers sitting at the tables and on the floor in their war gear. Every few minutes a voice gave out a serial number over the loud speakers and as each was called a unit moved off through a labyrinth of passages and companion ways to go out through one of the sally ports that had been opened in the side of the ship. I was the guide for my company.

The ship had been at anchor for a long time. We had been told that we were now part of the Eighth Army under General Montgomery and that we were going to land in Sicily; that was all. The men did not look as if the news had made any impression on them. There were quiet conversations and games of cards. Some men looked as if they were sleeping with their eyes open. The muffled detonations of gunfire came to us. Eyes looked up but I do not recall that anyone made a comment. The gunfire increased. There were louder bangs and sudden stabbing outbursts of noise from quickfirers. Sometimes a great flurry of explosions broke out then died away. One tremendous bang smote the side of the ship like an immense hand, so that the floor of the hold tilted slightly for a few moments amid a great clattering of locker doors thrown open and helmets sent flying. Even this did not rouse the men from their inertia. There was a lull in the noises. Our number was called. I set off up the wide staircase, the company following in single file. I saw the sally port, a big sunlit square, and stepped aside to wait for my section. I was standing next to the seaman who had taught me the route on the previous day. He told me that German 'planes were attacking in waves. A bomb had put the ship's port engine out of action. Another ship was burning.

I took my place and went down a gangway into an LCA (Landing Craft Assault). These were small, open metal boxes with fronts made to fall forward as ramps. We could hear aero-engines in the sky but there were no 'planes directly overhead. I caught a glimpse of the burning ship; after that I kept my eyes on the shore. We were running into a small bay at the foot of a wooded slope. LCA's were beaching on a narrow strip of sand. Men were scattering out of them, coming together in files and going up in threads through the wood. Our craft sidled in towards a stone mole. Each time we bumped it, men climbed the sides and leaped; we all ran for the shore. Strange officers shouted, "Get on there now!" to us and pointed to a track leading up through the wood. We went up it in file.

We came out on to a plateau and trudged along a country lane. Whichever way we looked across the fields we saw soldiers digging in. We were on a wide, fertile-looking plain patched with bright green plantations, brown fallow land and silvery groves of olive trees. Low blue hills ran to one side of us. A white cloud rested on the middle of this range, the only one in the pale blue sky. It was a wide, shallow cone. The shape puzzled me. I was also puzzled by a loud chirping sound that never ceased.

We were directed into a field and came to a halt at the top of it, against a low, dry-stone wall, beneath a belt of olive trees. Major Bell spoke to us. He said that the only enemy forces in this area were Italians and that they had been routed by troops who had landed before us. We had to look out for snipers, of whom there were a number about. The password for the day was "Desert Rats" and the countersign was "Kill Italians!"

We lay down, waiting for food and for spades. We were to get neither. They were on a truck which was stolen as soon as it was put ashore. Thus we learned at once that ruthless mutual robbery is the law within an army in the field. We had to live for several days on whatever we could forage from the fields; that turned out to be nothing but tomatoes and almonds. This diet made our bowels bleed.

The enemy aircraft came back several times. It was only in the newspapers that the British had air superiority in Sicily. The enemy had a ring of airfields round the town of Catania; their 'planes were over us a couple of minutes after they had taken off and most of them were deadly Focke-Wulf Fw190's. All we had were a few Spitfires from Malta with only enough petrol to stay over us for fifteen minutes.

The attacks went on all night. I had always been indifferent to air raids but it was a new and uncomfortable experience to lie on the ground amid a muddle of noises, explosions, throbbing engines, insistent automatic fire and the sound of showers of splinters slashing through foliage and whacking into the ground. Coloured lights streamed up over our heads and shimmering flares kept lighting us up boldly. At one time during the night I was disconcerted to feel myself trembling hard. My teeth chattered so loudly that I feared that I would wake up the man next to me, who was sleeping through the din. Only my body was affected. My mind was at ease and was indeed intensely interested in all that was going on.

When all the noise had died away I got up and walked along a track into a vineyard. Away from the trees, the landscape was bathed in bright moonlight. I explored on, coming out on to open grass and then to the edge of a low cliff. I lay down, looking out across a calm sea, the ships' anchorage hidden from sight by a headland. A wide, glittering track of moonlight ran across the sea toward me. My only thought was of how lucky I was to be here.

I had realised, at some point during the day, that the cloud resting on the hills was the snowcap of Mount Etna, and at another moment it had come to me that the chirping noise was made by cicadas. I had seen ancient Etna. The thought astonished me. And I had often read about cicadas in books. I had dreamed about foreign places since my childhood, when I had sent coupons away for Thomas Cook's brochures. These to me were only the material for dreams. So were all the books I read. Now I had been far out in the Atlantic and witnessed the monstrous power of the ocean, I had seen flying fish, I had sailed on the Middle Sea that Odysseus had sailed and that I had read about in Thucydides. In that time, when few people had travelled abroad before the war, I do not think that I was such an exceptional case. I was to have most of my romantic feelings knocked out of me in the six weeks of the Sicilian campaign but I have never lost my fascination with the island, nor ceased to enjoy the burn of the sun on my skin, nor failed to marvel at the brightness and infinite clarity of the southern light.

At first light I stood with another corporal, Billy Strachan, at the top of the field, looking down at a long, gentle slope in front of us. On our right trees made an irregular grove down the slope. At the foot of the slope the view was bounded by a dark wall of trees. In front of the trees the colour of the pale, parched grass was broken by a large patch of bright viridian green. Billy said, "That's water."

We were tired and dirty. The entire landscape was silent. A couple of sentries stood unmoving against the trunks of trees. The rest of the men were stretched out like a line of dead at the foot of the wall. Billy and I stepped over the wall, ran into the trees and skulked down the hill in their shelter. Soon we saw the gleam of water among the bright green. We reached it to find a large pond surrounded by reeds which also grew in dense patches in the water. We lay down with our faces over the water, washed ourselves and shaved. Refreshed, we were sitting up when a most gigantic bang smote in upon us, a wall of glistening water rose up from the pond in front of us and a hard downpour fell upon us. When it had stopped, Billy said, "I suppose this is what they call the baptism of fire."

I made a remark about snipers who fired shells; but Billy was pointing to something that protruded above the surface of the pond in front of us. It was a great, twisted sheet of metal, blackened by heat. We could see patterns of rivets on it. Mystified, we went back to the company lines. Later in the day we heard that the ship we had earlier seen ablaze had carried a cargo of ammunition and had blown up. A company of Pioneers had been sent into the ship to get as much ammunition out as they could; they had still been working in her when she went up.

*****

The Germans took over the defence of Sicily. Weeks of hard fighting followed on the plain south of Catania. An aspect of war that I had not foreseen was the occurrence of idle spells during which we sometimes seemed to have been forgotten. At these times I was able, also unexpectedly, to do more reading than I had for a long time.

Having read in so many narratives of the previous war that the young authors of these memoirs had taken a couple of slim volumes with them to the trenches in France, I had brought two slim volumes to Sicily. One was a copy of the Soviet Constitution of 1936, known as the Stalin Constitution. This was a little book about four inches by three in size, bound in soft grey leather with the title in gilt letters. It had been sent to me from Moscow before the war. I dare say other men had pocket Bibles just like it. I was still, then, solidly I would have asserted, one of the faithful. I lip-read to myself the clauses of this Constitution as if they were verses in Scripture. They proved to me that the Soviet Union was the freest country in the world. Here it was in black and white: freedom of religion, freedom of speech, even freedom for the republics to secede. The other slim volume now strikes me as an interesting contrast. It was *Les Fleurs du Mal*. This epitome of bourgeois degeneracy had stood untouched on my bookshelf since I had joined the YCL eight years earlier. I had picked it up, unthinkingly I am sure, blown the dust off its top edge and brought it with me. And Baudelaire's verses I read aloud to myself, too, to transport me away from dismal scenes.

I was also presented by Captain Walton with a metal box which was a boon in two ways. It was solidly packed with Penguin books, a gift from some welfare organization. The captain asked me to pass the books round among the men and I did so. I also read most of them. I cannot remember the titles but they must have comprised a fairly complete set of the early Penguin editions, a selection so admirable that it has earned a place in the cultural history of this country. The other advantage of this gift, far greater at certain moments, was that when I had sunk it into the earth at one end of a slit trench, it made excellent head cover.

It is not surprising that I found time to write a story during this campaign. It was a humorous anecdote, written only to obey an impulse and to amuse Nelly, to whom I sent it. I had no idea that it would ever be published. She passed it on, without my knowing, to the *Daily Worker* which printed it on the feature page. Four years later I went through the file of that newspaper in a public library in London, copied out the story and put it into one of my books as a matter of sentiment. When the book came out I regretted having done this, as the story is rudimentary, the sort of thing that appeared in pre-war holiday magazines.[1]

But then, as I try to understand the fluid state of my mind in that year, I realise that the reason why I did not know that the story had been published

---

1   The short story "The Toy Shop" was published in the Daily Worker, 19 Oct 1943. It was revised and published as the chapter "The Music Box" in *The Human Kind*. The original story is reproduced in Susie Thomas, Andrew Whitehead and Ken Worpole (eds), *So We Live: The Novels of Alexander Baron* (Nottingham, 2019), pp.82–5.

was that I did not see the *Daily Worker* at this time. The government had lifted the ban on it in August 1942, but although I still received batches of copies of *Challenge*, a paper which to me seemed more and more juvenile, I had hardly ever bothered to look at the *Worker* during our fevered year of training and did not arrange for it to be sent to me when I went abroad. Party members were passionately attached to the *Worker*. It was their life-line. I must have changed (unknowingly, I must repeat) a great deal already.

******

When the fighting ended we moved into the town of Catania. We took up our quarters in a poor street near the docks. We turned a commandeered tenement block into a barracks. It was built around a courtyard with an arched entry. A room on one side of this entrance served as a guardhouse. Round the corner more similar tenements faced the sea. The habitations in our street were only low, wooden dwellings standing in a range against some taller buildings. They looked like improvised shanties. The people in the street had suffered privation during the battle. They were hungry, many of them were ill, there was no work for the men and the street was filled with piles of rubbish that nobody tried to clear while we were there.

Only older men were to be seen. The young ones were all away at the war. Some were known to be prisoners. Women were in mourning for others. After a while some of the men were able to get an occasional day's work for the British Army at the docks but for the most part the men clustered in little clans on street corners or at the doorways of their dingy clubs, wearing their black jackets across their shoulders like cloaks and smoking cigarettes. I thought them a lot of conceited parasites on the women, who fascinated me.

The women of Sicily were to be the subject of my second novel. They lived a life of their own. They were more natural and knowing than English women. Those over forty all wore black. Those a few years older than that had faces as aged and seamed as my grandmothers'. The girls wore short print dresses faded by much washing. They walked clack-clack down the street on wooden sandals. They had a quick energy of movement and voice, emotions and tempers that flared easily and a way with men that was at once wary and frank.

I sometimes sat at the back of a little church watching the women tell their sorrows to the Virgin; and once in some back-street hall I sat squeezed on a bench among an audience of women who were all weeping loudly. The cause of their grief was the film that we were watching, "Wuthering Heights".

Figure 32 "The women of Sicily were to be the subject of my second novel." A photograph of an unknown Italian woman found among Baron's papers.

They rocked in sympathy with Cathy Earnshaw. From all parts of the dark hall they cried, "*Ah, la poverina, la poverina!*"

A demi-god came down among them. They adored him and rejoiced. He was our new medical officer, an Indian captain. He was a brave young man. He had been wounded three times. One day he gave us a lecture on the pleasures of being wounded and had the soldiers howling and choking with laughter. He was also strikingly handsome and when he started an informal surgery for the women they flocked to him, some bringing real complaints and some inventing ones just to see him.

The Italian language came to my tongue more easily each day. I had the help of an Italian grammar which my father had sent to me wrapped in the latest consignment of new woollen socks from my mother, but the language seemed simply to rise up inside me as if from a reservoir. I became a general factotum in the street, everybody's friend, and in particular the MO's interpreter. As my Italian vocabulary increased it included a disproportionately large number of gynaecological terms.

The company was kept busy. Clothing and equipment had to be inspected and replacements given out. Every day was a round of parades and barrack duties. Later, we began to train. The soldiers were kept strictly in hand, only being allowed out in parties, each for three hours at a time, on the condition that this concession would be cancelled if it was abused. In these restricted periods however, many of them were able to make friends in the town and even virtually to set up households with lonely women.

I and two other corporals struck up a friendship with a girl whose name I forget, a prostitute. She was eighteen, a small, slender, pretty girl. We were all wistfully fond of her but none of us made any advances to her. We used to sit with her at the table of a tiny café on the waterfront chatting about childish things. One day she picked up a British sailor. He, too, looked no more than eighteen years old, a big, innocent boy. She wore a sailor blouse and collar like his and they walked past us, going up to her flat, hand in hand like a brother and sister.

One day while we were training I took ten men to a beach outside the port for a bathing party. I was in company with Corporal Gray, who had another ten men. Eric Gray and Billy Strachan were my two most congenial companions among the corporals. They were both from the north of England, Gray having worked in a warehouse and Billy on a fishing quay. They both liked to have a serious talk and to borrow something sensible to read.

We went down the beach through gaps cut in barbed wire entanglements. Mines had been dug up and were stacked here and there. The sand was littered with Italian grenades of the kind known as Red Devils. These were

Catania - Lido Plaia.

Figure 33 "We went down the beach through gaps cut in barbed wire entanglements." Baron's postcard to his sister Ida, 12 September 1943: "I bathe in calm blue waters, and lounge on golden beaches."

like big red tin eggs. They were blast grenades; they exploded on impact and were used mostly to stun and confuse. The most dangerous thing about this grenade was the one lead pellet inside it which shot away like a bullet when it exploded. We undressed, left a man to stand guard over our weapons and clothes and went into the sea.

We were just outside the enclosing mole of the port. We swam out to the end of this; when we turned and started to swim back, we saw a party of soldiers from the Highland Division standing at the water's edge watching us. They were all short, thin men, wearing tam o'shanter caps. The HD men had a reputation for being sullen to outsiders and quick to get into fights with them. Many of the Jocks looked very young, like those on the shore in front of us, street boys from Glasgow perhaps, shovelled into the war and in a continuous state of anger. The Jocks on the beach began to throw Red Devils into the water in front of us. Shouting had no effect on them. Our sentry, whom they ignored, stood by, helpless. They kept on tossing the grenades which fell closer and closer to us, until we turned and swam out to sea again. Then at last we stopped and trod water, we saw that the Jocks were going away. We swam back to the shore, came out of the water and lay down to dry in the sun. Gray and I looked over our parties. One of my men was missing.

We went back into the water and for a long time searched and dived without finding him. We returned to the shore, dried and dressed ourselves in silence. We were now very late for our midday meal. I thought that my men must be famished. I said, "All right, get into the truck."

The men in my party did not move. They stood in a group looking at me. Gray came across to me and said, quietly, "You're a callous cunt."

I was taken aback. I had spoken in all innocence, meaning well. I asked for a volunteer to stay with me and a man stepped forward. My lance-corporal took the rest back to quarters. When they had eaten, he sent two men out to replace us and we continued for twenty-four hours to keep a vigil on the beach but we never found the body.

One day we were confined to barracks without warning, paraded and marched away. The women gathered on the pavements to watch us go and, as at the end of my Sicilian novel, many of them were crying. The men who had girlfriends in other parts of the town were not able to let them know. As far as these girls knew we just disappeared.

*****

We were loaded into a train at a railway halt outside the town. One of the group of officers conferring on the platform was a tall lieutenant-colonel.

He turned away from the group and came along the platform, preceded by the sergeant-major who was calling my name. I looked out of the carriage window as the colonel approached. I had last known him as Captain Morden in my first company. He pointed to the insignia on his shoulder and said, "Not bad, don't you think?" He asked me how I was. After I had replied, he said, "I know about your troubles. Keep smiling. You never know," and strode away to rejoin the group of officers.

We went aboard a ship in Syracuse harbour and for the next ten days sailed mysteriously about the Mediterranean. The soldiers slept on the open deck, some in the covered walks alongside the main superstructure, most of us lying like a human carpet on the open foredeck. The ship ploughed in and out of violent Mediterranean storms. Every downpour soaked us again. We slept soaked. There was a huge saloon in which officers passed the time of day. Men stood at the windows staring in like accusing spectres.

I went down with a fever. I was so weak and so hot that someone (I had no idea who) caused me to be taken down to the sick bay. The ship's doctor diagnosed malaria. I spent the next five days in a wonderful bed. The mattress was a foot deep and felt as if it was full of water. The only other men in the sick bay were both from my company, Corporal Docherty and Brett, my lance-corporal, who had done a year in the glasshouse for hitting a sergeant-major with a pick handle. I hardly knew where I was for most of the time. I can recall only the hot spells when I felt as if I was melting. By the time the ship docked I was weak but the attack seemed to have passed.

We were in Taranto harbour. (On the southern Italian mainland, it is only a few hours' sailing time from Syracuse.) All the medical orderlies were on deck. A seaman came in and left a big steaming dixie on the orderlies' table. As soon as he left we went to the table and found that the dixie was full of pork stew, enough for six. We ate it clean.

The company had marched away when we were taken off the ship and put into an ambulance. At the base hospital wounded were being brought in. The hospital was in a big *palazzo* standing in its own grounds. A busy medical officer met us at the foot of a grand marble staircase. He pointed to a space of empty floor in the angle of the staircase, and told us to kip down there until he had time to see us. As soon as he had gone away we walked out of the hospital. The sentry at the gate did not challenge us.

We tramped along a country road going north, hoping for a lift, but not a vehicle came along. The evening passed. It grew dark. A heavy downpour began. At last we saw a small truck parked on the verge. The driver appeared to be looking at a map with a flashlight. We crowded round the cab, one of us banging at the window. Then we all started to shout with laughter in the rain. We had found one of the company's trucks.

Figure 34 "We tramped along a country road going north, hoping for a lift, but not a vehicle came along." Baron in Sicily, 1943.

The company was in a field. The only shelter was afforded by some rolls of tarpaulin which had been thrown down here and there. The men were unwinding them and crawling into them. The rain was still falling in rods as we wandered about looking for a hospitable tarpaulin. We heard the major's voice booming in the darkness, "Where are those corporals?" He roared out our names one by one. We found him. He took us to a farmhouse, the officers' quarters. We followed him in. It consisted mainly of one big room with a stone floor. The room was packed with officers setting up camp beds or undoing bedrolls. A flight of five steps led up to a stone landing outside an inner door. The three of us took possession of this, lay down on the stone and slept soundly.

In the morning the Old Man (as we affectionately called Major Bell) marched the company back to Taranto and commandeered a cinema as a billet. We lay down in the rows between the seats. The men had a whip-round for ration tins and gave them to the projectionist, who ran incomprehensible films for his new patrons all day long.

After a wait of several weeks it turned out that a wild rumour was true. We were going back to England. We embarked; we would learn when we arrived home that Montgomery was back in England to prepare for the Second Front and that he had brought his Thirtieth Corps with him, three famous divisions and all their supporting troops.[2]

---

2   Montgomery (1887–1976). 'Monty', The best known of British Army commanders during the Second World War. Widely associated with the defeat of German forces in North Africa. Later the 1st Viscount Montgomery of Alamein.

Chapter 31

I was in a hammock in the deep hold of the troopship. Something woke me up in the middle of the night. It was silence. For two weeks the pounding and vibration of the ship's engines had been part of the natural order. I went up on deck. The ship was at anchor. The water around looked still and glassy. Clustered lights twinkled in a line, not far away. We were lying off Northern Ireland. The next day we dropped anchor in Gair Loch, in Scotland.

We went down the gangways. A train was waiting for us. Nice Scottish ladies came up and down the quay with trays of sandwiches and buns and jugs of hot tea. It was a grey November day. We all scribbled letters to our families. The ladies took them from us to post.

The train ran south all day without stopping. Scotland went by the windows, then England. Everyone knows the feeling of coming home from a holiday when all is ordinary once more, as if the holiday had never been. So it was with Sicily; for the present, all that was out of our minds.

Dusk came. I recognised the Sussex Downs in the distance. Then it was dark. A shimmer of white light outside the train brought us to the windows. Parachute flares were dropping. A German 'plane made a run over us, firing. We were not hit. We ran into a tunnel and stopped. When we came out at the other end the 'plane had gone.

We got down out of the train at Hailsham. We split up into parties and were taken in trucks to billets in the villages round about. With another soldier, a man named Brewster, I was put down outside a little bungalow. It was not unoccupied. It turned out that a batch of replacements were already waiting for the company and one of them was in the bungalow. We walked around, exploring, and he trailed behind us. We were in the little back garden when the night lit up once more and the bellow of a 'plane in a shallow dive sent Brewster and me flat on the lawn. The replacement stood over us laughing and calling us "charlie", which means cowardly. The 'plane flew away without dropping any bombs.

I cannot imagine that the German High Command had put on a reception for our little company. Perhaps they knew that Thirty Corps was moving into the South of England; or we might have come in for a couple of the random hit-and-run attacks that were taking place all over the Southern counties.

We were given fourteen days' leave. After I had seen my family I went to London. I called in at the YCL office and found that I had arrived in time for a meeting of the League's National Council. The members at this meeting looked terribly young to me; most of the boys were under military age. They seemed a bright, pleasant lot. The chairman announced that I was present and I stood up to an ovation. I fell back at once into the old rhetoric. I talked about the Eighth Army and told them that soldiers deserted from hospital to get back to the front, just like the Russian soldiers who, according to propaganda articles in communist newspapers, were doing this on a huge scale.

It was true that this took place but it was not true that the British soldiers were doing it out of eagerness to get back into battle. When we were on the Catania Plain lone soldiers used to come into the company lines on their way back to their battalions. They had indeed escaped undischarged from the base hospitals in Algiers and by mysterious ruses had been able to cross the Mediterranean undetected. They did so, however, because to a soldier the army was a vast, indifferent machine peopled by strangers who cared nothing for him; he would sooner be under fire with his own comrades and leaders than at the mercy of strangers.

Above all these men went back to the front with their wounds still raw to avoid being sent to the convalescent depot, about which fearful stories circulated among the troops. It was said to be staffed by brutes who were determined to teach the convalescents that a wound was no excuse for skulking and who made life worse than miserable for their victims.

It was during this leave that I met Otto Schling for the last time.[1] I had known him before the war as one of the leaders of the Czechoslovak Young Communist League who had served in Spain with the International Brigades before coming to this country in 1939. His English wife was a prominent and well-liked member of our own YCL. What I did not know

---

1   Otto Schling (Šling) (1912–1952). Leading Czech Communist. Active abroad in the Comintern in Spain and England. Returned to the Czech Republic in 1945 and became secretary of the Czechoslovak Communist Party in Brno. Arrested in 1950 and executed in 1952 as one of the defendants in the so-called Slánský show trial. Apparently, according to Alison Macleod in her *Uncle Joe*, Mick Bennett (qv) protested to both Harry Pollitt and John Gollan that Schling was innocent. But British Communists did not have the leverage in Prague or Moscow to influence events.

until the day in late 1943 that I was taken to see him was that he was the Rezident of the Communist International in Great Britain.

The Comintern kept a Rezident (the accent is on the last syllable) in every country to advise and assist the local Communist Party and of course to report on it to Moscow. The existence of this functionary was a close secret. Out of the forty or fifty thousand members enrolled in the British party in 1943 I doubt if more than a few score were even vaguely aware that such a personage existed. Perhaps a dozen knew the Rezident's identity.

After the war the Schlings went back to Czechoslovakia and Otto became one of the leaders of the new communist state, In 1952 he was one of the group of top communists arraigned on preposterous charges in one of the show trials that were ordered by Stalin throughout Eastern Europe to tighten his control over the region. Otto and several others were hanged.

Costa Gavras made a film, *L'Aveu*, about the trial, based on the testimony of a survivor.[2] In the film the part of Otto Schling is taken by someone who looks very much like him. He is shown in the dock continually pulling up his trousers because he has lost weight in prison and he is not allowed to wear a belt. This must be true to what happened. I, too, have sometimes played the part of Otto Schling; that is, as writers do, I have tried to think with his mind while unbelievable things are being done to him, right up to the moment when he feels the noose choking him.

According to Otto, when we met at the end of 1943, the official line – or policy – of the Comintern was now that the end of the war must see the completion of the world socialist revolution. The Comintern was only a speaking-tube for Stalin. In plain English, Stalin had decided on the conquest of Europe after the war and the establishment of communism throughout the world.

Stalin must at that very time have already been in the process of changing his mind about this, for it is a matter of record that in 1943 he was getting information about the British and American plans to make atom bombs. He set his own scientists to work with the same aim. But at the end of the war, although he put up an aggressive front in Europe and helped the Chinese communists in their last push for power, he avoided a conflict. The communist parties in the West had to execute secret about-turns and take part in or support capitalist governments, not without some confusion in certain countries.

---

2   *L'Aveu* (The Confession). A film made in 1970 by Costas Grivas, starring Yves Montand and Simone Signoret. It focusses on the Slanský trial through the fate of Artur London (1915–1980).

The Comintern, of course, had been officially dissolved several months before my leave. None of us took this seriously. Schling was still *en poste*. We now know that the Comintern leaders in Moscow simply moved with their staffs from one building to another, henceforth under the wing of the Foreign Department of the Soviet Communist Party.

*****

Nobody in the company doubted that there was soon going to be a Second Front, for when we came back from leave we moved to Southampton and we began to train at sea. Southampton was crowded with the soldiers and trucks of the three Thirty Corps divisions. In the canteens the soldiers exchanged information about their new training, which all pointed one way, and conversation dwelt on one question, "When d'you reckon, mate?"

One quiet Sunday morning I was out for a walk with Gray and Strachan. We went into a café in the Shirley district of the town. The only other customer was a soldier sitting at a table talking loudly to himself, ignored by the woman polishing cups behind the counter. He was laughing to himself and shouting, "Zeez-zeez-zeez — CRACK!" again and again, clearly meaning to imitate the fall of mortar bombs. After watching him for a moment I walked to his table. My friends followed me and we sat down with him. I said, "I owe you a cup of tea, corporal."

He wore the shoulder titles of some vanished regiment, the Northumberland Horse, but he was an anti-tank gunner. These old names were often preserved out of sentiment. I suppose I should have called him bombardier, the artillery rank indicated by two stripes. I had last met the man on the Catania Plain. I had been sent on with a small advance party to occupy a new location for the company. On one side of the location a battery of twenty-five pounders were slamming away at targets around Misterbianco. On the other, some tired infantry were resting at the foot of a tall cactus hedge. Some anti-tank guns were harboured against the hedge, their crews sprawling around them. As I walked past the gunners one of them, this corporal, called out to me and held out a mess tin of tea invitingly, perhaps because I, too, looked dog-tired, unshaven, plastered with dust, my face disfigured with desert sores widely daubed with gentian violet disinfectant and streaked with dried blood from a nick in my forehead. I squatted down next to him and we exchanged news while I sipped the boiling hot tea, a life-saver.

I was not surprised by this second encounter. Such unexpected meetings seemed often to occur in an army of millions. He remembered our meeting, appearing delighted. He calmed down but as we talked about Sicily and hit upon shared experiences he would again laugh loudly, in an odd, childlike way. He said, after a while, more quietly, "They should never have sent us home. It breaks your heart," and when we stood up to leave he said, "You keep your heads down next time, lads."

Parties of our men were sent to Portsmouth Dockyard, where naval ratings taught them the elements of seamanship. We took turns at sea in the Channel, sometimes on board our own British mother ship, HMS *Tasajera*, sometimes on American ships. We liked to sail with the Americans. Their galleys were open all day long, a real cafeteria service, with every kind of hot dish to be had for the asking, and coffee, cream, ice cream, cookies and soft drinks *ad lib* at any time.

We learned to handle landing craft. We were out one day running an LCA off the Isle of Wight. A dense white fog came down on us and we ran head-on into the end of Ryde pier. We backed off fast as the Pier Master leaned over the rail and shouted through a loud hailer, "Ahoy! Who's there?"

As we disappeared into the fog we answered with a great shout, "Monty's men!"

Those of us who were not at sea went into the Southampton docks, where we helped sappers to build a new type of landing craft, the Rhino. As these were launched we took them to sea and learned to work them. The Rhino was a huge raft made up of buoyant metal boxes welded together along struts of angled steel. It was propelled by two Chrysler Marine engines at the rear and had a small ramp at the front. It could take trucks, guns, small armoured vehicles and supplies ashore as well as troops.

By the Spring we were taking part in big exercises at sea, simulated assaults in which troops of all arms took part with gun support from the Navy.

I had one more short leave. In London I went to supper with Mick Bennett. He said, "There won't be a Second Front this year."

"How do you know?"

"Manny Shinwell told Pollitt." Shinwell was War Minister in the coalition Cabinet. He had once been a man of the Left and was still cautiously friendly towards them.[3]

A year before I would have plunged into argument and given an account of what we were doing on the south coast. Indeed I would have thought it

---

3 'Manny' Shinwell, Baron Shinwell (1884–1986). British Labour politician. In his later career he served as Minister of Fuel and Power, 1947–1950, Secretary of State for War (1947–1950) and Minister of Defence, 1950–1951. (On Pollitt and Bennett, see above.)

my duty earlier to let the Party know. Now I decided to take my cue from Manny Shinwell. I held my tongue.

After this, leave stopped. Now we had to hand letters in for censorship as we had when we were overseas. On the notice-boards was an Army Council Instruction forbidding us to talk even among ourselves about what was going on.

I had a moment of suspicion, then, when one day in the company office Major Bell and his second-in-command Captain Walton, asked me what I thought was going to happen. I wondered if they were testing me. We were alone; I decided that I was with friends and I told them.

At the time it was still assumed that an invasion of France would have to take place where the Channel is narrow. It is only twenty-one miles wide between Dover and Calais. The Germans took this for granted, too, and (though I did not know it) most of their troops were concentrated there. But, I said, Thirty Corps was here and it was an assault corps. We knew that the Americans were on our right in the western counties, and that they were practising at sea; we had sent a detachment to exercise with them, on an occasion when our men claimed to have seen Eisenhower and Montgomery on the beach.

I asked, what if we went across here? It was true that the Channel here was eighty miles wide and that there were no ports in front of us; but I had seen some strange contrivances being built in the docks, floating platforms with steel pillars at their corners which were secured by huge ring-bolts. If these bolts were pulled away the pillars would drop to the sea-bed and secure the platforms as floating piers. These piers were, of course, components of the Mulberry Harbour which was to be taken across in sections but I had no idea of that great undertaking.

Finally I suggested that airborne troops might be dropped to secure the flanks of the attack. Those on the right could seal off the base of the Cotentin Peninsula and start a drive on the great port of Cherbourg from inland.

This was a fair forecast of what was to happen. I was not a clairvoyant or a military genius. I had used my eyes, but what I had seen and surmised had all come together when I read a book that was published in 1943, *Paratroops* by F.O. Miksche. Miksche was a Czech communist who had been an officer with the Republican artillery in Spain.[4] His book was an argument for the use of parachute troops on a large scale, something which had not

---

4   F.O. Mischke. Born 1905. Served in the International Brigades in Spain. Writer on military themes. See *Blitzkrieg: The German Method 1939–41* (London, 1941) and *Paratroops: The History, Organisation and Technical Use of Airborne Formations* (New York, 1943).

yet been attempted. To illustrate his argument he postulated an Anglo-American invasion of France and he located it on the very stretch of Normandy coast that we were now facing and on which the Allies were to land on D-Day. He had a sketch map to explain it, showing airborne divisions landing on the left to make a flank (I do not recall whether or not he opted for the river line which was chosen in the event) and on the right at the base of the Cherbourg Peninsula.

I found time to write during these months. In Sicily, as well as the short story, I had written some articles which were printed in the *Eighth Army News*, a paper which was as keen as *Challenge* to get its readers to write for it. It was the only real soldiers' paper in the war; when a town fell to the Eighth Army the *News* crew followed the forward troops in, commandeered a press and brought out an issue.

I also started a novel. It was called *Death On A Troopship*. During the voyage to Sicily a rumour had persisted that the convoy was being followed by a submarine. One sunny day when we had reached calm southern waters, the convoy closed up into slow, stately lines. Three hundred of us were on an upper deck at the time doing physical exercises. While we were springing and knees-bending we heard the muffled boom of explosions and turned to see destroyers chasing between the lines of ships dropping depth charges. The P.T. instructor roared, "Never mind the side-show, my lads. Watch ME!" We were creatures of training and tradition and in an atmosphere of pride and high spirits we kept our eyes to the front as we once more bounced and flung our arms out, all in unison.

It was easy to elaborate a thriller from these events; quite a good one, as writers always think about the books they have failed to write. When I had free time I typed a chapter in a corner of the company office. I completed about fifty foolscap pages. I kept these in a manila folder which I used to stiffen the back of my big pack.

*****

We were sent on embarkation leave. I spent all of it with my family in Newbury. The days were sunny. I read and went for walks with my sister. I felt relaxed and at peace. I had decided not to go to London. I did not want to meet any Party people. This time I let my parents come with me to the station. We were alone on the long, open platform of Newbury Station. I shook hands with my father and kissed my mother on the cheek. They only said a few commonplace things; as usual they were both calm and smiling. As the train took me away I watched the two small figures receding.

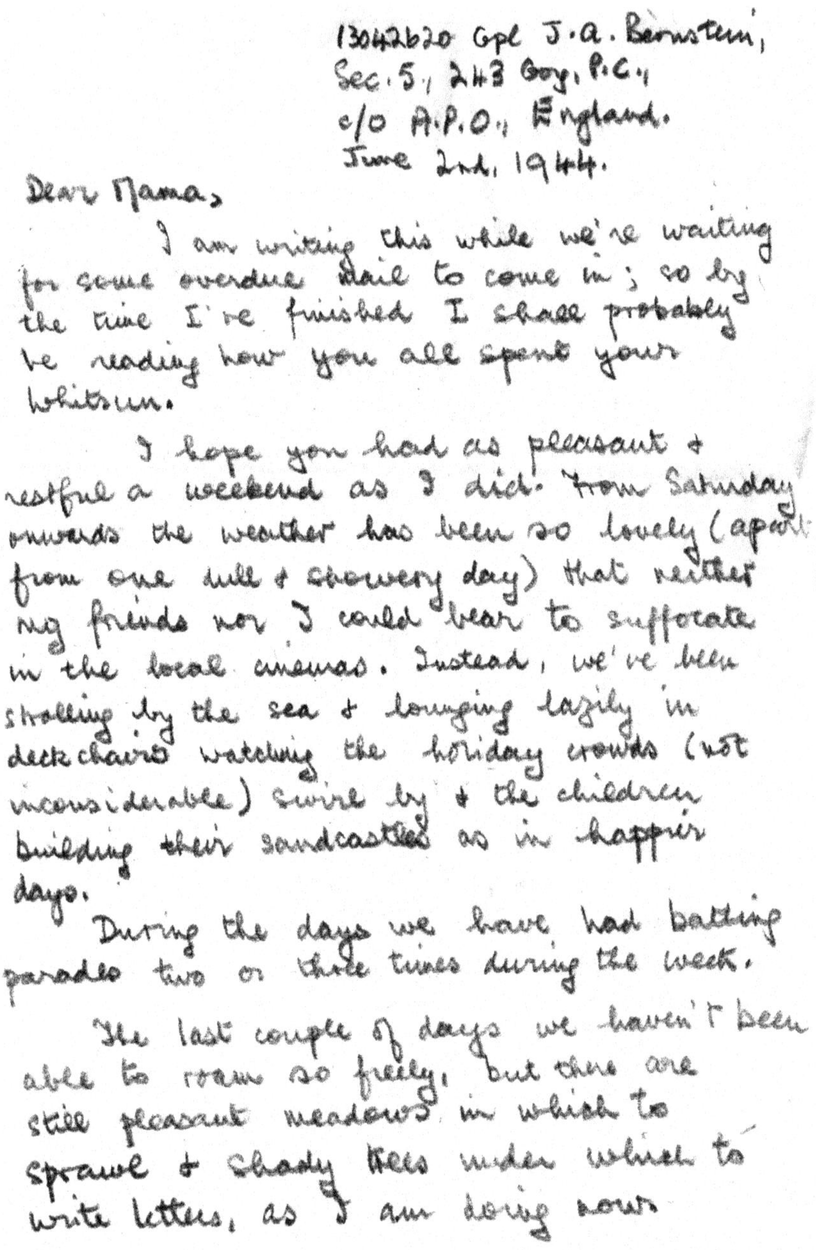

13042620 Cpl J.A. Bernstein,
Sec. 5, 243 Coy, P.C.,
c/o A.P.O., England.
June 2nd, 1944.

Dear Mama,

 I am writing this while we're waiting for some overdue mail to come in; so by the time I've finished I shall probably be reading how you all spent your Whitsun.

 I hope you had as pleasant & restful a weekend as I did. From Saturday onwards the weather has been so lovely (apart from one dull & showery day) that neither my friends nor I could bear to suffocate in the local cinemas. Instead, we've been strolling by the sea & lounging lazily in deck chairs watching the holiday crowds (not inconsiderable) swirl by & the children building their sandcastles as in happier days.

 During the days we have had bathing parades two or three times during the week.

 The last couple of days we haven't been able to roam so freely, but there are still pleasant meadows in which to sprawl & shady trees under which to write letters, as I am doing now.

Figure 35 Baron's final letter home before D-Day, 2 June 1944: "This may be the last letter I have time to write for some little while."

2

This may be the last letter I shall have time to write for some little while. I don't know; but if for a short period, my correspondence is not as regular as it has been, I know you won't worry.

Will you please start sending me bundles of papers again, as you used to? Send the Sunday papers + any issues of the dailies that Pop or you consider specially important. As soon as big events begin to happen, send the more weekly "Chronicle" + "Evening Standard" until the most spectacular period has passed. Also, I used to enjoy the "New Statesman" + the occasional "Times" you used to send.

In other words — now that I've wasted a lot of space in detailed explanations — the medicine as before.

My love to you all,

Yours,

Joe.

Figure 36 Baron and his NCO friends of the "Ginger Group", possibly on the Isle of Wight (see also Figures 6, 29 and 30).

I went to London some time later. It was on the eve of the invasion. I took a parcel of the company's documents to hand them over to the Second Echelon, a shadow organization that had been set up to take over most of the paperwork of units that were going into the field. It was a sure sign that we were about to go. I was glad that Major Bell had trusted me. I did not want to meet any Party people even by accident and stayed in the Second Echelon building until it was time to catch my train back. I did not give the matter thought. I had simply stopped trusting the Party.

The drivers, clerks and other auxiliaries left us, with all the vehicles. They were gathered with thousands like them, with a mass of vehicles, in a camp near the Port of London. It was meant to look like the main concentration of forces, and, according to the histories, it fooled the Germans. It also left the assault units unencumbered.

At last we got the expected order. Field Service Marching Order. Confined to billets. All kit to be jettisoned except the gear we wore and some small requisites. This last was unprecedented. Kit was usually collected into stores or kept to be sent on to us. Our billets were in a row of little houses. In the evening the men in my billet went out into the back garden and lit a bonfire.

Above our heads there was a thick grey blanket, the smoke screen that was now regularly put up over the town. We brought abandoned kit out of the house by the armful, trousers, tunics, underclothes, and good boots; we threw everything into the fire. Someone threw petrol on and the flames roared high. We were all squatting on the lawn like Boy Scouts in camp, drinking beer from the bottles that passed from one man to the next. We did not drink a lot but the act of flinging away kit was itself intoxicating and so were the flames. A soldier threw three or four nine-millimetre bullets into the fire. One by one they popped and squealed past us, each time provoking a loud whoop and shouts of laughter. I was standing at the back with the manila folder in my hands. Well, I thought, good-bye to all that, and threw my novel into the fire.

Next morning we were ferried across to the Isle of Wight. The officers moved into Cowes Castle, the men into a tented camp in the castle grounds which sloped down to the Solent. We looked out on the invasion fleet, a mass of ships at anchor that gave us heart.

On the last evening we assembled in a marquee. Major Bell gave us a briefing. He had been to a commanders' conference on the mainland. The arrangements were wonderful, he said, canteen ships galore and plenty of hospital ships. He was at his most genial and reassuring.

As the men dispersed the sergeant-major was already talking with a few of his cronies in the grimly affable way he had of imparting bad news.

Among them was my sergeant, Hughie O'Rourke, who passed it on to me in confidence. The Old Man had been shown a table of Casualty forecasts at the conference. We were down to lose eighty per cent. Another company had been trained to carry out the same task as us and would be passed in over us.

That night I was called up to the castle and shown into a room that was bare except for a small table and a chair. On the table was a large manila envelope. The Orderly Officer told me that I was to spend the night in the room with my submachine-gun, guarding the envelope. He left me. The envelope was not sealed. In it was the Thirty Corps Operation Order.

It was a thick wad of foolscap pages pinned together. It opened with the Corps Order of Battle and went on to give the breakdown into beaches, code names, the Corps objectives for each of the lower formations. There were maps, diagrams and appendices dealing with supplies, estimated casualties, reserves, communications, medical facilities and every other related matter. It all seemed very efficient. I read it through.

I was puzzled about my presence here. Was it a sign of trust or was it a concealed way of keeping me under guard for the night? If the major had distrusted me would he not have reported me to the security people after my forecast in the company office, the accuracy of which was now confirmed by this Order? In that case would I have been allowed to go free? Of course the document might not be genuine. The events of D-Day would throw light on that. But the army did not need to be roundabout or surreptitious in its dealings with a corporal. If I were not trusted I could have been detained without explanation here or elsewhere. I took the cheerful view. The Orderly Officer dropped in from time to time and stayed for a chat and a smoke. It was heartening to believe that I was going across among friends; and I must be the only corporal who knew the orders for an entire army corps.

Chapter 32

In two of my novels there are accounts of the landing in Normandy on D-Day, 6 June 1944. These are based on my memories but I read them today as if they were somebody else's story. My mind retains only the recollection that certain things took place but the detail of these is fading like old pencilled notes. To restore immediacy I shall turn to passages from the novels at some points in the account that follows. I clearly remember, for instance, that I was blown up, but when I turn back to what I wrote about it only a few years after the event, I see all in the scene that I have forgotten; I am, as it were, looking at a film about an actor who resembles me.

I and my nine men left the troopship in an LCA and within a mile of the shore we transferred to a Rhino which had been towed across the Channel by another ship. The company had provided crews for twenty-two Rhinos. Our task was to land on the heels of the lightly-armed assault troops to deliver their carriers, heavy weapons and trucks loaded with replenishments of ammunition and petrol. The carriers were small tracked vehicles, lightly-armoured, which could transport men and weapons across any terrain. The leading assault platoons touched down at 7.25 a.m. The first Pioneers beached twenty minutes later.[1]

Several carriers stood in the bows of our Rhino. Behind them their prospective passengers, a small crowd of infantrymen, squatted on the deck: Green Howards, an assortment of the lead battalion's odds and sods, not an officer among them. As we approached the shore a preceding company were moving off the beach. On our right the Hampshires were landing. At the top of their beach I saw a scatter of men falling like skittles. After the war I

---

1   Baron's Pioneer unit landed in the immediate wake of the first assault troops of the 6th Batallion Green Howards on Gold Beach, King Sector, below the German coastal battery at Mont Fleury, northwest of the village of Ver-sur-Mer. The Mont Fleury gun emplacements were still under construction at that time and had been subjected to intense naval bombardment in the preceding hours. They were stormed and captured by D Company, 6th Green Howards, soom after landing. Major Stanley Hollis won the only VC of D-Day for the action at Mont Fleury. See J. Sadler, *D-Day: The British Landings* (Stroud, 2019).

met a film director who had commanded a landing ship on D-Day. He told me that many of the Hampshires were young boys who clung to the ship's rails in terror when they saw men being killed in front of them. The sailors best their hands free with clubs and forced them down the ramps on to the beach.

I stood in the bows of our Rhino with two infantry corporals. Smoke was drifting across the beach from left to right. Black plumes, each with a flicker of red flame at its heart, were leaping up into the smoke, a salvo of mortar bombs exploding.

> The landing craft nosed inshore through a mass of floating rubbish. A dead sailor came floating out to sea, face and legs under water, rump poking upwards; then a dead soldier, his waxen face turned up to the sky, his hands floating palm upwards on the water; he was kept afloat by his inflated lifebelt.
>
> ...a party of Ordnance men were clearing the beach of mines. They ran a criss-cross of instantaneous fuse out over the sand: their sergeant waved his hand, they threw themselves flat on the ground and he fired the fuse. The fuse exploded with a flash, and here and there mines were set off, throwing up domes of dark brown sand. The men scrambled to their feet and went on with their work; all except one, who remained on the ground, wriggling like a cut worm, the victim of their sacrificial hurry.

Fifty yards or so to our right another Rhino kept abreast of us. It was carrying petrol and ammunition. Corporal Gray was aboard that one. I saw it hit.

> There was a small explosion and a dab of flame; then a great white detonation from stem to stern; a flash like the sun; the men disappearing; the whole shape of the craft disintegrating; an enormous, many-coloured upboiling of flame and black smoke; burning petrol cans sailing through the air; the heads of one or two men bobbing in the water, swimming slowly to the shore.

I returned my gaze to the shore. The Green Howards in front of us had planted a long cane with a yellow pennant at its top to indicate a safe place to beach. We were yawing away from this, to the left. Our coxswain was shouting some sort of appeal. I thought that he could not see the pennant (in fact one engine had cut out, swinging us to the left) and I hauled myself up on to the track of a carrier so that I could give him an arm signal. This movement saved me.

There was a bump, a faint lifting of the bows as we rode on to an obstacle and a sharp, not very loud bang. I remember seeing the steel deck open upwards in ragged petals, being lifted bodily from the track on which I stood, feeling myself lying on my back (I remember no impact) with seawater freezing through my clothes, my eyes being dazzled by the bright white-ness of the sky, the seeming slowness with which torn pieces of metal swooped down out of the whiteness, and the boots of my section clattering past me.

The deck was submerged, its plates torn open, the ramp was wrenched off its mountings and (it must have been as I got to my feet) I glimpsed the two infantry corporals lying beneath green water that was tinged with blood. One of them had his eyes open.

I have no recollection of how we got the carriers ashore or of crossing the beach. I may have been briefly out of my senses. I was deaf, I think, for a while. I am not aware of any other ill-effects.

Our last order had been to join up with the infantry if our Rhino was knocked out. At the head of the beach an infantry officer gave us directions and we made our way to the left, trudging past dead and wounded Green Howards. Some of the dead hung over a low bank beyond which a long field sloped up to the skyline. This field was the site of a German battery which we had expected still to be firing on us. The battery and the infantry defences around it had been stormed by a company of Green Howards with such dash that we were spared the slaughter which the sergeant-major had forecast. The infantry company had lost all but seventeen of its hundred and twenty men.

I remember leading my party up a lane that ran alongside this field. On our left was a high bank that supported a massive dense hedge, more a tangle of saplings than bushes. A heavy machine-gun was firing in our direction but we were below its level. It seemed to be traversing wildly, sometimes thrashing showers of leaves and branches out of the hedge. It shopped firing.

In front of us there was a gap in the hedge, about fifteen feet long. If the gunners had now laid their sights on the gap our best chance would be to bundle up and cross it in a rush, but before we reached it an armoured vehicle swerved into it and stopped broadside on. It was a converted tank with an open deck, it carried twin quick-firing Oerlikon guns with a shield, mounted on a rail. The gunners swung the Oerlikons round and as we passed behind them they began to pour shells into a copse from which the machine-gun was firing, on the far side of a ploughed field.

The lane brought us to a village where a sergeant hailed us and led us into an orchard on the left where the Regimental Sergeant-Major of the Green Howards, a tall, upright man, was organizing a perimeter defence for the village. He directed us to the far side, where we dug slit trenches. We were resting after this task when an infantry lieutenant arrived with his platoon. He told us to move farther up the hedge. We obeyed and started all over again, not even grumbling. We were too resigned to such things.

Our pits were up against another tall Normandy hedge. We were on top of a bank above a narrow sunken lane on the other side of which was a thick plantation of slender trees. Beyond this was a German strongpoint which held out for three days. A party of our men had gone in with the Canadians on our left. They did not come back to us until the strongpoint was subdued.

When they returned, one of them told me how he saw a leading battalion cut down by machine-gun fire. A battalion of *Québecois* went in over them, howling, with their fighting—knives out. Earlier, he related, when he and his comrades had come ashore, in a little fishing port, a desperate battle was going on all round them. Two of them jumped down into a crater, saw the exposed end of a big concrete drain, crawled into it and tucked into their assault rations while street fighting continued above their heads.

I cannot recall on which of the subsequent nights I had a trench blown in on top of me. I only have one picture of a slope of yellow ground, perhaps lit by the glare of an explosion. I know that I jumped into a German slit trench on top of another man and gasped, "Sorry," to him as another explosion followed and the trench caved in. It was well made, with baulks of wood to support the parapet. These were driven inwards above our heads and stopped the earth which tumbled in from burying us altogether. The other man was heaving and choking underneath me. I worked a hand up past a timber. It may have been seen. The baulks were suddenly lifted away and we were hauled out.

Two mornings after D-Day the missing Corporal Gray came back to us with three men. They had gone on too far and found themselves behind the German forward positions when night fell. A French farmer had hidden them. In my novel about Normandy, *From the City, From the Plough*, I have an incident in which a corporal returns after his friend has given up hope.

Gray and his men came back pulling a little handcart loaded with provisions which the farmer had given them. They had brought this through the German and British forward positions without being challenged. I did not put this in my story. There is a limit to what a writer can make his readers believe.

Astonishingly, only one of Gray's party had been killed when their Rhino blew up. Four others, wounded, were all recovered from the sea. I had lost two men on D-Day, both wounded. One came back to us from the dressing-station. The other, a boy of nineteen, went blind in hospital.

*****

The story of Major Keith begins in Sicily.

We had settled in beneath the trees that dotted one end of a field, a long stretch of parched grassland that was bounded by the usual low drystone wall. A line of taller trees made a screen between us and another expanse of grass which also had its bordering clumps of trees. A sister company of Pioneers moved in one day beyond the dividing trees. Like us, the men dug shallow sleeping pits against the wall or clustered under the trees, where they and their trucks would have some concealment from the Fw190's.

On the morning after their arrival we were astonished to see them drawn up on parade in the open centre of their field. They remained there for a long time, while NCO's fussed about getting the ranks perfectly aligned, while a rifle inspection was held and then while they simply waited. The sun was coming up in the sky all the time; the Sicilian sun that could kill. In the distance we could hear aero engines idling about the sky. Sometimes we could even hear the German 'planes running up their engines on the Catania airfields before they took off. We never assembled in the open. It was asking for trouble. The company beyond the trees was asking for it now and we were near enough to them to feel uncomfortable.

At last their company commander came out of a small stone cabin that must have been his quarters or his company office. He was a small, dapper man with sandy hair. His quick movements brought a terrier to mind. This was Major Keith. He stood for a long time addressing them in a high voice, in words inaudible to us, in what sounded like a tone of harangue.

There was no mingling between the men of the two companies in the days that followed. Troops in the field did not have canteens or time off for social life. The men were not allowed to wander far from their squads or platoons and they never had any wish to do so. However, drivers met on their runs to dumps and to headquarters and NCO's went to and fro on

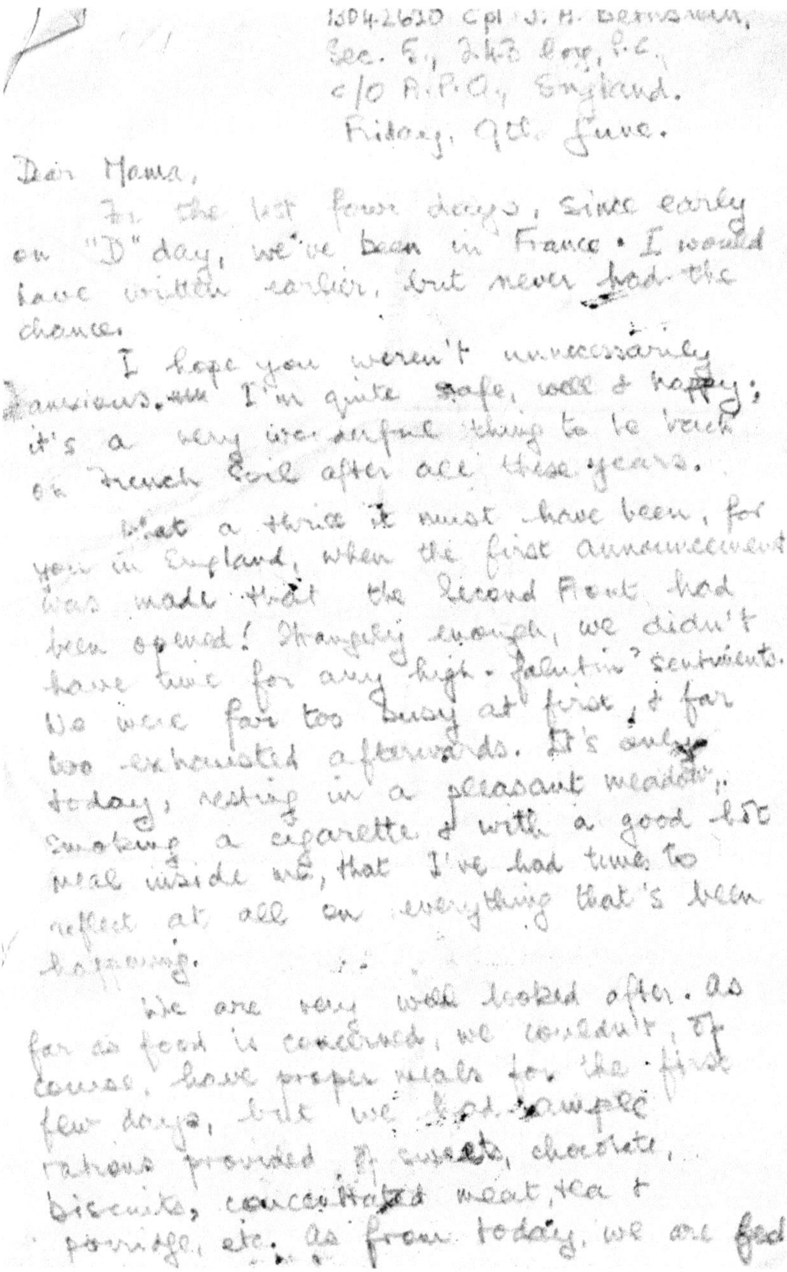

Figure 37 "I cannot recall on which of the subsequent nights I had a trench blown in on top of me." Baron's letter home, 9 June 1944, his first since D-Day, in which he comforts his mother: "I hope you weren't unnecessarily anxious. I'm quite safe, well and happy."

rather more substantially, on the famous "compo" rations — boxes from which each little group of men can make up three really good meals a day. For instance, I've just had pork, vegetables & potatoes, followed by golden pudding, tea, & biscuits. We are expecting our first mail in; & have newspapers, tho' rare as yet, get here in one day.

Please don't send any parcels, but lots of papers, as you did when I was in Sicily.

Keep well, don't worry, & write soon. I'll write, too, as often as I can.

My love to Pop, Sha & yourself,

Yours,

Joe

errands. Stories about Keith came to us. His men thought he was mad. Some of them feared him. He was always looking for trouble. He wanted to win a medal, they said. He kept them on parade while they could hear the German 'planes in the sky and jeered at them as cowards. Early every morning he came out of his hut and pranced about stark naked in full view of his men, doing physical jerks.

One day a new lieutenant was attached to our company, Mr. Logan. He was a man of about thirty, tall, lean, muscular and tanned; I am reminded of him when I see old Australian films about cattle drovers in the outback. He had no duties and simply pottered about. Hughie O'Rourke told me that he had come to us from Keith's company.

A friendly officer told me more about the newcomer. Events in Keith's company had come to a head. During one morning parade a private soldier had fixed his bayonet and charged out of the ranks towards Keith. Perhaps everybody was too dumbfounded to move; nobody did so. The soldier had almost reached the major when two men brought him down. Logan had suffered at the major's hands. After this incident he could stand it no more and had a tremendous quarrel with Keith, saying (or something like it) that he felt like finishing the job himself. The colonel sent him to us to cool off. Soon afterwards he was transferred away.

We saw nothing of Keith's company after that. I had forgotten about them until, in Normandy, some days after the landing I came across a Pioneer who was waiting with other wounded men to be taken out to a tank landing ship which would carry them back to England.

I went across to him, gave him some cigarettes and learned that he was from Keith's company. I asked how things had been. "I'm well out of it," he said. He had a splinter wound in the leg. "We got shelled to fuck."

I said, "Is Keith as crazy as ever?"

"He's snuffed it, thank God," he answered.

"A shell?"

"Some bugger shot him," he said. This, in the English of the streets, referred without any doubt to a man in Keith's own company. "He got us in the shit and then some bugger done him."

This was not the story that I found in the official records after the war. Keith's company had landed on the left flank and from the start came under frequent shelling. Keith's command post was under particularly heavy fire. One of the tasks performed by Pioneers in the advance from Normandy was to go out ahead of infantry attacks and to put up smoke in so-called shell screens, to make it more difficult for the German artillery to locate and break up the infantry when they came on. The men doing this job were protected by their own comrades deployed as infantry and they regularly came under shell and machine-gun fire. Two days after the landing Keith's men went out to put up smoke on the flank. Keith was with them. The official report was that he was one of those killed by the shelling.

The official report is probably true. I know what wild rumours flew about among the Other Ranks.. They saw him as a man looking for a medal. When they were given a dangerous job they assumed that it was his fault. "He got us in the shit." I could never know whether the wounded man's tale was the truth or wish-fulfilment.

It did not matter. One day the tale would emerge from my mind as the story of the Mad Major in my first novel.

*****

I did not go through Normandy with the outlook of an observer. Obviously I was storing up experiences. Even the most minute occurrences or remarks were snapped up and retained in some part of my mind, but it was without my knowledge. I was aware only of being a soldier among soldiers and my conscious mind was occupied only as theirs were.

The process of literary creation is partly unconscious, that of original conception sometimes entirely so. It was not simply that a clutter of memories was piling up in some mental attic. It seems to me that a secret craftsman in me was looking out for a master theme and even selecting here and there material for a structure. I may be deceiving myself, for it was not until three years later, in 1947, that all this seemed to come swiftly together in my mind.

At any rate, an incident in my Normandy novel, *From the City, From the Plough*, reproduces something that I saw in the early days of the campaign, a trivial enough event but I recognise it as the seed from which the novel grew.[2] An infantry battalion was trudging up to put in an attack, a straggle of bemused bumpkins toiling along under the weight of their gear in single file on the left-hand side of a lane, shepherded (as I say in the novel) by their tired, schoolmasterly officers who walked alongside them trying to keep up their spirits with feeble jokes and wise-cracks. I stood at the entrance to a field watching this. I am sure that without my knowledge a crucial matter was settled in my mind. I would write a book about the life and death of one of those unregarded county battalions.

---

2   *From the City, From the Plough* is Baron's first and highly successful novel, published by Jonathan Cape in 1948.

The battalion I watched may have been the same that I heard about soon after, of newcomers to the war who were caught by a terrible bombardment while they were trying to form up on a start line, lost three hundred men (half their fighting strength) and scattered, too demoralized to fight for days afterwards.

Writers combine separate events into a single scene for effect. So does memory. As I watched that battalion going by, I fancy that I recollect a field hospital being set up in the meadow behind me in readiness for the attack. It was a wide marquee under the trees, its front entirely open to reveal operating tables being installed and the paraphernalia of surgery being laid out. Perhaps I saw this on another day. But even if my recollection is of two occasions, on one of them I had my first flash of disgust with war as a human activity.

How utterly senseless it was! Here were these unhappy men, plodding along, unwilling but letting their legs carry them on toward the butchery, After them came a detachment of Pioneers with rolled stretchers on their shoulders who would pick up those who were mangled but still alive and bring them back to this field. In the marquee behind me was a sort of factory where repair jobs would be done on human bodies, people with saws, knives, needles and catgut, cutting parts off, rummaging inside to bring out lumps of lead or steel shards and stitching up where stitching was possible.

This idea, or revelation, could only have lingered for moments. Certain thoughts could not be permitted lest they weaken the will. The war had to be won, even though I agreed with the poet Day Lewis that it was to defend the bad against the worse.[3] And of course, I had been told by the Comintern Rezident that we communists had more war in store for the world, to bring about our final victory. I know that later on I thought of the possibility with revulsion. I do not know if I remembered it in Normandy.

*****

The infantry moved on. We remained a mile from the sea. Of the twenty-two Rhinos that our company had been tasked to land on D-Day, Gray's was one of five that had disappeared. Eight others had been knocked out during the landing, by hits or by running on to mines or on to the teeth of underwater obstacles called hedgehogs. Most of the other nine were damaged. Half the company was put to work lifting intact engines out of

---

3   Cecil Day-Lewis (1904–1972). Writer and poet who later moved away from his Communist sympathies. Appointed Poet Laureate in 1968. In common with some other Left intellectuals he wrote crime stories. In his case under the name Nicholas Blake.

the wrecked craft and removing every other component that could be used, so that the rest could be patched up and made seaworthy again. Another detachment was sent to do a similar job upon damaged tanks.

```
                                      13042620 Cpl.J. .Bernstein,
                                      Section 5, 243 Coy.,P.C.,
        Note new address              B.W.E.F.
                                      Monday, June 26th, 1944.

Dear Pop,
         During the last two days I've had a real beanfeast
as far as mail is concerned. Letters from Mama, Ida and yourself,
several bundles of papers, and your very useful parcels, for
all of which many thanks. With the air pillow, and with other
comforts that have accumulated recently in my underground
boudoir, I am living in princely luxury. Ida's letter was well up
to her old standard. My friends were puzzled at the explosive
cackles and chuckles I emitted while reading it. What a gift for
gossip that girl has! I also received letters from my friends,
as well as a book and a large box of cigarettes.

         Tell Mama I listen to the home radio every day. My
regular listening time is nine o'clock in the morning, when I
take down the news at dictation speed for our company newspaper
(now in its seventeenth issue).

         We drank your whisky (by the way, I was tickled at the
way in which you referred darkly to "my favourite throat medicine"
in your letter!) on the spot when I opened your parcel. We all
had a swig each and toasted those we'd left behind us.

         The news continues very good, doesn't it. As I write
the Russians have Viborg in the bag and Vitebsk ripe to follow.
Their offensive is spreading along hundreds of miles of front,
giving the hard-pressed Germans new headaches every day. On this
side, Cherbourg, though still just about holding out as I write,
is a foregone conclusion. Its possession will be an enormous
advantage to us. How much we need a big port like this you can't
imagine, though we have so far confounded the enemy by doing
successfully what they had previously declared to be impossible,
i.e., adequately supplying a big army off the beaches. You can
look forward to lots more good news from the West.

         How are you managing these days about getting up to
town.? I hope you're not finding it too exhausting in the
circumstances. And are the "buzz-bombs" much of a nuisance? --
are you getting any in Newbury?

         Thanks, all of you, for writing. I hope to hear
from you all regularly as I did in Sicily -- it is a
pleasure I can't adequately describe.

         Fondest love to you all,

                  Yours,
```

Figure 38 "We saw and took part in furious activity but we took everything as it came, a battle or a storm, without speculating about it." Baron's letter home, 26 June 1944, reassuring his father about his own welfare and the course of the war. It offers only the merest hint at his real experiences: "… and toasted those we left behind us."

As June went on the refitting of the Rhinos became more urgent. Although it was midsummer the weather, cold and cloudy from the start, worsened. The winds grew fiercer daily and the seas ran high. We entered into a period that some war historians have called The Great Storm. It became increasingly difficult to bring in supplies and reinforcements. It was an agonizing crisis but we knew nothing of it. We were sent back to the beaches. We saw and took part in furious activity but we took everything as it came, a battle or a storm, without speculating about it.

In the back of an open truck I returned to Mont Fleury, where we had landed. The grassy, gently-sloping expanse across which the Green Howards had dashed to storm the enemy battery was transformed. As far as I could see, a line of huge wooden loading platforms had been erected at the head of the beach. Offshore it seemed as if every tiny coaster in the British Merchant Marine had been collected here, fat little vessels each with a single funnel. Stranded by low tide, many of them lay on their sides in the mud. I had not known that such minuscule tubs existed. They were like children's toys.

Ducks ran to and fro. The Duck (DUKW: I have never found out what the acronym stood for) was an amphibian, a boat with wheels or a truck that floated. It was a long white craft (let me call it so) on high wheels with huge tyres. It ran down a track of steel mesh from the platforms to the sea and drove into the water, when a change of gear activated its marine propeller. An army of little brown figures swarmed on the platforms, soldiers unloading supplies from the Ducks as these arrived back from the ships, others running trolleys loaded with crates to the rear of the platform, where trucks arrived unceasingly from the front to be loaded up, turned round and sent back to the forward dumps.

I spent some days with a detachment that manned a small flotilla of Ducks. We ran out to sea and tied up alongside one of the ships that were moored in deeper water. Some of us swarmed aboard up rope ladders or scramble nets, surrounded the open hatches and set to work with a small crane to send load after load of food or ammunition crates down to our comrades in the Duck. When this was stacked hazardously high with crates, we left the ship and made a sensational return trip to the beach, joyously climbing great waves and plunging into troughs with Red Indian screams.

However stormy the day, we were sent out, unless it was certain that the raging sea would overturn or swamp any Duck. Then all activity would cease. Not a box of cartridges would come ashore. A dull silence would settle upon the beaches and the guns would sound more loudly, as if to give us some hint of the situation inland.

There was now a use for the patched-up Rhinos. I was turned out of my pit at five a.m. one morning and told to take ten men to the Mulberry. This was the great artificial harbour which the invading force had towed across the Channel in sections. We did not know that the storm had broken up the American equivalent of Mulberry. Ours stood fast. Dark clouds, beneath which rags of thinner cloud scurried, prolonged the gloom. Our truck ran westward past Duck Park, as the unloading area was called, and set us down on a quay in the Mulberry Harbour.

Three sappers were waiting for us, a corporal and two privates. A Rhino was tied up in the calm dock basin directly below the high quayside on which we gathered. The corporal told us that we were going out to one of the larger cargo ships that were hove to well out to sea. He must have seen a copy of the cargo manifest, for he explained that we were to unload twenty-five pounder shells.

The twenty-five pounder field batteries were the closest to the infantry. Sometimes it was their fire alone that broke up the fierce counter-attacks of the German SS divisions which were now arriving in Normandy. Casual as we were about our duties, we must have known that.

We set off on a heavy sea. The ship was four miles out. We tied up. A crane swung nets down to us filled with green metal cases that each held two shells. On our rolling deck we had to catch these loads as they swung violently to and fro, full of sharp-edged boxes, and unload them. Gradually a pyramidal stack of boxes rose on the deck. All the time the heavy sea was lifting up the Rhino and sending it to bang thunderously against the ship's side. This went on for a couple of hours. The corporal and I speculated quietly as to how long our reconstituted Rhino would stay in one piece under this treatment. The private soldiers seemed indifferent. The ship's captain had his own concerns. He came to the rails and informed us through a loud hailer that he was going to cast us off before we stove in the ship's plates. We started our engines, the lines flew away and as we backed off, the captain's voice boomed faintly through the gale, "Good luck!"

We spent several hours butting our way over heavy seas, trying in vain to make for the shore. The ship was long out of sight. We did not see any others. We wondered how far out to sea we were. Whichever way we looked we saw only an empty, mightily heaving waste of water. The poor light became gloom as the hours went on, the clouds darker, hard falls of rain obscuring our view.

Great slopes of green water rose and fell around us. The big raft rode up these and slid down them and we heard a creaking from its welded joints.

The wind rose, howling and whimpering. The gloom thickened into dusk. Soon the dusk was grained with darkness. As far as we could see we still had the English Channel to ourselves.

Sometimes one of the hills of water subsided on to our stern. In doing so, one of them stopped our engines. We lifted the cowlings back on their hinges to see if we could start the engines again. Another great roll of water tore off the cowlings and carried them away together with the improvised wooden deckhouse in which we had left our flares.

After that we drifted with no idea of direction until we were in black darkness. All we could see was the rise and fall of shining green walls of water. As the raft lifted and fell a crack sounded and, soon after, another. If enough welds went the raft would break up and we would all go down in a torrent of sharp steel boxes. The boxes were already on the move, edging a little this way and that with the movements of the raft. We all seated ourselves round the flat top of the stack facing outward, clamped our legs against the boxes to hold them in and joined hands to resist the waves.

Our hopes rose when we heard the throb of powerful engines and three motor gunboats in line astern came out of the night close by us, going out to sea at high speed. We halloo'd and ahoy'd but they went on past us and disappeared.

Depression set in. We were soaked and chilled and the gale battered at us. We sat in silence, listening for the next crack of a weld. The sapper corporal tried to raise our spirits by starting a song ("Bill Smith knew my father", to a hymn tune). We joined in but the gale snatched the sound away from our lips and we gave up. I was now in a state of lethargic melancholy but without fear. I imagine that we all were. We drifted on in this state for a long time until someone heard a faint voice through the ravings of the storm. Roused, we heard a faint, "Ahoy!" then another and we began to respond.

A tug nosed out of the darkness with a soldier standing in the bows, his hands cupped round his mouth, calling, "Ahoy! Ahoy, there!" The tug passed us, keeping well away for fear of being thrown on to us, and went round us. We could see the crew eyeing us and talking together. At last the tug took up a position in front of us. It had to surge away two or three times to avoid a collision, then it dropped back close enough to throw us a line. What followed for at least half an hour reminded me of a scene from Conrad. Time after time the tug's crew failed to get a line to us. Throughout all the failures and frustrations the men on both craft gave no sign of impatience or disappointment but kept trying with all the calm, persistence and deliberation of Conrad's seamen.

Once we made fast with a six-inch rope. As soon as it took the strain it snapped. The efforts began again, until two lines, one to each side of our bows, were made fast. The tug took us in tow. We all sat slumped on the shell boxes as if dreaming, for what seemed hours, until we passed between the high walls of a sea entrance to Mulberry. The Rhino glided over the still water of a basin. We caught lines, tied up and climbed with stiff legs up a high steel ladder to the quay.

It was midnight when we were back in the company lines. The Old Man was waiting up for us, as he did every night for the Rhino crews that were out, sometimes for so long that they were feared lost. They all returned and all, I imagine, found him waiting by the barn in which he had kept the cooks up with hot food for the exhausted crews.

I remember this episode more clearly and in more detail than any happening on land during the Normandy fighting.

*****

By August the Allies were pushing out in all directions. The end of the battle approached. We were left behind. We moved into an abandoned farm and some idle days ensued. At the entrance to the farmyard was a big mound, surrounded by a single strand of wire roughly fixed on slats of wood. The lid of a ration box was planted on the top of the mound, with the legend daubed on it 14 BRITISH. The farmhouse was HQ. The officers and sergeants must have found quarters there or in some little houses behind the farm. The Other Ranks settled down around the edges of a big field which sloped up from the farm-house. Each pair of men cut out a wide, shallow sleeping pit, a foot or two deep, around which they built up a low wall of ammunition or grenade boxes filled with earth, fastening waterproofs overhead as cover.

Another NCO and I found a pit left by the Germans, about six feet by four. It was clean, probably having been an ammunition pit. We covered the floor and walls with waterproof capes, used a quilt from a ruined cottage as a mattress, made recesses lined with wood in the walls, used a metal plate from a wrecked vehicle to give us head cover, resting it on a baulk of wood with hooks in it from which to sling our submachine-guns and laid turfs on top of the metal plate to camouflage it, with more waterproofs beneath them to keep the rain out. An escape hatch was closed by the lid of a ration box. I wrote a description of this shelter in a letter to my mother which, to amuse her or perhaps reassure her, was so grandiose that Captain Walton, who had been censoring the mail that day, strolled across to ask if he might inspect our luxury hotel.

I wandered off into the countryside when I had no duties, sometimes on the excuse of foraging, bringing eggs back and (for the Officers' Mess, which had the facilities to cook them) fresh vegetables. I had a chance at last to speak French and the pleasure of eating a six-egg omelette in a farmhouse, with a bottle of rough white wine, a glass of calvados and bread from a cartwheel loaf. I was misguided enough one day to bring a pack full of Camembert cheeses back to the company. The officers took a few and so did my friends out of loyalty. Other men, after trying them, spat the cheese out and commanded me to take the stinking French muck away. I ate two, doggedly, and buried the rest.

Butt and Riley were from Liverpool. We put them down as dock rats, sneak thieves who stole pickings from ships' cargoes. Butt was big and swarthy with thick lips; behind his back the men called him a half-breed Scouse. Riley, his hanger-on, had a face as white as the underside of a toadstool, unique in the company in being untanned by the weather. They were both in my section. Butt always had a curiously ingratiating manner towards me. One morning I woke up in my pit to see him grinning down at me in the aperture, offering me, on a ration-box lid, several buttered biscuits heaped with jam and a mug of tea that turned out to be fifty per cent rum, and announcing, "Breakfast is served, me lord."

The rum was stolen. These two had taken to raiding the convoys that passed us on their way to the forward area. They were generous with their loot. We all (whatever our opinion of them) enjoyed their gifts of tinned chicken and duck (for whom were these meant? Nothing like this reached our officers and the wounded in the hospitals certainly did not get it) and other exotic luxuries. Idleness bred mischief and other men joined them, only a few but enough to flood the company with good things.

One morning a truck drew up in the farmyard. An officer got out of the cab and several Military Police jumped down from the back. Major Bell and the captain came out of the farmhouse and engaged the officer in conversation. They did so with an apparent persistence that struck me even from a distance. Meanwhile the sergeant-major came into the field with his usual fussy, fast stride and conferred with sergeants. The sergeants scattered to all sides of the field. Soon there was a stream of men all hurrying in one direction, to the latrines.

Our company was proud of its latrines. A set of comfortable box seats was carried on a truck and was now installed against the trees to one side of the field, with a canvas screen around it. Behind it was a mound of excavated earth. Our latrines were always spotless, cared for by two sanitary men (shit-house wallahs) who were both given the rank of lance-corporal, to provide them with some extra pay and to protect them from too-rough teasing.

In a few moments the screen at the back of the latrines had been taken down, soldiers were throwing tins down into the pit and the sanitary men were hard at work shovelling in a cover of earth and chloride of lime.

When the Old Man could (as we presumed) detain them no longer, the Redcaps came round the field, looking in vein into our shelters. I do not remember if they visited the latrine but if so, they found the canvas screen back in place, the sanitary men seated on the mound enjoying a smoke and a row of soldiers installed in the latrine peacefully reading bits of newspaper.

There was another corporal in the company who was much respected by the men as a Christian who said his prayers and was a kind friend to anyone who needed help. He and I must have agreed that some antidote to idleness was called for. We gave out handwritten notices announcing that a meeting was to take place in the barn next day. At the head of each handbill was the subject in big letters: WOMEN.

The word proved to be a draw. The venue was one of those great Norman barns with interiors like those of churches; I believe that some early churches in England were based on them. Ladders ran up the high walls to several lofts. The floor was crowded with men. Others swarmed up the ladders and sat in rows on the edges of the lofts, their legs dangling. All had their weapons with them. It brought to my still-communist mind some painting I had once seen of a meeting of the Petrograd Soldiers' Soviet in 1917.

On the day before we had given out slips of paper with questions on them, for the men to talk about in their pits before they came to the meeting. First came the question with which I had opened my pamphlet in the far-off days of 1941: was "a piece of cunt" the way to talk about a woman? Other questions asked whether women could be soldiers, whether they should be allowed to join the same trade unions as men and whether they should get equal pay with men for doing equal work.

The two of us stood on a farm cart at one end of the barn. We read out the questions one by one but we took no part in the debates. All the talking was done by the men. There was no lack of speakers. Men jumped up to demand a hearing or shouted interjections. Someone stood up to deplore obscene talk about women. ("Don't forget, your mother is a woman.") Another man started a hubbub by declaring that "no decent woman enjoys it." All who spoke were against making any concessions to women in the workplace. There was a lot of joking and much laughter but almost everyone took the occasion seriously. A man who jeered at the proceedings was shouted down. "Chuck him out!" "Ignorant!" "Ignorant!"

*****

At about this time, in the culminating British attack in Normandy, an infantry brigade was fighting on Mont Pinçon, a commanding height whose capture opened the way for the breakout. The brigade suffered heavy losses and one battalion, the 5th Wiltshires, was almost wiped out.

I heard nothing about this action at the time. In the months that followed I met men from 43 Division who told me about it. In December I was in an infantry reinforcement camp waiting — so I thought — to be sent up the line. There I came across a man from 5th Wilts who had been recovering from a wound since August. He told me more. Fifteen months later, when I had been demobilised, I started to unearth all the information I could about the battle. It was the climax I needed for my novel. The 5th Wilts became the 5th Wessex. The story leading up to this climax would be a mosaic of my own experiences. Evidently these were typical, for a number of readers who had served with the 5th Wilts wrote to me recalling events in the novel as real, and characters whom they claimed to recognise. So did many others who had served in other battalions.

*****

We took part in the drive north after the retreating Germans, riding in RASC troop-carrier trucks. Thousands of German soldiers were still on the loose around the line of advance, some of them carrying out night raids, but at nights we slept on the ground around the trucks without (do I remember this rightly?) even putting out sentries. We were all sure that the war was as good as over.

We crossed into Belgium. The trucks came to a stop in a huge hanger, perhaps a bus garage. We had lived under the sky and hidden in holes in the ground for thirteen weeks, like beasts of the field, taking to it as a normal mode of existence. We lay down on the concrete floor of the hangar and once again slept under a roof.

Chapter 33

The Langestraat in Ostend is, as its name tells us, a long street. It is narrow and at nights in the autumn of 1944 there echoed between its high walls all the noises of the small hotels, bars and dance-halls that lined it. The bars and dance-halls were busy, although there was nailed to the door of nearly every one of them a printed notice: OUT OF BOUNDS TO TROOPS.

During the day they were silent and empty of soldiers. One Military Policeman patrolling the pavement was enough to keep them away. But at nights a tide of soldiers and girls surged in and out of them, flowing up and down the street on pavements and roadway while music of many kinds mingled, little bands thumping, pianos playing, the voices of singers amplified, all in the darkness, for there were no lights or neon signs, all windows were covered by blackout curtains and the opening and shutting of doors threw only momentary shafts of light across the pavements. From time to time the M.P.'s swooped in their little covered trucks to carry out a *razzia*, but they could do little against such a host, which melted away and, when they had gone, flooded in again.

Strange, sudden changes of fortune occur to soldiers in a war. We fell asleep in our garage, dirty creatures of the earth. We awoke to board our trucks again and were set down outside a hotel on the Langestraat, our next home.

It was, of course, stripped bare. The men slept on the floors of empty rooms and were forbidden to introduce any amenities. But we opened the kitchens and the dining room. The men sat down at tables and were served civilised meals. I struck up an acquaintance with the manager and persuaded him to open two lounges, one as a Sergeants' Mess and the other as a corporals' clubroom. He gave me a comfortable mattress which I laid on the floor of my room and folded back every morning with my kit neatly arranged on top of it.

Much tolerance was shown to me by our officers; I was allowed my mattress. I rented two radio sets for the sergeants and corporals. I cannot remember through what intermediary I found the man who provided them. He lived in a flat at the top of a dingy tenement house with a large family of all ages around him. Against the walls of the room an extraordinary collection of junk was stacked, old radio sets, electric irons, vacuum cleaners, saucepans, clothes horses and so on. One of the women in the flat, whoever she was, must have been at odds with him. She saw me to the door, slipped out on to the landing, and whispered to me that he had belonged to some police force which had worked with the Germans. He was now in hiding.

I gave no thought to this attempted denunciation. I took for granted that many of the civilians we saw were turncoats and all the soldiers knew well but cared nothing that the girls who danced and drank with them in the bars had been doing so with German soldiers until a few days earlier. It has only occurred to me for the first time now, as I write forty-eight years later, that our radio sets, and all the other loot, might have been the property of Jewish families whom the collaborator had arrested and sent to their deaths.

We were now in the Canadian sector. There was a little tramway along the coast from Ostend to Blankenberge, which was near enough to be almost a suburb. On the day we arrived the Germans were still in Blankenberge. They sent a tram loaded with explosives along the line. The Canadians sent it back and followed to mop the Germans up.

We stayed here for many weeks. Working parties went out every day to do trivial jobs; otherwise we were left alone. Round the corner from the hotel we found The Scotch Tea House. A British soldier had stayed behind to open it after the 1914–1918 war. His Belgian widow made us welcome. It was a home from home. We drank tea as mother makes it and ate rock cakes and hot buttered toast with jam. A few of us NCO's had our own ideas about this good fortune. We speculated that we might be enjoying the rest that preceded a really dirty job.

There was a brothel at the far end of our street. The pious Montgomery would not tolerate brothels in the British sector but this one flourished under the Canadians. My friends and I went there sometimes to drink a glass of beer.

We sat at small round tables in a room like a barn, its high walls were bare except for dirty, flaking yellow paint. The floorboards were bare and strewn with litter. A staircase open to the room ran up a side wall to a landing. A mass of men crowded on this staircase, making a lot of noise on the wooden treads. On the landing doors were banging open and shut all the time. Once in a while a girl came downstairs for a rest. The girls all looked like farm wenches with huge shoulders and fat, mottled red arms. Sometimes we offered one of them a drink. Wearing only, as far as we could see, a short dress and a pair of slippers, she would sit down heavily as if she had been doing a hard morning at the washtub. Not bothered by us with conversation she would sip her beer for a few minutes, then sigh, thank us, and go back upstairs.

There was a terrible mood of depression in the army that autumn. So far from coming to an end the war seemed likely to drag on for years. Rumour had it that there were eighteen thousand deserters in the British and Canadian sectors alone. I sat in a canteen one afternoon when a North American voice boomed from the doorway. "Sit down! Sit down! Everyone stay where you are." It was a Canadian Military Police officer with a megaphone. His men doubled into the room, some making for the lavatories which might afford a means of escape, others taking up posts around the room. We were ordered to produce our army identity books. Then the officer and his NCO's came to all the tables, inspecting the books, scrutinising our faces and sometimes lingering to question a man.

My friends and I did not talk about the war but we were all affected by this mood. Four of us, all corporals, were called in front of the Old Man. There was some scheme afoot to rest long-service NCO's. He had four jobs on offer, all soft billets in the rear areas. Each post carried the rank of sergeant. One of them, I recall, was that of guard commander at the NAAFI Officers' Shop in Brussels.

We all refused. Perhaps we were each restrained by the presence of the others but I do not think that we would have accepted even if we had been called in separately. The inducements did not weigh much against the separation from friends and from good officers. In the end the major picked four other NCO's, I think without consulting them, choosing them on compassionate grounds.

One morning I went with a working party to the port area of Ostend. In the railway sidings I saw a line of flat cars. On them, covered by tarpaulins that failed to conceal their shapes or their blue and white colours, were assault landing craft. I decided that I had seen the reason for our presence in Ostend.

This was confirmed the next day by Hughie O'Rourke, who had had it from his friend the sergeant-major. We were in for another assault landing. I was to keep it to myself.

I waited for the usual sequence of events, a bit of training, perhaps, a check-up on equipment, then the stand-to. Instead, Hughie told me another story, also from the sergeant-major. According to this the Old Man had gone before his superiors to protest that we had done our share of landings and that someone else should have a turn. "They chucked him out," Hughie said.

This aspect of the story remains a mystery to me. It was not unusual for an officer to warn his superiors that a task given to him would cost too many lives or would be altogether hopeless. But if he was not heeded he would do it. Above all, no decent officer – or any other man – would try to palm a dangerous job off upon another unit. Least of all would our sturdy Harry Bell. On the other hand, the sergeant-major was no idle gossip. Major Bell must have continued to be highly regarded by his superiors, for in the course of time he received a decoration.

There was no stand-to. Instead, at dawn a few days later I was sent to the port with a working party on a truck loaded with dixies of hot tea and a crate full of thick bully beef sandwiches.

On a quayside, sheltering from the thin rain behind stacks of military stores that awaited transportation, was a company clearly not long out from England. Their faces were guileless and they wore greatcoats that had never been slept in. They told us that they had been in a reinforcement park in Brussels, having a good time, when at short notice they had been trucked up here.

The LCA's were now in the water, tied up alongside the quay. We fed the Pioneers, helped them to get down into the landing craft, cast them off and as the little vessels sidled away into the mist, we shouted after them the catchphrase of a comedian of the time, "You lucky people!"[1]

This was all we saw of the operation to clear the Germans from the mouth of the Scheldt, which they were blocking. Their two strongholds were at Flushing and Westkapelle. Each was attacked on 1 November by a Commando with a Pioneer company in support. The force that set out from Ostend headed for Westkapelle, where a force of five thousand German infantry protected twenty-five heavy gun batteries.

Both the attacks were bloody affairs. The landing craft came under fire before they reached the shore. Some received direct hits and limped back with dead and wounded littering their decks. At Westkapelle the force went in from the seaward side, secured a lodgement and held on until evening when a Welsh infantry division took over. For the Pioneers it was a memorable and costly day. Afterwards, the commander of Second Army published an order praising their conduct. My mother listened to the BBC radio war report every evening, of course with me in mind. She had not received a letter from me for some days and when she heard about the Westkapelle landing she was convinced that I was there. She listened to a

---

1   "You lucky people!" The catch phrase of Tommy Trinder (1909–1989), a popular comedian of the pre-and post-war years.

recorded report by a BBC war correspondent who had gone in with the Commandos. She heard him ask a Commando for his impressions after the attack, to receive the reply, "You tell them about the Pioneers."

*****

At the end of the year we were on the outskirts of Antwerp, quartered in the glass-roofed sheds of an old factory which the Germans had occupied not long before. We burned the straw from their paillasses, filled the sacks with clean straw and bedded down on the concrete floors.

A bitter winter had set in, with thick snow on the ground and a film of invisible ice on the roads, which made marching a torment. Men slogged along in heavy greatcoats, the upper parts of their bodies burdened with gear, so that the leg muscles soon wearied and ached painfully with the effort of keeping a balance. When, inevitably, a man's feet shot away from under him, he went over, rifle and helmet clattering down, and often he knocked a couple of others over with him.

Everyone's spirits were lower than ever. The Germans had launched a shock offensive under von Rundstedt and had overwhelmed the Americans in the Ardennes.[2] Facing us, on the other side of the River Maas, was another large German force, including their best parachute divisions, which was said to be awaiting the word to deliver a right hook against us. If they captured our main forward base, Antwerp, the Germans might smash the western Allies. Even if not, the war might go on for ever.

My own mood was now greatly changed. I distinctly recall the first time I was forced to acknowledge it. On 1 November, after we had seen the landing craft off on their way to Westkapelle, I stood on the quay in the rain with my camouflaged oilskin cape flapping around me and I felt a great sag of bitterness at having been left behind. I had almost forgotten about the infantry transfer and the affair of the infantry commission but now they came into my mind to mock my futile dreams of attaining distinction. I felt an utter failure; after four years, a wretched Pioneer corporal.

The thought of the four years lingered with me. Until now I had not noticed the passage of time. Now I realised that four years of my life had

---

2   Gerd von Rundstedt (1875–1953). Entered the Prussian Army in 1892. Staff Officer in the German Army in the First World War. Field Marshal in the Wehrmacht in the Second World War. Charged with war crimes after 1945 but never faced trial on account of his age and frail health.

gone down the drain. I was twenty-six. It seemed like middle age to me. What had I achieved?

I thought that I was still a loyal communist. But if I had been, all the things that depressed me would have been of no account. As it was, the thought of an end to the war depressed me almost as much as its continuance. Then I would have to go back to the life of a Party professional, the life I had escaped from. I thought of it as a drudgery.

I was physically affected, too. I was tired all the time. And for the first time I was nervous. It did not occur to me that I had been concussed twice in Normandy. These experiences seem to have quite gone out of my mind. I did not dwell on my condition now. It only irritated me. It all seemed too ridiculous. I was not in a forward area. I was in the neighbourhood of a great city. But Antwerp was being hit, at short range, by a barrage of V1's and V2's that fell on the scale of a steady artillery shoot. The V1 was like a Cruise missile, but without the sophisticated electronic guidance of the Cruise, so that it landed at random. The V2 was a rocket that carried a ton of high explosives. Both were fired from sites in Holland. When the engine of the V1 cut out we knew that it was about to fall, perhaps on us. The approach of the V2, even more unnerving, was silent.

The people of Antwerp seemed to take no notice of these attacks. Whenever I went into the city I saw the pavements and cafés crowded. I first realised that I was actually frightened when I went into a big department store to requisition some supplies for the company. It was the kind of building which was not erected in Britain until at least twenty years later, a great tower of glass. There may even have been escalators between its many floors. It was packed with shoppers admiring the Christmas displays, all glitter, canned music and human noise. A wondrous experience for a slit-trench soldier. But as I went about with my pad of requisition forms I felt only unease. I looked out through the great glass walls at the rooftops of the city and heard the distant, prolonged roar as a V2 exploded and brought down a building. From then on I knew that I was scared. I was scared of the glass roof under which we slept in the factory. I felt, as I have written in a story, that innumerable fine wires inside me were being tightened on violin pegs. I longed for the forward area and for the safety of a slit trench.

A letter from a comrade at this time brought another matter to my mind. Bill Carritt was with the Fourteenth Army in Burma. He had given up a sergeant's stripes in the artillery to transfer as a private soldier to the infantry. He wrote from the jungle to say that he was happy in his new life but that he was dismayed by one thing about his comrades in the battalion, their bitter antisemitism. I was naively puzzled by this. I wondered what soldiers in Burma could blame the Jews for. I was also surprised at his discovery. I remembered the sly reference of a sergeant-major to Israelites in 1940, but in the four years since then not once had anyone in my presence made an antisemitic remark or referred to my being a Jew.

Ironically, such an incident occurred now. At eleven o'clock one night we were in our billet, confined to barracks as always at this hour. Butt and Reilly, the two dock rats, approached me. They wanted to slip out for a short while only, to see a woman who expected them. They told a tale about a loan they had promised to repay by tonight. I reminded them that the orderly sergeant would be round at midnight, perhaps a little earlier, to see if we were all present and correct. I gave them half an hour. They swore to be back by then and went off. Soon after, the sergeant-major walked in. He banged on the door with his stick to summon our attention and shouted, "Battle order, thirty minutes, jump to it." This meant that we were on thirty minutes' notice to move, dressed and equipped in battle order. I asked him what was up. He said, "Jerry's up the road. Move, my lads," and strode out.

We assumed that the big German attack had come. The men got busy with their gear, with no particular haste and showing no concern. As for me (I am sure of this) I was relieved. I was going to leave Antwerp, boredom and fear behind. We were soon ready for a move and settled down again to our cards, books, letters, catnaps or quiet conversations. Time passed. Eleven-thirty came and went. Butt and Reilly did not appear. Absence when required to go into action was a court-martial offence ranking with cowardice in face of the enemy. Midnight. The orderly sergeant walked in. I had no intention of being court-martialled with the two dock rats. The sergeant called out, "You corporals, all present and correct?"

I replied, "Two men absent, sergeant." He took down their names. At this moment Butt and Reilly came in, both the worse for drink.

The orderly sergeant said, "By God, you two are lucky. Another minute and you'd have been for it." He went out.

I said, "We're on thirty minutes. Get into battle order."

"You reported us," Reilly said. He turned to his mate. "He reported us."

Butt, the man who had brought me an open-air breakfast in bed in Normandy, said, "It's coming to something when Englishmen have to take orders from the likes of him."

They began to put their equipment on. Corporal Croft came across to me and said, "It was the drink talking."

I said, "That's when the truth comes out."

We went to sleep in our greatcoats, boots and equipment and were not roused until the morning. There had been no German attack. After the moment's pang of bitterness I did not dwell upon the incident. I did not take Butt and Reilly seriously.

It was not until after the war that I thought hard about the business of being a Jew. It was part of my rendering of accounts with the Communist Party. Jewish communists thought they were working to earn their tickets of admission to a fellowship in which race was forgotten and in which all were simply comrades. I saw that this was an illusion. I read, extensively for the first time, about the Holocaust. I was numbed with horror and, for a time, obsessed by it. Of course I was different, I saw now, and felt glad that I was. I was still an atheist. I could never be anything other. My prime attachment in life was to the English language and through it to England but I saw no difficulty about being a Jew, too.

Questions remain. How could I have lived through the years of the Holocaust, virtually forgetting that I was a Jew? How could I have not even wondered what I ought to do about the collaborator in Ostend? The fact is that being a communist had inoculated me with indifference. Even the most humane of communists took into themselves the brutal indifference of the Party towards human suffering. I have been told that the British Press paid little attention to the Holocaust. I did not see communist newspapers during the campaign in Europe but my father regularly sent me bundles of editions of the *News Chronicle*, the liberal newspaper which gave more space than any other to this subject. If I saw reports, my eye must have passed over them. Yes, the communist thought in those days, the Jews are suffering, poor devils. But millions of other people are being oppressed and massacred. The Jews' lot is only that of the rest. We shall save them all, save the whole world from suffering, give them all *les demains chantants* and all that.[3] *Staline, notre soleil!*

*****

A second irony. Now that my enthusiasm had waned I got my transfer to the infantry.

We were called on to supply a draft of reinforcements. We had done this before. Pioneers were experienced troops and were a reserve near at hand for infantry battalions which had suffered heavy losses.

---

3   "Les demains chantants." Does Baron mean "les lendemains chantants"? Those who uttered the cry, and Baron himself at the time of the Popular Front, believed their tactic would usher in "glorious tomorrows".

We were in a small town on the Dutch border, in a great open space surrounded by 15th-century buildings. After the war I saw the Breughel painting "The Massacre of the Innocents" and recognised the background of the painting as the same place.

My name appeared on the list of men whom an infantry officer had selected. In the past Major Bell had only let private soldiers go. This time two other corporals, Eric Gray and Will Christopher, were on the list; and our youngest officer, Mr. McKie, who had taught us about explosives at Devonport, had volunteered.

Major Bell sent for me. He said, "I'd like you to stay. Up there you'll be just another man with a rifle and pack. If you stay I promise I'll get you made up as a warrant officer." (Warrant officers are an intermediate stratum between NCO's and officers who hold the monarch's commission.)

Gray and Christopher were friends of mine. We had already decided to try to stick together. I said that I had better go with them.

We set off in a truck next morning. I was relieved to be going. The sun shone on snowy fields. All was peaceful. Something puzzling soon dawned on us. The front was to the north and we were going south. I should have been prepared by now for the ways of the army. We continued south to Bruges and were delivered to an Infantry Reinforcement Depot.

We were kept there for several days. There was a parade that took up the whole of each morning, with at least two thousand men hanging about in the cold in ragged lines while drafts were called out and marched away to go up the line. Most of the men were infantrymen returning from leave or from hospital. An occasional cluster of men in a new draft wore clean uniforms. Most of those around us had faded and stained greatcoats like ours, limp with being slept in or rolled up every day for six months. Many looked pale and unwell, with one or two wound stripes on their cuffs, sometimes with three, although we had imagined that men were not sent back to the front after a third wound. They talked quietly among themselves, searching out men from their own battalions, forever anxious for news. I heard one of them say, "I'll not be sorry to get back."

We were behind barbed wire and not allowed to leave the camp. Prisoners of war. One afternoon a party of us, all NCO's, formed ourselves up and marched smartly out through the gates as if on duty, a sergeant giving the step. We wandered about the town for a couple of hours and then marched back. The centre of Bruges under snow was charming. I have seen Flemish paintings that have reminded me of it.

I do not know what happened to the private soldiers from our company. Perhaps they were sent straight to the forward area. We three NCO's remained. At last our names were called. We climbed into the back of a truck once more. Once more it drove in the opposite direction to the war. We spent a night in an empty seaside villa with a party of front-line private soldiers going on home leave. They tore up the staircase plank by plank and banister by banister to keep a fire going all night. The house was a shell next day when another truck came for us and took us to Ostend where we went aboard a tank landing craft. The big bow doors were wide open like those of a modern car ferry. We walked in on to the corrugated metal tank deck, lay down on it and went to sleep. When we woke up next morning the ship was still tied up in port. We went up on to the open deck and discovered that we were at Tilbury in England.

I was apathetic by now. We might well be shunted about for days from one camp to another. To have set out for the front and found ourselves spirited away from the war seemed unreal. Ever since the end of the war I have had occasional war dreams. None have been about battles. Most of them have been about nothing else but senseless journeys of soldiers in trucks or ships. I wake up from them feeling depressed and inert.

A train took us to a reception centre in Surrey. It was another senseless dream-scene. Troops milled about in a succession of bare rooms, floors were carpeted with men who had lain down, covered themselves with their greatcoats and gone to sleep. No-one seemed to know where he was going. The three of us at last found a quartermaster sergeant sitting behind a trestle table. When we asked where we were supposed to be going, he said, "Home," and gave us papers for fourteen days' leave.

My mother and sister still lived in Newbury, in the little slum court. The street door opened into a small scullery from which a narrow staircase of bare wood led up to two rooms. My mother slept in one of the two rooms above, with my father when he was not in London. A door in the end of this room led into a tiny hutch of a room in which my sister slept.

I walked the short distance from Newbury station, still incredulous at being back in England. I opened the front door and saw my mother peeling potatoes in the scullery. She turned at the sound of the door and gaped for a moment, with a look that might have been taken for one of dismay. I stood in the doorway looking at her. Her hair had gone entirely grey. She smiled rather wanly and said, "I'll get you something to eat."

I said, "Hello, mum," and went to kiss her cheek. Then, "Do you mind, mum? I'm going to bed."

I went up the stairs to the first bedroom. I let my gear drop to the floor. I took off my boots and my outer clothes and climbed into the bed. I woke up at ten o'clock the next morning after sleeping for eighteen hours.

My father was downstairs. He had come home in the evening and had slept on the floor. My mother had shared my sister's narrow bed in the tiny room.

I spent most of the fortnight in Newbury, eating and sleeping. I did not tell my family that I was now in the infantry. I had not yet changed my cap and shoulder badges. I told them that I was home on a course.

I only spent three days in London. Ted Willis and his wife Anne had separated and though I had not seen him for a long time I had kept in touch with her. She was living at her mother's house in Edgware, an outer suburb of London. She insisted on giving up her bedroom to me. She was going to marry an American soldier. He had been reported missing in the Ardennes during the German offensive but he had now turned up alive. Her hospitality to me was prompted by simple friendship but I felt that she made a fuss of me as a little thankoffering on her part.

I had not seen a room like this before, a suburban lady's bedroom. The bed had silky sheets and a peach-coloured satin cover with frilly edges, the dressing-table had a little frilly skirt to match and the peach mirrors had designs engraved on them. I was tickled, as I went off to sleep in exquisite comfort. I did not talk about politics with Anne and I left London without even knowing if she was still in the Party.

I did not get in touch with any other former comrades, except for William Rust, the editor of the *Daily Worker*.[4] I called on him in company with an old YCL-er I met in a canteen, now an infantry sergeant on leave from Italy. We asked Rust if he would pass on to Willie Gallacher, the MP, a request to put in a word behind the scenes to get more warm clothing sent to the soldiers at the front, who were freezing. Rust sat in a low-slung chair warming his bottom with an electric heater. He told us not to worry about things like that. The Red Army was winning the war. We left in silence.

Otherwise, I pottered about the town, visiting my grandparents, lingering in bookshops and going to the cinema. On two evenings I went out with

---

4   William Rust (1903–1949). Early member of the British Communist Party. Went to Moscow in 1928 on Comintern duties. Active as a political commissar in the Spanish Civil War. See Rust, *Britons in Spain. The History of the British Battalion of the XVth International Brigade* (London, 1939). First editor of the *Daily Worker* (1930–1932) and assumed his editorial duties later between 1939 and 1944. Described as "round and pink and cold as ice." See https://spartacus-educartional.com and Andrew Flinn, "William Rust: the Comintern's Blue-Eyed Boy?" in John McIlroy, Kevin Morgan and Alan Campbell (eds), *Party People, Communist Lives. Explorations in Biography* (London, 2001).

Anne. I was alone on the final evening. Walking at random along St. Martin's Lane, I saw that the London Philharmonic was playing at the Coliseum Theatre. I had never been to a classical concert. There was a HOUSE FULL notice on an easel in the foyer. But as I turned away from it the house manager came up to me, asked me to follow him and installed me in a front seat in an empty box. He returned a few minutes later to usher J.B. Priestley into the box, with Tom Russell and two women. Russell was the secretary of the London Philharmonic and a Party member. I knew him by sight. I said, "Good evening." They did not answer. After that I did not turn round. They left at the interval.

When the Cold War set in a few years later, Russell was attacked in the Press for being a communist. Sir Adrian Boult, the conductor, warmly defended him. Ted met Russell at London Airport and said to him, "If the Party was in power and Boult was in trouble, would you do the same for him?"

Russell said, "Don't be naive."[5]

I got back to Anne's house late. It was silent and dark. I decided not to risk waking the family up and settled down on the doorstep, curled up in my greatcoat. Every house had a sandbag on the doorstep to put out incendiary bombs. I used the sandbag as a pillow. My greatcoat had kept me warm on many other nights in the bitter winter. I did not hear the milkman when he came in the early hours and set a bottle down next to my head. Anne opened the door at eight o'clock to take the milk in and found me fast asleep.

I returned to Surrey. My two friends and I went.to see the quartermaster sergeant in his office and asked what came next. "A nice rest," he said. He told us that we were going to a training battalion in the UK. We would stay there for six to eight weeks, then go back to "the other side."

---

5   The episode involving Tom Russell and Sir Adrian Boult which came to a head in 1952 is slightly more complicated than Baron suggests. Boult did at first defend Russell but then withdrew his backing, believing apparently that the London Philharmonic Orchestra where both worked would be jeopardised financially if Russell, a Communist, remained in post. Russell's remark, as reported second hand by Baron, is significant, however. Priestley, who accompanied Russell to the theatre is the well-known novelist, J.B. Priestley (1894–1984). George Orwell considered him to be a Communist sympathiser. MI5 believed Priestley resisted all attempts by the CPGB to enlist his support. See TNA KV2/3774-3775.

Chapter 34

We were sent to a battalion stationed in Northern Ireland. Hilly country surrounded the camp. Strong guards were kept up at the camp gates but anyone could get in through the three-strand barbed wire fence that surrounded the large perimeter. At night we chained up our rifles in a rack. The area was one day to become bandit country, an IRA domain. The people in Newry were all Republicans but we did not know it. Old women sitting in their doorways invited us to come in for a supper. For a shilling they gave us a pile of bacon rashers, two or three eggs, a big pot of tea and as much as we could eat of white bread and butter such as we had not seen for five years. The girls danced with us quite happily. As soon as our womenfolk at home heard that we were in the unrationed Land of Plenty they wrote asking us to buy roll-ons and nylon stockings.

On the morning after we reported to the battalion my two friends and I went before the Irish medical officer to be passed fit. When he had examined us he said, "All you fellows are fit for is the boneyard."

Every morning after that for a fortnight we went before breakfast to the MI (Medical) room and each had to drink a pint of milk with a raw egg whipped up in it.

We went on a night exercise in the hills. As we threaded our way along a high, narrow ledge, with the sound of a rushing stream far below us, I discovered that I had become night-blind (we used the term to describe reduced vision in the dark, which was said to be caused by vitamin deficiencies). I had said nothing about it; I must have assumed that a few weeks of good Irish food would put me right.

One day I was walking along the main camp road. As usual it was raining, a Scotch mist which made the asphalt slippery and glistening. There was a black interruption to life. I woke up on a table. I looked up at the MO's face. Hands came at me from both sides dabbing with swabs of cotton wool. I saw the medical orderlies working over me. The lumps of cotton wool were stained with blood and dirt.

The M.O. probed and palped. He kept urging me to tell him what I remembered. It was all a mystery to me. He asked me for my name and my army number. I told him. He then uttered some Irish saying, which I forget, the drift of which was that I was a lucky fellow. I was contused all over and I had a bit of concussion but nothing was broken.

A thirty-hundredweight truck travelling at forty miles an hour had come in off a side road behind me and skidded, tossing me out of the way and going on to demolish a Nissen hut. I had travelled nine feet through the air and landed on my head on soft ground. I knew about the nine feet because an officer had measured it with a tape, in readiness for a court of enquiry.

I spent a week in hospital in Newcastle, County Down. The medical orderlies had been with Wingate's Chindits in Burma, and were no doubt burned-out cases who were also here for a rest.[1] They were as gentle as young mothers. The officer in charge was a genial man; no sitting to attention in bed or six a.m. inspections for him. He sauntered round during the morning and said, "Anything we can get you?" However, he did not examine me. I felt like a hotel guest. Nothing suggested to me that my latest concussion might have been one too many.

I settled down to sleep one night. Low lights burned in the ward. An orderly sat at a table near the door. I woke up with my heart going like an electric bell. Sweat started out of me and trickled down my skin, as bad as when I had had malaria. It went cold and was unpleasant. I had come up out of nowhere to the sounds of a battle. I thought at first it was one of those startling dreams when the sleeper thinks he is awake; but I was awake. Those were twenty-five pounders; those were mortar bombs; that was small arms fire. I could hear the Bren bursts.

I sat up, wiping myself with my pyjama jacket. The orderly saw me and said, "It's all right. There's a big exercise on in the mountains of Mourne." He brought me fresh pyjamas and a cup of tea.

Back with the battalion I went rapid-firing at the butts and vomited over the breech of my rifle. The officer sent me to the MO who took me off duties to go for another examination.

The next day, having nothing to do, I strolled on to the grenade range. There was a row of sandbagged bays. A sergeant was in charge of each. Men went into the bays and threw grenades at a row of sticks thirty yards away, each stick in a circle. The object was to throw a grenade so that it fell inside the circle.

---

1   Orde Wingate (1903–1944). Senior decorated British Army officer. He created the Chindit operations against the Japanese in Burma, which involved guerrilla operations. Wingate was killed in a plane crash after inspecting Chindit-held bases in Burma.

I walked into a bay, took a grenade from a box, and pulled out the pin. The sergeant must have heard that (in the phrase then common) I had got a twitch on. He muttered, "Fuck this for a lark" and hurried away. Another sergeant came into the bay and gave me a reassuring grin. I only remember him as Ernie; before the war he had been a professional footballer with Manchester United. I was standing there, holding down the lever of the grenade and studying the stick in front of me.

I threw the grenade and stood watching. It hit the stick and fell to the ground. I stayed on my feet till the last second of the fuse. So did Ernie. Then we both as if joined together ducked behind the sandbags to the sound of the explosion.

An officer came across and said, "Well done! Would you like to have a go with the Piat now?" The Piat was a contrivance that fired an anti-tank bomb.

I felt exhilarated but once again my heart was going fast and I was sweating. I went back to my hut.

A few weeks passed before I had another medical examination. I was given a lower medical grade and sent to do light duties in England. My two friends were posted to battalions abroad, one to Germany and one to Burma.

I was lonely, miserable, angry, disappointed and tired. After more than five years the bottom had dropped out of my life and I knew that I no longer had a belief to sustain me. I went from one in-between place to another. At one of them I saw a notice asking for volunteers for Burma. Men were wanted in Demob. Groups 29 and upwards. I was in Group 29. I sent in my name but heard no more. I dare say the people in the office did not even forward my application.

The war in Europe ended. It was to continue for another five months in Burma. I could not settle down. I cannot remember in what place of transit I was on the night that the atom bomb was dropped on Hiroshima. I was in a large barrack-room full of double-decker beds. I always took the top bed in such places so that some drunken stranger would not vomit or urinate on me.

The room was crowded with men. None of them took any notice of a radio that babbled in the background. I could hardly catch the announcer's words but a few phrases came to me, enough to startle me, "Japan," "atomic device," "devastation."

A few of the men may have uttered idle comments before they looked down again to their cards but otherwise the news passed unnoticed. I lay on my bed, shocked and depressed. I am sure of this. It is not an invention of memory foisted on to the scene.

13042620 Cpl. J. A. Bernstein,
H. Q., 207 Coy., P.C.,
Midland Rd., Olney, Bucks.
Saturday, August 11th, 1945.

Dear Mama and Pop,

Isn't the news wonderful? It looks as
if the world war is really going to end long before any
of us had even hoped it might. I do wish I could have
come home this weekend!

I see, in the newspapers, that there were
celebrations, mainly by troops, in the West End as soon
as the first news of the surrender offer came through.
This is quite understandable. The end of the war with
Japan will be an even happier day for the troops, both
British and American, than the last VE-Day was. After
all, though on VE-Day civilians could relax at last,
the troops, although they were very happy about it,
nevertheless felt that there was still another big job
to be done. Now they can all start thinking of their
homes and future at last. That is, if developments
continue as at present — and it seems to me that they
must, as it would be very difficult for the Japanese
to back-pedal at this stage.

Mind you, although the end of the Jap war will
certainly mean a big speed-up in demobilisation, I don't
for a moment imagine that we will all come out with a
rush. There are masses of men in my own and lower age-
groups still scattered overseas, and shipping has to be
found to bring them all back to England before demobbing
of our groups can even begin. Then there will be the
enormous task of occupying all the widely-flung
territories overrrun by the Japs as well as Japan
itself, and rounding up the Jap armed forces. No, I
think the best I can hope for will be to be out by
Christmas or the New Year. Still, that would be wonderful enough, wouldn't it?

Figure 39 "I lay on my bed, shocked and depressed. I am sure of this." In contrast to his
actual reaction to the news of the dropping of the atomic bombs on Japan on 6 and 9 August
1945, Baron's letter home of 11 August is full of his usual reassuring words and optimism.

When Victory in Europe Day had come I had felt only empty and sick. Eric Gray had met me when he was on leave from Berlin and had told me a story which appears in my novel *The Human Kind* as "The Way a War Ends".[2] Two young soldiers, one British and one Russian, had fought to the death with knives. I had been sure for the last two years that the war with Germany would be followed by a war with Russia, the last fight which we were called upon to face in the chorus of the "Internationale". Gray's story was the image of it. It also made clear a conviction that had been forming at the back of my mind that madness and blood lust get out of control in a war and were now loose in the world. I had read about the Thirty Years' War and now I imagined Europe being laid waste in thirty days.

One day I could not get out of bed. There was nothing wrong with my body but my will had left me. Eventually I got up and was sent to see an extraordinarily kind psychiatrist. In his office, he said, "Let's get out of here," and we walked the streets talking. I was sent away for a long convalescence.

Of the months that followed I remember one sequence of happenings in particular, as if they all occurred on the same day, though they probably did not. Memory, the dramatist, has put them all together to form a single phantasmagoria.

I am walking about the streets of Birmingham. I realise that the grimy building on my left is the University. I go up steps into a long, wide entrance hall and read the notices pinned to many boards. Another world. When I was seventeen I stood in a hall reading notices like these, in University College, London. A handbill advertises a series of lectures on Modern French Literature. I go further into the building to ask about them and am sent from one room to another until I am standing in front of (so I am told) the Professor of French. He is sitting behind a table covered with books and papers. He seems irritated by my intrusion. I ask if I can come to his lectures. He says, "No. You are not a member of the University." Not a word more. I say, "Thank you, sir," and leave.

Later, I must have been walking for a long time. I am in a suburb. The roads are wide. Grand houses stand in their own grounds behind big gateways and gravel drives. I am invited into one of the houses. (By whom? Was someone standing at the gate?) I am taken through the house to a spacious conservatory which looks out on to the gardens. The conservatory has a lofty roof. The floor is of large patterned tiles. There is much greenery, some in tubs or hanging in baskets.

---

2   Baron's short story, "The Way a War Ends," appears in his collection of essays, *The Human Kind* (London, 2011), pp.149–53.

I sit alone on one side of the conservatory. On the far side is a group of five or six soldiers in hospital blue.(This consisted of a loose, ill-fitting jacket and trousers of bright blue cotton, worn with a white shirt and red tie. I was in convalescent dress, wearing my brown service blouse with the blue trousers.) These soldiers are all young, not one, I should guess, more than twenty years old. Every one of them has lost a leg, the amputations being of different lengths. Two pleasant ladies try to put us all at our ease. Two girls are in attendance. They bring trolleys to us and serve us with tea in cups of thin china, little sandwiches with the crusts cut off and pastries.

Why are there only the few of us in this large pavilion of glass? How does the time pass? Two of the *uni-jambistes* come swinging past me on their crutches accompanied by one of the girls. They go into the gardens. Time passes. One of the soldiers returns. As he clumps past me he mutters to me, "She takes the prick."

More time has passed. I see the cripples stand up, in a close group, their heads lifted back as if they are posing for a group of statuary. They start to sing. Their voices are cracked and wild. They look and they sound defiant and they are singing a bitter song which I have not heard before, a song which has spread throughout the Eighth Army in Italy, an army once lauded, now forgotten, of under-strength battalions denied reinforcements and freezing in the mountains. It is called "The D-Day Dodgers" and it is sung to the tune of "Lilli Marlene".[3] It begins,

> *We are the D-Day Dodgers, out in Italy,*
> *Always on the vino, always on the spree,*

and it ends:

> *Up there in the mountains, in the mud and rain,*
> *You'll see the scattered crosses, there's some which have no name.*
> *Heartbreak and toil and suffering gone, the lads beneath them*
> * slumber on,*
> *For they were D-Day Dodgers in sunny Italy.*

I am wandering in the streets again. It occurs to me that Denis Hoyland, the comrade whom I had once visited in Oxford, must live in a house like

---

3   Lili Marlene, sometimes Marleen, a German song made popular in the Second World War by Lale Andersen. By 1943 Marlene Dietrich was singing an English version to Allied troops.

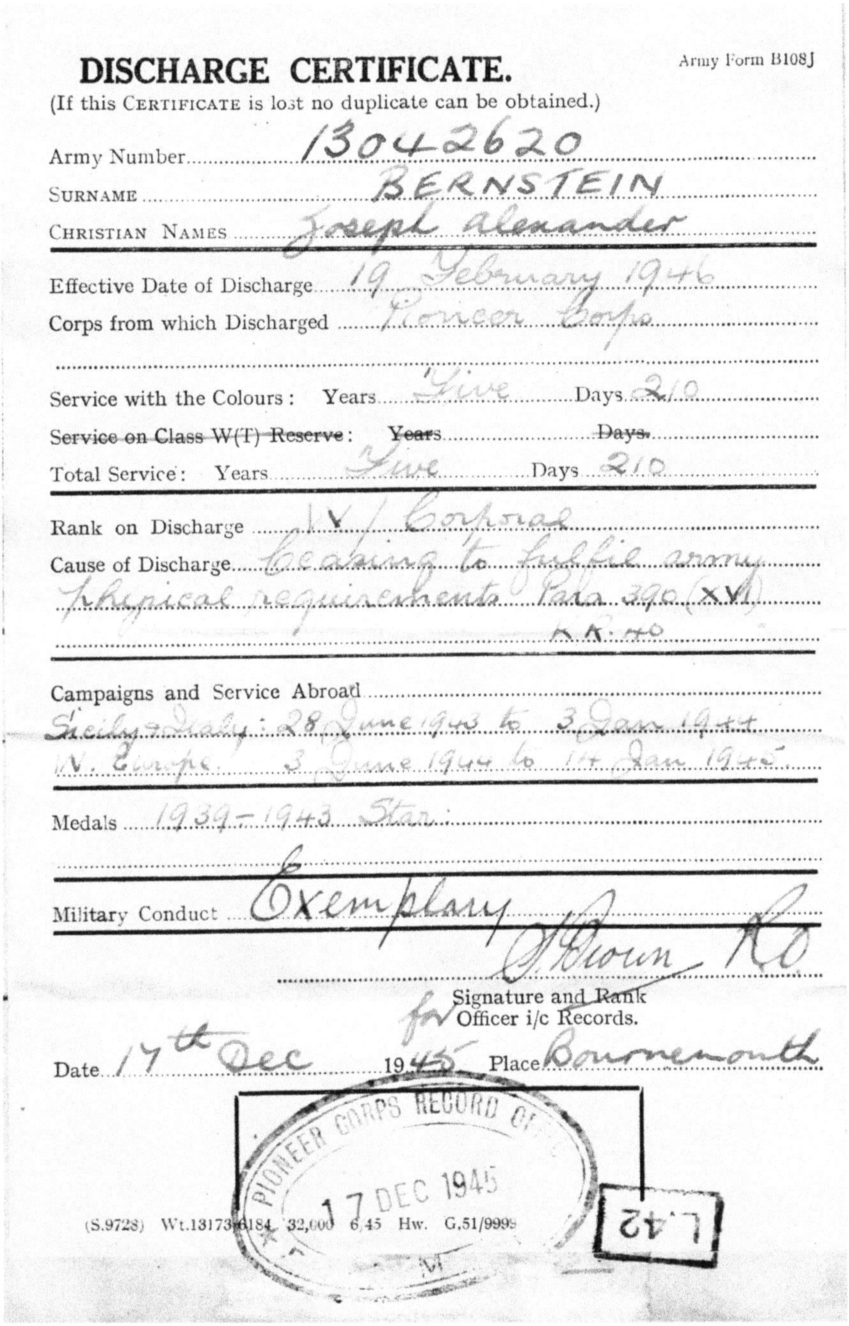

DISCHARGE CERTIFICATE. Army Form B108J

(If this CERTIFICATE is lost no duplicate can be obtained.)

Army Number: 13042620

SURNAME: BERNSTEIN

CHRISTIAN NAMES: Joseph Alexander

Effective Date of Discharge: 19 February 1946

Corps from which Discharged: Pioneer Corps

Service with the Colours: Years: Five Days: 210

~~Service on Class W(T) Reserve: Years Days~~

Total Service: Years: Five Days: 210

Rank on Discharge: L/Corporal

Cause of Discharge: Ceasing to fulfil army physical requirements Para 390 (XVI) K.R. 40

Campaigns and Service Abroad: Sicily & Italy: 28 June 1943 to 3 Jan 1944; N. Europe 3 June 1944 to 14 Jan 1945

Medals: 1939–1943 Star.

Military Conduct: Exemplary

J. Brown R.O.

for Signature and Rank Officer i/c Records.

Date 17th Dec 1945 Place Bournemouth

PIONEER CORPS RECORD OFFICE 17 DEC 1945

L.42

(S.9728) Wt.13173/6184 32,000 6/45 Hw. G.51/9999

Figure 40 "1946 began, a dreary year. I was due to be demobilized in April but I was given a medical discharge three weeks earlier." Baron's discharge certificate, December 1945.

these, perhaps in this suburb. I look up the directory in a 'phone booth, find a number and ring. A manservant answers. He says, "I'm very sorry, sir. Master Denis was killed in the war."

*****

1946 began, a dreary year. I was due to be demobilized in April but I was given a medical discharge three weeks earlier. I was awarded a small pension which I drew for a year and then renounced. I was interviewed by a committee who wanted to know if there was anything I needed to help me start life as a civilian. I said that I was a writer and wanted a typewriter.

I went to a demobilization centre and travelled up to London with an outfit of civilian clothes in a large cardboard box. I arrived at Waterloo Station. Not long afterwards I met a man who had been in the tanks, a hard-bitten fellow, who said to me, "It was lucky they'd taken my pistol off me, or I'd have shot myself sooner than walk out under that arch at Waterloo." I knew how he felt. I was reluctant and frightened when I walked out of the station.

Chapter 35

A few days after I was demobilized I went to the showrooms of the Imperial Typewriter Company in Kingsway with a voucher from the army. A salesman told me that there was a twelve-month waiting list for their portable model but that he would get me one in a month.

I came out of the showroom and was walking back toward Southampton Row when I heard a shout from across the street. Ted Willis came across the road. He asked me what I was doing in London.

I was in uniform. I told him that I was on six weeks' demob. leave. He said, "What are you going to do after that?"

"I don't know."

"Are you going anywhere now?"

"No."

"Come with me."

He had quit his post as a Party professional in, I think, 1942, to give all his time to writing. This was a drastic step for a member of the inner core, since writing was regarded at King Street as a trifling and contemptible occupation. On my last visit there in 1942 I had heard Ted spoken of as a deserter, although he was still a Party member. Since then he had been making his name as a dramatist. He was also writing film and radio scripts. During all this time I had only met him twice, fairly briefly; a matter of chance. He told me that he was on his way to a meeting with a documentary film producer in Soho Square. There was a film to be written about the army. If he got the contract, would I like to help him, for a share of the fee?

This job fell through but he had another to offer me. He was Artistic Director at Unity Theatre; they had launched a monthly magazine, *New Theatre*, and the editor wanted to move on. Would I like to take over?[1]

---

[1]   Unity Theatre started in 1936. It had links with the political Left, including the Left Book Club. See Colin Chambers, *The History of Unity Theatre* (London, 1989) and, more recently, Isabelle Seddon, *East End Jews and Left-Wing Theatre: Alfie Bass, David Kossoff, Warren Mitchell and Lionel Bart* (London, 2020).

I was glad of a chance to get my hand in at journalism again and started work a few days later. I spent two years at *New Theatre* and at Unity, the period during which I was coming to terms with civilian life, settling my accounts with the Communist Party and writing my first novel. It was in some ways a hard time for me. I knew little about the everyday world, having been out of it since I was a schoolboy of sixteen. I was in a bad mental and bodily state, too, for the first few years, although nobody ever knew of it except my parents who sometimes had to look after me, and Ted Willis and his new wife Audrey, who were kindness itself to me.

I enjoyed my work at *New Theatre*. During its short life it established itself as an authoritative journal in the theatre world. Eventually it brought various interested parties together to sponsor an impressive British Theatre Conference at which every group of workers in the theatre was represented and an array of celebrities attended including a Cabinet minister. In spite of the magazine's antecedents there was nothing communist about it. It catered for members of the profession and lovers of the theatre and gave space to every point of view. Its only politics was to call for generous State support for the theatre. Like all ventures of its sort, it declined and died when its initiators no longer had time to nurture it.

Unity was a political theatre run by a strong nucleus of communists. I was a trained Party worker, a valuable catch, and six weeks after I joined I was installed as chairman of the theatre.

Unity was an amateur theatre unlike any other. It put on shows all the year round like a professional theatre and its first nights were attended by the leading critics. It drew on a large body of volunteers for its casts and for all its services. Professionals, some of them famous, were glad to act or direct on its stages without payment.

I was a capable chairman and I was lucky to be appointed just at a time when a group of talented and energetic people came in to take over the artistic and business affairs of the theatre. During our tenure we wiped out a large and chronic debt, which must have been a feat unique both among fringe theatres and among organizations of the Left.

On *New Theatre* I had the pleasure of going to every play I wanted to see, anywhere in the country, a wonderful and restorative boon after the war. In Unity I was able to watch theatre people at work. But I was never more than a watcher. I was not a theatre person and never became one. I have never tried seriously to write a stage play, although in time I wrote movies and plays for television. My own nature kept me apart from a crowd who were serious in their intentions but imbued with all the scattiness and temperamental quirks that are to be found in theatricals.

I was a rigid sort of person, trained as a Communist of the Party machine and, after the army, a thorough-going NCO. Besides, I was preoccupied with other matters more important to me: my relations with the Party and the writing of my first novel. Late at night, after the show or at the end of some stormy meeting, when the theatre people streamed off to their pub, it would have been the sensible thing for the chairman to go along and mingle, but I always hurried off to walk a mile or two alone, to clear my head on the way home in preparation for the night's work on my book. Most of the members were not at ease with someone like me. At meetings I could not conceal my impatience with the tantrums and cliques that are part of theatrical life, or with the political verbiage in which amateurs of the Left indulge. I cut speakers short and behaved in general like a corporal. It was effective but it was not popular.

*****

By the time I met Ted Willis in Kingsway most of the thousand threads that bound me to the Party had been broken. I was doggedly sure that I would not go back into the Party machine and I had no wish to start life among the rank-and-file.

It was the chance meeting with Ted that took me back into the communist milieu of Unity; but I would in any case have sought out some Party resting-place at first. All the world outside was so strange to me that I would have alighted as a matter of necessity and habit on some Party twig, if only for a time.

That time lasted two years. It was not because of a struggle in my soul. I felt both determined and easy about leaving it all behind me. It was for a time, perhaps, cowardice and the inertia fostered by my relations with a few friends, in which shared assumptions had always been taken for granted. Mainly, however, it was because a change of heart or of attitude had by degrees taken me over in the last few years and had not been accompanied by any thinking. I now realised the nature of this change and thought it my duty to examine it. It was after all still the most serious matter in my life. I had to read, think things out, put arguments together and try them in contest.

But here I came face to face with a problem: contest with whom? It was not only the prospect of Communist Party life that repelled me, but that of plunging back into Communist Party discussion. In their internal debates communists can only recognise certain categories of thought, those in which they have been trained, and they can only express themselves in the private language of the Party, a dreary mechanical jargon that in itself limits their thinking. I did not want to speak this language any more or to have to listen to it.

Inevitably, there were occasions when I was with some Party official to talk about Unity Theatre affairs, or with some old Party friends, when I was provoked to reveal some of the new, heretical speculations that were churning about in my mind, but I met with such incomprehension and such a depressing gabble in response that I extricated myself quickly each time. In short, I learned to keep my mouth shut.

The only person with whom I argued seriously and often was Ted Willis, with whom I had shared a career that went back to our political beginnings in 1934. He and Audrey must have discerned the worn-out state in which I had come home and took me under their wing with determination. At their flat, on country walks, in the course of seaside outings, Ted and I again and again fell into argument, the two of us equally passionate. It was hard to turn a welter of thoughts and feelings into arguments but in doing so I gradually spelled out to myself what I now believed. The idea that the Party was an élite now seemed laughable to me: it was an environment of self-deception. Its mode of life had become repugnant. I could never again tolerate it. I had begun by objecting to this lie or that: now I saw communism as an entire structure of lies. I remembered how we had conditioned ourselves to accept absurd casuistries and realised how deeply we had degraded ourselves.

Since my return from the army I had been reading in every moment that I could spare, making up for years of lost time. I read novels, poems, plays, essays, memoirs, histories, politics and philosophy. Everything mattered to me; in one way or another everything I read helped to tear down my former beliefs. My mind was a chaos. New perceptions surprised it like flashes of light. Fragmentary ideas whirled, dissolved and assumed new shapes from one day to the next.

The word intoxication describes my condition aptly; it was akin to the state of liberation engendered by strong drink. All my diverse reading contributed to the one enticing brew, that of freedom. I could not convey this to Ted. I told him that he had forgotten what an open mind was. He replied that he had an open mind. Communists, he said, did not despise the inheritance of bourgeois thought. But the best of it only provided glimpses of what the communists saw clearly and completely. Nevertheless he read conscientiously every work about which I enthused.

Even to him I did not speak about a matter which I thought he would never understand, an idea that as a revolutionary Marxist he would consider too childish even to consider. This concerned the part that accident plays in human affairs. The Theory of Accident is only a phrase I jotted down while I was making notes for this memoir. But throughout the war I could not fail to see the determining part that chance played again and again in my life, as it had done earlier. When I looked at the war, especially at what I knew of it behind the scenes, the same was true, and whatever aspect of history I thought about, it was true again.

I could elaborate on this and contest both Marx's dictum that all history ("all" is the fallacious word) is the history of class struggles and the crazed belief of the Leninist communists that they possessed a science of history which would enable them to steer the human species into the future as if the Party were at the wheel of a great Historical Motor-Bus. This memoir is not the place for argument over such ideas and life itself, to use a favourite phrase of the communists, has now belied their contentions.

Clearly, though, I had come to a position which was incompatible with Marxism. My arguments with Ted occurred intermittently over a long time and were well advanced before I once again met John Gollan.

On my return to London I had called at Party headquarters and talked with a few of the old professionals. They had assumed that I was reporting for duty. In the weeks that followed I had turned down two offers of organizing jobs and an invitation to join the staff of the *Daily Worker*. After that I had kept away from them.

I had seen nothing of Gollan. He was in charge of the Party in Scotland. In 1947 he was appointed Assistant General Secretary and installed himself at King Street. He and Ted were still on terms of personal friendship and before long he invited Ted to lunch. He asked for news of me and was much put out to hear of my dereliction of duty. He said that it was time he saw me: he meant to settle matters with me. It was plain from Ted's account of their conversation that he had not made Gollan aware of my heresies. Ted had only told him that I seemed to be in a rather unsettled state. This, on Ted's part, was not the proper conduct for a communist. It did not occur to me that Ted's reticence in speaking about me might be a clue to his own state of mind.

I, in turn, went to lunch with Gollan. I was determined to be evasive. I was not ready to confront him. I feared that the man who had mesmerised me when I was sixteen might still be able, given my confused state, to scatter the thoughts that I was so painfully trying to assemble. I had visions of caving in and being beaten back into the fold.

When we met he soon came to the point. He said that he understood my need for a rest but that enough time had gone by. It was unworthy of a comrade like me to waste his time in "that theatre". I needed a responsible job to pull me together. He invited me to join him at King Street as his assistant; my principal task would be to take over the Party supervision of the youth movement, which it was now time to rebuild.

I prevaricated. He pressed me. I said, "I don't want to go back to Party work."

He insisted that I explain myself. At last I confessed to something about which I had not yet said a word to anyone. I said, "I'm writing something," and added, "a novel."

"A novel?"

"That's what I want to do. I want to write."

He said, in a sickened tone, "Oh, Christ!" Then, in his old persuasive way, "That's not a job for you. What does a writer do, even a good writer, even one of ours? He describes the world. You are one of the people who have to change it. And one day to run it."

I said nothing.

He leaned across the table and went on, "Look at me. An Edinburgh slummie. I am one of the five hundred men who matter most in the world." Later he said, "I don't care about that Willis. He's all right on a platform with the lights on him. But you are one of us."

I did not reply to this. Eventually he said, "Will you do one thing for me? Will you see a Party doctor?"

The doctor turned out to be a psychiatrist. She told Gollan that I was disturbed and should be left alone for a year or two. He said that he would respect this. When I saw Ted afterwards I only referred to the occasion with a few dismissive remarks. I did not tell him what Gollan had said about him and I did not mention the novel.

A little more than a year later I had my last argument with Gollan, one which constituted my final break with the Party.

He had asked once more to see me. Ted Willis invited us both to his home for supper. I have little recollection of what Gollan and I said in a long argument; but this time I was no longer in awe of him or tongue-tied. I was for once as fierce and eloquent as he was.

I remember that he employed a familiar argument, that the Party had made me, that I owed to it whatever qualities I had, and that I had no right to make away with them for my own purposes. I recall, too, that when I presented him with some facts about Stalin's misdeeds he cried, "Don't tell me! Don't tell me what I know. I could tell you a thousand times worse! I'm saying this to you, but outside this room they could tear my nails out one by one and I wouldn't open my mouth."

He was polite enough when he left but Ted remarked that he was white-faced with emotion.

I only saw Gollan once more, many years later, when he was General Secretary of the Party. I was crossing the forecourt which then existed at King's Cross Station when a taxi pulled up in front of me and he stepped out of it. He did not seem to have changed except that he was wearing a passable suit, a neat shirt and a tie. He was carrying the old, huge black briefcase that I remembered, the kind that I used to think of as a Moscow briefcase, packed out with his necessities. He saw me and his face brightened with the smile that I remembered from old times, his eyes lighting up and his mouth opening wide as if in surprise and welcome. He chatted gaily with me. He asked me if I was married. Had I a family? I told him that we had a baby boy. He said, "That's good. Good. It's no life without them." After a few minutes he shook hands with me, wished me luck and went off to catch a train to Edinburgh.

*****

The discussions with Ted had continued up to my final encounter with Gollan. Soon after that Ted and I engaged in one more argument. It must have led up to my saying something that provoked Ted, some reference perhaps to the time, only a few years earlier, when we had not merely approved of Stalin's blood purges but glorified them, asserting that it was right to shoot a hundred people on the chance that there might be one enemy among them.

Ted said, "I'd shoot a thousand on that chance."

I remarked that a thousand was a bit much.

Ted was silent for some moments, then he said, "I've been having you on. I've been arguing with you for a long time now to clear my own head. I reckon I'm about six weeks behind you in my thinking."

Not long after that he left the Communist Party quietly and rejoined the Labour Party. He continued to live his twenty-four-hours-a-day life. He was the most prolific of writers, he became prominent in show business and television and in many aspects of public life; he worked hard for Labour and advised the party on arts and entertainment policies. In 1963 he became Lord Willis, awarded the life peerage by a Conservative government on the recommendation of the Labour leader Harold Wilson.[2] He died in 1992. Near to the end of his life he agreed with me that the years of our youth were the most

---

2   Harold Wilson (1916–1995), Lord Wilson of Rievaulx. British Labour politician. Prime Minister 1964–1970 and 1974–1976. See the classic biography by Ben Pimlott, *Harold Wilson* (London, 1992), which as its dustcover reproduces Russell Spears's striking portrait of Wilson, completed in 1974.

intensely-lived of our lifetimes and that beside them everything since, the writing, the achievements, the rewards, even the fortunate family lives that we both enjoyed, sometimes seemed pallid, an improbable daydream. At other times it was the communist years that seemed like a dream.

*****

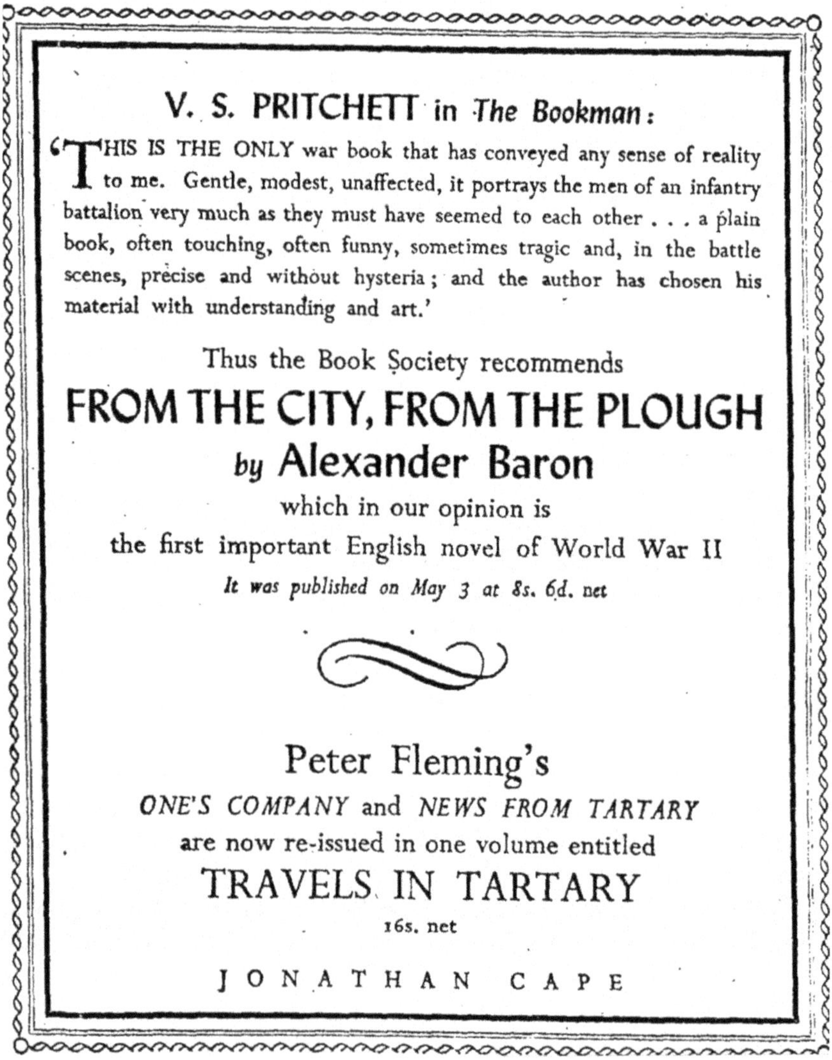

Figure 41 "I started to write *From the City, From the Plough* in the second half of 1946." Book Society recommendation, published in *The Times*, 11 May 1948, p.7.

I started to write *From the City, From the Plough* in the second half of 1946 and finished it in the Spring of the following year. I did not have to make a resolve to start it. By now it was ready inside me and only had to be written down. One night I put a sheet of paper into the typewriter and began to do this, as naturally as I might sit down to my supper. I usually worked for about three hours from midnight.

When it was finished I put it away in a drawer. I suppose I thought it would be wonderful to see it printed as a book one day but I did not make any plan to bring this about. I did not know how to, but I could have enquired; by this time I knew a number of left-wing writers. I simply felt satisfied that the book was out of me. Perhaps I was afraid that it would be rejected. I have always dreaded the moment when I have to show a piece of work to other people.

I do not know how long the book lay in the drawer. I was out one evening with Ted and Audrey Willis. I may have drunk a glass or two more than usual of red wine, for in reply to a remark by Ted that I ought to get down to writing a novel, I blurted out that I had already written one. After that I had to give the book up to them. Ted read it and, knowing that I would not believe him if he praised it, enlisted another friend, Roger Woddis, who later made a name for himself as a topical versifier.[3] The two of them came to me some days later and insisted that I send it off. They gave me the names of three publishers. The first two wrote nice things about it but turned it down. The third was Jonathan Cape.[4]

I had known the house of Cape since I was a schoolboy when I had written to them to get their free house magazine and received every issue proudly, feeling that I was the regular reader of a real literary journal. The cover of *Now and Then* was always illustrated by an engraving of the fine Georgian doorway of Cape's premises at 30, Bedford Square.

One morning I opened a letter and read an invitation from Cape to come in and talk to him about my book. I remember the deep impulse of joy I experienced at the thought that I was going to walk in through that doorway, which for all those years must have stayed in my mind as the entrance to a world that I dreamed of. When, a year later, I held the printed book in my

---

3 Roger Woddis, born Nehemiah Salem (1917–1993). Author, journalist and scriptwriter. He had a connection with Unity Theatre and hence to Ted Willis. Member of the CPGB until the Soviet invasion of Czechoslovakia in 1968. See *Oxford Dictionary of National Biography*, online (accessed 28 March 2019).

4 The publishing house of Jonathan Cape had been founded in 1921 by Herbert Jonathan Cape. He remained in charge of the firm until 1960.

Figure 42 "Since then I have given all my time to writing." Publicity for Baron's second novel, *There's No Home*, in *Reynold's News*, 1950.

hands and, after that, saw the evidences of success coming in, I felt nothing as profound; only a tired, slightly incredulous, slightly ironic satisfaction.

Cape introduced me to the reader who had advised him to publish the book, Daniel George, who for several years after was a literary mentor and a friend to me.[5] He turned down the title that I had used, "The Fifth Battalion". We beat about for a long time trying to think of another. In the end Cape's wife suggested the title under which the book came out.

I had sent the book in under a pen name, John Masterman. I wanted to divorce this freak enterprise from my known identity as a communist. Cape explained to me that John Masterman was the name of a famous academic who had published several books.[6] He invited me to pick another of not more than five letters so that it could be printed in fair-sized letters across the spine of the book. I took Baron from the facia of a shop. The book came out in the year that I severed my last tie with the Party and I seized the chance to shed my communist identity and start life again with the new name.

Six weeks after the book came out Cape asked me to come and see him again. The downstairs office housed a band of smart and beautiful girls who made much of me and told me that the book was going into its fifth impression. Upstairs, Cape handed me my first glass of publisher's sherry and instructed the counting-house, through a box device on his table, to send up a cheque for five hundred pounds made out to Mr. Alexander Baron. I opened my first bank account with this cheque.

Good reviews poured in, followed by unbelievably better ones from the United States. New impressions followed one another off the press. The postman kept bringing me more translation contracts. That year, now out of the Party, I left my job at *New Theatre*. Since then I have given all my time to writing.

---

5   "Daniel George" was Daniel George Bunting (1890–1967). Author and critic who wrote under the name Daniel George. He often read manuscripts for Jonathan Cape.

6   John Cecil Masterman (1891–1977) Sportsman, writer and one-time Vice-Chancellor of Oxford University (1957–1958), His first book was a thriller, *An Oxford Tragedy* (London, 1933). His best-known work came later. See *The Double Cross System in the War of 1939–1945* (London, 1973).

APPENDIX

NOTES FOR REVISION OF MEMOIR (1997–99)

Baron wrote his memoir *Chapters of Accidents* in the mid-1990s. He finished the first draft in August 1996 and a second, slightly revised draft in November 1997. During the next two years he frequently jotted down further notes for revisions in a small red Silvine notebook (his habit was to carry small notebooks with him everywhere) as well as on loose scraps of paper. In the last two years of his life, Baron's eyesight was failing rapidly and he was unable to produce a third draft of the full text. After his death in December 1999, these rough notes for revisions to the memoir formed part of a collection of his private papers retained by his family (the bulk of his papers were subsequently deposited at the University of Reading Archive).

In preparing the memoir for publication, the editors have now integrated some of Baron's proposed revisions into the main text where these entailed minor stylistic amendments or straightforward corrections or clarifications of points of fact.

In many of his notes, however, Baron offered commentaries or elaborations on the text rather than proposing specific changes to it. In some of these notes, Baron recorded additional, newly-remembered details called to mind on re-reading passages of the memoir (not always identified in the notes); through conversations or correspondence with old acquaintances and comrades; in the course of reading memoirs and scholarly studies; or that perhaps came to him spontaneously. In other notes, he recorded doubts concerning the text, calling into question the accuracy of his earlier recollections, yet without offering corrections. In still others, he drew out inferences from certain passages about his own character and career, reflecting – often self-critically – on how his early experiences shaped or prefigured his later life.

Throughout these later reflections, Baron frequently drew attention to the operation of chance in determining his life-history, as he deliberated further on his own informal 'theory' of historical contingency – a resolute rejection of his earlier Marxist faith in historical determinism (see Chapter 31, also endnote to p.335 below) – that had informed his choice of the memoir's title: *Chapters of Accidents*.

Very few of these notes are dated and many are elliptical or fragmentary. One, for example, states: "Marie-Louise! At least this story may point to an explanation of why there are such gaps in my memory." There is nothing in the memoir, or in his notes, to indicate who Marie-Louise was, nor any hint as to what the story might have been that her name recalled to him, and that seemed so significant to him at the moment he jotted down this note. Marie-Louise remains a mystery. The editors have not included in the appendix notes like these. After the memoir's publication, all Baron's notes for revision will be available for consultation by researchers in the University of Reading collection of Baron's private papers.

In this appendix, the editors have reproduced a selection of Baron's notes, where we have been able to identify the relevant passages in the text with which they are associated, and where we feel that they add materially to the value and purpose of this edition as a whole. That's to say, we present extracts from his notes when we feel that they might offer further insight into Baron's early life and political activities, his wartime experiences, his later career as a writer, and the processes of memory and self-reflection that, in his old age, shaped the composition and writing of this memoir.

In Baron's notes reproduced here, the author's original spelling and punctuation have been preserved. Notes are undated, unless otherwise stated.

****

Page 37   *"A name loses its potency after it has been used for a while."* In his notes, Baron pondered:

"Should I make more of my childhood fears of war?

1. How old was I when, at night in bed, I heard the drone of bombers? It was the RAF on exercise, as I knew, to see if … (as Baldwin said after it: 'The bomber will always get through') (age 12?).
2. As a child (1928/9 onwards – age 10 or so –) I had got hold of all those war books. Perhaps when I heard Aunt Esther.…
3. Then at school – the book *Nie Wieder Krieg* – age 13/14?
4. It surfaces (secretly) at Munich time.
5. But I am free of it when war breaks out. I am a good soldier."

Page 48   *"My father also became a master craftsman."* A note indicated the catalyst of this recollection:

"I am reminded [of this] by Philip Roth's *American Pastoral* on glove-making. The maestri. The incredible skill, picking, matching, stretching the furs, the fine cuts, a surgeon or an artist could not equal the design. How I took these for granted when small and at the same time was in awe. And when older, felt small because he was a worker who could do, make, devise *anything*."

Page 56 *"Most of my memories, however, are of indoors, looking out from our room."* Further memories and reflections on East London street culture in a short note:

"'Won't you buy by pretty flowers?', 'I've been 7 years in a prison…'. Other ballads – Victorian London, Dickens' London – continued until the war scattered a way of life in 1939."

Page 58 *"When I was five my mother took me to a hospital…"* Baron expanded in a note on how his mother's gifts of second-hand books from a stall in the Royal Waterloo Hospital's waiting-room had shaped his outlook on English history and nature.

"The old geography book my mother bought me for a penny. I was 5 or 6. How vivid a picture I have always retained of what it was like when 'England' was 'the workshop of the world'. And when D. and I drove that evening (other memories connect here) from Hove to Chislehurst and I was filled with peace and joy by the lovely unexpectedly hilly countryside, I remembered 'the garden of England.'"

The initial "D" stands for Delores (née Lopez-Salzedo), whom he married in 1960. Soon afterwards, Baron and his wife moved to Hove, on the south coast of England, where they lived until returning to London in 1972.

Page 66 *"My sister and I called him Zaida B."* For Baron's further reflections on his attraction to the music hall, see endnotes to pp.87 and 126.

Page 71 *"Five of her ten children lived at home."* Baron's note on this passage indicate a slightly different number of children and expand on memories of his family. Jack Agass, mentioned in the note, was the protagonist of Baron's novel *Rosie Hogarth*, which, he suggests here, was the second book written after *From the City, From the Plough* (although *Rosie Hogarth* was published third, in 1951). The initials "TNH" refer to *There's No Home*, his second published novel (1950). It is possible that Baron did not write these two novels in the order in which they were published, or that he misremembered the dates and order of their publication when writing this note.

> "Of 11 aunts and uncles – 4 were simple and inarticulate. Blunted, fragmentary speech of such naivety that I, even as a child, knew… Yet I didn't distinguish them from the others, who were alert and intelligent, one of them (the schoolmaster) clever and shrewd. When I think of Jack Agass, who says 'It's all right for them as got the words', I recall them, and my sympathy for them. I wonder if this led me to make it my second novel, even tho' TNH was already in my mind…

> Charlie: Auntie Annie's White Slaver. A smart, good-looking fellow, not young, touches of grey in sideboards. His attire. (Cf. later, Otto Katz the Comintern man!!). [For Otto Katz, see Chapter 21, p.169, footnote 10 – Ed.] Through an innocent matchmaker?

> A 'tec [detective – Ed.] warns my grandfather ('Old Levvy'). My letter. 'Long words, dear.' Brachycephalic anthropoid. I explain, 'fatheaded ape.' Fat cheeks shining, she claps her hands with joy."

Page 73   *"A tall, strong man…"* Baron left two fragmentary notes about his maternal grandfather Isaac Levinson:

> "I stood before him as if looking up at a great oak – then he took me and hoisted me up high above his head, the gleam of a smile lighting his stern, moustached face, saying…."

> "…and it goes without saying that he, too, was chaste in his speech, allowing himself only a little latitude when he hoisted me up high, saying 'And how goes the little *pisher*?'"

Page 76   *"We were hypocrites on the day of the great fast…"* A brief note on his father's dress and conduct on the Jewish day of fasting:

> "Yom Kippur. His best suit – watch and chain, celluloid collar and knitted tie. The 'old lady'. Gave her his arm."

Page 82   *"My parents often had company in the evenings."* In a note, Baron alluded to his uncle Jack, who was also a carpenter and also played jazz piano, so it is possible that he is muddling uncles here.

> "How my uncle Jack taught himself to play jazz. Minimum of fingering, maximum smashing of chords. The band. Alf the tailor

(ex-soldier), Jack the carpenter, Esther, a fine, taught pianist (more about her if I haven't already got it). The Netherlands Club. Market porters (bodies like cubes of meat and bone). Dockers. Street sellers of salt and pickled herrings from the big barrel."

Baron's only other mention of his Aunt Esther was an elliptical allusion in another jotted note (see endnote to p.37 above).

Page 86   "*There were reasons at that time for his sensitivity about anti-semitism.*" Baron's notes include a reflection on Jewish identity and self-identification, and how this forms writers and the subjects of their writing. He indicated that these thoughts were prompted by reading Alfred Kazin's essay on the American Jewish writer Bernard Malamud, 'A Single Jew', *New York Review of Books*, 9 October 1997.

"1. My meeting with Malamud. When I had put my question to him, he replied, 'Can you imagine what it is like for a Jew like me—' put his left hand on his chest, '—me, to walk around a campus with beautiful girls on my arm?'

2. Kazin's reminiscence of the flash of resentment in his [Malamud's – Ed.] eyes when a writer (a Gentile) greeted him as Bernie. Kazin comments, he was an artist and wanted his due. I remember: 'I am Gerda Charles!'

3. Kazin recalls Malamud's Jewish grocer. And that recalls to me the day when I, a small boy, stood outside the shop in Hare Street saying, 'Shop shut, shop shut,' because he [Baron's grandfather – Ed.] was on the sofa, tired. Why did I never see this as a story?

4. The Jewish butcher in the Gentile neighbourhood. His children have to take out leaflets in Yiddish. Again, Kazin on a Malamud story brings this to mind also as the seed of a tale. Where did I read or hear about it? Mick Bennett?"

Gerda Charles was the pseudonym of Edna Lipson (1914–1996), an Anglo-Jewish author and longstanding acquaintance of Baron's. Baron's fourth point above mentions Mick Bennett, who appears frequently later in the memoir.

Page 87   "*When my parents went to visit friends for an evening my mother's sisters Hetty and Annie came to sit with us.*" Baron's notes suggest that Hetty and Annie also introduced him to the theatre:

"1. Going up West. Top of open bus. Coloured lights.

2. Hetty and Annie, the gallery girls. I was a small boy. Sitting in

solemn fascination. Looking down on a cube of yellow light in which reduced people did things like goldfish in a tank. Voices floated up with an unreal ring. I heard names – Fred and Adele Astaire – Layton and Johnstone – The last show at the old Empire. *Lady be Good.*"

Baron refers here to music hall performers Turner Layton and Clarence 'Tandy' Johnstone. The last show at the old Empire was in 1926. The following year the theatre was largely demolished to be redeveloped by MGM as a cinema.

Page 87   "*I took the unmarried state of these two aunts for granted.*" On Annie's husband Charlie, see endnote to p.71.

Page 91   "*We were a reading family.*" A further note on his early reading. On Baron's childhood visits to libraries, see also endnotes to pp.95 and 135.

> "Dickens. I had only read *Barnaby Rudge* (its effect on me as a small boy – lurid, a phantasmagoria, those Gordon Riots – the unspeakable ecstasy of reading books you cannot understand when you are small) – *Pickwick* (its effect on me), *Copperfield.* The Library (Northwold Road). Mum and I. Weekly expedition with oilskin shopping bags. Our reading. My father's reading (James Jeans, etc.)."

James Jeans was a British scientist and author of several popular works on astronomy and cosmology in the 1920s and 1930s.

Page 92   "*On Saturdays, after an early lunch, we hurried to the cinema...*" Baron's notes include a long reflection on the role of cinema in his life.

"1. Did cinema educate me as a writer? From childhood I had been one of the enthralled mass in the dark bound together by the shared sensation of emotion.
2. In the YCL, during those years when I read no (heretical) literature, my relief was in snatched visits to the cinema. It wasn't a film buff's interest. I was a movie-goer like the others. It comes to me now that cinema, which entered then into the marrow of my bones and is still there, was the influence that guided me to find the form for my first work.
3. The prologue to *From the City* ... What guided me, soon after I had begun to assemble those odd chapters, to write that

suspenseful passage which, reprised, will lead up to the climax, almost at the end? Then Chapter I is the beginning of the long flashback. Surely, movies?

4. I'd joined the London Film Society (a landmark body in film history in England) when I was 15. I'd read books about cinema as an art, and in those years saw all the great Russian directors. But this was before the age of the film buff. I wasn't one. I'd read about montage but I had no conscious interest in technique, certainly not in story technique. I had just come to look with eyes accustomed to movies...

5. And it comes back to me (I forgot till now) that just before I was demobilised I saw *Laura* and was spellbound. I'd suddenly started to see how it was made. The first scene. What the camera was doing. So the desire to get into films when I was demobbed ran through me like electricity. But when the time came I couldn't get an ACT ticket, even though I was mixing with Communist directors, fellow writers, etc.

6. My one script for Crown Film Unit, then Crescent Films.

7. But I was also writing *From...*"

Baron's sixth point mentions Crescent Films. This was Unity Theatre's short-lived film company. According to Unity's historian Colin Chambers, Crescent Films made only one film, *Century of Song*, written and produced by Baron and directed by Fritz Weiss, but never released (*The Story of Unity Theatre* (London, 1989), p.290). According to the British Film Institute's website, the film was in fact titled *Ta-ra-ra Boom De-ay* and it was made in 1945; the director's name is given as Fred Weiss. The film was based on Unity's popular theatrical show *Winkles and Champagne*, about the history of the music hall, written by Bill Owen (who also starred in the film adaptation). There is no further information on the script that Baron stated here that he had earlier written for the Crown Film Unit, a government agency producing public information films.

Page 94   "*I could not think of anyone nicer than my Uncle Harry in those years.*" In one of Baron's notes, recollection of the loaned Shakespeare volume prompted other thoughts:

> "How old could I have been when Harry lent me his Shakespeare? I came across 'Venus and Adonis' and 'Lucrece'. I remember – I do – how I burned (a blush of all of me) – yet I must have been quite ignorant. Or, if I was already 10 (still at Shacklewell) unable

to believe what a boy had told me in the playground. Monstrous! Impossible! I surely didn't know how a girl differed from me. (I remember that, too.) Yet I was aroused. And I must have been flooded (that blush) with the realisation that some great secret was being withheld from me."

Page 95 *"To me being a journalist meant being a writer."* Baron's notes include a reflection on how his early reading served as a formative influence on his life:

"Tit-Bits: Sent articles, aged 12. Like Arnold Bennett before me. Writing as some kind of destiny filled my head from some time quite early in childhood, but as it gradually took shape as an ambition, I dared to aspire no higher than 'writing for the papers'.

The Library: A fair walk to the nearest. We went every week or two with tickets we'd got in our father's name, too. Four from grown-ups' library and two from children's. I enjoyed children's books, all massively bound, seemed to go back to Victorian times. G.A. Henty, then, later, Percy F. Westerman and early PageG. Woodhouse (Psmith) – about one of the vast army of clerks which still existed, now swelled by women typists, who were the cleverer children of working-class families which were proud of their status (escaped!) although almost all worked for wretched wages, often in Dickensian offices.

Papers: The Labour *Herald* must have reviewed books but it was not till we took the *News Chronicle* (its liberal pedigree) that we had book reviews to guide us. Great, decent newspapers. Lynd, Priestley, Stanley Baron's country articles and maps for ramblers (I used them), and great correspondents like A.J. Cummings and William Forrest. Circulation about 2 million (?) – to a great body of people it was an educator and guide.

Then, age 13/14, I learned of the existence of the *New Statesman*. At reading room. Down-and-outs and solitary old pensioners came in for the warmth. I'd hover angrily while one of them sat dozing over it.

My own path: I believe it was these influences that prepared me for communism. The view of Russia since Revolution – sympathy for working–people, as they believed, trying to carry out a Great Experiment. Tolerance for 'mistakes'. Refused to believe stories

in right-wing press, easily discredited … Cummings in Moscow
believed the confessions. Stalin, peasant, master of deception
(Roy Howard). Potemkin villages, etc. Some on the paper I now
know to have been CP or fellow-travellers (so what?). Honest
people, deceived by their own hunger for a Great Good Place –
who in turn deceived us."

Page 101 *"I had always been happy at the Shacklewell…"* Three notes
present Baron's further recollections of his friends from primary
school and neighbourhood streets:

"On my friends there. The 'rough' boys in jerseys and shorts half-
way down thighs, with cropped heads and pudding basin fringes.
Bert Long – skinny, starved face with dirty white skin, a cut-down
jacket and trousers, trained and frayed, from some dustbin,
the jacket down to his knees. Adores and boasts of his dad the
burglar – 'We 'ad a chicken last Christmas" […] In the
playground. I played 'Release' and (almost as violent) 'Jimmy-
Knocker'. (Bookish and solitary boy but with a disposition to
violence and risk.)"

"My childhood friends apart from Arthur. At school, as well as
Fred Johnson, Edwin Veasey. Both their fathers were killed in the
war. I went to play with Edwin's little working (stationary) steam
engine. Made for him by an uncle (mechanic). He came to play
with my fort. Made for me by Uncle Jack, carpenter. And my toy
soldiers. In our street there were also two boys whose fathers had
been killed in the war. Vic Howells (joined up as a boy solder
when 14. Smart in his uniform: pipe-clayed belt, etc.), and Stanley
Fredman, the quiet boy. With Stanley, Edwin (and, of course,
Arthur Gold, who was more like a brother than a mere friend),
after school we would go to the other's house and take for granted
that we would be fed with a substantial tea, with lots of bread and
butter in doorsteps, perhaps a boiled egg, or sliced ham or meat.
Stanley was spoken of as 'slow' or 'simple'. A quiet, intelligent boy,
he spoke slowly and deliberated before he spoke, even about the
simplest of matters."

"In the street. I was a happy member of the community of street
children. Mostly boys. Two or three girls joined us in hopscotch,
the chalked 'field' always renewed. I was storyteller. Our
expeditions. 'Look behind you!' Pails of dung. Stealing flowers.

Innocent fun. Constituted ourselves as a football team (other streets)."

Page 103 *"We waited in a classroom until the Head entered."* A succinct note hints at the strong impression made on Baron by the poetry of John Masefield (1878–1967), which he encountered first as a child and then later on the bookshelves of the Grocers' School Headmaster Jenkyn Thomas.

"Childhood – and at school – Jenkyn Thomas. *Salt-Water Ballads.* The long poems. 'Reynard'. 'Everlasting Mercy'. 'Dauber'."

Salt-Water Ballads was a 1902 volume of poems by Masefield. The other titles listed in the note are long poems by the same poet: 'Reynard the Fox: or the Ghost Heath Run' (1919), 'The Everlasting Mercy' (1911), and 'Dauber: A Poem' (1912).

Page 112 *"The School Theatre was not used in those days for plays…"* Baron's memoir refers to one or more older relatives who were accomplished musicians (see p.82 and associated endnote above), but only twice mentions the fact that he too had been a proficient piano player since his childhood (from his teenage years, always favouring jazz).

"Social club: our own little jazz band. We had a fine pianist. When he rested, I took a turn. Owed this to my music teacher, pretty Miss [illegible – Ed.], taught me to read and write music and plug away at Czerny's 100 Exercises, an imitator of my uncle Jack. And an echo at Barton Stacey…".

Barton Stacey was the Hampshire army camp where Baron played piano in the Corporal's Club (see Chapter 29).

Page 116 *"The same September I was starting my third year at the Grocers…"* On newspapers and their role in Baron's literary and political development, see endnotes to pp.95 and 135.

Page 118 *"However, this disappointment had a lasting and beneficial effect."* Two loose slips of paper among Baron's notes discuss the meaning that a French poem, which he first encountered as a schoolboy, held for him, and offer insight into his self-characterisation. The poem was 'La Mort Du Loup', by Alfred Victor, Comte de Vigny (1797–1863). In the first note he claimed that already as a teenager he identified with the poem's solitary, proud protagonist, the wolf.

However, in the second note, presumably written on a later occasion, he questioned this. Baron's annotated school copy of *The Oxford Book of French Verse* remains among his private papers. The first note also contains a cryptic reference to a personal bereavement – he omitted the name, presumably deliberately – which he claimed had little emotional impact on him (although he still pointedly recalled it over four decades later). This short, introspective note seems to reflect a man at peace with himself in his old age.

> "'La Mort du Loup' by de Vigny (*The Oxford Book of French Verse*, p.301). I adopted this at 15 (before I became a communist). It explains – even without my born shyness and my war injuries (brain and eyes) – the whole course of my later life – refusal to send out my books, etc. Never felt the loss of ……. I had my wife, my son and my few cherished friends. Had done my work. Had more years than I had ever expected.'

> "Did I identify myself with this poem when I first read it? I was 14 or 15. If so, why? There was nothing in my life to recommend to me the silent endurance of pain and death. I did not feel an outcast, a spurned or rejected one? Since I kept the volume with me and read it during and after the war, could I have only seen myself in it then?"

Page 126   *"Always on the prowl to find the intellectuals I had read so much about..."* Baron's notes qualify this description of his search for 'high' culture:

> "Wednesday afternoons. It wasn't only in search of high culture that I bunked off. I went to Leicester Square to see the new non-stop variety shows, for a few pence, from the gallery. My father had loved the old music-halls in their golden age, of which saw the dying embers when I was small. He went on taking us to every vaudeville show that reminded him of music-hall, and I loved it. I had known Flanagan (Ruby Weintrop) and Allen – Florrie Forde every year. Now, the newly-formed Crazy-Gang – I continued a fan for years. After the war (*New Theatre*), Victoria Palace..."

On *New Theatre*, see Chapter 35 and endnote to p.332.

Page 135   *"I could not have been very attentive..."* A further note on the local public libraries that Baron visited so often as a boy. Baron stated here that his decision to go to Stoke Newington Public Library one morning in February 1934 – because he could get hold of newspapers more easily there than in the library nearest to him – was one of the 'accidents' that determined his future biography. It was while returning home from there that he saw a Labour Party poster advertising the talk where he was first drawn into left-wing political activities.

> "1934. Why I chose to go to Church St. Library instead of the much nearer Hackney reading room. Hackney (Mare St.) was always full of old men and out-of-works keeping warm and passing time. Some looked at job adverts. Others studied the racing form. The old men fell asleep. I wouldn't get near a paper. This decision / choice / act started a chain of consequences that set the future course of my life."

Page 147 *"In the League of Youth we went out canvassing for the Labour Party..."* In a brief note, Baron pondered whether to correct an omission from the memoir text. There is no further information on Baron's first girlfriend, a Labour Party activist. Clearly, Baron's 1971 novel *The In-Between Time* was in part inspired by his romantic as well as political experiences as a teenager.

> "Refer to my girlfriend? Sweet – sensible – supported me but stubborn to reject communism = but I never tried to convince her. As I got busier with meetings farther apart, we parted."

Page 155 *"Until I became too busy with national work..."* Baron's notes on revisions for the memoir include the following press clipping, presumably relating to one of the "local actions and escapades" in which he participated with the LLY:

> "Scene at Youth Meeting.
> Songs, Shouts and Blows.
>
> There was pandemonium at a 'Youth Meeting' in the Memorial Hall, Farringdon Street, E.C., last night, when members of five political parties were to debate on 'Whither Youth?'
>
> The 'Red Flag' was sung, youths came to blows, girls shouted and screamed.
>
> When Mr. William Joyce, a young Fascist, rose to speak, about 100 young people began to sing, and at the back of the hall there were several scrimmages.

At the end of the meeting half the audience trooped down the stairs, singing and shouting."

Daily Herald, Friday, 5 April 1935.

Page 168   *"The Young Communist League at this time called itself a school for heroes."* In a brief note, Baron reflected on his use in the memoir of the phrase "the honour of the communist":

> "Chekhov said, 'We all know what a dishonest deed is, but what is honour?' 'Blut und Ehre' – the SS fought to the death to conform to/uphold a certain definition of honour."

Page 170   *"They pushed me forward."* In his notes, Baron described Malraux's charisma:

> "Nearly all those who came in direct contact with him fell under his spell – and I am not only talking here of naïve schoolboys but of famous writers, some of whom were twice his age, as well as eminent thinkers, statesmen, leaders of men, saintly monks, cunning old politicians, glamorous socialites, cynical journalists, unworldly priests [...] 'The Great Bamboozalum.'"

Page 219   *"We had chosen the location for the press..."* Baron's notes give further information on the communists' secret activities and associates at this time:

> "Where we hid out stock of paper in 1940. It was in the Snake House at the London Zoo. This was by courtesy of Dr Geoffrey Vevers, the Superintendent of the Zoo. He was a Party member, whether 'open' or not I don't know. I think he had written or been mentioned in the *Daily Worker*. I was not told ('need to know' – and to protect Vevers). Information from Mick Bennett – my visit in autumn of 1996."

Page 233   *"Most of the men in the company were Londoners..."* In one note, Baron mused on the derogatory concept of *Grobbe Yidden*. The three men referred to in the first line were Baron's two grandfathers and his father.

> "Grobbe Yidden? These three men, the mechanic, the cobbler and the fur cutter, often referred to certain people as Grobbe Yidden. Included – gambled, swore, spoke gutter variety of Yiddish, had bad manners, were loud and assertive – also they

[the three men – Ed.] assumed that most Jewish traders and workshop bosses were like this…".

Page 234   *"I heard nothing about my transfer."* In his notes Baron wrote further about his army friendships:

"I made friends [in the army] as I never had in the YCL. Except for the officers and a cadre of NCOs, almost the entire company consisted of 22 year-olds, most of whom were Londoners. Quite a few were already in unions, or took for granted that they would join one when they were older. Some, I found, had experience of local 'barneys' (fights) with Mosley's Blackshirts. But above all there was a current of working-class London pride, humour and sheer sauce that united them all. They quickly sorted themselves out into local sets. A head appears around my barrack-room door. 'Any Dalston boys 'ere?' I call 'Me', and I have found a new group of ready listeners and, as time will show, supporters."

In another note, Baron gave a slightly different account of this incident:

"When we arrive at the billet. Introduce Bob Chapman (his name in memoir?). Ch: 'Where you from?' Me: 'Dalston.' Ch (door, yells): 'Where's Freddie Carvell? 'Ere Fred, 'ere's another Dalston boy for you.' Carvell that day appointed himself our cook. He was that type of 'Dalston boy'. The benefits to me."

Neither Chapman nor Carvell appear in any draft of the memoir. But Baron's friends were not just Londoners. The memoir later frequently mentions Corporals Billy Strachan and Eric Gray, two northerners (see endnote to p.260).

Page 241   *"In the meantime I was enjoying my present life."* Two notes on Baron's enjoyment of the companionship of the army during his period of training:

"*Alouette!* Those long route-marches which I loved, over the chalk downs of southern England, on hot summer days. Where did they learn – not only to whistle, but to roar the responses: '*Et la tête – Alouette!*' This alone elevated my status in the company."

"I played a harmonica (a cheap one), but not badly, in my first company. I didn't think about it. It wasn't to ingratiate myself. I was just given it, tried it, learned the tricks and played, sometimes, of an evening round the stove, in the Nissen hut or (in Hampshire) in the billet. This was one of the things I had never done before and have never done since, like climbing to the high board at the swimming pool in Andover and diving. And playing the prank in the Corporal's Club. I went egg-stealing in early days. This wasn't done to ingratiate myself with 'the lads' either (as a communist!!). I did it without thought. Fun. Adventurousness. Innocent. A reversion to the flower-stealing [see endnote to p.101 – Ed.] of my childhood."

Page 250   *"Not long after this I met Springhall by chance..."* A note presents more information on Peter Zinkin's clandestine activities on behalf of Moscow:

"Peter Zinkin. Also a Soviet agent. 1. When retired from 'D.W.' [*Daily Worker* – Ed.], said to his successor, who refused with horror, 'Would you like my other job?', etc. (E[rik] Scott, [Allen] Hutt's [illegible word – Ed.], to Alison [Macleod]). 2. Peter Fryer came upon him one night writing a report on the rest of the staff. His activities before the war, e.g. forming a network of aircraft workers without telling the Party, which was outraged but obviously powerless. 4. Book by Nina Fishman has stuff on him, the import of which N.F. doesn't understand. 5. The post of Industrial Organizer was obviously a Russian prerogative. His successors, [Bert] Ramelson and [Mick] Costello ... but I can't say this, they're still alive..."

Page 260   *"A small group of the keenest NCO's formed..."* In a note, Baron offered a lengthy reflection on the reasons for his social reticence while in the army. He started by recalling that the 'Ginger Group' started corresponding with his younger sister Ida in 1942:

"...perhaps after I'd taken Harry Forrest home with me for a meal. He reported that my sister was a smasher. [...] Evacuated to Newbury, she had responded to the call-up of women for war service and was a secretary at an army Military Transport training centre. She sent them her photo. The first I knew was when they confronted me with it. She was indeed a smasher. Gray and Strachan were the principals, but some of the others joined in the fun. How come an ugly mug like me had a smasher like this for a sister? And they claimed to be reporting all my doings to her."

"Why I was reserved? I was not displeased at this. One or the other of them spoke freely about their lives now and before the war. I had little to say in return. I did not want to appear a dark horse and this collective good-humoured flirtation with my sister put me, too, into a more human relationship with them.

There was little, indeed, I could tell them about myself. I said that I had been a journalist on labour papers. What else? A rank-and-file member of the Party could chat freely about it and his life in it. But I couldn't talk about the apparatus, etc.

And then there was my pledge. I had handed in an undertaking to give up even the citizen's right which I possessed to talk politics, and had asked 'them' in return to let me go overseas and to get any promotion that I earned. Well, it had met with silence from the unknown people who watched me, but I was a corporal, I was going and did go overseas, I did have a dozen men to lead in action, better than none, and if I was denied an infantry transfer or a commission, I was to have the occasional chance of action. So, I didn't want to be drawn into talking at length with them about politics, apart from the generalities and brief comments we all indulged in.

Of course, when Major Bell told me (overseas) to round up all the men who were idling by their pits, not out on detachment, and give them a lecture on world politics or how the world was going, I did so.

Another reason. Besides, as time passed, I remained as faithful as ever to the Party (after all, there was the 'Russian glory' before my eyes, the heroic Russian troops and partisans – to me a demonstration that socialism, theirs, must be their inspiration) but I saw more and more all the dark things, the base and unpleasant things, which I had taken for granted or glibly approved of. And more and more inclined to feel at least relieved at the growing distance between me and all that.

Nor could I go on believing that the people amongst whom I had been were the human elite. The rough-and-ready lot around me, the soldiers, were no elite, but they showed up better to me than many of my former comrades.

So how could I talk about all that?"

Page 263   *"None of my friends had ever been to a smart restaurant before..."* One of Baron's notes reflected on his earlier experiences of drinking wine:

> "Wine. My tiny silver goblet. These [Baron's family – Ed.] were poor people – slum alleys and courts. Rare occasions. A toast. Beautiful and civilized. Do I recall this when in Plymouth? – the Italian restaurant (such as none of us had patronised) – my comrades had never drunk wine. In Sicily – as if it was beer!"

Page 282   *"We were given fourteen days' leave."* Two notes offering further thoughts on the social profile of CPGB members:

> "1942 – 'In Ted's Time'. People nowadays who imagine communists have no idea of the transformation in the Party when rich people, celebrities, etc. joined it or gave it money. (Leonid Krasin in 1907, 'We Bolsheviks are positively bon ton.') The daughters of two quite famous generals joined, and the daughter of a Minister of State at the War Office went out to sell *Challenge* in the streets towed by 2 Afghan hounds on long leashes. Cf. earlier – Dr. Vevers – Snake House." [On this, see endnote to p.219 – Ed.].

> "YCL – Had been a big increase in membership – sons and daughters of generals and Tory ministers – ! Mick is secretary. Ted gone (saw little of him)."

Page 284   *"He wore the shoulder titles of some vanished regiment..."* Baron's notes describe the prelude to his first encounter with the corporal in Sicily:

> "En route: the shell. Knocked flat on my back. The officer looming above. The sergeant glimpsed on the ground. I totter back to the truck. Some of my party, who have jumped down to help me, tumble aboard, one of them with my helmet. The head pains (a few days)."

Page 285   *"A year before I would have plunged into argument..."* In his notes, Baron expanded on his account of this meeting:

> "Mick Bennett – 'There'll be plenty of dark nights over there.' When I had told him that that a leading Trotskyist had just joined my company. I would never have done it. But earlier I'd have told myself that he was only joking (knowing that he wasn't). By early

(Spring?) 1944 I just heard it as ridiculous and gave no further thought to it. So the threads went on snapping...."

Page 301   *"The process of literary creation is partly unconscious..."* Baron's notes offer further reflection on the inter-relations between experience and literature:

> "It happened that when we were overseas I enjoyed a freedom that was extraordinary for a corporal, who ought at all times on duty to be with his section. This was accorded to me by the favour of Major Bell, who never uttered a word of explanation to me but who, I reckoned, was determined to go on treating me as if I were still an officer candidate; thus, he devised for me a variety of errands and assignments, some for his benefit, as when I roamed the countryside foraging for fresh food, and some, presumably for my own, as when he arranged for me to spend time with the infantry. 'It'll be experience,' he once curtly remarked. Taking my liberty for granted I also thought up tasks for myself which enabled me to roam the countryside in and out of the forward area.

> It could not of course have entered his mind that he was helping in my preparation to become a writer. It did not enter into mine. I am convinced that I did look upon the infantrymen in whose company I found myself as material for 'copy' (as lay people call it). I only knew that I was living the life that I had tried for ever since the third day of my military service in 1940. But the experiences entered into me, I suppose to germinate undetected. It was only in 1946, in the months after I had left the army, that the purpose of my life since childhood overmastered me and I began to scribble, and when I did it was the experiences of that summer in Normandy, seeds that were now bearing fruit as something more than simple memory, that burst forth and took form on paper.

> **Should I also enlarge on the fact that the essence of my experiences is in the battle scenes of *From the City?***

> And that the book is, not a disguised memoir, but a fairly sophisticated piece of writing? Quote Michael Howard in the Cape history.

> This is not boasting. He or she who is fated to be a writer does not start off with a tyro's work but appears showing his or her

best, even maturity will bring its results ... Say here or elsewhere? – how I began by writing fragments or episodes which were not recollections but already stories ... how I naively stood in Foyles' looking at recent novels to see how they were made, how long the chapters were, whether I could have chapter titles as in old-fashioned books (I did), etc. But when I came to the prologue to Mont Pincon I saw that this must repeat the same words set down at the very start of the book. Throughout all that comes before, the reader must be warned from the start that he is being brought to this fateful moment. The fact is that it doesn't need writers' courses, etc. The new writer who is a writer finds his craft coming to him as he works. Instinct points out necessities and he creates the solutions."

Page 308   "*I wandered off into the countryside when I had no duties...*" See endnote to p.301 regarding Major Bell's granting to Baron an unusual freedom of movement.

Page 327   "*When Victory in Europe Day had come I had felt only empty and sick.*" In Baron's notes, he described another cause of general demoralisation at the war's end:

> "Soldiers had taken satisfaction, if not pride, in the red service chevrons on their cuffs, gold wound stripes and ribbons with a star for every campaign. The terms you had to satisfy to get a star. Then, immediately war ended, [it was] announced that everyone who had spent 24 hours in a theatre of war got a star!! Another NCO to me, 'Now Joe Loss and his band'll get the lot!'"

Page 332   "*I enjoyed my work at New Theatre.*" A note on Baron's first postwar employment:

> "*New Theatre*. I studied theatre ... on our board, Michel Saint-Denis ... and the 21-year-old Peter Brook. Harley Granville-Barker a guide to us. Down to Stratford every year. Bea and Dickie H. [unidentified – Ed.] at the Mucky Duck. The cast at their country house. Part of my healing."

For Baron's involvement in Unity Theatre (as Alex Bernstein), see Colin Chambers, *The Story of Unity Theatre* (London, 1989). See also endnote to p.92.

Page 334   *"The word intoxication describes my condition aptly..."* According
to one note, Baron's exploration for a new political compass after the
war also drew him towards anarchism:

> "Iain Sinclair, [*Lights out for the Territory* (Granta, 1997) – Ed.]
> pp.26–29 *and passim* references to the covens of anarchists
> (various shades) in Hackney and Stoke Newington, including
> some (the Angry Brigade and others?) in Amhurst Road,
> reminded me that in my first post-war years when I roamed
> London, I sometimes felt a vague pull towards anarchism, drop-
> ped in at the Freedom Bookshop near Red Lion Square, and
> bought stuff."

Page 335   *"I could elaborate on this..."* Baron's notes for revision include
thoughts on expanding this paragraph:

> "Consequences. My little piece on the Theory of Accident is
> incomplete unless I add a paragraph on consequences – it is these
> which are unpredictable and often (see Engels) undesired. This
> extends the theory to history and refutes Marxist history. The
> paragraph need not be long."

Page 339   *"When it was finished I put it away in a drawer."* A note dated
June 1998 on the vagaries of literary funding.

> "Only the other night I remembered that I applied for an Atlantic
> Award soon after I had got *From the City* typed in two copies.
> What was offered? It would have encouraged me. It [the type-
> script – Ed.] came back to me within a few days. It could not have
> been read – perhaps someone dipped into it or looked at the first
> few pages. Mervyn Jones got one, I'm sure deservedly. His first
> published novel was a fine piece of work. He'd written two before
> that. But there was Maurice Carpenter, a literary hanger-on. I met
> him in the company of known writers and he obviously knew a
> lot of others. Never published. He got one. He said to me, 'They'll
> give it to anyone they know.'"

Baron refers here to Mervyn Jones (1922–2010), a journalist and
novelist, son of psychoanalyst Ernest Jones, and one of Baron's closest
personal friend from the postwar period onwards. Jones and the
historian William E. Fishman (1921–2014) gave the eulogies at
Baron's funeral at Golder's Green Crematorium in December 1999.
Baron's claim that Maurice Carpenter was "never published" seems

to be incorrect. A search on the integrated online catalogue of all major British libraries returns the titles of nearly twenty published works credited to Carpenter between the mid-1940s and late 1970s, mainly original poetry and critical essays on poetry, plus a 1976 memoir *A Rebel in the Thirties.* He was a friend of Edith Sitwell, and had written for the YCL cultural magazine *Alive!* in 1939–40, though Baron does not mention encountering him at this time. A very brief biography of Carpenter can be found in Graham Stevenson's online 'Encyclopedia of Communist Biographies': https://grahamstevenson.me.uk/2008/12/16/john-miles-maurice-carpenter/ (accessed 6 May 2022).

Page 341   *"Since then I have given all my time to writing."* Baron's notes contain his own brief career summary, mainly covering the period addressed in this memoir, and a set of reflections on his literary output, proposing that, to be fully understood, his novels need to be read as one body of work and in the light of his early experiences of childhood, politics and war that the memoir describes.

> "**Alexander Baron.**
> Born December, 1917. Grew up in Hackney. Educated at the Shacklewell School (Elementary) and Hackney Downs School. Joined the Labour party at the age of sixteen and was active in it and in the Communist Party until 1940, gaining some prominence in both. 1935–1938: worked as a clerk for the London County Council and in spare time edited a Labour Party youth journal. 1938–1939: assistant editor of "Tribune." 1939–1940: editor of "Challenge" (Young Communist League weekly). 1940–1946: Army. Served in Sicilian campaign. Was with leading troops on D-Day, 1944, and took part in NW Europe campaign. 1946–1948: edited a theatre magazine. On success of first novel, *From the City, From the Plough,* became a full-time writer. 1992: Elected Honorary Fellow of Queen Mary and Westfield College, University of London.
>
> **A Note On My Work**
> When I left school in 1935 I gave up an ambition to study history in order to plunge into the politics of the day. (This was at the urging of one of the leaders of the Communist Party). History has remained my obsession. I was, after all, up to my neck in it from 1934 to the end of the Second World War (see the biographical note). The presence of history impregnates all my

stories. They are connected by a web of cross-references. My three war books constitute a single body of work in which the broadening exploration of the theme can be seen. Premonitory thoughts about tribalism led to two studies of it, both in a London working-class setting, *Rosie Hogarth* (1951) and *King Dido* (1969). *King Dido* is set in the Coronation year of King George V, as is *Gentle Folk*, a visionary novel about the future of the twentieth century. The pair represent the Two Nations at that time. Another novel still unpublished, *The Trumpet Call*, takes up the visionary exploration of the theme, "Where are we going?" Two novels set in Spain, *Franco is Dying* and a companion volume not yet published, *The War Baby*, take Spain as a cockpit in which the theme of war is re-examined and something is said about the conflicts and destiny of the century. I have just finished writing my memoir, *Chapters of Accidents*, which deals with my life up to the publication of my first novel. It is meant to provide a background and a key to my novels.

Throughout my career I have been encouraged by the support of a number of critics and, in recent years, by the attention my books have begun to receive from some academics. However, they have always been looked upon as disconnected works and, most of them, as realist essays upon London life or upon war. I wrote the memoir and now this note because I would like one day to see the entire *oeuvre* considered in their light. Such as study would bring out what is distinctive about my work."

Milton Keynes UK
Ingram Content Group UK Ltd.
UKHW021430050124
435531UK00031B/288